THE CAMBRIDGE COMPANION TO
BLACK THEOLOGY

This volume discusses normative theological categories from a black perspective, and argues that there is no major Christian doctrine on which black theology has not commented. Part I explores introductory questions such as: what have been the historical and social factors fostering a black theology, and what are some of the internal factors key to its growth? Part II examines major doctrines which have been important for black theology in terms of clarifying key intellectual foci common to the study of religion. The final part discusses black theology as a world-wide development constituted by interdisciplinary approaches. The volume has an important role in bringing Christian thought into confrontation with one of the central challenges of modernity, namely the problem of race and racism. This *Companion* puts theological themes in conversation with issues of ethnicity, gender, social analysis, politics, and class, and is ideal for undergraduate and graduate students.

Dwight N. Hopkins is Professor of Theology at the University of Chicago Divinity School. He has published several books, which include *Being Human: Race, Culture, and Religion* (2005), *Heart and Head: Black Theology Past, Present, and Future* (2002), and *Global Voices for Gender Justice* (2001, co-editor with Ramathate Dolamo and Ana Maria Tepedino).

Edward P. Antonio is the Harvey H. Potthoff Associate Professor of Theology and Social Theory, and Associate Dean of Diversities at the Iliff School of Theology in Denver, Colorado. He is editor of *Inculturation and Postcolonial Discourse in African Theology* (2006).

CAMBRIDGE COMPANIONS TO RELIGION
A series of companions to major topics and key figures in theology and
religious studies. Each volume contains specially commissioned chapters
by international scholars, which provide an accessible and stimulating
introduction to the subject for new readers and non-specialists.

Other titles in the series

Continued at the back of the book

THE CAMBRIDGE COMPANION TO

BLACK THEOLOGY

Edited by Dwight N. Hopkins
and
Edward P. Antonio

CAMBRIDGE
UNIVERSITY PRESS

University Printing House, Cambridge CB2 8BS, United Kingdom

Cambridge University Press is part of the University of Cambridge.

It furthers the University's mission by disseminating knowledge in the pursuit of education, learning and research at the highest international levels of excellence.

www.cambridge.org
Information on this title: www.cambridge.org/9780521705691

© Cambridge University Press 2012

First published 2012

A catalogue record for this publication is available from the British Library

Library of Congress Cataloguing in Publication data
The Cambridge companion to Black theology / edited by Dwight N. Hopkins,
Edward P. Antonio.
    p.   cm. – (Cambridge companions to religion)
Includes bibliographical references and index.
ISBN 978-0-521-87986-6 (hardback) – ISBN 978-0-521-70569-1 (paperback)
1. Black theology.   I. Hopkins, Dwight N.   II. Antonio, Edward P.
BT82.7.C36 2012
230.089′96–dc23
2012015436

ISBN 978-0-521-87986-6 Hardback
ISBN 978-0-521-70569-1 Paperback

Contents

Contributors

Edward P. Antonio is the Harvey H. Potthoff Associate Professor of Theology and Social Theory, Associate Dean of Diversities, and Director of Justice and Peace Programs at the Iliff School of Theology in Denver, Colorado. He is currently working on a book on the modernist roots of black theology. He is editor of *Inculturation and Postcolonial Discourse in African Theology* (2006). In addition, he has published articles on race and sexuality, empire, black theology, religion and the environment in Africa, Aristotle on slavery, and Nietzsche and race, among others. Antonio's areas of research are black and African theologies, philosophical theology, continental philosophy, social theory, and postcolonial discourse.

Garth Baker-Fletcher is Associate Professor of Religious Studies at Texas College. He is the author of, among other books, *Somebodyness: Martin Luther King, Jr. and the Theory of Dignity* (1993); *Xodus: An African American Male Journey* (1995); *Dirty Hands: Moral Ambiguity and Christian Ethics* (2000); and *Bible Witness in Black Churches* (2009).

Allan A. Boesak is Honorary Research Associate at the University of KwaZulu Natal, Theologian in Residence at the University of the Free State, and Extraordinary Professor of Systematic Theology and Research Fellow at Stellenbosch University, South Africa. He is Chair of the Senior Advisory Council of the Trans-Atlantic Roundtable on Religion and Race. His most recent publications are: *Dreaming a Different World: Globalisation and Justice for Humanity and the Earth – The Challenge of the Accra Confession for the Churches* (co-editor with Johann Weusmann and Charles Amjad-Ali, 2010) and *The Divine Favour of the Unworthy: Probing New Frontiers in Black Liberation Theology* (forthcoming).

Michael Joseph Brown is the Director of the Malcolm X Institute of Black Studies and Associate Dean of the College at Wabash College, Crawfordsville, Indiana. He is the author of *Blackening of the Bible: The Aims of African American Biblical Scholarship* (2004) and *The Lord's Prayer through North African Eyes: A Window into Early Christianity* (2004).

James H. Cone is Charles A. Briggs Distinguished Professor of Systematic Theology at Union Theological Seminary, New York, and a founder of black theology of liberation. He wrote the first two books on liberation theology from the perspective of African American religious experiences. From his seminal first text, *Black Theology and Black Power* (1969), to his widely read *Martin and Malcolm and America: A Dream or a Nightmare?* (1991) to his latest work, *The Cross and the Lynching Tree* (2011), Cone has continued to teach systematic theology at Union Theological Seminary, New York City, and write and lecture globally.

Cyprian Davis, OSB is Professor of Church History at the School of Theology at Saint Meinrad College, Indiana, and, since 1951, a Benedictine monk of Saint Meinrad Archabbey. He is a founder of black Catholic theology, and his books include *The Church a Living Heritage* (1982); *The History of Black Catholics in the United States* (1995); and *"Stamped with the Image of God": African Americans as God's Image in Black* (co-editor with Jamie T. Phelps, 2004).

Riggins R. Earl, Jr. is Professor of Ethics and Theology at the Interdenominational Theological Seminary in Atlanta, Georgia. *Dark Salutations: Ritual, God, and Greetings in the African-American Community* (2001) and *Dark Symbols, Obscure Signs: God, Self, and Community in the Slave Mind* (2003) are two of his many publications.

Noel Leo Erskine is Professor of Theology and Ethics at the Candler School of Theology, Emory University, Atlanta, Georgia. He is the author of *Decolonizing Theology: A Caribbean Perspective* (1998) and *From Garvey to Marley: Rastafari Theology* (2007).

James H. Evans, Jr. is Robert K. Davies Professor of Systematic Theology at Colgate Rochester Crozer Divinity School, Rochester, New York. He is the author of *We Have Been Believers: An African American Systematic Theology* (1993) and *We Shall All Be Changed: Social Problems and Theological Renewal* (1997).

Dwight N. Hopkins is Professor of Theology and Director of MA Studies at the University of Chicago Divinity School. He is the author of *Shoes That Fit Our Feet: Sources for a Constructive Black Theology* (1993) and *Being Human: Race, Culture, and Religion* (2005) and editor of *Black Faith and Public Talk: Essays in Honor of James H. Cone's "Black Theology and Black Power"* (1999). Hopkins founded the International Association of Black Religions and Spiritualities, a fourteen-country network embracing India, Australia, Japan, Fiji, Hawaii, the USA, Brazil, Jamaica, Cuba, the UK, Zimbabwe, South Africa, Botswana, and Ghana.

Julian Kunnie is Professor of Religious Studies/Classics/Africana Studies at the University of Arizona. He is a former Director of Africana Studies at the same university and was Director of African Studies at Kalamazoo College from 1992-1994. He has taught at Valparaiso University, the University of California, Berkeley, and the Graduate Theological Union. Conference presenter on five different continents, his numerous publications include *Models of Black Theology: Issues in Class, Culture and Gender* (1994), *Is Apartheid Really Dead? Pan Africanist Working Cultural Perspectives* (2000), and *Indigenous Peoples Wisdom and Power: Affirming our Legacy Through Narratives* (with Nomalungelo Goduka) (2006), and *Globalization and Its Victims: Wars Against the Earth and the Impoverished of the World* (forthcoming in 2013). He is the producer of four documentary films, *Umoya: The Spirit in Africa* (2000), *Black* *and Brown: An Afro-Latino Journey* (2006), *We Belong to Mother Earth: Dineh Elder and Hataali Jones Benally Speaks* (2011), and *Global Indigenous Peoples Performing Arts Festival* (2011).

Mokgethi Motlhabi is one of the founders of black theology in South Africa; he published the first book on black theology in South Africa – *Essays on Black Theology* (1972). Some of his other works include *The Theory and Practice of Black Resistance to Apartheid: A Social-Ethical Analysis* (1984); *Challenge to Apartheid: Toward a Morally Defensible Strategy* (1988); *Toward a New South Africa: Issues and Objects in the ANC/Government Negotiation for a Non-Racial Democratic Society* (1992); and *African Theology/Black Theology in South Africa: Looking Back, Moving On* (2008).

Walter de Oliveira Passos teaches history at the Colégio Estadual Tereza Conceição Menezes, Salvador, Bahia, Brazil. In addition he is an ordained pastor of the United Presbyterian Church of Brazil. His areas of research include black theology, slavery, African diasporas, and the economic and social history of Africa and Brazil. He is author of three books: *Teologia Negra: A Revelação* (*Black Theology: The Revelation*, 1995); *Anegrando: Tornar-se Negro* (*Becoming Black*, 1995); and *Bahia: Terra de Quilombos* (*Bahia: Land of Quilombos*, 1996). Passos is President of the Conselho Nacional de Negras e Negros Cristãos (CNNC).

Anne Pattel-Gray is Chief Executive Officer of Ngaran Goori Limited, Port Adelaide, South Australia, and is the first Aboriginal person to earn a PhD in Australia. She is the author of *Through Aboriginal Eyes: The Cry from the Wilderness* (1991) and *The Great White Flood: Racism in Australia* (1998).

Raúl Suárez Ramos is Director of the Martin Luther King, Jr. Memorial Center in Havana, and one of the first promoters of black theology in Cuba. He is an ordained Baptist clergyman, a national church leader in Cuba, and an international leader in global Christian networks. He is the author of *When You Pass through the Waters* (2007).

Anthony Reddie is Research Fellow in Black Theology for The Queen's Foundation for Ecumenical Theological Education, Birmingham, UK, and is a leading developer of black theology. His books include *Black Theology in Transatlantic Dialogue* (2006); *Black Theology in Britain: A Reader* (co-editor with Michael N. Jagessar, 2007); *Postcolonial Black British Theologies* (co-editor with Michael N. Jagessar, 2007); and *Working against the Grain: Black Theology in the 21st Century* (2008). Reddie is the editor of *Black Theology: An International Journal*.

J. Deotis Roberts is President of the J. Deotis Roberts Research and Library Institute, and one of the founders of black theology. He has a PhD in philosophical theology from the University of Edinburgh, and taught for many years at Howard University, Washington, DC. He is the author of *A Black Political Theology* (1974); *Roots of a Black Future: Family and Church* (2002); and *Liberation and Reconciliation: A Black Theology* (2005, 2nd edn.).

Linda E. Thomas is Professor of Theology and Anthropology at the Lutheran School of Theology at Chicago (Chicago, Illinois). She is the author of *Under the Canopy: Ritual Process and Spiritual Resilience in South Africa* (2007);

editor of *Living Stones in the Household of God: The Legacy and Future of Black Theology* (2003); and co-editor with Dwight N. Hopkins of *Walk Together Children: Black and Womanist Theologies, Church and Theological Education* (2010).

Dennis W. Wiley is pastor of Covenant Baptist Church in Washington, DC, and has a PhD in theology. His essays include "Black Theology, the Black Church, and the African American Community"; "Howard Thurman, the Church, and the Poor"; "Black Theology in Praxis"; "The Meaning of the African American Church"; and "Spirit in the Dark: Sexuality and Spirituality in the Black Church."

Delores S. Williams is Paul Tillich Professor Emerita at Union Theological Seminary, New York City. She is one of the founders of womanist theology and the author of *Sisters in the Wilderness: The Challenge of Womanist God-Talk* (1993).

Gayraud S. Wilmore is Emeritus Professor of Church History at the Interdenominational Theological Center in Atlanta, Georgia, and former President of the Society for the Study of Black Religion. He was at the first meeting that eventually published the July 31, 1966 theological statement on "Black Power." Among his sixteen written or edited books are *Black Religion and Black Radicalism: An Interpretation of the Religious History of Afro-American People* (1998); *Pragmatic Spirituality: The Christian Faith through an Africentric Lens* (2004); and *Black Theology: A Documentary History*, 2 vols. (co-editor with James H. Cone, 1979, 1993).

Jeremiah A. Wright, Jr. is the Emeritus Senior Pastor of Trinity United Church of Christ in Chicago, Illinois, and has degrees from Howard University, the University of Chicago Divinity School, and the United Theological Seminary. He is the author of *What Makes You So Strong?* (1993); *Africans Who Shaped Our Faith* (1995); *Good News: Sermons of Hope for Today's Families* (1995); *When Black Men Stand Up for God* (1997); and *A Sankofa Moment: The History of Trinity United Church of Christ* (2010).

Preface

The Cambridge Companion to Black Theology aims to fill a void in the intellectual study of black religious experiences in different parts of the world. Nowhere is there a volume that critically analyzes black theology of liberation in its varied manifestations and deepens normative theological categories from a black perspective. The two volumes on black theology (1993) edited by James Cone and Gayraud Wilmore consist of a collection of topical, primary documents from 1966 to 1992. In fact, their two volumes are titled a *documentary history* of black theology. And the aim of various introductions to black theology of liberation was not to present a systematic exposition of the key doctrines of black theology as a discipline. Nor was their mission to delve into forms of black theology indigenous to other countries. Hence the uniqueness of the present volume.

Indeed, this *Cambridge Companion* entails three parts. Part I explores the overall introductory matters about black theology. What have been the historical and social factors fostering a black theology? What are some of the internal nuances key to black theology's growth? And what other disciplines have impacted the doing of black theology? Part II examines some of the major themes or doctrines that have been important for black theology in terms of clarifying key intellectual foci common to the general study of religion. And Part III presents global expressions of black theology. As an established body of knowledge and practice, black theology has grown in conversation with similar contexts and related disciplines. Black theology is a global phenomenon in dialogue with interlocutors who have developed the discipline in their own contexts, based on their own warrants. By presenting black theology in relation to its global settings, this text situates black theology as a world-wide development constituted by interdisciplinary approaches.

This *Companion* will meet the needs of both undergraduate and graduate courses. It goes well with classes centered on: religious studies, comparative models of theology, black studies, women's studies, systematic and constructive theologies, comparative religions, the study of interdisciplinary models, and international studies.

We would also like to acknowledge the assistance of several people who helped with various aspects of this book. Rachel Harding played a crucial role in helping us make initial contact with Walter Passos in Brazil and Sergio Varela at the Cambridge University Press office in Brazil helped us maintain the contact. Gary W. Bunch translated the essay by Passos from Portuguese into English. My former research assistant at Iliff, Robyn Henderson-Espinoza, prepared the index. Two other Iliff doctoral students helped with the book. Néstor A. Gómez-Morales translated the essay on black theology in Cuba by Raúl Suárez Ramos from Spanish into English and Jason Wesley Alvis helped with the initial editing of some of the chapters.

Dwight N. Hopkins would like to thank his former research assistant and doctoral student, Karl W. Lampley, who graduated in 2012. We also want to thank Kate Brett, Laura Morris and Anna Lowe of Cambridge University Press for their expert help and guidance as we worked on the book. Edward Antonio is grateful for the encouragement and assistance of his wife, Gladys. The contributors to this book are located in different parts of the world. Without their timely responsiveness and their commitment to the book, coordinating the project would have been very hard and the global portrait of black theology that the book presents would certainly have been significantly attenuated. We are grateful to all the contributors.

Finally, we give profound thanks to John W. de Gruchy (Cape Town, South Africa) who first had a conversation with Dwight in 1999 about the possibility of doing a companion volume on black theology. John also introduced Dwight to editors at Cambridge University Press.

Part I

Introduction

1 General introduction

DWIGHT N. HOPKINS

Black theology of liberation interweaves three related experiences. "Theology" signifies the long tradition of the various forms of Christianity beginning with the life of Jesus in, what we today call, northeast Africa or west Asia. "Liberation" designates the specific mission of Jesus the Anointed One on earth; that is to say, liberation of oppressed communities to attain power and wealth. And "black" means the multiple manifestations of black people's socially constructed worldviews, aesthetics, and identities. In brief, black theology of liberation answers the question: how does Jesus' Gospel of liberation throughout the Christian tradition reveal itself in black culture? Ultimately, arising out of the particularity of the black experience, the goal is to help craft healthy communities and healthy individuals throughout the world.

Rooted in the Christian tradition, following the path of Jesus, and affirming black culture, black theology of liberation derives from both modern and contemporary contexts.

THE MODERN CONTEXT

By "modern context" we mean the historic encounter between European missionaries, merchants, and military, on the one hand, and the indigenous family structures of the darker-skinned communities of the globe (i.e., the greater part of the world), on the other. Bold European explorations made contact with what would later become Africa, Asia, the Caribbean, Latin America, and the Pacific Islands. Depicting these diverse regions as qualitatively different, Europe then forged itself into a normative cartography called "Europe." The modern context solidified many European nation-states while colonizing, removing wealth from, and stifling the cultural growth of the rest of the world.

For example, we can symbolically, if not substantively, specify 1441 as the beginning of, perhaps, the largest displacement, forced migration, and genocide in human history – the European Christian slave trade in

Africa. In 1441, the first group of Africans were taken from the West African coast bound for the Christian land of Portugal. Upon the ship's return to its home port, the Africans were given as trinkets to Prince Henry, sovereign of a Christian country. Portugal, indeed, held the first slave auction in 1444.

Subsequently other Catholic states (such as Spain and France) and Protestant countries (such as England and Holland) joined in the physical hunt for the sale of black skins. Consequently, popes blessed the European slave trade and both Catholic and Protestant clergy accompanied the slave vessels that went forth to do the work of Jesus in Africa.

And then, of course, 1492 expresses the paradigmatic marker of modernity. Precisely in the 1492 rise of European modernity, we see the confluence of Columbus, the European Christian church, and African slavery. Even before the historic voyage of 1492, a papal bull issued in 1455 commended Prince Henry of Portugal "for his devotion and apostolic zeal in spreading the name of Christ." At the same time, this decree gave the Prince "authorization to conquer and possess distant lands and their wealth."[1] Here a pattern was set that was to undergird Columbus' voyage as well as that of every other European slave ship on the way to the west coast of Africa.

Indeed, a brief look at the commission received by Christopher Columbus prior to his first trip reveals the European mindset toward non-European peoples and their lands. On April 30, 1492, Spain's King Ferdinand and Queen Isabella wrote:

> For as much as you, Christopher Columbus, are going by our command, with some of our vessels and men, to discover and subdue some Islands and Continent in the ocean, and it is hoped that by God's assistance, some of the said Islands and Continent in the ocean will be discovered and conquered by your means and conduct, therefore it is but just and reasonable, that since you expose yourself to such danger to serve us, you should be rewarded for it.[2]

In this commissioning, we have the joining of several factors. First, Columbus does not venture forth as a solitary voyager. He is authorized by the state, the highest authority in the civil and political realm. Furthermore, his charge is by definition to discover, conquer, and subdue foreign lands. And very importantly, given this definition and the will of the state represented by Columbus, God would assist the victory of European peoples over non-European populations.

What is the reward offered to Columbus for his labors? Ferdinand and Isabella continue:

> Our will is, That you, Christopher Columbus, after discovering and conquering the said Islands and Continent in the said ocean, or any of them, shall be our Admiral of the said Islands and Continent you shall so discover and conquer ... You and your Lieutenants shall conquer and freely decide all causes, civil and criminal ... and that you have power to punish offenders.[3]

Thus he receives personal titles of nobility and, with "God's assistance," the authority to decide and punish any persons who would disobey his command. With this commission in hand, Columbus set forth on August 3, 1492. He wrote in his journal that the inhabitants of the New World would make good Christians and "good servants" for Spain. When Portugal protested this commission to Columbus, the arbitration of this territorial dispute fell not to an international tribunal of lawyers or heads of state but only to the European Christian church.

On May 4, 1493, Pope Alexander VI issued a papal bull in Spain's favor. In it, the pope first acknowledged Columbus, who "with divine aid and with the utmost diligence sailing in the ocean sea, discovered certain very remote islands and even mainlands." Regarding Ferdinand and Isabella, the pope wrote:

> And in order that you may enter upon so great an undertaking with greater readiness and heartiness endowed with the benefit of our apostolic favor, we, of our own accord, not at your instance nor the request of anyone else in your regard, but out of our own sole largess and certain knowledge and out of the fullness of our apostolic power, by the authority of Almighty God conferred upon us in blessed Peter and of the vicarship of Jesus Christ ... should any of said islands have been found by your envoys and captains, give, grant, and assign to you and your heirs and successors ... forever together with all their dominions, cities, camps, places, and villages, and all rights, jurisdiction ... all islands and mainlands found and to be found.[4]

From the European church's perspective, at the dawn of modernity, clearly, conquering and subduing are a corollary to the act of discovering foreign territory and peoples. Moreover, as theological justification, the pope draws on the authority of "Almighty God," the "vicarship of Jesus Christ," the tradition of "apostolic power," and the premier role of Peter. This gets at the heart of the modern context for the subsequent rise of black theology of liberation. Certain elements of European power (a trinitarian alliance of Christianity, the state, and world discovery) were compelled to ape their God or justify their attempts at economic, cultural, and spiritual domination of the earth's darker-skinned peoples. The impulse is one of normative claims rationally leading to spreading the Cross and culture to black people. This sector of modern European power would tell dark-skinned peoples what they could believe and what they could think about their beliefs.

The papal bull closes with these words:

> Let no one therefore infringe, or with rash boldness contravene,
> this our recommendation, exhortation, requisition, gift,
> grant, assignment, constitution, deputation, decree, mandate,
> prohibition, and will. Should anyone presume to attempt this, be
> it known to him that he will incur the wrath of Almighty God
> and of the blessed apostles Peter and Paul.[5]

The European Christian slave trade of the fifteenth to nineteenth centuries (that is, from 1441 to 1888, when slavery was abolished in Brazil) in West Africa forever disrupted the balance of material resources in world history. West African (and North American, Brazilian, Jamaican, and Cuban) black labor (through cotton and other commodities) coupled with European Christian appropriation of Africa's raw materials built the British and North American industrial revolutions and facilitated their concomitant technological innovations.[6] And, in the long view of history, the foundation of North America's superpower emergence was laid by taking the indigenous people's land and eliminating human populations to near extinction.

And after 400 years of legal chattels, it is no accident that the nineteenth-century legal end of European Christian, international slavery was followed by the 1884–85 Berlin Conference. Here, Western European powers (with the American government's knowledge) carved up those African land areas to be colonized by European countries. Before this conference, a map of Africa reflected vast land areas with somewhat fluid boundaries. After Berlin, the African map was redrawn with color-coded countries created and controlled by European nations. By 1902, European powers controlled, at least, 90 percent of the entire continent. While a fruitful harvest of wealth transfer from Africa and other parts of the world to Europe and North America was being reaped, the reverse happened with regard to religions. Because of the consolidation of European modernity's global expansion by the late 1890s, it is no accident that Western powers regarded the nineteenth century as one of the high points of their

Christian missionary activity. With the military and merchants securing the beachhead, missionaries followed closely behind. Sometimes they accompanied the armies and the business sectors. The West took the wealth of the rest and exchanged it for their Cross of Jesus.

Again, Africa fell to immense material and human resources transfer and Christian missionary activity. The development of Western modernity led to the underdevelopment of the continent. And, at the same time, the nineteenth century saw an onslaught of ideological attacks on the natural and God-given humanity of Africans and the global dark-skinned diaspora. The nineteenth-century European creation of the racial theories of the "science of man," and the disciplines of anthropology, philosophy, and missiology, to name only a few, heralded two plumb-line questions in the theoretical and religious imagination of some major European thinkers.[7] Are Africans and the darker-skinned global peoples (1) naturally human and (2) created in the Christian God's image? The first query points to a scientific matter; the second to theology.

The questioning of biological evidence's particularity and the Genesis narrative's universality not only hounded the "being-human" status of Africa and its internationalized descendants. We find questioning of the humanity of darker-skinned people throughout the earth. For instance, the 1770 voyage of British explorer, navigator, and cartographer James Cook marked the first European contact with the eastern coast of Australia. He was also the first European to see the Hawaiian people in 1778. Those daring trips brought Europe into close contact with what Cook cited in his diary as people of very dark or black color.[8] Eventually, Britain colonized the indigenous people of Australia, and US missionaries and entrepreneurs overthrew the internationally recognized kingdom of Hawaii.

And so the questions of whether black people were human since they lacked what Europeans called a civilized culture and whether they were capable of having an authentic religious faith endured throughout modernity, throughout the world. Any group of animals can have a culture, but was it human culture? Any group of people can worship all kinds of things, but was it Christian worship? Could they be black (i.e., remain faithful to their indigenousness) and religious (i.e., as defined by European Christians)?

CONTEMPORARY CONTEXT

The contemporary context provides the second major backdrop for the rise of today's black theology of liberation. Key to this theological context was the first written statement by black pastors on Jesus, power, and the church. Published in the *New York Times*, this "Black Power" document of July 31, 1966 did not, however, fall from the sky as if by magic. Rather, within the political, cultural, and religious dynamics of the 1950s and 1960s, we encounter direct incentives for the emergence of the July declaration penned by African American clergy. This public statement stands for the exact beginning of the emergence of contemporary black theology of liberation.

The civil rights movement (1955 to late 1960s), known globally because of the Baptist preacher and theologian Martin Luther King, Jr., comes as the first incentive. The Revd. Dr. Martin Luther King, Jr. combined black slave theology (that God is justice, protest, and freedom), national liberation movements (the initiative of underdeveloped countries toward self-determination), Gandhian nonviolence (thus expressing solidarity with the world's darker-skinned people), and the lofty ideals of the US Constitution and Declaration of Independence (concerning the rights of modern citizens).

King's theology and African American church practice were new. They made the fight for freedom the defining objective of Christianity and called upon faith communities to actively change the world, even at the risk of physical harm. Consequently, Americans could not call themselves Christian if they violated the full humanity of other human beings. This was a revolutionary change from the prevailing American Christianity that had promoted, in the main, the ideology of profit and individualism. King's life was emblematic of the civil rights movement, from the moment of his December 5, 1955, elected leadership of the Montgomery, Alabama, bus boycott against legal segregation to his assassination on April 4, 1968 in Memphis, Tennessee. At the end, King interpreted the life of Jesus as liberation of the poor and the oppressed. Demonstrable evidence for this claim exists in his final twin goals: supporting the black working class in Memphis, Tennessee, and organizing a multiracial poor people's campaign to camp out in Washington, DC, with the explicit purpose of disrupting the national government.

The appearance of Black Power (on June 16, 1966), symbolized as the resurrection of Malcolm X's thought after his February 1965 murder, constituted the second incentive for the emerging black theology. While the civil rights initiatives linked Christianity with justice and church militancy, the black power movement situated the cultural identity of blackness at the center of any real justice for African Americans. That meant the right of self-identity: the right to name one's black and African self independent of white control; and the right of self-determination: to control black communities unhindered by white power. Unlike the civil rights effort's limited terrain, black power swept every region of the country and affected every quarter of the African American community.

A third contemporary incentive for the rise of today's black theology of liberation was the publication of Joseph R. Washington's book *Black Religion* in 1964. Civil rights and black power movements came from the streets. Washington's theoretical argument, in contrast, surrounded itself in the sanctity of the hallowed halls of the academy. Moreover, he was an African American religious leader who emerged out of the black church. This insider argued as follows. Because of segregation, white churches were the authentic inheritors of the Christian tradition from Europe. White religion was genuine because they had faith in Jesus Christ. Linked as they were to the correct tradition with faith in the correct object meant that white believers had the capacity to renew their belief and practice by comparing contemporary living with the tradition and the founder. White theology, therefore, entailed reflecting critically on tradition and faith in Jesus.

Segregation produced the opposite effect for black communities. Outside of authentic white churches, and white Christian tradition, black churches, furthermore, had "belief." Belief meant belief in anything, including justice for the poor. But, for Washington, the Christian word "faith" had a limited and singular meaning – faith in Jesus Christ. If black people did not have authentic churches (as a result of segregation, which meant separation from white worshippers) or an authentic lineage to Christianity through European churches, and they had no faith in Jesus Christ (in contrast to a generic belief in anything), then blacks did not have a theology. Again, theology is critical reflection by a community on their relation to their faith in Jesus as this community exists in an authentic church connected to the European church traditions. Hence, the direct challenge became – no such thing as a black theology existed. Understandably, part of the incentive for the rise of contemporary black theology of liberation, at least on the academic front, was a refutation of Joseph Washington's thesis of denial.

Washington wrote specifically for the 1960s US Christian community. Yet the logic of his argument elevating "true" white and European Christianity and subordinating indigenous folk religions revealed the same negative global attitudes that helped give rise to other black theologies and other forms of progressive theologies from the earth's darker-skinned peoples.

However, the incentives of the civil rights and black power movements outside of the academy and Joseph Washington's book from the academy existed within larger global and historical currents. Black theology, a pioneering liberation theology indigenous to the USA, started in the global context of a shift in world order, particularly after World War II – the second major violent conflict on European soil in the contemporary era. A combination of international and domestic factors came together to provide the backdrop for the origin of black theology in the mid 1960s. Black theology did not descend willy-nilly from the heavens but burst onto the North American domestic scene (and globally) through a combination of local and international influences.

For instance, the post-World War II era positioned the US government and its monopoly corporations as the undisputed champions of capitalism and American-style democracy in the non-communist world. The war's end also had an immediate effect on 1950s black civil rights efforts in the southeastern United States. Black Americans supported this seductive ideology of liberation from fascism and communism. These systems were based on either racial superiority (such as Nazism) or human rights violations (owing to state dominance). If the world's greatest government had stopped Hitler's blitzkriegs and fought to make the world safe for democracy, then surely this same government would soon resurrect its own black citizens from the death of racial apartheid at home.

The rhetoric and worldview championed by North American power structures abroad were taken very seriously by African Americans fighting against white supremacy and voting discrimination at home. But when black soldiers came back home, reality soon set in. Blacks began asking how the US government, which apparently seemed so sympathetic to people millions of miles away, could neglect, if not oppress, its own black citizens – many of whom lived a stone's throw from the White House in Washington, DC. And so an evolving postwar debate about freedom, democracy, and equality helped give rise to the civil rights movement.

Indeed, talk of a better world did help start the African American mass efforts for justice. But so too did the concrete reality of the numbers of black Americans who fought abroad against Nazism and biological supremacy; it made a deep imprint on the historical experience of collective black America. African American GIs returning from tours of duty after World War II and the Korean War had accumulated firsthand knowledge of the world, especially about racial relations. They learned that it was possible for white working-class youth from Mississippi (Ku

Klux Klan country) to live, work, sleep, and play with black working-class youth from backwoods Georgia (post-slavery land).

The two antagonists could reconcile their differences and function as equals in the midst of waging war for a higher cause. All the white eugenics theorists, all the social determinist professors, all the propagandizing politicians, and all the white theologians had been wrong, absolutely wrong. Life experiences proved not racial irreconcilability but rather racial unity grounded in a justice goal. At minimum, war forced a functional unity for co-human survival.

Furthermore, black soldiers abroad felt free for the first time, relative to their home experiences. The only segregation the French sought was to identify and isolate the hated Brown Shirts. Unless instigated by American whites, the word "nigger" did not pass from the lips of white Europeans when they saw a black person in one of Uncle Sam's uniforms. On the contrary, black soldiers felt so liberated while in Europe they even experimented with interracial relationships with French and other white European women. Unlike in small-town Alabama, no cries for lynching were heard.

To be seen by whites in Europe as simply other humans was a revolutionary education for black GIs. The unthinkable – that divine creation, mental endowment, cultural incompatibility, natural antagonism, and human tradition did not prevent black and white equality – had occurred. Discharged from duty, African Americans re-entered civilian life in the United States determined not to let legal segregation prevent them from building a healthy community for their families and for all people.

The domino effect of global decolonization also fanned the flames of black church-led 1950s civil rights initiatives and the 1960s black power challenges. African American communities and churches were well aware of the struggle for self-determination being fought by brown, yellow, and black peoples in the international arena. As early as 1938, for example, numerous black churches rallied to defend Ethiopia from Italy's invasion. India's independence from Great Britain in 1947 conveyed some of the first signs of hope. Mao Zedong's wave of Red Guards successfully moved the People's Republic of China out of the capitalist orbit in 1949. And starting with Ghana's independence ceremonies in 1957 and Nigeria's in 1959, European colonial administrations in Africa gave way to indigenous ruling structures. Also in 1959, just 90 miles from the US mainland, mountain guerrillas began the process of resituating Cuba as an independent nation with a substantial African citizenry.

Restated, World War II so captured the attention and resources of European colonial powers that it gave nations on the global, political, and economic periphery an opportunity to assert themselves as independent actors. Thereafter, the Cold War between the United States and the Union of Soviet Socialist Republics further opened the crack of opportunity for newly developing nations to fight for independence and national liberation.

In the 1960s and 1970s, black theology centered the concept of "liberation" within religious and theological dialogue. This language was directly influenced by the national liberation speeches and slogans of Third World nations, both nonaligned and socialist, as they called for national independence against structures of (white) colonial powers (during the 1950s and 1960s). Similarly, black theology was the first religious movement to clearly equate Jesus the Anointed One with the liberation of the oppressed in North America in the struggle against structures of (white) domestic power. It did so because African American theologians were heavily influenced by national liberation fronts that were fighting against (white) colonialists around the world.

In the language of global resistance organizations, *liberation* had an exact meaning that was adopted by black theology into the Christian conversation about protest for equality. An oppressed nation, by the standards of both the United Nations and the former Communist International, had the right to separate from systematic restrictions that victimized its people.

Third World peoples were nations because of unification by a common language, territory, culture, tradition, and (perhaps) racial or ethnic stock. This liberation discourse resonated with black pastors' understanding of the Old Testament vision of slaves liberated from oppression and Jesus' New Testament earthly mission to liberate the poor and the oppressed. Drawing on the grammar of international organizing for independence, black theology combined this talk with a Christian framework of Jesus the Ultimate Liberator. Although not all black theologians advocated an absolute separation or independence from America as the final goal, all agreed that blacks had the right to self-identity – for instance, name change, African culture, linguistic style, slave tradition, racial lineage; and the right of self-determination – that is, controlling their political destiny and physical communities.

Two other dynamics helped nurture the civil rights and black power movements and, in turn, the birth of black theology. One was the 1954 US Supreme Court decision that declared separate facilities for blacks and whites as inherently unequal. This *Brown* v. *Board of Education* verdict emerged partly from a reassessment of the world theater by the US government and its multinational corporations. To expand post-World War II American hegemony, it was necessary to modify the apparent contradictions between domestic apartheid – violent structures against black people sanctioned by the federal administration – and US rhetoric about America being the land of opportunity. However symbolically intended by some, the Supreme Court decision nevertheless provided a major incentive for African American struggles for citizenship and full humanity.

The last factor was the Marshall Plan. This post-World War II scheme allowed American multinational corporations to penetrate Europe and helped boost the American economy back home. With the domestic economy improving, American citizens became more positive about the future. Like other Americans, blacks experienced rising expectations about their education and standards of living. As a result, the belief that each generation of children would improve beyond the lifestyle of their parents increased tremendously. Global macroeconomic realities suggested national microeconomic expectations. The international payoff of progress for white Americans spurred the impatience of African Americans domestically.

Against this global backdrop, black theology emerged from the work of a group of radical African American pastors and religious educators whose faith challenged them to link Christianity and the black struggle for social transformation. It was an attempt to redeem the soul of, and reorganize, the North American system. Starting in July 1966, black theology rose with close links to the thrusts of the two major movements of the 1950s and 1960s: the goals of racial equality (black power) and real democracy (civil rights).

The ad hoc National Committee of Negro Churchmen, the signatories of the July 31, 1966, black power statement, announced that African Americans had the right to think theologically and that all God-talk inherently advanced notions of racial power. Published in March 1969, James H. Cone's *Black Theology and Black Power* was an inaugural book on liberation theology. Using the lens of the African American experience, he argued that the core message of the Bible paradigmatically expressed by Jesus the Anointed One was liberation of the materially poor. Consequently, ecclesial formations, educational venues, and civic society were called by God to focus on the liberation of the least in society: the broken-hearted, the wounded, working people, the outcast, the marginalized, the oppressed, and those surviving in structural poverty. Based on biblical theological criteria, Cone claimed, white churches and most African American churches had failed their vocational assignments regarding their faith and their witness. This text offered the first sustained theological argument relating to issues of liberation, racial cultural identity, and a new material kingdom on earth in the interests of society's majority. This pioneering work, along with his subsequent publications, meant that Cone is generally cited, nationally and internationally, as the father of contemporary black theology of liberation.

Since its origins in the 1960s, black theology of liberation has matured into a body of knowledge defined by its own origins, traditions, norms, global indigenous forms, and kindred disciplines. In this sense, black theology takes place wherever darker-skinned peoples in the world reflect on their faith and liberation within their own local contexts. Specifically, throughout the 1960s and 1970s, blacks in Africa, Asia, the Caribbean, Latin America, and in the United States of America initiated and participated in various social-justice movements. Such movements included different dimensions of protest; however, one commonality was the issue of race or the discrimination suffered by darker-skinned people in various countries. Many churches, ecclesial leaders, and professors began to respond to these social movements and, consequently, began to raise theological questions. For instance, what does the Gospel of Christianity have to say about the changes in the contemporary political and cultural scenery? What is theological about the emergence of once-silenced voices? The first move was to conclude that, in general terms, the theology of former colonizers and former slave masters was insufficient. Thus, the second move: black Christians and theologians created a new way of doing theology from their own perspectives in their own particular countries.

Though many forms of oral and written faith beliefs in Africa, Asia, the Caribbean, Latin America, the Pacific Islands, and in the USA preceded the contemporary period of black theology, not until the 1960s do we encounter the *name* "black theology" and the attempt to initiate and maintain such an *academic* discipline. Consequently, as a *self-identified* scholarly endeavor and social movement, an analysis of black theology has to return to the July 31, 1966 *New York Times* manifesto written by an ad hoc group of African American clergy.

This full-page newspaper declaration responded to the moral, cultural, economic, political, and psychological challenges posed by a young black power movement. On June 16, 1966, black youth workers of the American civil rights movement broke with the gradualist integrationist model of race relationships championed by the Revd. Dr. Martin Luther King, Jr. Instead, the youth workers articulated a new voice of black power and liberation of the poor. They assumed that African Americans as a black people needed to accept their own "racial" history, rely on their own culture, and move toward attaining their own group power. The sharing of power in society, they believed, would best facilitate an ethical relation between different racial groups. Black power advocates, furthermore, perceived intentionally the global connections of their movement by linking their efforts to colonial and postcolonial struggles of African and other peoples of the "Third World." Restated, a similar cultural and political ferment was developing among black peoples in various parts of the world, and the US black consciousness advocates consciously saw themselves as part of this global growth of heretofore left-out voices of dark peoples.

Hence, contemporary black theology of liberation originated with a specific history constituted by peculiar cultural and political contexts confronted by definite social and spiritual challenges. The July 31, 1966 statement set the initial contours of black theology. The article declared that race relations inherently entail theological issues of which groups have and which groups lack power. Specifically, whites in the USA had too much power and little conscience, while blacks had an abundance of conscience and no power. Furthermore, it confronted the assumption that American democracy accented only individual rights, while, in fact, it secured white people's group rights over black Americans' God-given rights as a people.

As we saw above, in 1969, black theology received its first coherent theological book with Cone's *Black Theology and Black Power*. Cone argued that the heart of the Christian message was liberation of the poor, who struggled against concrete structures preventing them from attaining their full humanity. And, pursuing this new liberation theology logic, he claimed that the American black-power movement was actually the Gospel of Jesus Christ. Methodologically, theology arose from and occurred within the black poor communities of the USA and poor black communities throughout the world. At the same time, because of the varied nature of black poor folk's lives, black theology needed to engage various disciplines, such as politics, psychology, culture, language, international analysis, economics, and other social sciences. Thus, the global aspect and the interdisciplinary approach of black theology continued to surface in the foundational documents of the discipline.

Similar factors of structural white racism in the Christian community and lack of culture and economic power in the black community, coupled with a new youth movement, took place in South Africa. In

1970, the South African University Christian Movement established the Black Theology Project. South African black theology was a direct off-spring of its own Black Consciousness movement headed by Steve Biko. Theological issues of liberation of the poor as the hub of the Christian discourse, Jesus Christ as liberator, and the black poor as the site of faith and a new humanity permeated South African black theology.

Black theology is an academic discipline, among darker-skinned peoples, which has grown into a global dynamic. In various parts of the world, black Christians or people of faith are developing constructive theological statements regarding their belief in and practice with a God of cultural, political, and individual liberation. They hold in common several factors.

First, they agree that the norm of black theology is a complete and integrative liberation, including the cultural right to self-identity and the political right of self-determination. Both rights flow from a moral imperative. That is to say, Jesus calls us to build healthy human communities and healthy individuals on earth. Second, the starting point is a God of liberation dwelling with and acting on behalf of the poor. More specifically, black theology begins with race, the dark-skinned peoples at the bottom of societies. From this locus of the black poor, one opens up a host of interrelated theological concerns (such as gender, class, land, inheritance, etc.).

Third, methodologically, all forms of black theology concur with the important interplay between issues that arise out of poor black people's lives and the role that theology serves in discerning the depth of prophetic faith in these lives and movements. Therefore, black theology appears on a global stage whenever dark-skinned peoples in their own indigenous countries link societal claims with theological claims. From the local context, each manifestation of black theology links to similar international conversational partners. Fourth, another distinct characteristic is black theology's simultaneous relationship to various publics – the academy, the local church, and civic community focused on religion and justice. Black theology began out of church and community concerns. It then brought to bear the expertise of the academy. Black theology, in this regard, perceives a very broad constituency and audience comprising scholars and intellectuals, as well as ecclesial and civic leaders and lay populations.

Fifth, they agree that the racial category of "black" is both a social and phenotypic creation. True, social contexts define whether one is considered black in a definite country. So, too, does phenotype, in the sense that once race is socially and contextually defined, all who fit a certain phenotype are then understood as black. It is no accident that wherever black theology arises, the darker-skinned peoples are usually at the bottom of each society, whether one speaks of Africa, Asia, the Caribbean, Latin America, the Pacific Islands, Europe, or the USA.

Perhaps on a global human scale, black theology touches the intellectual depths and emotional yearnings of all communities and all individuals, regardless of race or ethnicity, who are concerned about issues related to what it means to live responsibly in today's world. All people are searching and questioning the nature of their faith in today's commodified and consumerist culture – a fast-paced, get-rich-quick, you-can-have-it-now, superficial culture. Although we emerge from unique cultural backgrounds, we all face similar issues: who are we and how are we related to our families, the ecology, and the cosmos? What do we do in relationship to our neighbors? What does the future hold in our turbulent times of pain and struggle, sadness, and joy?

Essentially, black theology grapples deeply and sincerely with the human questions of today. And, with much passion, it searches for definite answers to these challenges, because many of those questions across the world are exacerbated when they pertain to the darker-skinned communities. And so emotional passion, intellectual clarity, and a life-and-death sense that there is something at stake characterize the contributions and longevity of black theology. When all human beings, thirsting for a new way to be human, encounter these questions and answers, and discover that they are addressed with heart and head, they have the opportunity to open themselves to the reality of humane and just living with blacks and with all brown, red, yellow, and white people. In our mutual humanity, based on commitment to the freedom of poor folk, we all thirst for some safe and comforting space where we in our families can open ourselves to intellectual interrogation of our existential feelings. Black theology achieves precisely that: it brings together pain and pleasure, sacred and secular, and heart and head.

In addition, a black theology of liberation reminds everyone continually of the necessity of experiencing a passionate love for people, especially those without voices. To love another is to recognize oneself in the face and life of another. To love someone is to immerse and expose oneself in the context and conversation and culture of another. Love is the ultimate risk of faith – a faith grounded in liberation of all humanity; a faith with a vision for a new heaven and a new earth where each person can achieve the fullest realization of his or her calling as it serves their families and the greater collective human, ecological, and cosmological whole. To have such a love is to have a hope that springs from living in a balance and harmony found within the human being and in relation to all there is and has been.

Through the ups and downs in the course of human history, what is it that sustains us? Even when it looks as if all the world is going in different, fractured directions, this hope can carry a people through. Faith, hope, and love embody a black theology of liberation. But more than that, they are what continue to keep poor and marginalized folk alive and seeking a better life for themselves, their children, and their grandchildren. Black theology attempts to make intellectual sense of all of this to help bring about a healthy human community for the poor and, indeed, for all the world's humanity.

Notes

1   Lamin Sanneh, *West African Christianity* (Maryknoll, NY: Orbis Books, 1983), p. 21.
2   H. S. Commager (ed.), *Documents of American History to 1898*, vol. 1 (New York: Appleton-Century-Crofts, 1968), p. 1.
3   Ibid., p. 1.
4   Ibid., p. 3.
5   Ibid.
6   Robert E. Lucas, Jr., *Lectures on Economic Growth* (Cambridge, MA: Harvard University Press, 2002); Joseph E Inikori, *Africans and the Industrial Revolution in England* (Cambridge University Press, 2002); Eric Hobsbawm, *The Age of Revolution: Europe 1789–1848* (London: Weidenfeld & Nicolson, 1962). We should not forget the immense exploitation and innumerable deaths caused by brutal working conditions and child labor in European countries and the USA. In fact, white workers in Europe and North America have a historical commonality of structural victimization as seen in the industrial revolution periods.
7   Dwight N. Hopkins, *Being Human: Race, Culture, and Religion* (Minneapolis, MN: Fortress Press, 2005), ch. 4.
8   See Cook's diary entry for April 22, 1770, preserved at the National Library of Australia.

2 Historical perspective

GAYRAUD S. WILMORE

BLACK RELIGION

From the earliest years of their captivity, transplanted Africans, denied access to other forms of self-affirmation and collective power, have used religion and its various institutions as the principal expression of their peoplehood and their will both to exist and to improve their condition. Black religion, characterized by fluctuation between moods of protest and accommodation, and protesting in the context of accommodating strategies, has contributed considerably to the ability of African American people to survive the worst forms of oppression and dehumanization. Beyond mere survival, as leaders and followers became more sophisticated about how to make the most of their religion, it has helped them liberate themselves, first from chattel slavery, then from ignorance and degradation, and finally – though still imperfectly – from civil inequality and subordination, to go on to greater heights of personal and group achievement.

In a classic essay on black religion, W. E. B. DuBois wrote: "Three things characterized this religion of the slave – the Preacher, the Music, and the Frenzy."[1] Although this classic description captures the dynamic of the Africans' earliest appropriation of evangelical Protestantism on both sides of the Atlantic, contemporary historical studies reveal a more complex and comprehensive pattern of religious development. From a perspective that includes not only what DuBois called "an adaptation and mingling of heathen rites ... roughly designated as Voodooism,"[2] but also the institutionalization of incipient slave worship in black American churches of the nineteenth and twentieth centuries, three dominant themes or motifs stand out as foundational from the August 1619 Jamestown, Virginia, landing of the first forced arrival of Africans to the present. They are survival, elevation, and liberation.[3]

THE AFRICAN HERITAGE

It seems incontrovertible that religious traditions brought from West Africa gave early comfort and consolation to the slaves as they were slowly acculturated to the new religion of Christianity in North America. In the beginning, African traditional religions functioned as a survival strategy for the captives struggling to maintain life and sanity under bondage to white people who regarded them as little more than beasts of burden. The first Africans who were transported in the seventeenth and eighteenth centuries brought religious beliefs and practices that prevented them from being totally dehumanized by chattel slavery. In their homeland they had shared, within many linguistic groups, certain ancient ways of life – rituals, wise sayings, and ethical teachings – that had been handed down from generation to generation.[4] Ancient beliefs, folklore, attitudes, and practices provided a holistic view of reality that made no radical separation between religion and life. There was in the affairs of the everyday no consciousness that at one moment one was being religious and at another moment nonreligious or secular. There was no sense that certain understandings of time, space, human activities, or relations between human and divine beings belonged to science or philosophy rather than to religion; to the life of the mind rather than the life of the spirit.

It may be almost impossible for modern people to understand fully the way of life out of which the slaves came. We have to change our entire habit of thought about the difference between being and doing, between reflection and action, the commonplace, ordinary affairs of daily existence and what we vaguely call the "spiritual life." Only in this way can we begin to appreciate the comprehensive, unitary character of the African consciousness. Of course, some scholars contend that the past was almost completely obliterated for the slaves brought to North America. But let us argue, for the moment, that for those who did remember anything about their former lives (and it is unreasonable to assume that everything was immediately forgotten once they disembarked on the quays of Jamestown, Virginia, or Charleston, South Carolina) there was no separation between religion and life, between the sacred and the profane. Experience was truth and truth was experience. The single entity – what we might call "life-truth" – comprehended the totality of existence. Reality was, at one and the same time, immanent and transcendent, material and spiritual, mundane and numinous.

From the beginning, certain men and women who possessed power for both good and evil, skilled in sorcery and divination, exercised extraordinary influence over the slaves. In some slave narratives and reports of white missionaries, they occasionally appear as the first recognized leaders of the community, men and women respected and feared by both slaves and masters. Through these specialists in magic, conjuration, and the healing arts, what was left of the old African religions was transplanted and integrated into the new culture of enslavement. At a deeper level, the reinterpretation and synthesis of transplanted and newly acquired religious systems, mainly evangelical Protestantism, produced a distinctive African American religious consciousness. Out of this mystical, survival-oriented consciousness, part African and part European, the shout songs and spirituals, expressing the loneliness and sorrow of a stolen people, emerged on the plantations. But with no less charismatic force the slaves' religion celebrated the sheer fact of survival despite constant brutalization in the fields, and death and disease in the living quarters.[5]

THE CHRISTIANIZATION OF THE SLAVES

Any analysis of black religion in America must begin with two issues of critical importance: the attitude of white Christians toward the Christianization and emancipation of the slaves, and the nature of the earliest slave religion. The first recorded baptism of an African in the American colonies occurred in Virginia in 1624, but there was no systematic evangelization until the eighteenth century. Even then, the colonists were in no hurry to introduce their slaves to Christianity. The British rationalized the enslavement of both Africans and Indians because they were different in appearance to themselves and because they were heathens. When it became evident that blacks were becoming believers despite widespread neglect by official church bodies, Virginia was the first of the colonies to make short shrift of the matter by declaring in 1667 that "the conferring of baptisme doth not alter the condition of the person as to his bondage or freedom."

It was difficult enough to induce a healthy state of religion among the white population. Attempts by the Society for the Propagation of the Gospel in Foreign Parts, an outpost of the bishops of London, to encourage planters to provide religious instruction for their slaves were largely unsuccessful, but almost from the beginning some blacks attended public worship and requested baptism. By the American Revolution, starting in 1776, a few had become Anglicans, Presbyterians, Baptists, and Methodists. In South Carolina, one missionary, the Revd. Samuel Thomas of Goose Creek, reported as early as 1705 that he had given religious instruction to at least a thousand slaves, many of whom could read the Bible and were memorizing the creed.

Taking the Gospel to blacks helped to ease the consciences of the colonial religious establishment about slavery, but it did not solve the problem completely. All of the American churches wrestled with the issue and, with the possible exception of the Quakers, finally compromised their ethical sensibilities. Bitter contention raged between Northern and Southern churchmen, and as early as 1837 there were splits among the Lutherans and Presbyterians. In 1844 the Methodist Church divided North and South over slavery, followed by the Baptists in 1845. The antislavery American Missionary Association virtually split the Congregational Church in 1846. The Presbyterians finally set up Northern and Southern branches in 1861, and a fissure opening up in the Episcopal Church was aborted in 1862 by the refusal of Northern Episcopalians to recognize that any controversy existed. Both the Episcopal and Roman Catholic churches, with some difficulty, were able to maintain structural unity throughout the Civil War.

THE EVOLUTION OF BLACK CHRISTIANITY

During the anguish in the white churches over slavery, the special nature of black Christianity asserted itself. We do not know when the first slaves stole away from the surveillance of the masters to worship in their own way. Two conjectures seem reasonable. First, it must have been early in the seventeenth century, for Africans would not have neglected practicing their ancestral religion altogether, and the whites did little to induce them to adopt theirs. Second, it is unlikely that the worship they engaged in was devoid of transplanted survivals from Africa. Today most scholars accept the position of W. E. B. DuBois and Melville Herskovits that fragments of African religion survived the Middle Passage and the "breaking-in" process in North America, to reappear under disguise in the early religious meetings of the "Invisible Institution" – the proto-church of the slaves. One contemporary secular scholar writes:

> In the United States, many African religious rites were fused into
> one – voodoo. From the whole panoply of African deities, the
> slaves chose the snake god of the Whydah, Fon, and Ewe. Symbolic
> of the umbilical cord and the rainbow, the snake embodied the
> dynamic, changing quality of life. In Africa it was sometimes the

god of fertility and the determiner of good and ill fortune. Only by worshipping the god could one invoke his protective spirit.[6]

There is scant evidence that Voodoo or some discrete form of reinterpreted African religion synthesized as effectively with Protestantism in the English colonies as it did with Roman Catholicism in the Caribbean and Latin America. Nevertheless, reports of missionaries and slave narratives show that the African conjurer and medicine man, the manipulation of charms and talismans, and the use of drums and dancing were present in the slaves' quarters as survival strategies, even after conversion. Selective elements of African religions were not easily exterminated. A Presbyterian missionary, the Revd. Charles C. Jones, described what he encountered among the slaves as late as 1842:

> True religion they are inclined to place in profession, in forms and ordinances, and in excited states of feeling. And true conversion in dreams, visions, trances, voices – all bearing a perfect or striking resemblance to some form or type which has been handed down for generations, or which has been originated in the wild fancy of some religious teacher among them.[7]

Revd. Jones warned his fellow missionaries that the blacks displayed sophisticated perversions of the Gospel accountable only to the influence of African survivals. So impressed was he with their covert resistance to white Christianity that he compared their objections to "the ripe scholarship and profound intelligence of critics and philosophers." African religion – childlike?

The dark and contrary side of black religion must be understood as an alternative form of spirituality. It is a fundamental aspect of what we may call the survival tradition and was indelibly imprinted on a persistently heterodox form of Christianity that came down through the African American churches, sects, and cults into the twentieth century.

THE FIRST BLACK CHURCHES

Although there was a black congregation on the plantation of William Byrd III, near Mecklenburg, Virginia, as early as 1758,[8] the first black-led churches formed along the Savannah River in Georgia and South Carolina in the 1770s, and in the North at about the same time. Immediately following the 1776 American Revolution, black imitations of white Baptist and Methodist churches appeared in Philadelphia,

Baltimore, and New York City. But in the Sea Islands off South Carolina and Georgia, in Louisiana, and on scattered plantations across the Southeast, a distinctive form of black folk religion flourished and infused the adopted white evangelicalism with retentions of African spirituality. A new and implacable African American Christianity was being created, much less puritanical and otherworldly than its white counterpart. For example, the three best-known slave revolts were led by fervently religious men – Gabriel Prosser in 1800 (Virginia), Denmark Vesey in 1822 (South Carolina), and Nat Turner in 1831 (Virginia). Studies of the music of the early black church show that hidden rebelliousness and a desire for emancipation were often expressed in song. The independent black churches – particularly the African Methodist Episcopal (AME) Church and the African Methodist Episcopal Zion Church (AMEZ) – were "freedom churches" in the sense that their latent, if not manifest, concern was liberation from slavery and elevation to a higher status through education and self-help.

David George, who served as de facto pastor of an independent black congregation at Silver Bluff, South Carolina, before 1775; George Liele and Andrew Bryan of the First Colored Baptist Church in Savannah, Georgia; Josiah Bishop of Portsmouth, Virginia, and other preachers – from 1760 to 1795 – were all former slaves who ministered in hostile territory under the sponsorship and with the encouragement of radical white Baptist preachers. Some among them, such as the full-blooded African "Uncle Jack," "Black Harry" Hosier, who served the Methodist bishop Francis Asbury, and the many illiterate preachers mentioned in missionary reports and other sources, are almost legendary.[9]

Many of their sermons dealt with the deliverance of Israel from Egyptian captivity, the stories of heroism and faithfulness in the Old Testament, and the identification of Jesus with the poor and downtrodden masses. Though mainly untutored, but rarely unsophisticated, they told "many-a-truth in a joke," as the saying goes, slyly philosophizing about how "God don't like ugly," and "everybody talkin' 'bout heaven ain't goin' there," obliquely reassuring their congregations of the ultimate vindication of their suffering. These homiletical folk pronouncements reaffirmed black people's belief in a God who would punish the slave masters one day. Moreover, many animal tales, adages, and proverbs that make up the corpus of black folklore were repeated from the pulpit as homiletical devices, as, passed down through the oral tradition, one preacher said, to "explain the unexplainable, define the indefinable, and unscrew the inscrutable."

The theological motif of these early preachers was survival by virtue of supernatural power available to believers. They were preoccupied with maintaining their people's sanity, keeping them alive, helping them to retain some semblance of personhood and self-esteem in the face of massive dehumanization. Blassingame writes:

> One of the primary reasons the slaves were able to survive
> the cruelty they faced was that their behavior was not totally
> dependent on their masters ... In religion, a slave exercised his
> own independence of conscience. Convinced that God watched
> over him, the slave bore his earthly afflictions in order to earn a
> heavenly reward. Often he disobeyed his earthly master's rules
> to keep his Heavenly Master's commandments ... Religious
> faith gave an ultimate purpose to his life, a sense of communal
> fellowship and personal worth, and reduced suffering from fear
> and anxiety.[10]

DEVELOPMENT OF THE NORTHERN CHURCHES

A somewhat different tradition developed among black churches in the North. Many of their pastors also emerged from slavery and humble rural backgrounds. But in the freer atmosphere of the North the theological content of their religion took a different turn. It tended toward the ethical revivalism that took hold of white Protestant churches following the Second Great Awakening (1790–1815). It was more urbane, more appealing to those blacks who were beginning to enjoy a relative measure of prosperity and greater educational opportunities.

After Richard Allen and Absalom Jones protested racial segregation by walking out of St. George's Methodist Church in Philadelphia in 1787, they founded a quasi-religious community organization called the Free African Society, which was replicated in other cities. In Baltimore, New York, Providence, and Boston, these associations – dedicated to the educational, moral, and religious uplift of Africans – became the scaffolding of the black churches of the North. Immediately following voluntary or forced separation from the white churches, African Americans demonstrated an overarching interest in social, economic, and political advancement by making their new churches the center of such activities. They were aided by white friends such as Anthony Benezet and Benjamin Rush of Philadelphia in organizing and funding their benevolent societies, but their churches were the main engines driving all "secular" enterprise. The primary impulse behind these Northern developments was a desire for autonomy, racial solidarity, self-help, and personal and group elevation.

Thus, Peter Spencer formed a new denomination, the Union Church of African Members, in Wilmington, Delaware, in 1813;[11] Richard Allen became the first bishop of the African Methodist Episcopal Church, founded in Philadelphia in 1816; James Varick, the first bishop of the African Methodist Episcopal Zion Church denomination, founded in New York in 1821. These men, together with Absalom Jones, rector of St. Thomas Episcopal Church of Africans in Philadelphia; John Gloucester, pastor of the First African Presbyterian Church of the same city; Peter Williams, Jr., the first ordained black priest of the Episcopal Church in New York; and Thomas Paul, founder of the first black Baptist Church, also in New York City, were all strong, progressive leaders who, in the first two decades of the nineteenth century, promoted education and social betterment as a religious obligation. They encouraged Northern laypeople to undertake racial progress programs. We can speak of these Northern church leaders, therefore, as elevationists in the sense that their concerns went beyond mere survival. Although a physician and journalist, Martin R. Delany, of Pittsburgh, is a good example of the elevationist orientation. For Delany, education, self-help, a desire for equality and racial advancement were ladders of black elevation and "the means by which God intended man to succeed."[12]

The concept of elevation appears by name in black literature throughout the nineteenth century. Black men and women, clergy and lay, envisioned a broad horizon of racial uplift or advancement through religion.[13] They were the ones who dominated the free black communities of the North and led such causes as the boycotting of goods produced by slave labor, resistance to efforts of the American Colonization Society to return them to Africa, and conducting activities at a time when public meetings of blacks were forbidden in the South and even preaching was prohibited except under white supervision.

Some of the most ardent champions of the doctrine of racial elevation were black women. Concerned about the stability of the family, the education of children, and the cultivation of Christian morality, they organized female societies and auxiliaries alongside of the churches and other male-dominated institutions. The sermons and writings of Amanda Berry Smith, Maria Stewart, Frances Ellen Watkins Harper, Fannie Barrier Williams, Lucy Craft Laney, and Nannie H. Burroughs bear eloquent testimony to the special emphasis black women put upon uplifting black folk, making the church more responsible for "racial promotion," and training young women for parenting and leadership roles in church and community.[14]

As the clergy became more distracted by ecclesiastical responsibilities, the secular organizations that they had spawned gradually became autonomous, although still under the parental influence of the larger churches. Such was the case of the American Moral Reform Society and the National Negro Convention movement. The latter first met in a church in 1830 and held seven consecutive annual convocations on elevationist issues. Many of these meetings were attended by liberal whites, to whom they provided an opportunity to continue a fellowship with blacks (and to exercise subtle control) that had been made more difficult by the development of separate black churches. The regional and national conventions devoted to abolition and moral reform also represented the liberation motif that was nurtured by a black middle class anxious for upward mobility. It soon extricated itself from the direct control of the preachers. Its real impetus was to come from church-related, but intellectually independent laymen and women – from Paul Cuffee, the Massachusetts sea captain, to Maria Stewart, Booker T. Washington, and W. E. B. DuBois. In the antebellum period (before 1860) the themes of liberation and racial elevation were sponsored by relatively wealthy laymen such as James Forten, Robert Purvis, William Whipper, and William C. Nell. The most influential among them was the journalist David Walker, whose incendiary *Appeal to the Colored Citizens of the World* in 1829 inspired former slaves such as Frederick Douglass and William Wells Brown, and such "free born" propagandists as Martin R. Delany, William H. Day, and H. Ford Douglass.[15]

A COMPARISON OF MOTIFS

There is, obviously, an intricate and dialectical relationship between the survival, liberation, and elevation traditions in the black community. All three were seminal in the churches of the nineteenth century and continued into the next century in various configurations and degrees of tension, depending upon the situation that existed in different geographical areas. In the ghetto of Los Angeles, between 1906 and World War I, the survival-oriented followers of William J. Seymour and other charismatic evangelists produced an unprecedented display of African religious retentions that had lain dormant for a hundred years in the interstices of black rural society. Thus a black Pentecostalism was born that had been nurtured in the "Invisible Institution" (i.e., the secret worship services of the enslaved), but almost extinguished by the middle-class Negro churches and the white missionaries who came South with the Union Army especially after the end of the Civil War (1861–65). Holiness or Pentecostalism claimed 34 percent of the black churches in New York City in the mid 1920s. In twelve other Northern cities in 1930, 37 percent of the churches were storefront missions that fostered a volatile combination of survival and liberation hermeneutics. During and after World War I this distinctive strain of lower-class religion, derided and repudiated by the elevation-oriented churches of the established middle classes, was radicalized, and in the white-hot, purifying fires of its African-like forge metamorphosed into various religio-political sects and cults, including blackenized versions of Judaism and Islam.

The liberation and elevation traditions began with the determination to survive, but they go beyond "make do" to "do more," and from "do more" to "freedom now" and "black power." All three strategies have to do with "making and keeping life human." They are basic to African American life and culture, and are intertwined in complex ways throughout the history of the diaspora. All three traditions are responses to hard reality in a dominating "white man's world." All three arise from the same religious sensibility that crystallized in African American Christian, Afro-Islamic, and Afro-Judaic sects and cults since the mid eighteenth century.

Beginning in 1955, it was the genius of Martin Luther King, Jr., that brought the three motifs or traditions together again in a prophetic ministry that wedded the deep spirituality and will to survive of the alienated and impoverished masses, with the sophisticated pragmatism and will to achieve equality and liberation that characterized the parvenu urbanites and the Negro intelligentsia – the "New Negro" of the Harlem Renaissance (which began in the early years of the twentieth century in New York City). King embraced all three of these tendencies and created a multidimensional movement, inseparable from the black church that set in motion social, political, economic, religious, and cultural forces that have not yet run their full course. Martin King stands, therefore, at the pinnacle of black religious and political development in the twentieth century. He was not alone in pointing the way to a new future; for the black Muslim minister Malcolm X forced a decisive break between moderate accommodationism that compromised the liberation ideal and a form of protest that was truly revolutionary, which ultimately radicalized King. But in King was the confluence of all the complex and variegated tendencies and orientations that are summed up in the three motifs of survival, liberation, and elevation. Other leaders were to come out of the sacred ground upon which he stood, yet beyond him lay unexplored heights that could not have been seen without standing on his shoulders.

The publication in 1969 of James H. Cone's thunderous challenge to Euro-American theological scholarship, *Black Theology and Black Power*,[16] made room for an alternative strategy for the black church and an intrusive new tenant in the halls of academia. This method of theologizing had not been altogether absent during the years before King, but had sulked in the shadows outside the mainstream black churches and the ivy-covered walls of their schools and colleges. Cone's first book gave a name to this neglected and ignored stream of African American religious thought that probably came into existence when the first slave tossed all night on his straw mat, wondering why he should be expected to believe in a God who ordained all blacks to perpetual bondage. The name given by Cone to what he found pulsating just beneath the surface of King's more conciliatory Social Gospel was "black liberation theology," the religious first cousin to the Black Power philosophy enunciated and popularized by Stokely Carmichael and Charles V. Hamilton.[17]

Before the end of the 1960s the liberation theme had once again regained ascendancy and proliferated far beyond the black ghettoes of the United States. Liberation theology took root among oppressed campesinos and barrio-dwellers in Latin America, among black Christians in South Africa, white feminists and black womanists in the United States. It rapidly became a major topic among theologians on both sides of the Atlantic and in such ecumenical circles as the World Council of Churches. But the discussion was not limited to seminaries and church councils. A small but belligerent movement for black religious power and social transformation broke out under the aegis of a new coalition of African American church executives, pastors, and academics that called itself the National Committee of Black Churchmen (NCBC) – a Northern version of King's Southern Christian Leadership Conference (SCLC). The watchword in important segments of the African American religious community was liberation – freedom from racism, poverty, powerlessness, and every form of white domination. Liberation became a theological code word for the indigenous religious genius of the oppressed masses. On their part, African American theologians, freed from dependence upon priestcraft and deference to ecclesiastical authority, even within the black church, began to teach and write a revolutionary Christianity that began with Jesus, whom they called the Black Messiah. Jesus was the Oppressed Man of God who challenged the hypocrisy of Jewish religion, recapitulated in white Christianity and the corruptions of Negro religion, and the unjust power of the Roman state, recapitulated in the world-wide political and economic hegemony of American capitalism at the end of the twentieth century.

FACING THE PRESENT CRISIS

The holistic character of black religion was fractured after King and Malcolm, and both the black church and black culture, previously inseparable, lost that essential connection. Today they find themselves, in the first instance, in the throes of a crisis of faith; and in the second instance, in the grip of a crisis of meaning.

We still need a definitive study of how Black Power and the contemporary expression of black theology closely related to it, attempted to draw out the dialectical character of black religion implied and illuminated by King's leadership. He was never prepared to acknowledge those implications, or admit that he had made a contribution to the radical rethinking of black Christianity. The new black theology, however, is grounded in the liberation tradition of one important segment of the mainline black church to which he belonged. It seeks to learn from and assimilate the values of the black consciousness form of the survival tradition that he enlisted by the appeal made to the urban masses within and outside of the churches. The two streams of liberation and survival point to the diverse perspectives in the black theology movement today. If it still holds together such divergent points of view as that of Albert B. Cleage, Jr., Cornel West, J. Deotis Roberts, and James H. Cone, it is because this way of doing theology in the post-civil rights black community stands astride of both Martin Luther King, the tenderhearted liberationist, and Malcolm X, the tough-minded survivalist.

Perhaps the time has come to reassert the great black religious tradition we have been examining; to insert values that are truly Afrocentric (that is, to take seriously the role of Africa in world civilizations); and to rescue the inheritance of Martin and Malcolm – the strategies of survival, liberation, and elevation – from moral and spiritual debasement by children who never knew them and who, shamefully, were never taught the truth about who they are and how they came to this sorry plight.

This, I take it, is one of the goals of black theology. If the Church will return to basics and tap once again into that ennobling and enlightened religion that brought blacks through the civil rights period (from 1955 well into the 1960s) and helped them amass a modicum of Black

Power (from 1966 well into the 1970s), perhaps the crisis of these years into the twenty-first century will be surmounted and they can go into the next with integrity and hope. Martin King anticipated this possibility. Indeed, it was a part of his dream – an embracing of enduring values, a profoundly religious reorientation, a rejuvenation of the spirit of blackness. This may well be what he was talking about when, at the end of his last book, he wrote these words:

> This is our challenge. If we will dare to meet it honestly, historians in future years will have to say that there lived a great people – a Black people – who bore their burdens of oppression in the heat of many days and who, through tenacity and creative commitment, injected a new meaning into the veins of American life.[18]

Notes

1 W. E. Burghardt DuBois, *The Souls of Black Folk* (New York: Fawcett Publications, Inc., 1961), p. 141.
2 Ibid., p. 145.
3 See Gayraud S. Wilmore, *Black Religion and Black Radicalism: An Interpretation of the Religious History of African Americans*, rev. 3rd edn. (Maryknoll, NY: Orbis Books, 1998).
4 Richard F. Burton, *The Proverbs: Wit and Wisdom from Africa* (New York: Negro University Press, 1969), p. 25.
5 See Wilmore, *Black Religion and Black Radicalism*; and Dwight N. Hopkins, *Down, Up, and Over: Slave Religion and Black Theology* (Minneapolis, MN: Fortress Press, 1999).
6 John W. Blassingame, *The Slave Community: Plantation Life in the Antebellum South* (New York: Oxford University Press, 1972), p. 33.
7 Charles Colcock Jones, *The Religious Instruction of Negroes in the United States* (Savannah, GA: T. Purse Company, 1842), p. 125.
8 Mechal Sobel, *Trabelin' On: The Slave Journey to an Afro-Baptist Faith* (Westport, CN: Greenwood Press, 1979), p. 296.
9 James Melvin Washington, *Frustrated Fellowship: The Black Baptist Quest for Social Power* (Macon, GA: Mercer University Press, 1991).
10 Blassingame, *Slave Community*, p. 206.
11 Lewis V. Baldwin, *The Mark of a Man: Peter Spencer and the African Union Methodist Tradition* (Lanham, MD: University Press of America, 1987), p. 15.
12 Martin R. Delaney, *The Condition, Elevation, Emigration, and Destiny of the Colored People of the United States and Official Report of the Niger Valley Exploring Party* (Amherst, NY: Humanity Books, 2004; originally published in 1852 and 1861).
13 Delores Williams combines the survival and elevation motifs into a dyadic emphasis, which she terms "the survival/quality-of-life

tradition." This, she concludes, is a female-centered tradition originally appropriated from the Bible and emphasizing God's positive response to the black family rather than capitulation to the degrading, hopeless conditions of black existence during and after slavery. Delores S. Williams, *Sisters in the Wilderness: The Challenge of Womanist God-Talk* (Maryknoll, NY: Obis Books, 1993), p. 6.

14   For example, see Amanda Berry Smith (Introduction by Jualynne Dodson), *An Autobiography: The Story of the Lord's Dealings with Mrs. Amanda Smith the Colored Evangelist*, Schomberg Library of Nineteenth-Century Black Women (New York: Oxford University Press, 1988); and Marilyn Richardson (ed.), *Maria Stewart, America's First Black Woman Political Writer: Essays and Speeches* (Bloomington, IN: Indiana University Press, 1987).

15   See Henry Highland Garnet, *Walker's Appeal, with a Brief Sketch of His Life* (New York: J. H. Tobitt Co., 1848); Herbert Aptheker, *"One Continual Cry," David Walker's Appeal* (New York: Humanities Press, 1965).

16   James H. Cone, *Black Theology and Black Power* (New York: Seabury Press, 1969).

17   See Stokely Carmichael and Charles V. Hamilton, *Black Power: The Politics of Liberation in America* (New York: Random House, 1967).

18   Martin Luther King, Jr., *Where Do We Go from Here? Chaos or Community* (New York: Harper & Row, 1967), p. 134.

3 Black theology and liberation theologies
EDWARD P. ANTONIO

Black theology like other liberation theologies claims to be committed to fighting social injustice of every kind, everywhere: homelessness, unemployment, racism, sexism, homophobia, lack of access to healthcare and education, the marginalization of indigenous peoples, declining mortality rates, economic and other social impediments to ownership of property, hunger, economic inequality within and between nations, particularly between nations of the North and those of the South, human rights violations, discrimination of religious minorities, malnutrition and undernutrition, as well as environmental degradation and its impact on the poor. Granted that the list of injustices is not exhaustive we might say, then, that black theology is "related" to liberation theology, or is indeed a theology of liberation by virtue of its commitment to resist and eradicate all the injustices in the list. There are three significant features of this list to which I want to call attention. First, it is important to notice that it is comprehensive enough to include social, political, economic, environmental, cultural, and religious injustices. Second, at least on the face of it, it delineates a pluralistic understanding of modes of oppression. Third, the modes of oppression divide up into two categories: what has been called "struggles for recognition" centered on issues of race, identity, gender, sexuality and other forms of cultural injustice, and "economic oppression" centered on so-called "material inequality." Dividing up oppression in this way is not new. It has been around for a long time in social theory. Today it expresses itself in the debate between those who argue that oppression must be understood in terms of economic or class relations and those who demand and struggle for different forms of social recognition (racial, sexual, gender, and so on). The debate has famously entered theology through the insistence of Latin American liberation theology and other forms of black theology that oppression must be understood in primarily socioeconomic terms. Leonardo and Clodovis Boff have argued, for example, that a correct understanding of oppression and how different forms of oppression are related requires supremely privileging socioeconomic causes.[1] Thus while broadly true, the conclusion that black theology is "related" to liberation theology, or is indeed a theology of liberation by virtue of its commitment to resist and eradicate all the injustices listed earlier, turns out both to be somewhat premature and to fail to tell us anything about how black theology undertakes its struggles against various forms of oppression. Does it do so on the basis of the "struggles for recognition" or on the basis of economic oppression or, again, on the basis of both? And if recognition is the desired starting point, the question becomes, which recognition? Is it recognition of race, sexuality, or gender? As we shall see, practitioners of black theology sometimes disagree both among themselves and in their conversations with Latin American liberation theology about which starting point to privilege.

This chapter suggests that the field of liberation theologies is marked by a wide-ranging methodological pluralism. This pluralism is not merely a matter of fashion, style, or variation in emphasis among practitioners of liberation theology, but rather a reflection of genuine differences in history, content, experience of injustice, and of methods and approaches for identifying, analyzing, resisting, and overcoming the oppression that causes such injustice. The dissimilarities mirrored in this pluralism in turn lead to serious differences in how the concept of liberation itself is understood and deployed. Evidence for this methodological pluralism is global. It can be seen in the existence of liberation theology in Latin America, black theology in various parts of the world such as South Africa, Britain, Brazil, the Caribbean, and others. Asia has produced its own varieties of liberation theology (Minjung in Korea, Coconut theology in the Pacific, Dalit theology in India, the theology of struggle in the Philippines, and so on). The methodological pluralism of liberation theology includes countries of the global North, where it sometimes manifests itself as white feminist theology, queer theology, and political theology. In addition there are theologies such as mujerista, and womanist theologies. As Peter Phan has pointed out, these theologies crisscross the globe and are not confined to any one particular country or region.[2] There have been three approaches to this pluralism. The first approach celebrates the differences it represents and sees them as part of a common and shared history of oppression; the second approach also accepts and celebrates these differences but stresses not a common and shared history but the radical uniqueness of each. According to this approach the methods, experiences, interests, contexts, perspectives, and goals of different liberation theologies are not interchangeable, they are not clones of each other. The third approach, while accepting difference, argues not for a shared history or radical difference but for methodological commonality constituted by what Peter Phan calls "the essential elements of their method ... [the] resources liberation theologians make use of, their hermeneutical approaches, and their criteria of truth." The question I discuss in this chapter is where black theology fits into this methodological pluralism, and to address this question I revisit an old debate on the relationship between race and class in liberation and black theologies. The debate is important for several reasons. First, it provides a way of thinking about the relationship between black theology and liberation theology that goes beyond the three approaches just described by locating its possibility not in commonality (methodological or identitarian) but in the necessary politics of contestation, which mark difference not as external relation but as the "constitutive limit" of identity – social and economic.[3] Contestation is endemic to social life. It organizes how power, wealth, culture, politics, and so forth are negotiated. Second, the race versus class debate is important precisely because, instead of pointing to methodological commonality within theologies of liberation, it points to serious methodological difference. Third, the debate opens up a space to rethink both the internal structure of black theology, that is how, on the one hand, black theology addresses difference (beginning with race and class, and broadening out to include gender, sexuality, and so on) within itself, and, on the other, how it fits into the global methodological pluralism represented by liberation theologies.

Following the suggestion of the conjunction "and" in the title of this chapter, I shall start with the question: in what way is black theology related to liberation theology? We should notice several things here before proceeding. First, we should notice that this question assumes that there is something that generically answers to the description "liberation" and that there is a theology associated with it. This association somehow effects or produces the existence of liberation theology. Second, the question assumes that black theology is somehow not a part of liberation theology, that it is something different that stands in some sort of external relationship to the latter. This second assumption begs the question of black theology's difference from liberation theology. Notice also that "liberation theology" is characterized in the singular. Again, I suspect that deploying the singular to describe "liberation theology" is the result of both an implicit desire for the security of an originary paradigmatic model of liberation, and an affirmation of the popular view that such a paradigm can, in fact, be found in Latin American liberation theology. After all, the assumption proceeds, is Latin America not the place where liberation theology started? It is exactly this popular image of liberation theology as essentially a Latin American phenomenon that has come to acquire global status that many people, including practitioners of black theology, have in mind when they talk about liberation theology. Indeed, the image is reinforced by scholars, including Latin American theologians, who privilege this model as the historical starting point of liberation theology. We need, however, to reject all these assumptions because, in the first instance, there is no generic, universal, or uncontested referent that stands for the idea of "liberation" and, in the second instance, because black theology itself has from its beginning always claimed to be a theology of liberation.

One way of understanding the methodological pluralism I have attributed to theologies of liberation is to take seriously Alistair Kee's statement that "Liberation is largely defined by the domination which it opposes, and it would appear that those who suffer under one form of domination may themselves be responsible for imposing another form of domination on some other group."[4] Kee goes on to argue that domination is a worldview, a mindset or ideology buttressed by assumptions about power, privilege, and advantage. As such it is more than the sum of its instances. Thus the effective elimination of domination must proceed from recognition of the interrelatedness of its various aspects.[5]

As we shall see later, black theologians have often historically charged that the Latin American version of liberation theology has methodologically tended to ignore the problem of racism in preference to that of class analysis. Womanist theologians have, in turn, critiqued black theology itself for its gender blindness, and queer theology has critiqued straight theologies for their heterosexism. The difficulty before us then is this: Latin American liberationists, womanist, feminist, and black theologians are very likely to reject the use of one paradigm in defining the concept of liberation, since their understandings of it are determined by different histories and experiences. Class domination, the argument runs, is not the same as racial oppression, or sexism, or homophobia, just as these three are not necessarily part of any one organizing essence.

It follows, on this argument, that differences in perception and experience of oppression "determine" differences in construing the object of the struggle against domination.

Very roughly, the problem can be stated in the following terms: according to some black theologians, the centrality of social analysis as itself an elemental property of liberation theology has been discussed by, for example, South American liberation theologians as if its value consisted merely in rendering possible a critique of the nexus between capitalism and oppression, that is, to the exclusion of the experience of racism as oppression. In other words, the focus of social analysis in South American liberation theology was for a long time narrowly circumscribed by the problems generated by the capitalist mode of production in such a way that racism was not featured as an autonomous, let alone a separate problem.[6] In one sense this is the old debate about the relationship between class and race as appropriate ways of describing oppression. The problems here are, of course, well known, as indeed is the fact that this whole area constitutes a minefield. Here I shall do no more than briefly outline the main features of the problem before proceeding to discuss its appearance and impact on the issues that concern me in this chapter.

The issue, as John Rex has put it, is "whether class really does have some kind of superior ontological status to race, and whether there is not a sense in which 'race war' is not a more important central structural and dynamic principle in sociology than the class war."[7]

We can perhaps best approach the problem by distinguishing between primary and secondary oppression. In their book *Sexism, Racism, and Oppression*, Brittan and Maynard identify two levels at which primary oppression is functional: primary oppression, they write "refers to the direct consequences of the unequal possession of biological capacities, and/ or economic, cultural, and social resources."[8] Thus in the case of biology, biological determinism is used to explain the oppression of women and out-groups such as blacks;[9] and in the case of social and economic oppression it is the mode of production and class that are regarded as final determinants of all other kinds of oppression. On this view, racism and sexism are reducible to, or explainable in terms of, the mode of production or "class." Unlike biological determinism, however, social and economic oppression does not necessarily appeal to inevitability.[10]

Secondary oppression, say Brittan and Maynard, "is always something other than it appears to the naïve consciousness of the oppressed person." Hence when women complain about exploitation on the basis of gender or blacks on the basis of pigmentation they are laboring under false consciousness as to the real cause of their social disadvantage, namely, exploitative relations of production. This, according to Brittan and Maynard and John Rex, in the book referred to earlier, constitutes the Marxist approach to the problem of oppression, an approach in which the state of the question has traditionally been considered in terms of how far women and out-groups fit into an overall causal framework of domination.[11]

There are of course two other approaches apart from the Marxist one: the first approach attempts to incorporate race and gender into a system of stratification defined a priori. On this view, gender and race are more or less significant variables within a predetermined social structure of, say, class relations but neither actually brings about qualitative change in the predefined structure. The second approach regards race and sex as autonomous variables: as separate classes.

That this debate has not left theology unaffected is clear from the fact that those theologies – whether political or liberationist – that have adopted a Marxist class analysis to explain oppression find themselves logically and existentially confronted by the need to account for the existence of different experiences of oppression; they must say whether race is reducible to class, whether it is simply a fraction of class or an underclass,[12] or indeed whether it is an independent explanatory variable in its own right.

The tension resulting from the disagreement between black and, say, Latin American liberation theologians as to which of these – race or class – is the most apposite category for understanding oppression can be discerned in both South African black theology and in the proceedings of the Ecumenical Association of Third World Theologians and the 1975 Detroit conference on theology in the Americas. We shall deal with South African theology first because South African society was until not long ago explicitly ordered on the basis of the political economy of race and class, supported by philosophical and theological arguments; and also because this debate about race and class has, interestingly, occurred within black theology itself.

A comprehensive account of this problem can be found in Sebidi's essay "The Dynamics of the Black Struggle and Its Implications for Black Theology." Here Sebidi makes the assertion that black theology has been shaped by race analysis, or by the view that the category "race" sufficiently explains the nature and dynamics of social conflict in South Africa.[13] "Race" is an explanatory and analytical key.

The race analyst in South Africa, says Sebidi, argues that the basic problem of his society can be explained, not in terms of class, but of the "primacy of racial ideology" contained in the deliberate racial segmentation of groups, which thus manifests itself politically as a "pigmentocracy," and economically as the "unmistakable criterion of differential incorporation into the South African social system," a criterion that determines the level and quality of participation in the productive process.[14]

Because of this, race analysts see the struggle as a nationalistic struggle, since for them it is blacks as a people, not as a class, that suffer oppression.[15] Moreover, the primacy of race is evident in the colonial nature of the situation: a white settler community subjugating a black indigenous community. For the race analyst, colonialism is necessarily collective exploitation of a whole people, not just classes.[16]

The class analyst, on the other hand, rejects this account as superficial and neglectful of the reality of capitalist exploitation proved by the existence of multinational corporations.[17] To reduce the South African problem to race alienates blacks, working blacks especially, from the workers' movement.[18] A good example of the position being described here is that of B. Moore, who argued that in order to avoid psychologizing the problem of South African society we must begin by placing the question of race in its proper social context. For Moore, this context is that of the class struggle.[19] "I would argue," he writes, "that 'race' is a problem in any society only to the extent that 'race' is 'built into' the character of the class struggle."[20]

Thus, when South African blacks claim that their oppression is due to the color of their skin they are talking nonsense, they are mystifying reality. Black theology's social analysis is therefore "false consciousness" because, says Moore, it fails to see race as an ideological reflex of class.[21] Like Moore, Sebidi accuses the race analysts of idealism, of putting too much emphasis on ideas, on the view that reality is a product of consciousness. Indeed Sebidi appears to include the entire Black Consciousness movement in this critique by attacking what is essentially the latter's strategy in the struggle. Strategically, says Sebidi, the idealist focuses on changing the mind and ideas in the hope that this will result in social change; the race analyst employs the psychological tools of education, preaching, and persuasion to influence social change.[22] The opposite of this idealism is materialism, and this is what characterizes the position of class analysts.

Sebidi, however, rejects the race/class dualism fostered by both these extremes. According to Sebidi, the class analysts are correct in drawing attention to the material conditions of life as the cause of social conflict in South Africa, but they err in denying any role to beliefs and ideas, which have played such a powerful part in shaping how South Africans think about their own problem.[23] Given the presence of both racism and capitalism in South Africa, Sebidi proposes the phrase "racial capitalism"[24] as an adequate way of describing the South African situation.

RACE AND CLASS IN THEOLOGY IN THE AMERICAS

The problem of the relationship of race to class has also surfaced elsewhere. For example, Sergio Torres, who in 1975 organized a conference on theology in the Americas, which took place in Detroit, Michigan, informs us that the various "interest groups" at Detroit complained that those engaged in liberation theology were white and their experiences particularly Latin American and thus were not aware of the theological contribution of blacks and women.[25] In particular, it was Latin American theology's often exclusive reliance on class analysis that, as Harnett et al. have shown, caused offence.[26] It is also this over-reliance on class that the black philosopher/theologian Cornel West has attacked. West does not deny the importance and utility of Marxist analysis for understanding the international economic order and the operation of capitalist economies. In fact, he sees a certain convergence between black theology and Marxist thought in their mutual concern for the poor and their use of a dialectical methodology, which in the case of black theology is latent, implicit, and undeveloped, and in Marxism is conscious and explicit.[27] This implicit/explicit distinction in the use of dialectic accounts for the absence of an active dialogue between the two camps and for the distortion of the similarities between them. But if West is quite sympathetic to the use of Marxist analysis, he is at the same time not uncritical of it.

According to West, by consistently underplaying the importance of the liberating aspects of oppressed cultures, Marxist analysis shows itself to be of a piece with oppressive European civilizing attitudes toward the people of color. As we have just seen, West is on the whole sympathetic to Marxism. But this does not mean that all black theologians are. For instance, Herbert Edwards is skeptical about its analytical value, although he does not deny its attractiveness for the exploited and marginalized. Indeed, he thinks that this appeal lies in the critical distance that Marxism is able to maintain between itself and the norms and mores of the oppressing culture, and in the fact that it presents a vision of the world that contradicts the one on which this culture is based. For Edwards, however, ideological changes have not made any significant difference to the situation of blacks in America.[28] He justifies his position thus:

My skepticism about the use of Marxism as a tool of analysis in our context is due simply to this: In our history in this country, whether one was Marxist, non-Marxist, pre-Marxist or post-Marxist, if he was white, he was also racist; if he was black he was oppressed.[29]

It is not clear whether West and Edwards are arguing that the failure of class analysis to account for culturally generated modes of domination is a necessary feature of Marxist social ontology, or whether it is simply an accident explainable in terms of the historical rather than the onto-logical subordination of race to class in what is, after all, a predomin-antly white society. For if West and Edwards are ontologizing – albeit negatively – the subordination of race to class, then it seems they are at least inadvertently conceding to the Marxist that class does indeed pos-sess ontological superiority over race. This, of course, is what Edwards at least wishes to eschew. According to him, the problem of race and its conditioning effects on responses to it in terms of the demand for justice far outweigh the undoubtedly significant role played by eco-nomic factors. In other words, for Edwards "the racial factor has been the most important single determinant in the responses ... to the black American's demand for justice."[30] But here again it is necessary to ask whether Edwards is simply saying that, given a social structure shaped by political economy and its relations of production, race can be ascribed a determinant role within that structure, or whether he is saying more: that race is a parallel mode of oppression with its own conditions of gen-eration. To be sure, Edwards sees the need for historical and structural analysis, for understanding both the present order and for building a new one; and he even speaks of the value of analysis for comprehending what he calls "the interdependent character of the unfolding events of history and the formation of social structures."[31]

I have chronicled this debate at some length for a variety of reasons. The debate has not been resolved. It continues to fuel heated discussion on the left and to influence liberationist thinking across the world such that race or class, identity or economic exploitation, cultural justice or redistributive justice continue to be taken for granted by the contest-ants as radical discursive binaries that orient different understandings of liberation. Liberation theologies are no exception to this despite the false sense of settlement into which they have descended in the name of commonality and solidarity. According to this false sense of settlement it is enough to assert recognition of the interdependence of modes of oppression as a sign of a good liberation theology. Social complexity is proclaimed but hardly every analyzed.

Three conclusions follow from this discussion. First, black theology, qua theology of liberation, is related to other liberation theologies by participating in the debates on the nature of oppression. Participation in these debates means that black theology has an *interest* (in the technical sense of the term) in both the shape and form of liberation, in how the concept of liberation is understood.

Second, black theology, qua theology of liberation, is related to other liberation theologies by being committed to the same goals that other liberation theologies espouse – justice, equality, freedom, deliverance from all forms of exploitation, and full economic and political enfranchisement. Hence the claim of virtually all practitioners of black theology that all oppression is interrelated and that the theoretical adequacy and its ultimate practical efficacy require this presupposition.

Third, black theology, qua theology of liberation, marks a particular kind of discursive difference by the manner in which it inscribes race at the center of its analysis of oppression. This difference defines its mode of belonging to the field of liberation theologies. It is within this difference that it seeks to encompass and account for the multiplicity of experiences of oppression and its relationship to other theologies.

Notes

1   Leonardo Boff and Clodovis Boff, *Introducing Liberation Theology* (Maryknoll, NY: Orbis Books, 2007), p. 25.
2   Peter Phan, "Method in Liberation Theologies," *Theological Studies* 61 (2000): 40–63.
3   Judith Butler, "Merely Cultural," *New Left Review* 1(227) (January/ February 1998). See also Nancy Fraser, "From Redistribution to Recognition? Dilemmas of Justice in a 'Post Socialist' Age," *New Left Review* 1(212) (July/August 1995).
4   Alistair Kee, *Domination and Liberation: The Place of Religion in Social Conflict* (London: SCM Press, 1986), p. x.
5   Ibid., pp. x–xi.
6   See Cornel West, "The North American Blacks," in Sergio Torres and John Eagleson (eds.), John Drury (trans.), *The Challenge of Basic Christian Communities. Papers from the International Ecumenical Congress of Theology, February 20–March 2, 1980, São Paulo, Brazil* (Maryknoll, NY: Orbis Books, 1981), pp. 255ff. Pierre van der Berghe has argued that race has "little claim for autonomous theoretical status." *Race and Racism: A Comparative Perspective* (New York: John Wiley and Sons, 1967), p. 6. See also W. J. Wilson, *Power, Racism, and Privilege: Race Relations in Theoretical and Sociological Perspective* (New York: The Free Press, 1973), pp. 3–4.
7   John Rex, *Race Relations in Sociological Theory* (London and New York: Routledge and Kegan Paul, 1983), pp. 1–2.
8   Arthur Brittan and Mary Maynard, *Sexism, Racism, and Oppression* (Oxford and New York: Blackwell Publishing, 1984), p. 1.

9 Brittan and Maynard use the term "out-groups" without defining it.

10 Brittan and Maynard, *Sexism, Racism, and Oppression*, p. 2.

11 For a description of various Marxist accounts of the relationship between race and class, see Rex, *Race Relations* and Brittan and Maynard, *Sexism, Racism, and Oppression*.

12 Brittan and Maynard, *Sexism, Racism, and Oppression*, pp. 45ff. An attempt to relate the notion of an "underclass" to race can be found in G. L. Rolison's "An Exploration of the Term Underclass as It Relates to African-Americans," *Journal of Black Studies* 21(3) (March 1991): 287–301.

13 Lebamang Sebidi, "The Dynamics of the Black Struggle and Its Implications for Black Theology," in Itumeleng Mosala and Buti Tlhagale (eds.), *The Unquestionable Right to Be Free* (Maryknoll, NY: Orbis Books, 1986), pp. 20ff.

14 Ibid., pp. 15–20.

15 Ibid., pp. 15–16.

16 Ibid.

17 Ibid., p. 17–19.

18 Ibid., p. 16.

19 Basil Moore, "Theological Perspectives on Racism." Paper delivered at the AAC Consultation at Lincoln College, North Adelaide, South Australia, May 30, 1978, pp.1–5.

20 Ibid.

21 Ibid., pp. 3–4.

22 Sebidi, "Dynamics of the Black Struggle," p. 44.

23 Ibid., pp. 51–54.

24 Cf. B. Magubane, "Race and Class Revisited: The Case of North America and South Africa," *Africa Development* 12(1) (1987): 5–42.

25 Sergio Torres, "Opening Address," in Sergio Torres and John Eagleson (eds.), *Theology in the Americas* (Maryknoll, NY: Orbis Books, 1976), pp. 267–68.

26 Anne Marie Harnett, S.N.J.M. *et al.*, "A Theological Quest. Synthesis of the First Stage of Theology in the Americas," in Torres and Eagleson (eds.), *Theology in the Americas*, pp. 242–52, at pp. 247ff.

27 Cornel West, "Black Theology and Marxist Thought," in G. S. Wilmore and J. H. Cone (eds.), *Black Theology: A Documentary History*, vol. 1, *1966–1979* (Maryknoll, NY: Orbis Books, 1979), pp. 552ff.

28 Herbert O. Edwards, "Black Theology and Liberation Theology," in Torres and Eagleson (eds.), *Theology in the Americas*, pp. 177–91, at p. 189.

29 Edwards' contribution to the black theology panel at the theology in the Americas conference, in Torres and Eagleson (eds.), *Theology in the Americas*, pp. 355–56.

30 Edwards, "Black Theology and Liberation Theology," p. 184.

31 Ibid., p. 177.

4 The social sciences and rituals of resilience in African and African American communities

LINDA E. THOMAS

INTRODUCTION

This chapter has several goals. First, it seeks to show how the social sciences can make a positive contribution to theology. In the process of achieving this goal I will also examine why theology has, until fairly recently, failed to make constructive use of social scientific methods. Second, I will show that the emergence of a variety of liberation theologies, with their strong commitment to the social and to social reality, represent an important opportunity for theology to engage the social sciences. Third, I will seek to apply the social sciences, and particularly my own discipline of social anthropology, to theology by investigating the responses of two different marginalized communities to social and political oppression. The first is a black South African community in the township of Guguletu, just outside Cape Town, and the second is an African American community on the South Side of Chicago. Over the course of analyzing these communities, I will appropriate the social sciences to theologize within a womanist framework. In other words, I take womanism as both an organizing experience and as a fundamental social category through which to deploy the social sciences in and for theology.

I begin with the claim that historically and presently, traditional academic theological inquiry does not adequately address issues and methodologies related to the social sciences. I will argue that the presence of African American male and womanist theologians, collectively with feminist, Latin American, Asian, and queer theologians, has begun to introduce social, historical, political, cultural, and economic issues into the formal field of theology. Moreover, I will suggest that although progress is slow, the presence of alternative, non-dominant theologies is changing the field of theology so that it must increasingly address the social scientific methodologies, concepts, and evidence that it has traditionally excluded. I will conclude by demonstrating the benefits of the increased presence of the social sciences to the field of theology.

TRADITIONAL THEOLOGY DEFINED AND CRITIQUED

Theology, by definition, focuses on the discussion of – and rational and systematic inquiry into – concepts and issues that theologians choose to associate with God. When one surveys the curricula of graduate theology courses, the dominant topics of study are conceptual. They include, in varying orders and degrees, historical doctrines, ideas, and movements concerning creation, human nature, the nature of God, sin, redemption, salvation, and eschatology, to name a few. Theological study in the North American Christian context generally proceeds by examining the ways that earlier scholars have dealt and wrestled with these primary topics, spurring change in the ways these topics are considered, espoused, taught, and implemented in theological education and, by extension, in the parishes and congregations of Christian communities.

In this regard, two obvious facts regarding theological inquiry and its academic pursuit must be recognized. First, the field of theology is a field of ideas. It is not rooted in or primarily concerned with issues or methodologies directly related to the social sciences. Academic theology, which forms the primary training of most Western religious leaders, is not significantly concerned with concrete social realities. The abstract nature of traditional theological inquiry ensures that in the majority of theological classrooms there is very little discussion of politics, class, race, gender, sexuality, poverty, ecology, and so forth, except in passing or during a class session or two devoted to "alternative" approaches to theological inquiry.

Theology is focused almost exclusively on the study of ideas – of systematic conceptual frameworks – for understanding questions of religious interest; that is, the nature of the divine, presence and power of the divine, relational aspects of the divine, and the divine's proverbial "end game." It has not, generally and in terms of historical practice, been a field of academic inquiry that is interested in, or familiar with, issues affecting daily life. This is a claim that many liberation theologians have made about traditional theology. It does not employ qualitative or quantitative social scientific methodologies or sources. A further indication of academic theology's dissociation from social events and structures is the fact that most seminaries and divinity schools maintain a separate "practical theology" department, not-so-subtly suggesting that "pure" theology must never burden itself with practical concerns.

The second obvious yet noteworthy reality of academic theology is that most of the theologians included in its course syllabi inhabit the clichéd, but searingly accurate, category of old dead white men. The theological curricula at most divinity schools in North America are dominated by thinkers such as Augustine, Aquinas, Luther, Schleiermacher, Barth, Tillich, and others of the same sex and race. Rarely are the social contexts of these scholars brought into the discussion of how they developed their particular theological constructs. However, the emergence of African American, womanist, Latin American, Asian, and queer theologians in academia is slowly beginning to change this.

THEOLOGY, SOCIAL CONTEXT, AND THE SOCIAL SCIENCES

While "informal" theologies from the perspectives of people of color and other marginalized groups/experiential modalities have long been written into the fabric of religious life of these persons and communities, formalized theologies written by, and overtly related to the experience of, women and persons of color did not emerge until the 1960s. The scholars behind these theologies actively deconstructed many of the ideological and epistemological blind spots of traditional theologies because they had experienced firsthand the real-life consequences of academic and practical theologies dominated by a Eurocentric, patriarchal perspective. They brought to the writing desk and to the classroom the acute awareness that historical context and social location radically and thoroughly shape and affect discourse about God and directly related theological practices. The experience and theological inquiry of non-dominant persons and communities in academic theological circles required that sources and methodologies outside those of the clichéd old dead white men be reinterpreted and reintegrated into a new understanding of theological education and constructive theological work.

For African American male and womanist theologians, neither scholastic tradition nor scripture could be claimed as the primary/dominant sources for discerning the nature of God or God's will for creation. Rather, the experience of oppression forced upon black persons and communities became the primary arbiter of theological authority. In the words of James Cone, "it is this common experience among black people in America that Black Theology elevates as the supreme test of truth. To put it simply, Black Theology knows no authority more binding than the experience of oppression itself. This alone must be the ultimate authority in religious matters."[1]

Cone placed theology squarely into the realm of social context. He redefined theology as the "rational study of the being of God in the world in light of the existential situation of an oppressed community, relating the forces of liberation to the essence of the Gospel, which is Jesus Christ."[2] The primary question that must be asked and answered is "What does the Christian Gospel have to say to powerless black men [*sic*] whose existence is threatened daily by the insidious tentacles of white power?"[3] This is a considerable departure from the detached, abstract questioning that has dominated academic theological inquiry for centuries.

Cone points directly to social reality as the appropriate focus for theological inquiry. He writes that the "righteousness of God is not an abstract quality ... it is rather God's active involvement in history."[4] Countering the white, patriarchal historical tradition still taught in most divinity school curricula, Cone claims that "Christian theology is never just a rational study of the being of God. Rather, it is a study of God's liberating activity in the world."[5] By rooting the fundamental task of theology *in the world*, Cone exploded the framework of a field accustomed to studying ideas abstractly, and inaugurated the need for theologians to call upon, utilize, and learn for themselves the methodologies and content of social science.

Moreover, the work of theologians such as Cone ruptures the boundary between theology and "practical theology," inextricably linking all theology to the social concerns and lived realities of marginalized persons. For instance, in addressing the traditional theological topic of soteriology, one is forced to recognize that salvation is only valid as a theological concept if it speaks directly to immediate social experience. The focus must shift from God's theoretical saving of souls to the far more concrete imperative to save hungry, dying, oppressed people.

As soon as questions of, and explanations about, creation, divinity, sin, and redemption are rooted in social issues such as racism, sexism, or economic justice, theology and the social sciences are joined at the hip. Indeed, Cone recognizes that "[t]he language of theology challenges societal structures because it is inseparable from the suffering community."[6] Thus, theology's critical and prophetic engagement with the systems that perpetuate injustice becomes necessary: "Theology can never be neutral or fail to take sides on issues related to the oppressed."[7] Needless to say, this type of social, constructive approach stands in stark contrast to the abstract "objectivity" of traditional academic theology.

In conversation with Cone and other black theologians, Latin American, Asian, womanist, and queer scholars also developed formal theologies of liberation. Each of these theologies, written expressly from a particular social and historical context, binds theology to earthly life and social structures. Cone cites the rise of black theology as being "due primarily to the failure of white religionists to relate the Gospel of Jesus to the pain of being black in a white racist society."[8] By extension, I suggest the same etiology for other liberation theologies: the inadequacy of the traditional theological academy's intransigent assertion that theology need not – and should not – be rooted in a particular social and historical context.

These waves of liberation theologies required that new sources of theological inquiry be considered – social scientific sources, to be precise. Such socially oriented theologies would not be well served by the methods of a historical theological tradition that reifies the hegemonic imaginary and rarely includes the lived experiences of marginalized persons. The search for new theological sources and resources demanded that this new wave of theologians reach out to the social sciences for help. Accordingly, liberationist scholars have increasingly turned to anthropology, social history, political science, and even geography to help make the case for theologies rooted in the social justice too often denied or ignored by white patriarchal theologies.

WOMANIST THEOLOGY AS A FRAMEWORK FOR INTEGRATING THEOLOGY AND THE SOCIAL SCIENCES

In examining this social scientific turn in theology, my own vantage point, as both an African American womanist theologian and anthropologist, places me in a position to study, analyze, and exegete within a multiplicity of method, experience, and perspective. Considered broadly, womanist theologians are African American feminist scholars who draw together the particularity of their own sacred experience with the universal implications of these experiences. Womanists interrelate issues of race, gender, class, sexual orientation, and ecology within their communities, thereby speaking (out of particularity) to community formation around issues of universal human conditions. Finally, womanist theologians seek balance among all issues impacting their well-being and the well-being of other marginalized communities – in a sense, the practical integration of religion and the social sciences.

Thus, according to Delores Williams, womanist theological method is "informed by at least four elements: (1) a multidialogical intent, (2) a liturgical intent, (3) a didactic intent, and (4) a commitment both to reason and to the validity of female imagery and metaphorical language in the construction of theological statements."[9] In particular:

Multi-dialogical intent allows Christian womanists to engage in many conversations with different people from various religious, political, and social communities. The desire of womanists in these exchanges is to focus on the "slow genocide" of poor African American women, children and men, caused by systems of exploitation. Liturgical intent means that black female religious scholars and clergywomen will develop a theology relevant to the African American church, especially its worship, action, and thought. At the same time, womanist theology challenges the black church with the prophetic and critical messages coming from the practice of black women. In a word, black church liturgy has to be defined by justice.

Didactic intent points to the teaching moment in the theology of the black church as it deals with a moral life determined by justice, survival, and quality of life ethics. All of these concerns commit us to a language which is rich in imagination and reason, and filled with female stories, metaphor, and imagery.[10]

Extending Williams' claim, I have argued that:

The method of womanist theology validates the past lives of enslaved African women by remembering, affirming, and glorifying their contributions. After excavating analytically and reflecting critically on the life stories of our foremothers, the methodology entails a construction and creation of a novel paradigm. We who are womanists concoct something new that makes sense for how we are living in complex gender, racial, and class configurations. We learn from the rituals and techniques our foremothers originated to survive in hostile environments and from how they launched new perspectives, reconstructing knowledge of a liberative approach for black women's lives. This self-constituting dynamic is a polyvalent, multi-vocal weaving of the folk culture of African American women.[11]

Furthermore, womanist methodology uses ethnographic approaches, which allow black woman scholars to enter the actual communities of poor black women in order to discover pieces to create a narrative for the present and the future. It is precisely in connection with this commitment to using ethnographic approaches and to the practical integration of religion with the social sciences discussed earlier that I will use my own work as an example of one way in which the social sciences can benefit theological understanding.

APPLYING THE SOCIAL SCIENCES TO THEOLOGY: AN EXAMPLE

With the foregoing womanist framework in mind, I will now illustrate how we might integrate the social sciences, and especially anthropological methodologies, with theology by demonstrating how I have integrated my own social scientific training within my primary field of religion/theology.[12] I do so by analyzing two different marginalized communities – one in Cape Town, South Africa, and the other on the South Side of Chicago, Illinois.

First, South Africa. For ten years, I conducted field research in black South African townships, primarily one located outside the city of Cape Town. This township is called Guguletu, which means "Our Pride." As an outsider attempting to understand religion in South African black townships, I have found Clifford Geertz's concept of culture as "webs of significance" that require "thick description" to be helpful.[13] However, Geertz's notion by itself is not sufficient and needs to be supplemented because it is too focused on interpretation, the symbolic, and thus on knowledge and the cognitive.

I view culture, particularly in the case of South Africa, as a collective or communal cognitive or symbolic phenomenon whose effects, namely knowledge, are shaped, structured, distributed, and controlled differently along economic and political lines in different racial communities in South Africa. In other words, knowledge is created and framed in an asymmetrical system by the ideology of white supremacy. This ideology underwrites white economic power and is itself underwritten by that same power. This is despite the fact that South Africa is now a democratic republic with a multiracial government and a black South African president.

In keeping with the old saw that knowledge is power, the impact of knowledge in South Africa (especially how it functions to elevate whites over blacks and other persons of color) produced and produces generations of people whose minds are colonized. This is why it is important to take seriously Geertz's understanding of culture in terms of the symbolic function of knowledge. But, to enhance Geertz's notion of culture as webs of significance requiring thick description, I add Roger Keesing's analysis, which suggests that culture is a material social process directly linked to the power of political economy in which cultural meanings are produced, thereby raising critical questions about who creates and defines cultural meaning and what these meanings intend.[14] As such, one must take seriously even in a new democratic South Africa, the power relationships of this country's sociocultural system, which is characterized by economic inequality and political disparity among the poor, including unequal access to cultural production.[15] All of these factors affect religion and its various expressions.

An example of the way in which culture, knowledge, power, and religion overlap is found in the notion of *ubuntu*. *Ubuntu* is a term used in South African black cultures to express what it means to fully *be* human in the context of community. I initially heard of *ubuntu* when I visited South Africa in 1985, and I noted its frequent use during subsequent research trips. In 1985, I experienced firsthand the turmoil in African townships in Johannesburg, Bloemfontein, Cape Town, and Durban that stemmed largely from the state of emergency imposed by the apartheid regime. The meaning of *ubuntu* became clear to me as black people's actions displayed defiance against the brutal system of apartheid, which violated them daily. Having experienced the effects of over three centuries of tragic usurpation of structural power by whites, black South Africans employ *ubuntu* as a concept to claim their "people-hood" despite their wilderness experience, which began in 1652 with the arrival of Jan van Riebeeck and the Dutch East India Company.[16] *Ubuntu* describes the cultural values of traditional African people and, in particular, the centrality of human beings in society. This value of *ubuntu* is substantially different from Western individualism. As a manifestation of the theoretical and practical synthesis of African moral and cultural values, *ubuntu* frames my larger project by informing my analysis of the two black communities I describe below. This analysis poses two primary questions about culture: (1) "How do different cultural systems work?" and (2) "How have cultural systems come to be as they are?" As I contextualize these questions for the study of religion in South Africa, my questions have become, "How does religion as a cultural system display itself among poor black South Africans?" And, in addition, "How has the system come to be as it is?"

RITUALS OF *UBUNTU* AS RESOURCES FOR SPIRITUAL AND POLITICAL RESILIENCE IN GUGULETU

My book *Under the Canopy: Ritual Process and Spiritual Resilience in South Africa* records the reality of life for poor black South Africans and the rituals they use to help relieve misery related to the structural oppression of race. Specifically, my work analyzes and records the ways in which African Independent churches empower black South Africans to deal with everyday struggles caused by remnant apartheid structures and to participate in the reconstruction and development of the new South Africa. While South Africa has entered a democratic era, apartheid ideology and structures are just beginning to be dislodged. As a consequence, many black South Africans find themselves trying to survive in an environment in which they suffer massive unemployment, scant resources, inadequate housing, deficient education, and little control over their existence.

For many black South Africans, African Independent churches serve as vehicles of resistance to the oppressive variables in their lives, offering a space in which to worship and create life-giving rituals. These "evangelical"[17] churches, which attract the poorest of the poor, utilize Christianity in ways that transform people's lives in order for them to become empowered social actors.[18] In my writing about the role of African Independent churches, I have aimed to dispel the notion that "evangelical Christianity" has little role to play in South Africa. Rather than playing an escapist role, these churches help black people to face the issues that are most important and most pressing in their lives.

The social environment for blacks in South Africa, where most blacks fall well below the poverty line, often gives them a sense of pollution in their lives: a lack of well-being is manifested spiritually, physically, socially, and psychologically.[19] In such circumstances, black South Africans often find relief in the Independent churches, where biblically based Christian theology, a sense of personal empowerment by the Holy Spirit, community support and concern, and a focus on healing help to address their issues, and consequently provide a sense of hope.[20]

St. John's Apostolic Faith Mission, the African Independent church in Guguletu where I conducted field research, is a typical African Independent church in that its members have an orthodox theology.[21] They believe God is all-knowing and the ultimate power of the universe. They profess Jesus as the incarnation of God and that Jesus' suffering, death, and resurrection particularly assist people who suffer in their day-to-day lives. The Holy Spirit (*umoya*) is central to the theology of St. John's because members experience its presence in worship services that have a Pentecostal flavor.

Furthermore, healing rituals are a central feature in the ministry of African Independent churches as members seek relief from the oppressive variables in their lives.[22] The Old and New Testaments provide members with a solid biblical theology for their ritualistic activity.[23]

John 5, which describes Jesus' healing of a disabled man who sat by the pool at Bethesda, is the central scripture for healing rituals at St. John's Apostolic Faith Mission. Indeed, the utilization of water for healing anchors all of the healing rituals at St. John's. Throughout the week, church members and other community people receive blessed water to drink, bath in, vomit up, and use for enemas.

Interviews with members suggest that through baptism, regular attendance, and participation in healing rituals, those who suffer various sicknesses are healed physically and, more often than not, are transformed emotionally.[24] People are usually drawn to St. John's because they are sick or are experiencing some other hardship, such as unemployment, inability to conceive, or wayward children. The understanding of illness exhibited among St. John's members indicates how apartheid structures contribute to members' malaise, or as medical anthropologist Mamphela Ramphele puts it, "affects people's sense of well-being."[25] Those who have been healed enthusiastically share their experience. Many people come to St. John's because they have heard about others who have been healed. In addition to the rituals of healing, the church also provides food and shelter, child care and other services, and, most importantly, a sense of community. By providing basic resources to its members, the church helps to both meet their needs and empower them. Thus, through community support, a commitment to a Christian life, and spiritual, social, and physical healing, members experience a more fulfilling life. Independent churches like St. John's are growing rapidly in South Africa because poor black South Africans spread the news that new life and health can be found in these "evangelical" Christian congregations.

RITUAL PROCESS AS A RESOURCE FOR SPIRITUAL AND POLITICAL RESILIENCE

Moving from Cape Town to the shores of Lake Michigan, my project "Ritual Process among Black Christians on the South Side of Chicago" centers on an economically depressed Chicago community called Englewood. The communal milieu for many African Americans on the South Side of Chicago, a setting where many blacks earn incomes that fall below the poverty line, often gives them a sense of inadequacy in their lives; a lack of self-confidence that is manifested religiously, bodily, communally, and emotionally.[26] In this project, I examine the ways that African Americans understand their lives and make meaning in light of the various structural oppressions that are a part of this community's life. The aim of this project is to analyze and record the ways in which black churches, on the South Side of Chicago, empower black Christians to (1) deal with structures that cause them to be adversely affected by race, gender, and class and, at the same time, (2) participate in the reconstruction and development of a positive black self and community. I am interested in interrogating how cultural systems of race, gender, and class are constituted on the South Side of Chicago, and understanding the ways in which African American Christians deal with these forces in their everyday lives. This line of inquiry opens up many questions for the social scientist: in a pluralistic democracy, in the most powerful nation in the world, how is it that, despite the reforms initiated by various programs and agencies within this society during the last fifty years, socioeconomic disparities based on race, class, and gender continue to exist? Why do the lives of the people who are adversely affected by these phenomena continue to be challenged by asymmetrical systems despite our "advances"?

Like their counterparts in South Africa, black Chicagoans living on the South Side are determined to change the marginalizing forces in their lives. Many attend congregations and actively participate in uplifting and revitalizing rituals in black churches. These churches fashion, form, and embody Christianity in various ways to alter and reimagine people's lives, and in so doing, equip them to use their personal agency as well as the institutional structures of the church to enhance their everyday lives. By writing about the role of the African American churches, my project explores the means by which black Christians deploy ritualistic forms and religious substance to play a major role in the development of the black community and the city of Chicago more generally. African American churches have historically helped black people to face the issues most critical in their lives. Many black Chicagoans on the South Side seek support in churches where the Bible plays a central role, where the Holy Spirit is actively present, where the community is supportive and concerned, and where there is a belief in and hope for liberative change in the conditions of life.

The South Side of Chicago is riddled with storefront churches and cathedrals on the blocks of most thoroughfares. One trait shared by most of these congregations is – as with the African Independent churches – an orthodox theology. They believe God is all-knowing and the ultimate power of the universe. They profess Jesus as the incarnation of God and that Jesus' death and resurrection will lend assistance to people who figuratively and literally suffer death day to day. The

Holy Spirit is central to their theology, as members experience its presence in worship services. Rituals are a central feature in the ministry of black churches as members seek relief from the continuing crucibles of life. The Old and New Testaments provide the congregations with a solid biblical theology for their ritualistic activity. Moreover, members testify that through baptism, regular attendance, and participation in church activities, those who suffer various challenges are healed and, more often than not, are transformed inwardly.

Why are so many people drawn to these churches? One hypothesis is that the cultural experience of oppression (including hardships such as unemployment, gang activity, violent death, and family instability) contributes to members' uneasiness and disquiet about both macro and micro societal structures, and has a negative impact on their sense of security. Members who have been supported by these congregations earnestly communicate their stories of spiritual uplift and awareness of a change in their lives with others. Many people come to these churches because they have heard from others who have been assisted spiritually, and otherwise. For instance, quite a number of these churches also provide food for the homeless, child care, and, most importantly, a feeling of kinship. By providing food, shelter, and clothing to people, these churches help women and men to "be somebody" – a person made in God's image – in a world that tries to destroy their humanity. Thus, through a nexus of support, a focus on Christian life, and a sense of renewal, adherents more ably manage their lives. These churches are growing as members tell others that restoration and strength can be found in these congregations.

Notes

1 James H. Cone, *Black Theology and Black Power* (New York: Seabury Press, 1969), p. 120.
2 James H. Cone, *A Black Theology of Liberation* (Philadelphia, PA: J. B. Lippincott, 1970), p. 1.
3 Cone, *Black Theology and Black Power*, p. 32.
4 Cone, *A Black Theology of Liberation*, p. 2.
5 Ibid., p. 3.
6 Ibid., p. 4.
7 Ibid.
8 Ibid.
9 Delores Williams, "Womanist Theology: Black Women's Voices," in James H. Cone and Gayraud S. Wilmore (eds.), *Black Theology: A Documentary History*, vol. II, *1980–1992*, 2nd edn. (Maryknoll, NY: Orbis Books, 1993), pp. 269–70

10 Dwight N. Hopkins and Linda E. Thomas, "Voices from the Margins in the United States," in Gregory Baum (ed.), *The Twentieth Century: A Theological Overview* (Maryknoll, NY: Orbis Books, 1999), pp. 209–10.

11 Linda E. Thomas, "Womanist Theology, Epistemology, and a New Anthropological Paradigm," in Thomas (ed.), *Living Stones in the Household of God: The Legacy and Future of Black Theology* (Minneapolis, MN: Augsburg Fortress, 2004), p. 40.

12 My formal academic training consists of a Master's in divinity from Union Theological Seminary and a PhD in anthropology from American University. However, I currently serve as Professor of Theology at the Lutheran School of Theology at Chicago.

13 Clifford Geertz, *The Interpretation of Cultures* (New York: Basic Books, 1973), pp. 5–7.

14 See Roger Keesing, "Anthropology as Interpretive Quest," *Current Anthropology* 28(2) (1987): 161–76.

15 William Roseberry, *Anthropologies and Histories: Essays in Culture, History, and Political Economy* (New Brunswick, NJ: Rutgers University Press, 1989), p. 11.

16 Riebeeck was a one of the first Dutch colonial settlers in South Africa. He arrived in Cape Town on April 6, 1652, with eighty-two men and eight women, and founded a European settlement there.

17 The application of the term "evangelical" in this context is contested both by some so-called "mainline" evangelical churches and by some independent churches seeking to distance themselves from the mainline churches.

18 Linda E. Thomas, *Under the Canopy: Ritual Process and Spiritual Resilience in South Africa* (Columbia, SC: University of South Carolina Press, 1999), pp. 120–22; Jean Comaroff, *Body of Power, Spirit of Resistance: The Culture and History of a South African People* (University of Chicago Press, 1985), pp. 252–53; Itumeleng Mosala, "African Independent Churches: A Study in Socio-Theological Protest," in Charles Villa-Vicencio and John W. De Grutchy (eds.), *Resistance and Hope: South African Essays in Honour of Beyers Naude* (Grand Rapids, MI: Eerdmans, 1985), pp. 103–11.

19 Harriet Ngubane, *Body and Mind in Zulu Medicine: An Ethnography of Health and Disease in Nyuswa-Zulu Thought and Practice* (New York: Academic Press, 1977), p. x; Francis Wilson and Mamphela Ramphele, *Uprooting Poverty: The South African Challenge* (Cape Town: David Philip, 1989), p. 176.

20 Bonganjalo Goba, *An Agenda for Black Theology: Hermeneutics for Social Change* (Johannesburg: Skotaville, 1988), p. 22.

21 Malcolm J. McVeigh, *God in Africa: Conceptions of God in African Traditional Religion and Christianity* (Cape Cod, MA: Claude Stark, 1974), p. 172; Goba, *An Agenda for Black Theology*, p. 49. See also Mosala, "African Independent Churches," pp. 103–11.

22 O. N. O. Kealotswe, "Spiritual Healing and Traditional Medicine in Botswana," in G. C. Oosthuizen and Irving Hexham (eds.), *Afro-Christian*

Religion in Southern Africa (Lewiston, NY: Edwin Mellen Press, 1991), pp. 184–90; Matthew Schoffeleers, "Ritual Healing and Political Acquiescence: The Case of the Zionist Churches in Southern Africa," *Africa* 60(1) (1991): 1–24; M. L. Daneel, "Charismatic Healing in African Independent Churches," *Theologia Evangelica* 31(3) (1983): 27–44.

23 Mosala, "African Independent Churches," pp. 103–11.

24 Thomas, *Under the Canopy*, pp. 62–85.

25 Mamphela Ramphele, personal communication, August 12, 1992. Dr. Ramphele is a medical doctor and anthropologist who has practiced and conducted research among poor populations in South Africa. See Wilson and Ramphele, *Uprooting Poverty*.

26 As of 1996, there were 170,000 blacks (as compared with 78,000 whites) between the ages of 18 and 64 living below the poverty line in Chicago. Linda E. Thomas, unpublished lecture, Garrett-Evangelical Theological Seminary, December 1996.

5 Black theology and womanist theology

DELORES S. WILLIAMS

Womanist 1. From womanish. (Opp. of "girlish," i.e., frivolous, irresponsible, not serious.) A black feminist or feminist of color. From the black folk expression of mothers to female children, "You acting womanish," i.e., like a woman. Usually referring to outrageous, audacious, courageous or *willful* behavior. Wanting to know more and in greater depth than is considered "good" for one. Interested in grown-up doings. Acting grown-up. Being grown-up. Interchangeable with another black folk expression: "You trying to be grown." Responsible. In charge. *Serious*.

2. *Also*: A woman who loves other women, sexually and/or nonsexually. Appreciates and prefers women's culture, women's emotional flexibility (values tears as natural counterbalance of laughter), women's strength. Sometimes loves individual men, sexually and/or nonsexually. Committed to survival and wholeness of entire people, male *and* female. Not a separatist, except periodically, for health. Traditionally universalist, as in: "Mama, why are we brown, pink, and yellow, and our cousins are white, beige, and black?" Ans.: "Well, you know the colored race is just a flower garden, with every color flower represented." Traditionally capable, as in: "Mama, I'm walking to Canada and I'm taking you and a bunch of other slaves with me." Reply: "It wouldn't be the first time."

3. Loves music. Loves dance. Loves the moon. *Loves* the Spirit. Loves love and food and roundness. Loves struggle. *Loves* the Folk. Loves herself. *Regardless*.

4. Womanist is to feminist as purple to lavender.[1]

In this full definition, Pulitzer Prize-winning novelist Alice Walker begins to show us what she means by the concept "womanist." The concept is presented in Walker's 1983 *In Search of Our Mothers' Gardens*, and many women in church and society have appropriated it as a way of affirming themselves as *black* while simultaneously owning their connection with feminism and with the African American community, male and female. The concept of womanist allows women to claim their roots in black history, religion, and culture.[2]

What then is a womanist? Her origins are in the black folk expression "You acting womanish," meaning, according to Walker, "wanting to know more and in greater depth than is considered 'good' for one ... outrageous, audacious, courageous and willful behavior." A womanist is also "responsible, in charge, serious." She can walk to Canada and take others with her. She loves, she is committed, she is a universalist by temperament. Her universality includes loving men and women, sexually or nonsexually. She loves music, dance, the spirit, food and roundness, struggle, and she loves herself. "Regardless." Walker insists that a womanist is also "committed to survival and wholeness of entire people, male and female." She is no separatist, "except for health." A womanist is a black feminist or feminist of color. Or as Walker says, "Womanist is to feminist as purple to lavender."

Not only did Walker's definition of a womanist accomplish what feminist and black theologians had not – to provide an image of black women's experience in their works – but she also offered tools for the analysis of culture in the United States, so that black women's culture, experience, and history could be lifted from obscurity into visibility. At last black female theologians found some of the "material needed" to make a theology of women's experience that "fitted" black women. Walker provides an introduction to black womanhood that affirms mothers and children, and is grounded in African American culture. She situates her definition of a womanist in a family context: a mother giving advice to her female child. Inasmuch as the father is not mentioned, one can assume that this may be a single-parent family like so many black families in the USA.

While Walker celebrates and emphasizes black women's culture and way of being in the world, she simultaneously affirms black women's historical connection with men through love and through a shared struggle for survival and for productive quality of life (i.e., "wholeness"). This suggests that two of the principal concerns of womanist theology should be survival and community building and maintenance. The goal of this community building is, of course, to establish a positive quality of life – economic, spiritual, educational – for black women, men, and children. Walker reminds the Christian womanist theologian that her concern for community building and maintenance must ultimately extend to the entire Christian community and beyond that to the larger human community. Yet womanist consciousness is also informed by womanist determination to love themselves. "Regardless." This translates into an admonition to black women to avoid the self-destruction of bearing a disproportionately large burden in the work of community building and maintenance. Womanist consciousness further directs black women away from the negative divisions prohibiting community building among women. For the womanist, mothering and nurturing are vitally important.

Walker has provided the cultural themes womanist theologians needed to unearth black women's experience and history embedded deeply in androcentric US culture, white and black. These cultural themes are: family, with female relationships emphasized; single-parenthood; women's intellectual pursuit ("wanting to know more than is thought good for a female child to know"); "colorism,"[3] which is the foundation of racism; women's leadership roles; women's resistance patterns; the objects of women's love (the folks, food, roundness, nature, dance, hospitality, men, women, and the spirit); sexual preference; women's community work with men in survival and liberation struggles; and the organic relation between womanist and feminist.

The womanist theologian must search for the voices, actions, opinions, experience, and faith of women whose names sometimes slip into the male-centered rendering of black history, but whose actual stories remain remote. This search can lead to such little-known freedom fighters as Milla Granson and her courageous work on Kentucky and Mississippi plantations. Her liberation method of conducting a midnight school for slaves broadens our knowledge of the variety of strategies black people have used to obtain freedom.[4] Women like Harriet Tubman and Granson used subtle and silent strategies to liberate themselves and large numbers of black people.[5] By uncovering as much as possible about such female liberation, the womanist begins to understand the relation of black history to the contemporary folk expression: "If Rosa Parks had not sat down, Martin King would not have stood up."[6]

WOMANISM AND FEMINISM

I believe there are five primary reasons that other black women have taken part in the changed spelling of our theological name from "feminist" to "womanist" theologians.

(1) There was tension between how African American women defined women's experience and how they thought white feminists wanted black women's experience defined. In their understanding of women's experience, African American women included both their struggle alongside all women in the women's rights movement and their experience with black men in the liberation struggle for all black Americans: females, males, and children. Black sociologists such as Elsa Barkley Brown criticized white feminists for not wanting to include black women's racial experience as women's experience and for not wanting to include race among women's issues. Black liberation theologian Jacquelyn Grant[7] also criticized white feminist theologians in the USA for not devoting time and energy to eradicating racism.[8]

(2) Some black women had reservations about white feminist definitions of patriarchy as the primary cause of *all* the oppression *all* women experience. They doubted that this description had "enough material in it" to define adequately the kind of *systemic* oppression black women experience in the USA. They felt they needed a description that not only identified men as oppressive decision-makers and functionaries managing the systems controlling their lives but they were also very clear about the participation of upper-class women with upper-class men in the exploitation of black women's labour, especially black female domestic workers. Most definitions of patriarchy provided in the USA were silent about white men and white women of every social class working together to maintain white supremacy and privilege.

African American women who had traveled around the world had discovered that there are many forms of "master and mistress" rule. Patriarchy is only one way for the powerful to control the powerless. In the African American community there were also women who, with black men, participated in the oppression of other women. Black women needed additional language to name and describe the ways of "master and mistress" rule they had experienced over the years.

(3) Many African American women became womanist theologians because they needed their own theological voice to affirm different cultural foundations for identical assertions made by both feminists and black women who later became womanists. An example is Rosemary Radford Ruether's normative principle of the "full humanity of women." A womanist affirmation of this principle is based on a cultural foundation of black resistance that white

American women neither have nor need. Womanist theologians, in asserting "the full humanity of women," are resisting and denying a negative idea about all black humanity that prevails in the USA even to this day, in addition to resisting the contention that women are not in the image of God.

(4) Living and working among the poor, some black women became womanist theologians as they struggled to do God-talk that emerged out of that social, cultural and historical context. They tried to produce theology whose construction, vocabulary, and issues took seriously the everyday experience, language, and spirituality of women. This kind of struggle needed its own theological ideas, framework, and vocabulary.

(5) African American women could not limit their concern, definitions, struggles, and goals to the survival, liberation, and well-being of women. The entire African American family – mother, father, children, and black kinsfolk – was oppressed and confronted by systemic violence. Feminist observations about the growing "feminization of poverty" were astute, but not much mention was made of the thousands of homeless, jobless, poor black men and black families (fathers, mothers, and children) living on the streets of the USA. Nor was theological attention being given to the violence destroying African American communities – caused mostly by drug-trafficking, which is controlled by non-black forces. Young black people, especially young black men, were being killed at an alarmingly high rate. Numerous black women were falling victim to drug addiction, and their rate of incarceration has increased dramatically. Black people claimed the black family was under siege by drugs and poverty. African American women needed a theology conscious of these facts at every moment. Black people's survival was at risk, but no Christian theology (feminist and black liberation theologies included) had made survival one of its primary issues.

Black women also needed a theology that was conscious of the sexism in the African American community. In 1979 Jacquelyn Grant wrote an article in which she claimed that black women are "invisible in black theology":

In examining black theology it is necessary to make one of two assumptions: (1) either black women have no place in the enterprise, or (2) black men are capable of speaking for us. Both of these assumptions are false and need to be discarded. They arise out of a male-dominated culture which restricts women to certain areas of the society. In such a culture, men are given the warrant to speak for women on all matters of significance. It is no accident that all of the recognized black theologians are men.[9]

Other black female theologians began to recognize the qualitative difference between the experience of black women and of black men even though they both experienced racial oppression in the United States. My own work discusses the uniqueness of black women's experience in terms of the surrogacy roles they have been forced to fill from slavery to this day. The surrogacy experience provides a different lens through which to envision the task of womanist theology and provides different questions to be asked about God's relation to the world.[10]

WOMANIST THEOLOGY AND METHOD

Womanist theology is defining the categories and methods needed to develop along lines consistent with the sources of that theology. Christian womanist theological methodology needs to be informed by at least four elements: (1) a multidialogical intent, (2) a liturgical intent, (3) a didactic intent, and (4) a commitment both to reason and to the validity of female imagery and metaphorical language in the construction of theological statements.

A multidialogical intent will allow Christian womanist theologians to advocate and participate in dialogue and action with many diverse social, political, and religious communities concerned about human survival and productive quality of life for the oppressed. The genocide of cultures and peoples (which has often been instigated and accomplished by Western white Christian groups or governments) and the nuclear threat of omnicide mandate womanist participation in such dialogue/ action. But in this dialogue/action the womanist also should keep her speech and action focused upon the slow genocide of poor black women, children, and men by exploitative systems denying them productive jobs, education, health care, and living space. Multidialogical activity may, like a jazz symphony, communicate some of its most important messages in what the harmony-driven conventional ear hears as discord, as disruption of the harmony in both the black American and white American social, political, and religious status quo.

If womanist theological method is informed by a liturgical intent, then womanist theology will be relevant to (and will reflect) the thought, worship, and action of the black church. But a liturgical intent will also allow womanist theology to challenge the thought/worship/action of the black church with the discordant and prophetic messages emerging from womanist participation in multidialogics. This means that womanist theology will consciously impact critically upon the foundations of liturgy, challenging the church to use justice principles to select the sources that will shape the content of liturgy. The question must be asked: "How does this source portray blackness/darkness, women, and economic justice for nonruling-class people?" A negative portrayal will demand omission of the source or its radical reformation by the black church. The Bible, a major source in black church liturgy, must also be subjected to the scrutiny of justice principles.

A didactic intent in womanist theological method assigns a teaching function to theology. Womanist theology should teach Christians new insights about moral life based on ethics supporting justice for women, survival, and a productive quality of life for poor women, children, and men. This means that the womanist theologian must give authoritative status to black folk wisdom (e.g., Brer Rabbit literature) and to black women's moral wisdom (expressed in their literature) when she responds to the question, "How ought the Christian to live in the world?" Certainly tensions may exist between the moral teachings derived from these sources and the moral teachings about obedience, love, and humility that have usually buttressed presuppositions about living the Christian life. Nevertheless, womanist theology, in its didactic intent, must teach the church the different ways God reveals prophetic word and action for Christian living.

These intents, informing theological method, can yield a theological language whose foundation depends as much upon its imagistic content as upon reason. The language can be rich in female imagery, metaphor, and story. For the black church, this kind of theological language may be quite useful, since the language of the black religious experience abounds in images and metaphors.

The appropriateness of womanist theological language will ultimately reside in its ability to bring black women's history, culture, and religious experience into the interpretive circle of Christian theology and into the liturgical life of the church. Womanist theological language must, in this sense, be an instrument for social and theological change in church and society.

WOMANISM AND BLACK LIBERATION THEOLOGY

Inasmuch as womanist theology is dialogical in the black community, first we pose the question: what does womanist analysis have to say to black liberation theology? There are at least three areas in which womanist theology can dialogue with black liberation theology: theological method, certain areas of Christian doctrine, and ethics. New ethical tasks are identified when black theology takes African American women's experience seriously.

Theological methodology

Womanist analysis raises methodological issues that either enlarge upon or challenge the methodological perspectives contained in some of black liberation theology. The methodological issues with which we will be concerned are the use of the Bible, the understanding and function of experience in black liberation theology, and the notion of the theological task in the same theology.

The Bible and black liberation theology

A womanist rereading of the biblical Hagar–Sarah texts in relation to African American women's experience raises a serious question about the biblical witness. The question is about its use as a source validating black liberation theology's normative claim of God's liberating activity on behalf of *all* the oppressed. James Cone asserts that

> the biblical witness ... says ... God is a God of liberation, who speaks to the oppressed and abused and assures them ... divine righteousness will vindicate their suffering ... [and that] it is the Bible that tells us that God became human in Jesus Christ so that the kingdom of God would make freedom a reality for all human beings.[11]

The Hagar–Sarah texts in Genesis and Galatians, however, demonstrate that the oppressed and abused do not always experience God's liberating power. If one reads the Bible identifying with the non-Hebrews who are female and male slaves ("the oppressed of the oppressed"), one quickly discerns a nonliberative thread running through the Bible. In the Genesis stories about Hagar and Sarah, God seems to be (as some Palestinian Christians today suggest about the God of the Hebrew testament) "partial and discriminating."[12] God is clearly partial to Sarah. Regardless of the way one interprets God's command to Hagar to submit herself to Sarah, God does not liberate her. In Exodus, God does not outlaw slavery. Rather, the male slave can be part of Israel's rituals, possibly because he has no control over his body as Hagar had no control over her body. Thus "the Lord said to Moses and Aaron, 'this ordinance of the Passover: no foreigner shall eat of it; but every slave that is bought for money may eat of it after you have circumcised him'" (Exod. 12:43–44);[13] but "no sojourner or hired servant may eat of it" (12:45). The sojourner and hired servant can refuse to be circumcised, but the slave cannot because the slave master owns the slave's body.

The point here is that when non-Jewish people (like many African American women who now claim themselves to be economically enslaved) read the entire Hebrew testament from the point of view of the non-Hebrew slave, there is no clear indication that God is against their perpetual enslavement. Likewise, there is no clear opposition expressed in the Christian testament to the institution of slavery. Whatever may be the reasons Paul advises slaves to obey their masters and bids Onesimus, the slave, to return to his master and later advises the master to free Onesimus, he does not denounce the institution of slavery. The fact remains: slavery in the Bible is a natural and unprotested institution in the social and economic life of ancient society – except on occasion when the Jews are themselves enslaved. One wonders how biblically derived messages of liberation can be taken seriously by today's masses of poor, homeless African Americans, female and male, who consider themselves to be experiencing a form of slavery – that is, economic enslavement by the capitalist American economy. They may consider themselves outside the boundaries of sedentary, "civilized" American culture.

Womanist theologians, especially those who take their slave heritage seriously, are therefore led to question James Cone's assumption that the African American theologian can today make *paradigmatic* use of the Hebrews' exodus and election experience as recorded in the Bible. Even though Cone sees that for the Hebrews "election is inseparable from the event of the exodus," he does not see that non-Hebrew female slaves, especially those of African descent, are not on equal terms with the Hebrews and are not woven into this biblical story of election and exodus.[14] The nonliberative strand in the Bible and the tension it apparently places upon black liberation theology's norm for interpreting scripture (i.e., God's liberating action on behalf of all the oppressed) make it difficult to understand how the Bible can function today in the way that James Cone suggests: "It matters little to the oppressed who authored scripture; what is important is whether it can serve as a weapon against oppressors."[15] Equivocal messages and/or silence about God's liberating power on behalf of non-Hebrew female slaves of African descent do not make effective weapons for African Americans to use in "wars" against oppressors.

Though there may be problems with his view of the overwhelmingly liberative work of God demonstrated in the Bible in relation to *all* the oppressed, James Cone is right to emphasize the significance of the community of faith for influencing the way the community's theologians use the Bible. He reminds the reader that "the theologian brings to the scripture the perspective of a community," and

> ideally the concern of that community is consistent with the concern of the community that gave us the scriptures. It is the task of theology to keep these two communities (biblical and contemporary) in constant tension in order that we may be able to speak meaningfully about God.[16]

Black theologians – in order to present a true rendering of the faith of the African American Christian community – must not be concerned only about the tensions between the contemporary black community and the biblical community. They must also reveal the tensions in the community's faith, so that the African American Christian community can become aware of how these tensions affect its theology and life. The community will see, on the basis of its way of appropriating the scripture, that it expresses belief in a God who liberates (the God of the enslaved Hebrews) and a God who does not liberate (the God of the non-Hebrew female slave Hagar). It may be that spasmodic participation of the African American denominational churches in the African American struggle for social change stems as much from unconscious tensions in their faith as from the growing bourgeois attitude of many of their congregations.

If black liberation theology wants to include black women and speak on behalf of the most oppressed black people today – the poor homeless, jobless, economically "enslaved" women, men, and children sleeping on American streets, in bus stations, parks, and alleys – theologians must ask themselves some questions. Have they, in the use of the Bible, identified so thoroughly with the theme of Israel's election that they have not seen the oppressed of the oppressed in scripture? Have they identified so completely with Israel's liberation that they have been blind to the awful reality of victims making victims in the Bible? Does this kind of blindness with regard to non-Hebrew victims in the scripture also make it easy for black male theologians and biblical scholars to ignore the figures in the Bible whose experience is analogous to that of black women?[17]

If black liberation theologians want to respond to these questions about black liberation theology's bias against black women, they must assume an additional hermeneutical posture – one that allows them to become conscious of what has been made invisible in the text and to see that their work is in collusion with this "invisibilization" of black women's experience. Therefore, in the use of scripture, theologians should initially engage a womanist hermeneutic of *identification-ascertainment* that involves three modes of inquiry: subjective, communal, and objective. Through an analysis of their own faith journey with regard to its biblical foundations, theologians discover with whom and with what events they personally identify in scripture. Through an analysis of the biblical foundation of the faith journey of the Christian community with which they are affiliated, Christian theologians determine the biblical faith, events, and biblical characters with whom the community has identified. Biblical aspects of the community's faith journey are revealed in sermons, songs, testimonies by the people, liturgy, ritual, and in its sociopolitical-cultural affiliations in the world. This subjective and communal analysis acquaints theologians with the biases they bring to the interpretation of scripture. Then theologians engage the objective mode of inquiry that ascertains *both* the biblical events, characters, and circumstances with whom the biblical writers have identified *and* those with whom the biblical writers have not identified, that is, those who are victims of those with whom the biblical writers have identified.

By engaging this womanist hermeneutic of *identification-ascertainment*, black liberation theologians will be able to see the junctures at which they and the community need to be critical of their way of using the Bible. Engaging this hermeneutic allows black theologians to see at what point they must be critical of the biblical text itself, in those instances where the text supports oppression, exclusion, and even the death of innocent people. Womanist theologians, in concert with womanist biblical scholars, need to show the African American denominational churches and black liberation theology the liability of its habit of using the Bible in an uncritical and sometimes too self-serving way. This kind of usage has prohibited the community from seeing that the end result of the biblical exodus event, begun in the Book of Exodus, was the violent destruction of a whole nation of people, the Canaanites, described in the Book of Joshua. Black liberation theologians today should reconceptualize what it means to lift up uncritically the biblical exodus *event* as a major paradigm for black theological reflection. To respond to the current issues in the black community, theologians should reflect upon exodus from Egypt as *holistic story* rather than *event*. This would allow the community to see the exodus as an extensive reality involving several kinds of events before its completion in the genocide of the Canaanites and the taking of their land.

The community would see the violence involved in a liberation struggle supposedly superintended by God.

What is suggested here is *not* that black theologians in their use of scripture ignore the fact of black people's identification with the exodus of the Israelites from Egypt. This is part of African American Christian history and should be remembered by the community. Nor should liberation language and liberation ideas be lost to black theology. However, I suggest that African American theologians should make it clear to the community that this black way of identifying with God *solely* through the exodus of the Hebrews and Jesus' reported words in Luke belongs to the black historical period of American slavery. To build contemporary systematic theology only on the exodus and Luke paradigm is to ignore generations of black history subsequent to slavery – that is, to consign the community and the black theological imagination to a kind of historical stalemate that denies the possibility of change with regard to the people's experience of God and with regard to the possibility of God changing in relation to the community. Pointing out these problems with the use of the Bible in black theology might also show theologians that in order to respond to the tensions in African American faith and to suggest woman-inclusive correctives, they might have to rely upon non-Christian and non-Jewish sources to interpret texts and shape their talk about the community's understanding of how God relates to its life.

Black experience

Equally important as the use of the Bible in black liberation theology is the issue of the nature and function of experience. Something called the black experience is the point of departure for the anthropology in black liberation theology. Black experience, however, is limited in its naming of experience as far as black women are concerned. The black experience and theological tasks described therein (as well as the view of history) presuppose and perpetuate black androcentrism. The introduction of black women's experience expands our knowledge of the character of black people's existence in North America.

Womanist analysis suggests another kind of history to which black theology must give attention if it intends to be inclusive of black women's experience. This is "women's re/production history." It involves more than women birthing children, nurturing, and attending to family affairs. Though the events and ideas associated with these realities do relate, "women's re/production history" has to do with whatever women think, create, use, and pass on through their labor for the sake of women's and the family's well-being. Thus black women's resistance strategies belong to black women's re/production history – just as the oppressive opposition to these strategies from dominating cultures belongs to this history. Through the lens of black women's re/production history we can see the entire saga of the race. We see the survival intelligence of the race creating modes of resistance, sustenance, and resurrection from despair. We see the exploitation of the community's spiritual, material, and intellectual resources by extra-community forces met by the uncanny, redemptive response of the religion black women created in the African American denominational churches.

Theological tasks

To deepen the theological tasks, womanist religious scholars carry out theology by starting with the black community and then moving to the academy. Moreover, to broaden the theological task, black liberation theology needs to be mindful of global coalition work.

Womanist Old Testament scholar Renita Weems began her biblical scholarship taking cues from the community of black women rather than solely from the academy. She has brought the academy and grassroots black women together as she retells biblical stories from the perspective of these women in a language they can understand. In her book *Just a Sister Away: A Womanist Vision of Women's Relationships in the Bible*, Weems uses her skills as a professionally trained biblical scholar and ordained minister to bridge the gap between church and seminary.

Another womanist New Testament scholar, Clarice Martin, uses a methodology that moves from women's issues in the church to academic scholarship, rather than imposing the world of the academy on the world of women. The exchange between these two worlds is evident in her first published booklet, a study guide on the Acts of the Apostles, produced for women in the Presbyterian Church (USA), *Tongues of Fire: Power for the Church Today*.

Sociologist of religion Cheryl Townsend Gilkes has shown how African Americans transformed fragments of scripture so that gender equality was achieved.[18] Gilkes, an ordained Baptist minister and womanist scholar, devotes much scholarly attention to unearthing cultural clues in black history and the black church, which help women own and recover their contributions to African American community life.

Jacquelyn Grant and Kelly Brown Douglas are contributing profoundly to womanist Christology as they develop their notion of Christ as a black woman.[19] A difference between their positions is that Grant sees Christ specifically as a black woman, whereas Douglas postulates a Christ living in the face of black women engaged in working toward the unity and wholeness of the community. Douglas' position is open-ended, in that it leaves space for Christ also to be living in the face of black men engaged in the same activity.

The development of women's theological voices in the United States has by no means been monolithic. Women in various cultural and racial communities have produced their own ways of talking and writing about women's relation to the divine. The womanist way produced by African American women is not something to be imposed imperialistically on women from other cultural contexts.

The hope of many womanist theologians is that communities of women from various cultures and countries will develop theologies consistent with their own experiences and cultural heritages. Then women from around the world can come together to share and exchange strategies for women's survival, liberation, and leadership in the churches. This kind of exchange will bring the spirit of the kingdom closer to our lives and lead to a more liberated world in which women and men live together in the image of God's freedom and grace.

Notes

1   Alice Walker, *In Search of Our Mothers' Garden: Womanist Prose* (New York: Harcourt, 1983), pp. xi–xii.
2   Stephanie Y. Mitchem, *Introducing Womanist Theology* (Maryknoll, NY: Orbis Books, 2002); Diana L. Hayes, *And Still We Rise: An Introduction to Black Liberation Theology* (Mahwah, NJ: Paulist Press, 1996); Diana L. Hayes, *Standing in the Shoes My Mother Made: A Womanist Theology* (Minneapolis, MN: Fortress Press, 2010); Monica A. Coleman, *Making a Way Out of No Way: A Womanist Theology* (Minneapolis, MN: Fortress Press, 2008); A. Elaine Brown Crawford, *Hope in the Holler: A Womanist Theology* (Louisville, KY: Westminster John Knox Press, 2002); and Dwight N. Hopkins, *Introducing Black Theology of Liberation* (Maryknoll, NY: Orbis Books, 1999).
3   Colorism exists in the black community when the community values lighter skin blacks over darker skin blacks. See Kathy Russell *et al.*, *The Color Complex: The Politics of Skin Color among African Americans* (New York: Anchor, 1993).
4   See   www.brooklynmuseum.org/eascfa/dinner_party/heritage_floor/ milla_granson.php.

5 Sarah H. Bradford, *Harriet Tubman: The Moses of Her People* (New York: Hesperides Press, 2008).

6 Rosa Parks, *Rosa Parks: My Story* (New York: Puffin Books, 1999).

7 Jacquelyn Grant, *White Women's Christ and Black Women's Jesus: Feminist Christology and Womanist Response* (Atlanta, GA: Scholars Press, 1989).

8 In the 1990s, white feminists, including Letty Russell and Elizabeth Bettenhausen, and black womanists worked together in an antiracism program sponsored by the Women's Theological Center in Boston. In the 1970s and 1980s, Beverly Harrison developed rigorous antiracism components in some of her courses at Union Theological Seminary, as did Carter Heyward at Episcopal Divinity School.

9 Jacquelyn Grant, "Black Theology and the Black Woman," in James H. Cone and Gayraud S. Wilmore (eds.), *Black Theology: A Documentary History*, vol. 1, *1966–1979* (Maryknoll, NY: Orbis Books, 1979), p. 420.

10 Delores S. Williams, *Sisters in the Wilderness: The Challenge of Womanist God-Talk* (Maryknoll, NY: Orbis Books, 1993).

11 James H. Cone, *A Black Theology of Liberation*, 2nd edn. (Maryknoll, NY: Orbis Books, 1990).

12 Naim Stifan Ateek, *Justice and Only Justice* (Maryknoll, NY: Orbis Books, 1989), p. 77.

13 All biblical quotations are from the Revised Standard Version.

14 Cone, *A Black Theology of Liberation*, p. 2.

15 Ibid., p. 31.

16 Ibid., p. 36.

17 For instance, it is most alarming that Cain Hope Felder, in his critique of biblical scholars' failure to give attention to the significant role of Africa and Africans in the Bible, gives *very little* attention to the African Hagar. Felder, a Christian testament scholar, does not allude to Hagar in the Christian testament. Though he cites countless references from the Book of Galatians, he never alludes to Hagar's inferior place in that book. This is a clear instance of the invisibility of "the oppressed of the oppressed" (e.g., the nonruling-class women and female slaves of African descent) in scholarship by black males. See Cain Hope Felder, *Troubling Biblical Waters: Race, Class, and Family* (Maryknoll, NY: Orbis Books, 1989).

18 Cheryl Townsend Gilkes, "Mother to the Motherless, Father to the Fatherless: Power, Gender and Community in an Afrocentric Biblical Tradition," *Semeia* 47 (1989): 47–85.

19 See Grant, *White Women's Christ and Black Women's Jesus*; Kelly Brown Douglas, *The Black Christ* (Maryknoll, NY: Orbis Books, 1994).

Part II

Themes in black theology

6 God

DENNIS W. WILEY

INTRODUCTION

In order to talk about God in black theology, one must understand that black theologians are not a homogeneous group. There is diversity in black theology just as there is diversity in white or any other form of theology. Before the discussion begins, two preliminary questions must be answered. The first is, "Which major phase of black theology are we talking about?" When one speaks of black theology, it is essential to establish from the outset whether one is referring to historical, homegrown, unsystematic black theology that existed prior to the 1960s black power movement, or to the contemporary, academic, systematic black theology that emerged in response to it. Although these two phases are integrally related, they represent two distinct approaches to the theological task. Historical black theology has often been an instinctive, unconscious, oral and written theology that emerged from ordinary, unlettered black people struggling to survive the multifaceted onslaught of a racist and oppressive environment. Contemporary black theology, on the other hand, has tended to be an intentional, intellectual, written theology that began among an ecumenical group of black clergy and was soon appropriated and further developed, primarily, by black theological scholars. Although there is no way to sharply separate contemporary black theology from the historical black theology on which it is based, this discussion will focus on the early stages of the former as a point of departure in considering the doctrine of God according to black theology.

The second question that must be answered before discussing God in black theology is, "Whose black theology are we talking about?" While there is some agreement, the fact is that there are as many perspectives concerning God as there are black theologians. With this in mind, I have chosen the theology of James Cone as a point of reference to guide these reflections on God in black theology. The reason for this selection is that much of what has been written by black theologians about God since the late 1960s, or about any other related topic for that matter, has been written in response to the writings of Cone. This reality can be attributed to two basic factors.

In the first place, Cone, the undisputed "father of black theology," was the first to publish a book on black theology.[1] In fact, not only did his first two books precede any other books specifically addressing this subject, but also they each employed the term "black theology" in their titles and in their content. His groundbreaking classic, *Black Theology and Black Power*, was originally published in April 1969, and his more systematically developed second book, *A Black Theology of Liberation*, was published in 1970.[2] In addition to the fact that he was first out of the starting blocks with these two major publications, his impeccable scholarship, critical analysis, lucid writing, and provocative style set a standard and a tone for black theological inquiry that could not be ignored.

This leads me to my second, and perhaps even more important, reason for choosing Cone as a reference point. With the possible exception of Albert Cleage, Cone was clearly considered by many to be the most radical of the early black theologians.[3] Combining his mastery of Western theology, his love for the black church, and his passion for racial justice, he minced no words as he attacked white theology and challenged the church (both black and white) to be faithful to the Gospel of Jesus Christ. Because he was astute enough and fearless enough to push the proverbial envelope of appropriate, acceptable, and "objective" theological discourse, his message demanded serious engagement from opponents and proponents alike.

With this in mind, this chapter will lift up three major aspects of God in black theology and touch on critical issues that are related to each aspect. If the question is, "Who is God, according to black theology?" the three major answers offered here are (1) God takes sides, (2) God is a liberator, and (3) God is black.

A GOD WHO "TAKES SIDES"

Cone's view of God mirrored, in some degree, his own impassioned approach to the theological task. For instance, he wrote in his introduction to *Black Theology and Black Power*:

> This work, then, is written with a definite attitude, the attitude of an angry black man, disgusted with the oppression of black people in America and with the scholarly demand to be "objective" about

it. Too many people have died, and too many are on the edge of death. In fairness to my understanding of the truth, I cannot allow myself to engage in a dispassionate, non-committed debate on the status of the black–white relations in America by assessing the pro and con of Black Power. The scholarly demand for this kind of "objectivity" has come to mean being uninvolved or not taking sides.[4]

In *A Black Theology of Liberation*, Cone further elaborated on this connection between passion and commitment:

Because black theology is survival theology, it must speak with a passion consistent with the depths of the wounds of the oppressed. Theological language is passionate language, the language of commitment, because it is language which seeks to vindicate the afflicted and condemn the enforcers of evil. Christian theology cannot afford to be an abstract, dispassionate discourse on the nature of God in relation to humankind; such an analysis has no ethical implications for the contemporary forms of oppression in our society.[5]

In fact, Cone went so far as to say, "The sin of American theology is that it has spoken without passion."[6]

This business of speaking with passion, making a commitment, and "taking sides" was important to Cone because it unequivocally demonstrated one's solidarity with oppressed humanity and one's revolutionary commitment to eradicate that oppression. Therefore, the same litmus test that was applied to theologians could also be applied to God. This is why he could later declare, "Blacks want to know whose side God is on" and "blacks have no time for a neutral God."[7] In order to further develop this notion of God in a comprehensive fashion that included all victims of oppression, regardless of color, Cone wrote his most mature systematic theological text entitled, *God of the Oppressed*.[8]

While all are not comfortable with this notion of a partial God, there does appear to be general consensus among black theologians that it is not the task of black theology to become bogged down in abstract theological ruminations. Black theology is concrete, not abstract. And it is interested in a concrete God, not an abstract God. The word "concrete," as used here, should not be misinterpreted to mean "rigid" or "inflexible." Instead, it refers to a theology and to a God *concretely* involved in the day-to-day lives and affairs of God's people.[9]

Cone gives one of the reasons for black theology's resistance to abstract theological discourse when he says, "The reality of God is presupposed in black theology. Black theology is an attempt to analyze the nature of that reality."[10] J. Deotis Roberts makes a similar point when he asserts, "The question of existence in reference to God is not the real issue for blacks."[11] In other words, probably due to the fact that the African ancestors of African Americans were introduced to God long before they were brought to this land as slaves, the *givenness* of God is a nondebatable assumption for most black theologians. Instead, they have been more concerned to distinguish the *true* God from the *false* God, that is, the God of black liberation from the God of white supremacy, the God of the slave from the God of the slave master, and, stated more universally, the God of the oppressed from the God of the oppressor.[12]

Because "God is,"[13] black theology has not been preoccupied with hypothetical musings on the so-called "death of God,"[14] ontological proofs for the existence of God, philosophical debates about the reality of God, or metaphysical speculations concerning the essence of God. To the contrary, black theology has sought to determine what can be said about the God of biblical revelation in light of the oppression of black people. Instead of focusing on questions such as "Does God exist?" black theologians have been more interested in asking, "Does God care?"[15] or, more pointedly, "What is God doing to alleviate the suffering of black humanity?"[16] Consistent with their understanding of the God of the Bible, they have been less concerned with the *being* of God *beyond* history than with the *activity* of God *within* history. The questions black theologians have raised about God are inseparable from the context in which black people have found themselves.

In *God of the Oppressed*, Cone reminds us of the contextual nature of theology: "Theology is not universal language; it is *interested* language and thus is always a reflection of the goals and aspirations of a particular people in a definite social setting."[17] Theology, or "God-talk," is not God talking about God, but human beings talking about God. Therefore, our understanding of God is shaped by our existential circumstances.

Cone's context, like that of most academic black theologians, was one in which, although he was raised and nurtured in the black church and black community, he was theologically educated in a white seminary and steeped in the Western theological tradition. Unfortunately, as with most of his theological peers, he received little if any education regarding black history or his African heritage. In fact, he says that during his entire time in seminary, "not one text written by a black person was ever used as a required reading for a class."[18] Thus, when as a young theological professor at a small, remote, predominantly white college in Michigan he found himself compelled to respond to the crisis of urban rebellions ("riots"), the assassination of the Revd. Dr. Martin Luther King, Jr., and the growing influence of the black power movement, he eventually discovered that although his personal study had exposed him to some rudimentary knowledge of black history, his early attempts to develop a black theology betrayed his excessive reliance on white theological sources. This was one of the critiques lodged against Cone by other black theologians after the publication of his first two books. His next two books, *The Spirituals and the Blues* and *God of the Oppressed*, reflected his effort to learn and grow as a result of this criticism.

CRITICAL ISSUES

A transcendent and immanent God
In black theology, as in African theology, there is a balance between God's transcendence and immanence.[19] While God is not identical with God's creation in a pantheistic sense, neither is God separate or aloof from God's creation in a deistic sense. Perhaps this balance between God's transcendence and immanence is best captured in the distinction between God and Jesus, as expressed in the Negro spirituals:

> God is experienced as Almighty and Sovereign and is often removed from the day-to-day affairs of people. But Jesus is experienced as a comforter in time of trouble who is readily available and always at hand.[20]

Whether one makes this sharp distinction between God and Jesus or not, black theologians are overwhelmingly unified in their belief that, in accordance with philosophical personalism, "God is both transcendent and immanent, both free and personal, both creative and moral." This God "is not abstract thought or a thought-process, but a person, a self, a thinker."[21]

A personal God
James Cone attests that, "Belief in a personal God and in the dignity and worth of the human person has always been a deeply held conviction

in the African-American community."[22] Apparently, this view among black people has its roots in Africa, because Joseph Washington reports that, according to West African belief, "God is not merely a power but [God] is a person."[23] One finds rare consensus among black theologians regarding this issue. Jones claims, "Of God alone can one speak of a self-existent, absolute reality who is also a good and loving person."[24] Roberts says that God "is a personal God of infinite compassion and suffering love."[25] And James Melvin Washington declares, "God feels and responds to the oppressed."[26]

This affective understanding of God renders the traditional divine attributes of "impassibility" and "immutability" particularly problematic for black theology.[27] Although God is not capricious, God is one who hears our cries, feels our pain, and answers our prayers. Indeed, God is *affected* by our welfare and, consistent with scripture, may even change his mind. Furthermore, it should be clear that, for black theology, this *personal* God is not a God of *individualism*. God cares for the *person*, but God also cares for the *community*. This is why Cone can say:

> The "I," then, who cries out in the spirituals is a particular black self affirming both [one's] being and [one's] being-in-community, for the two are inseparable. Thus the struggle to be both a person and a member of community was the major focus of black religion.[28]

A God of love and wrath

Whereas Cone believes that God is love, he also believes that God's love cannot "be properly understood without focusing equally on the biblical view of God's righteousness."[29] Cone, who often uses "wrath" and "righteousness" interchangeably, also says, "Most theological treatments of God's love fail to place the proper emphasis on God's wrath, suggesting that love is completely self-giving without any demand of obedience." In his opinion, this is what Dietrich Bonhoeffer called "cheap grace."[30] Hence, "A God without wrath does not plan to do much liberating." In fact, God's wrath is the flip side of God's love as it is applied to those who stand in opposition to the liberation of the oppressed.[31]

A GOD OF LIBERATION

Liberation is the term that perhaps best defines the God of black theology and best differentiates this God from the God of white theology.

Not only does this term accurately point to the liberating activity of the God of Israel, as revealed in the biblical text, but it also describes the goal for which African Americans have continually quested ever since the first twenty Africans were put ashore as indentured servants at Jamestown, Virginia in 1619.[32] It is a holistic concept that refers not simply to physical liberation, but to spiritual, psychological, emotional, social, political, and economic liberation. Cone recalls that in 1969, he was invited to become a member of the Theological Commission of what was then known as the National Committee of Black Churchmen (NCBC)[33] and to join the other members in Atlanta for the purpose of writing a black theology statement:

> At the time I was working on my second book, *A Black Theology of Liberation*, and thus the word "liberation", though found in *Black Theology and Black Power*, was now the central theme for articulating the gospel of Jesus. I suggested defining black theology as a theology of black liberation. It was accepted without dissent.[34]

That document, dated June 13, 1969, is entitled "Black Theology" and includes a section subtitled "What Is Black Theology?" that begins, "Black Theology is a theology of black liberation." It further states, "It is the affirmation of black humanity that emancipates black people from white racism, thus providing authentic freedom for both white and black people." Finally, it also says, "The message of liberation is the revelation of God as revealed in the incarnation of Jesus Christ. Freedom IS the gospel. Jesus is the Liberator!"[35]

Roberts agrees that "Black Theology is a theology of liberation," even though he believes that "reconciliation" should receive equal emphasis. While the NCBC excerpts above use the terms "liberation" *and* "freedom," Roberts makes the following distinction: "Unfortunately, freedom has been so 'white-washed,' misapplied, delimited, and discriminating in usage in America that it has little meaning of importance for the black man." He goes on to proclaim, "Freedom sums up what *is*. Liberation is revolutionary – for blacks it points to *what ought to be*."[36]

Nevertheless, although "liberation" is decidedly the term of preference, black theologians still sometimes use the word "freedom" instead. For instance, Joseph R. Washington, in his pioneering though controversial book, *Black Religion*, stressed the commitment of Negro folk religion to freedom and equality.[37] C. Eric Lincoln, a sociologist of religion who provided invaluable early encouragement and support to Cone,

including helping him to get his first book published, partnered with
Lawrence H. Mamiya to write the following reflections on freedom:

> A major aspect of black Christian belief is found in the symbolic
> importance given to the word "freedom." Throughout black
> history the term "freedom" has found a deep religious resonance
> in the lives and hopes of African Americans. Depending upon
> the time and the context, the implications of freedom were
> derived from the nature of the exigency. During slavery it meant
> release from bondage; after emancipation it meant the right to be
> educated, to be employed, and to move about freely from place to
> place. In the twentieth century freedom means social, political,
> and economic justice. From the very beginning of the black
> experience in America, one critical denotation of freedom has
> remained constant: freedom has always meant the absence of any
> restraint which might compromise one's responsibility to God.
> The notion has persisted that if God calls you to discipleship, God
> calls you to freedom. And that God wants you free because God
> made you for [God's]self and in [God's] image.[38]

This statement is faithful to the spirit of black theology, whether one
perceives the divine to be a God of liberation or a God of freedom. The
bottom line is that black people, poor people, and all people have been
created by God for freedom and liberation, not for slavery and bondage.

As Cone sees it, "The point of departure of black theology is the
biblical God as related to the black liberation struggle" and "God-talk
is not Christian-talk unless it is *directly* related to the liberation of the
oppressed." He believes the "two hermeneutical principles" for the doctrine of God are as follows:

(1) The Christian understanding of God arises from the biblical view
of revelation, a revelation of God that takes place in the liberation
of oppressed Israel and is completed in the incarnation in Jesus
Christ.

(2) The doctrine of God in black theology must be of the God who is
participating in the liberation of the oppressed of the land.

Finally, Cone says,

> Because God has been revealed in the history of oppressed Israel
> and decisively in the Oppressed One, Jesus Christ, it is impossible
> to say anything about God without seeing [God] as being involved
> in the contemporary liberation of all oppressed peoples. The God
> in black theology is the God of and for the oppressed, the God who

comes into view in their liberation. Any other approach is a denial of biblical revelation.[39]

A God of reconciliation

In addition to a God of liberation, black theologians have also viewed God in a variety of other ways, for example, as a God of hope, redemption, and survival.[40] However, the most serious early challenge to Cone's emphasis on liberation came from J. Deotis Roberts. Although Roberts agreed that "Black Theology is a theology of *liberation*,"[41] he also believed that "Reconciliation is always to be placed in conjunction with liberation."[42] While Cone does not generally reject the concept of reconciliation, the debate between them has centered on three questions: (1) What does reconciliation mean? (2) Who sets its terms? (3) When does it occur – *before* or *after* liberation? Regarding the first point, Cone makes a distinction between "the objective reality of reconciliation," that is, "from God's side," and "the subjective reality of reconciliation," that is, "on the human side."[43] The former as it pertains to blacks and whites, "means that God is unquestionably on the side of the oppressed blacks struggling for justice."[44] On the human side, reconciliation for black people means that they "must participate in God's revolutionary activity" against oppression. On the other hand:

> White people must be made to realize that reconciliation is a costly experience. It is not holding hands and singing "Black and white together" and "We shall overcome." Reconciliation means *death*, and only those who are prepared to die in the struggle for freedom will experience new life with God.[45]

Concerning the second point, only black people can define the terms of reconciliation between blacks and whites and, in reference to point three, liberation must *precede* reconciliation, unless one is referring to reconciliation *among* black people.[46] Cone believes that the differences between him and Roberts on this issue may be attributed to the fact that "Roberts belongs to the 'integration period,' and I belong to the era of 'Black Power.'"[47]

A violent or nonviolent God?

Roberts's identification with "integration" and Cone's (as well as Cleage's) alignment with "Black Power" help to explain their different stances on the issues of violence and nonviolence. Kelly Brown

Douglas was right when she concluded, "While Cleage's Black Christ strongly supported violence, and Cone's allowed for violence, Roberts's precluded violence."[48] It could also be said that while Cleage was heavily influenced by Malcolm X and Roberts was a devoted disciple of Martin Luther King, Jr., Cone was inspired by both. Cone was soundly criticized because he did not close the door on violence. His adoption of Malcolm's phrase "by any means necessary" meant not only that he, but also his God, refused to eliminate violence as a revolutionary option for the poor and oppressed. His rationale was that (1) America was a nation founded and built on, and sustained through a history of violence; (2) only the oppressed can determine whether violence is justified in any given situation; and (3) even if Jesus was nonviolent in first-century Palestine, the victims of oppression should not be bound by what the historical Jesus did *then*, but led by what God, through the resurrected Jesus, is doing *now* to liberate the oppressed. This, says Cone, is "the risk of faith."[49]

GOD IS BLACK

One cannot talk about God in black theology without at some point coming to a discussion of the color of God. Although color is a physiological trait that is technically inapplicable to a spiritual being, black theologians have understood the symbolic significance of attributing color to God, especially within the black church and the African American community. At least three reasons account for this significance. First, the creation story in the first chapter of Genesis states that human beings were created "in the image of God."[50] Although this account does not necessarily imply a *physical* image, it is difficult to disassociate the word "image" from the notion of visual perception. Just because God has no *literal* color does not mean that God may not have a *symbolic* color. Second, even though the Bible says that "God is spirit,"[51] it also maintains that Jesus, the Son of God, "became flesh and lived among us."[52] Flesh has color. But while it may seem impractical to attribute color to God the Parent, it is not impractical to attribute color to God the Son. Finally, this issue is significant because in the vast majority of churches, black and white, biblical characters, both human and divine, have traditionally been depicted as white, whether these depictions have occurred in stained-glass windows, paintings on the walls, or pictures in Sunday school literature, on the backs of bulletins and fans, or within the biblical text itself.

In her book *The Black Christ*, Kelly Brown Douglas examines how three black theologians, all of whom agree that Jesus Christ was/is black, interpret his blackness in different ways.[53] Her selection of theologians and her analysis of their approach to the divine color issue are instructive. But before turning to these theologians from the early stages of contemporary black theology, it should be understood that the assertion "God is black" did not begin with this phase. There were some black theologians in the *historical* phase who also lifted their voices in support of a black God. Two shining examples are Bishop Henry McNeal Turner of the African Methodist Episcopal Church and Marcus Garvey, founder and president general of the Universal Negro Improvement Association and organizer of the African Orthodox Church. On February 1, 1898, Turner, a fiery and outspoken black nationalist minister, published an article entitled "God Is a Negro." In it he asserted that black people have just as much right to portray God as "a Negro" as white people have to portray God as white. Why?

> Every race of people since time began who have attempted to describe their God by words, or by paintings, or by carvings, or by any other form or figure, have conveyed the idea that the God who made them and shaped their destinies was symbolized in themselves, and why should not the Negro believe that he [or she] resembles God as much so as other people? We do not believe that there is any hope for a race of people who do not believe they look like God.

While Turner conceded that the color of God was not really a big issue for black people, he made it clear that they could not stand by silently while God was depicted as being white.[54]

Garvey, another gifted black nationalist orator who in the early twentieth century organized "one of the most phenomenal social movements in modern history,"[55] also weighed in on the color of God:

> Whilst our God has no color, yet it is human to see everything through one's own spectacles, and since the white people have seen their God through white spectacles, we have only now started out (late though it be) to see our God through our own spectacles ... We Negroes believe in the God of Ethiopia, the everlasting God ... That is the God in whom we believe, but we shall worship [our God] through the spectacles of Ethiopia.[56]

Not only did Garvey articulate the need for black people to see the divine through their own spectacles, but he satisfied this need through his church "with a black hierarchy, including a Black God, a Black Jesus, a Black Madonna, and black angels."[57]

Three contemporary black theologians who have concluded that God is black are Albert Cleage, James Cone, and J. Deotis Roberts. While Roberts would be considered the more conservative of the three, Cleage and Cone would be seen as more radical, although for different reasons. Cleage is much more literal in his understanding of color as it relates to God, Jesus, and the biblical nation of Israel. According to him, "Jesus was a revolutionary black leader, a Zealot, seeking to lead a Black Nation to freedom."[58] Concerning God, Cleage argues that if mortals were created in the image of God, we must look at them to know what God looks like. Since humans are a variety of colors – black, yellow, red, and just a tinge of white (based on the relatively smaller population of whites in the world) – and if we view God as a "person,"[59] then God, who is a mixture of these colors, must be black, not white. As he explains, "In America, one drop of black makes you black. So by American law, God is black."[60]

At the opposite end of the black theology spectrum, Roberts also believes God is black, but only symbolically. Like Cleage, his major emphasis is on the black Messiah, but he rejects Cleage's "view that Christ is *actually* black in a literal-historical sense."[61] In language not unlike Turner's and Garvey's above, Roberts claims:

> Most [people] will depict the image of the ultimate in the visible form native to their own culture and ethnic group. It follows that the white Americanized Christ is alien to black [people] and this is the reason for the search for a black Christ.[62]

Roberts views the issue of the color of Christ as having both universal and particular significance. In a universal sense, Christ is colorless, but in a particular sense, the "symbolic" or "mythical" color of Christ is determined by the context of the religious experience. Thus, in keeping with his liberation/reconciliation theme, he says, "The *black Messiah* liberates the black [person]. The universal Christ *reconciles* the black [person] with the rest of [humanity]."[63] Essentially, what Roberts says about the color of Christ can also be applied to the color of God, because Roberts believed that "God was in Christ"[64] and that it "is through the window of the cross that we see the face of God."[65]

James Cone deals with the color of both God and Jesus Christ extensively. Since, however, this chapter is concerned primarily with God, our discussion will be limited accordingly.[66] It should be established, however, that for Cone, as for Roberts and Cleage, Jesus is the key for everything he says about God, because Jesus "is the plenary revelation of God."[67] In his second book, *A Black Theology of Liberation*, Cone includes a critical footnote that clearly explains his use of "blackness" as it refers to human or divine reality. In the first instance, it is a *physiological* trait referring "to a particular black-skinned people in America" who are the victims "of white racist brutality." In the second instance, it is an *ontological* symbol "for all those who participate in [or, one might say, *identify with*] liberation from oppression." As he explains:

> This is the universal note in black theology. It believes that all human beings were created for freedom, and that God always sides with the oppressed against oppressors.[68]

Many miss this "universal note" in Cone's early theology and assume that, whenever he talks about the blackness of God or of God "taking sides" with black people in their struggle against white racist oppression, he is automatically excluding whites from any meaningful role in black liberation. But his emphasis on ontological, and not just physiological, blackness means that black is more than a color – it is a symbol that points to a condition of suffering, humiliation, and oppression that demands liberation. Anyone can participate in this liberation, whether physically white, black, or any color in-between. But whoever participates – including God – must at least be black *ontologically*. For the word "God" is also a symbol "that opens up depths of reality in the world." And, argues Cone, "[i]f the symbol loses its power to point to the meaning of black liberation, then we must destroy it."[69] The development of Cone's universal perspective can be further detected in his fourth book, *God of the Oppressed*, in which he places less emphasis on the color of God, but rather addresses God's solidarity with oppressed humanity, especially the poor, regardless of color.[70] It is significant that, unlike his first two books, the title of this book includes neither the word "black" nor "theology."

A CRITICAL ISSUE

Is God a white racist?
This provocative question was raised by William R. Jones in his book of the same title.[71] Essentially, Jones' critical challenge to black theology was launched in the form of the classic question of theodicy, having to do with the justice of God: "If God is all-good and all-powerful, why do innocent people suffer?" With specific regard to black theology,

Jones asked, "If God is a God of liberation, having delivered the biblical Israelites from Egyptian slavery, what is the contemporary liberation/ exaltation event that verifies God's liberating power?" He argued that if black theology cannot point to such an event, then based on the disproportionate suffering and oppression endured by black people, God must be a white racist.

Cone offered at least three responses. First, he acknowledged the undeniable validity of Jones' critique and conceded that the problem of evil was a mystery to which there was no definitive answer. Second, he offered the liberating power of the resurrected Jesus Christ as the contemporary liberation/exaltation event, even though he knew that answer would not satisfy people outside the Christian faith. Finally, he responded that even if black theology could not conclusively respond to Jones' question, it still offered oppressed people the hope and incentive to fight against oppression rather than fall into a state of resignation and despair.[72]

This is why, despite the problem of suffering, "it was easy, almost natural, for [Martin Luther] King to embrace the philosophy of personalism," as discussed above. In so doing, however,

> he rejected [Edgar S.] Brightman's concept of the finite God as an explanation for the existence of evil. King's commitment to the faith of the Negro church was too strong to allow him to embrace a limited God.[73]

King, like black theologians and black people in general, found it difficult to embrace a God limited in either goodness or power. Although one may not understand why an all-good and all-powerful God would permit black people to suffer as they do, it is believed that we shall "understand it better by and by,"[74] because "God works in a mysterious way"[75] and "God's ways and thoughts are higher than our ways and thoughts."[76] In the meantime, black people of faith refuse to believe that God is a white racist, because, as King would say, even though "the arc of the moral universe is long, it bends toward justice."[77]

CONCLUSION: A GOD WHO IS BOTH UNIVERSAL AND PARTICULAR

The God of black theology is a God who takes sides, is a God of liberation, and is black. This God is a God of particularity who meets black people in their oppressed condition and who, in "the manifestation of Jesus as the black Christ ... provides the necessary soul for black liberation."[78] At the same time, this God is a God of universality in whom a growing number of diverse, marginalized groups – regardless of race, ethnicity, class, gender, sexual orientation, age, ability, and so forth – are finding refuge as victims of oppression. As we move further into the twenty-first century, the challenge for black theology will be whether its God will be *universal* enough to embrace *all* of suffering humanity in its rich diversity while remaining *particular* enough to respect and affirm the unique cultural, sociological, and contextual integrity of every child of God. When this happens, all of us – whether black, brown, yellow, red, or white – will finally be able to shout, "Free at last, free at last; thank God Almighty, we are free at last."[79]

Notes

1   Note that Joseph R. Washington, Jr.'s *Black Religion: The Negro and Christianity in the United States* (New York: University Press of America, 1964) and Albert B. Cleage, Jr.'s *The Black Messiah* (New York: Sheed and Ward, 1968) were precursors to the formal, contemporary black theology movement. Also, in his *Black and White Power Subreption* (Boston: Beacon Press, 1969), Washington used the term "black power theology" in reference to "radical black theologians," including Cone and Cleage. For more on this, see James H. Cone, *For My People: Black Theology and the Black Church* (Maryknoll, NY: Orbis Books, 1984), pp. 19–20.

2   See James H. Cone, *Black Theology and Black Power* (Maryknoll, NY: Orbis Books, 1997) and *A Black Theology of Liberation: Twentieth Anniversary Edition* (Maryknoll, NY: Orbis Books, 1990).

3   Because Cleage was a pastor in the church rather than a scholar in the academy, his work was not always taken as seriously as the writings of black theologians in the academy.

4   Cone, *Black Power*, p. 2.

5   Cone, *Liberation*, p. 17.

6   Ibid., p. 18.

7   Ibid., p. 70.

8   James H. Cone, *God of the Oppressed* (Maryknoll, NY: Orbis Books, 1997).

9   For example, Nicholas C. Cooper-Lewter and Henry H. Mitchell observe, "Omnipotence is an abstract term, but it represents God's concrete action in living history." See their *Soul Theology: The Heart of American Black Culture* (San Francisco, CA: Harper & Row, 1986), p. 43. Also, in referring to the abstract nature of the traditional "eternal and intrinsic attributes of God," John S. Mbiti notes, "Broadly speaking, African thought forms are more concrete than abstract." See his *African Religions and Philosophy* (London: Heinemann, 1969), p. 30.

10   Cone, *Liberation*, p. 55.

11   J. Deotis Roberts, *Liberation and Reconciliation: A Black Theology* (Philadelphia, PA: Westminster Press, 1971), p. 82.

12   One black theologian who would take exception to this statement is Cecil Cone, who, citing reports by Bishop Daniel Alexander Payne of the African Methodist Episcopal Church in support, claims that "the absurdity of slavery forced many devout slaves to raise the question about God's existence." See Cecil Wayne Cone, *The Identity Crisis in Black Theology* (Nashville, TN: AMEC), p. 41.

13   See Major J. Jones, *The Color of God: The Concept of God in Afro-American Thought* (Macon, GA: Mercer University Press, 1987), p. 46. It should also be noted that a gospel song by this name, "God Is," is popular in many black churches.

14   Refers to the 1960s "death of God" debate among Euro-American theologians.

15   Jones, *Color*, pp. 21 and 52.

16   *Historical* black theology does record some exceptions to this tendency, among black theologians, not to question the existence of God. For example, Cecil Cone notes, "While most slaves did not take the option of open rebellion against God, the absurdity of slavery forced many devout slaves to raise the question about God's existence." See his *Identity Crisis*, p. 41. In this same text, Cecil Cone also quotes Daniel Alexander Payne, a former bishop of the African Methodist Episcopal Church, as questioning the existence of God. Ibid., pp. 40–41.

17   Cone, *Oppressed*, p. 36.

18   James H. Cone, *My Soul Looks Back* (Nashville, TN: Abingdon), p. 36.

19   See Dwight N. Hopkins, *Shoes That Fit Our Feet: Sources for a Constructive Black Theology* (Maryknoll, NY: Orbis Books, 1993), pp. 16–17; and Mbiti, *African Religions*, p. 29.

20   Cecil Cone, *Identity Crisis*, p. 36.

21   Kenneth L. Smith and Ira G. Zepp, Jr., *Search for the Beloved Community: The Thinking of Martin Luther King, Jr.* (Valley Forge, PA: Judson Press, 1974), pp. 100–03.

22   James H. Cone, *Martin and Malcolm and America: A Dream or a Nightmare?* (Maryknoll, NY: Orbis Books, 1992), p. 29.

23   See Joseph R. Washington, Jr., *Black Sects and Cults* (Garden City, NY: Doubleday, 1972), p. 29, where he quotes Geoffrey Parrinder, *West African Religion* (London: Epworth Press, 1969), p. 25.

24   Jones, *Color*, p. 46.

25   J. Deotis Roberts, *A Black Political Theology* (Philadelphia, PA: Westminster Press, 1974), p. 109.

26   James Melvin Washington (ed.), *Conversations with God: Two Centuries of Prayers by African Americans* (New York: HarperCollins, 1994), p. xlv.

27   See an excellent discussion of this issue in Daniel L. Migliore, *Faith Seeking Understanding: An Introduction to Christian Theology*, 2nd

edn. (Grand Rapids, MI: William B. Eerdmans Publishing Company, 2004), pp. 82–84.

28 James H. Cone, *The Spirituals and the Blues* (New York: Seabury Press, 1972), p. 68.

29 Cone, *Liberation*, p. 69.

30 Ibid. For more on this concept of "cheap grace," see Dietrich Bonhoeffer, *The Cost of Discipleship*, 2nd edn. (New York: Macmillan, 1959), pp. 45–60.

31 Cone, *Liberation*, pp. 69–71.

32 See John Hope Franklin, *From Slavery to Freedom: A History of Negro Americans* (New York: Alfred A. Knopf, 1980), p. 54.

33 Later the organization became known as the National Conference of Black Christians. For more on this, see James H. Cone and Gayraud S. Wilmore (eds.), *Black Theology: A Documentary History*, vol. 1, 1966–1979, 2nd edn. (Maryknoll, NY: Orbis Books, 1993), p. 16; and Cone, *For My People*, p. 210, n. 3.

34 Cone, *My Soul*, p. 53.

35 Cone and Wilmore, *Documentary History*, p. 101.

36 Roberts, *Reconciliation*, pp. 26–27.

37 Joseph R. Washington, *Black Religion: The Negro and Christianity in the United States* (New York: University Press of America, 1984), pp. 29, 34 *passim*.

38 C. Eric Lincoln and Lawrence H. Mamiya, *The Black Church in the African American Experience* (Durham, NC, and London: Duke University Press, 1990), p. 4.

39 Cone, *Liberation*, pp. 60–61.

40 For each of these emphases, respectively, see Major J. Jones, *Black Awareness: A Theology of Hope* (New York: Abingdon Press, 1971); Olin P. Moyd, *Redemption in Black Theology* (Valley Forge, PA: Judson Press, 1979); and Delores S. Williams, *Sisters in the Wilderness: The Challenge of Womanist God-Talk* (Maryknoll, NY: Orbis Books, 1993).

41 Roberts, *Reconciliation*, p. 27.

42 Roberts, *Political*, p. 220.

43 Cone, *Oppressed*, ch. 10.

44 Ibid., p. 215.

45 Ibid., pp. 218–19.

46 Ibid., pp. 218–19 and 224–25.

47 Cone and Wilmore, *Documentary History*, p. 430.

48 Kelly Brown Douglas, *The Black Christ* (Maryknoll, NY: Orbis Books, 1994), p. 76.

49 See Cone's comprehensive discussion of this issue in his *Oppressed*, pp. 199–206.

50 Gen. 1:27.

51 John 4:24.

52 John 1:14.

53 See Douglas, *Black Christ*, especially ch. 3.
54 Bishop Henry M. Turner, "God Is a Negro," in John H. Bracey, Jr., August Meier, and Elliott Rudwick (eds.), *Black Nationalism in America* (Indianapolis, IN: Bobbs-Merrill Educational Publishing, 1970), pp. 154–55.
55 Hollis R. Lynch, "Introduction to the Atheneum Edition," in Amy Jacques-Garvey (ed.), *Philosophy and Opinions of Marcus Garvey* (New York: Atheneum, 1986), n.p.
56 Marcus Garvey, "The Image of God," in Jacques-Garvey (ed.), *Philosophy*, p. 44.
57 Cleage, *Messiah*, p. 8.
58 Ibid., p. 4.
59 Cleage does not intend to suggest here that God is a *literal* person. Instead, he is referring to the fact that "we are taught in the Christian religion to think of God as a person, as a personality capable of love, capable of concern, capable of purpose and of action." Ibid., p. 42.
60 Ibid., p. 43.
61 Roberts, *Reconciliation*, p. 137.
62 Ibid.
63 Ibid., p. 140.
64 This was the title of a book that made a tremendous impact on Roberts' Christology. Ibid., p. 142. See also D. M. Baillie, *God Was in Christ: An Essay on Incarnation and Atonement* (New York: Charles Scribner's Sons, 1948).
65 Roberts, *Reconciliation*, p. 145.
66 For an excellent summary of Cone's views on the color of Jesus Christ, see Douglas, *Black Christ*, pp. 58–60.
67 Cone, *Liberation*, p. 30.
68 Ibid., p. 204., n. 5.
69 Ibid., p. 57. See also a critique of Cone's concept of ontological blackness in Victor Anderson, *Beyond Ontological Blackness: An Essay on African American Religious and Cultural Criticism* (New York: Continuum, 1995), especially ch. 3 entitled, "Ontological Blackness in Theology."
70 Cone, *Oppressed*. Perhaps as a result of Cone's growing sensitivity to those who may have missed the universalism hidden in his first two books, he uses neither the word "black" nor "theology" in the title of this book. For more black theological thought on this subject, see Jones, *Color*.
71 William R. Jones, *Is God a White Racist?* (Garden City, NY: Anchor Books/Doubleday, 1973).
72 See Cone's extended response to Jones's critique in his *Oppressed*, pp. 150–78; and in Cone and Wilmore, *Documentary History*, pp. 436–38.
73 Cone, *Martin and Malcolm*, pp. 29–30.
74 A popular hymn in the black church.
75 A popular saying in the black church.
76 Isa. 55:9 (NRSV), paraphrased.
77 Smith and Zepp, *Search*, p. 113.

78 Cone, *Liberation*, p. 38.

79 The climactic words of Martin Luther King, Jr.'s famous "I Have a Dream" speech, delivered at the historic 1963 March on Washington. As King notes, these are the words of an old Negro spiritual. See James Melvin Washington (ed.), *A Testament of Hope: The Essential Writings of Martin Luther King, Jr.* (San Francisco, CA: Harper & Row, 1986), p. 220.

7 Jesus in black theology: the ancient ancestor visits

JULIAN KUNNIE

INTRODUCTION

For too long, Judeo-Christianity has been viewed as a Western Christian tradition mediated by the entrepreneurial agents of colonial missionaries from Europe for the "enlightenment" of the vast majority of the world's people, most of whom are overwhelmingly of color. Since Christianity as we know it in most places in the world today, with the exception of places such as Egypt, Ethiopia, Iraq, Jordan, Palestine, India, and other places in close proximity to the confluence of the African-Asian world, has generally been a Western European transmission with its concomitants of colonization and slavery, much of the world has ineluctably been indoctrinated with the hegemonic ideological imposition that Jesus of Nazareth was a "white man" so depicted in the plethora of books, paintings, pictures, and stained-glass windows around the world.

This chapter takes issue with this lethal Eurocentric definition and depiction of Jesus of Nazareth in Palestine. Because Christianity has essentially functioned as an ideological ploy by Western colonialism to proclaim the superlative distinction of Christendom in contrast to other traditions as part and parcel of the fabrication of the supremacy of European cultures in comparison to other world cultures, Western Christianity has always speciously claimed that it was derived from a tradition of unadulterated essentialist Judaic tradition that signified divine intervention in the lives of Judeo-Christians unparalleled in any other people's history.[1] So supercilious was this claim of theological monopoly that the defining moment of world history separated temporal spheres into "before the Christian era" and "in the Christian era" so that all successive generations would be compelled to subscribe to this historical demarcation wrought by the Christ event of the first century. Most scholars of Christian theology, including those who engage in historical and archaeological research on the biblical world, insist that the influences of Egyptian culture on early Christianity was essentially "Roman Egypt."[2] Such is the power that Western colonialism wields in the world of contemporaneity and in recent human history. What is palpable is that the current imperialistic powers of the world define history, confirming the view of Latin American liberation theologian, Gustavo Gutierrez, when he wrote, "History was written with a white hand."[3]

This essay will demonstrate that the Jesus of history points to a person of African-Asian culture who reflected the ethos of the civilizations of the ancient Egyptian/African world of the first millennium BCE, and that the Jesus of theological proclamation was a construction of Roman imperial hegemony institutionalized in the fourth century CE during the reign of Constantine, who moved from the radical decree of persecution of all adherents of the Christian faith to the outlawing of all religious traditions outside of Christianity within the confines of the Roman Empire. It is with the onslaught of this historical Roman imperialistic fiat that the grounds for the imperialization of Christianity were firmly established in Europe and subsequently propagated as an ideology justifying Western European colonial invasion and occupation of the world, what came to constitute the confluence of the Cross and the sword in the forced subjugation and enslavement of peoples in Africa and in the Western hemisphere in particular, marking an era of genocide unprecedented in world history.[4]

The Jesus of black theology is none other than a person of African-Asiatic extraction,[5] who signified the return of the ancestors to a people who have never disregarded the defining role that ancestral spirits play in their lives in every sphere, particularly those who are indigenous and of African descent. In the words of Lame Deer, a Lakota spiritual elder, Jesus was "a good medicine man."[6] It is for this reason that the association of Jesus with spiritual and physical healing has been so foundational for black people who are Jesus followers around the world. The chapter will subsequently illuminate black theological conceptualizations of Jesus Christ and finally conclude with the black Jesus of today and the implications for the twenty-first-century world.

ANCIENT EGYPTIAN AND AFRICAN-ASIATIC ROOTS OF JUDEO-CHRISTIANITY

As the renowned Egyptologist Theophile Obenga reminds us, Egypt is an integral part of Africa and the ancient civilizations of Egypt were closely interwoven with the cultures of the rest of Africa.[7] E. A. Wallis Budge, another Egyptologist, contends that African cosmological beliefs are very similar to those found in the ancient Egyptian world. For instance, he writes:

> In West Africa the belief in the DUAL-SOUL, i.e., the soul of the body, and the soul as we may call it, the "Spirit-Soul" is well-nigh universal. The soul of the body, the Egyptian Ba, is mortal, but the Spirit-Soul, the Egyptian Khu, is immortal. Nothing is soulless to the African, and even matter is thought to be a form of soul, of a low order it is true, which souls of a higher nature can make use of.[8]

What Budge is referring to as the immortal soul is the Ka, a cornerstone of ancient Egyptian metaphysics. It was this belief in the immortality of the soul that was transmitted to the Hellenistic Christian world of the first century CE, and that provided the basis of the Christian doctrine of redemption. So too, the belief in the resurrection of the body, intrinsic to the Christian belief system and inspired by the Easter event of Jesus' resurrection from the dead following his crucifixion, has much in common with the resurrection of Osiris in the ancient Egyptian mythological world, following Osiris' death in a chest that drifted into the Mediterranean, after which his body was returned to Egypt by his wife, Isis, and reconstituted after it was cut into fourteen pieces by Seth, the evil spirit.[9] This resembles most closely the core Christian ritual of the Holy Communion, where adherents consume the bread and the wine, symbolic of the body and blood of Jesus that is intrinsic to the Christian doctrine of redemption from the nature of human sin.

The concept of the Christian trinity associated with the belief in the divine revelation has strong antecedents in ancient Egyptian religio-cultural beliefs where trinitarian formulas underscored the way that chapels were constructed and the manner in which the gods Ptah of Memphis, Ra of Heliopolis, and Amun of Thebes were venerated as a single whole. Bojana Mojsov observes:

> The trinity of Ptah, Ra, and Amun were also a unity that symbolized all the gods of the country. The concept of the triad suggested plurality: in Egyptian writing three lines denoted the grammatical plural. Plutarch wrote: "We are accustomed to express 'many times' also as 'three times'; just as we say 'thrice blest' and 'bonds three times as many,' that is innumerable."

Within religious doctrine, the number three symbolized the three souls of god: name, appearance, and essence. The three-fold aspect of god was paralleled by the three souls of man. Amun, Ra, and Ptah represented all the gods of Egypt while being at the same time three aspects of one god. As a reaction to Akhenaton's monotheism, there developed a concept of the unity of the cosmos, of a single god who lay hidden in the multiplicity of things and whose name remained secret from both deities and humans. A Ramesiside hymn expressed this explicitly: "Three are all the gods: Amun, Ra, and Ptah. He who hides his name is Amun, he who is visible is Ra, and his body is Ptah."[10]

At the chapel especially designated for Osiris, the Mysteries of Osiris occurred:

> The three "mystery" chapels reiterated the theme of the trinity of Osiris, Isis, and Horus. They probably contained statues and sacred relics associated with each of them. In the central chapel of Osiris the resurrection of the god was celebrated in rituals that harkened back to the Middle Kingdom, if not before. The content of the rituals can be inferred from the wall reliefs, among them, an image of the dead Osiris lying on a bier. On both sides of the bier stand mourning women. Above Osiris's recumbent body hovers Isis in the form of a kite, receiving from the risen god the seed of his son. The resurrection of Osiris was represented as the sexual union of Osiris and Isis, the engendering of the savior-child.
>
> The unity of Osiris and Ra was underlined by the theme of the trinity. It is at this time that the worship of Osiris explicitly encompassed the doctrine of One in Three: The Resurrected Redeemer, the Holy Mother, and the Savior Child.[11]

These accounts vividly recall the birth of the savior-child, Jesus, celebrated at Christmas time, the resurrection of Jesus, where women gathered at the tomb on Easter morning, and the emergence of the doctrine of the Trinity in Christian tradition: Father the Creator, Son the Redeemer, and Holy Spirit, the Sustainer. It is for this reason that Omar Ayyad, a scholar of Coptic Christianity, asserts that the roots of Coptic Christianity lie in the ancient Egyptian world some two and a half millennia before the birth of Jesus, including the elevation of the symbol of the Cross as signifying blessing and redemption, akin to the ankh, employed by the Egyptian pharaohs in dispensing blessings to people and wishes for long life.[12]

JESUS OF BLACK THEOLOGY

The word "theology" is derived from the Greek concepts of "theos" – meaning God and "logos" – meaning word. Theology, then, signifies the word about God in the world. Theology in itself has limitations precisely because of its Hellenistic background that has been transmitted over the generations to the realm of contemporary knowledge via the Western European colonial world that insisted that the Western world as we know it can trace its history back to classical Greece. The problem with this historical hermeneutic is that it overlooks the fact that (1) Western Europe itself is a recent concept and (2) it places Greece at the center of ancient classical civilizations, even though we know full well that the pinnacle of ancient civilizations resided in ancient Egypt some 2,500 years before the era of Aristotle, Plato, Aeschylus, Euripides, and Sophocles. There is no fundamental continuity between ancient Greek civilization and the contemporary Western European world because Greece was shaped by its interactions with the ancient African and Asian world, as Theophile Obenga notes in his *African Philosophy during the Period of the Pharaohs*, in critical areas such as metaphysics, philosophy, astronomy, medicine, mathematics, and science.[13]

We would thus argue for the past origin of black theology in the ancient African world of Egypt, Nubia, and Cush, contiguous with the hinterlands of eastern, western, and southern Africa. Black theology, if we do need to employ the term, is as old as human civilization itself. The problem is that Western colonial, economic, and military hegemony has distorted our very basis of epistemology and forced us to accept the primacy of Europe as the foundation of all knowledge. Nothing could be further from the truth.[14] Robert Hood, author of *Must God Remain Greek?*, charges in this regard:

> Examples of the Graeco-Roman legacy that we in the West
> take for granted abound. We assume uncritically that there are
> fundamental, unchanging "principles" that anchor humanity
> and cultures. We speak of "truth" as a natural given in human
> affairs and discourse. It is customary to think of "action based on
> one's principles" and to speak of the "spiritual" being dissimilar
> to the "material," of "essences" in contrast to "becoming."
> Theologians and other intellectuals like to talk about "being" and
> "God as the ground or source of being," about "Jesus Christ as the
> Logos," about "God as the alpha and omega," about "essences and

accidents," and about "form and matter." All of these demonstrate the conquest of Greek metaphysics and philosophical patterns of thought in our ordinary and conceptual lives.[15]

The African world that is the ontological basis of blackness possessed radically different understandings of the spirit world, and understood the role of divinities and nature spirits actively and directly involved in the lives of human beings.[16] Everything in the world, earth, the four-leggeds, the birds, fish of the sea, trees, rivers, forests, valleys, planets, sun, moon, and other celestial phenomena were imbued with divine spirit and intervened in human affairs, as the preceding section on ancient Egyptian civilizations illustrated.

It was this indigenous African world that was violently disrupted, interrupted, invaded, and violated with the onset of Western European colonialism and enslavement of Africans, forcibly kidnapped and transported across the Atlantic to work as slave labor for European merchants and property owners, on lands stolen from indigenous red and brown people in the Western hemisphere.[17] African people were separated from their kith and kin, forced to survive in a brutal world under the yoke of chattel slavery, beaten by the whip and the lash by white slave masters determined to subordinate African women, men, and children and exploit their bodies as forced free labor in the cotton fields and sugar plantations of North America and the Caribbean, often violating African women sexually as part of this orgy of subjugation. The result over time was the loss of the languages of West and Central Africa that Africans had brought with them on slave ships.

It was during this time that a Europeanized colonial Jesus was introduced to Africans. It was also during this period of the holocaust of enslavement that theologies of liberation emerged, spawned in the crucible of chattel slavery.[18] During slavery, as Albert Raboteau explains in *Slave Religion*, Africans were prevented from practicing their indigenous religious ceremonies and observing their traditional customs.[19] The drum, cornerstone of African culture, was strictly prohibited under the regime of slavery. There were those who practiced their Islamic faith, as Richard Brent Turner describes in *Islam in the African American Experience*.[20] For enslaved Africans, Christian teaching was initially forbidden. After believing that a Christian ideology of a white Jesus could pacify the restless African women and men on the slave plantations, white plantation owners gradually permitted the teaching of the Africans by itinerant white preachers, albeit under the watchful eye of the white slave master.[21]

In what may have appeared to be a simplistic theology that affirmed black personhood and elevated the centrality of Jesus as the crucified and resurrected one of God, African Christians began to appropriate the Christian teaching in ways that addressed their abnormal condition of enslavement, servitude, and brutality under the yoke of forced labor. How could a loving God who cared about all of creation, they questioned, sanction the violence of family fragmentation and unmitigated repression as extant in the institution of slavery? Would heaven be segregated between black and white, they asked? The spirituals that continue to be sung in black churches are precisely the legacy of a radically different theological assertion among African Christian communities that embraced liberation motifs, that urged "fleeing from bondage in Egypt" and "stealing away to Freedom," and the power of a Deity who was able to overcome all obstacles of human oppression and suffering.[22]

It is in this context that the figure of Jesus assumed primordial significance, where the Africans who viewed themselves as being unjustly beaten by the lash of enslavement and trapped by the confines of the slave cabin began identifying with the suffering and struggling Jesus of history, besieged as a poor working-class Palestinian living under the tyranny of Roman colonial occupation.[23] The spiritual, "Were You There When They Crucified My Lord?" captures this sentiment. Soon, black churches centering on Jesus spread all over places where enslaved Africans lived, the first being the African Baptist Church in Savannah, Georgia in 1773. Richard Allen and Absalom Jones walked out of St. George's Methodist Episcopal Church in Philadelphia in 1787 and formed the African Methodist Episcopal Church in 1816.[24] Essentially, these churches were places were black people could be themselves and worship Jesus in the cultural way they saw fit.

Black theologies of liberation were manifest in the concrete acts of rebellion waged by African leaders who were bent on insurrection, such as Gabriel Prosser in 1800 (Virginia), Denmark Vesey in 1822 (South Carolina), and Nat Turner in 1831 (Virginia), and in revolutionary anti-slavery involvement by Henry Highland Garnet in 1816 and David Walker in 1829, with the writing of *The Appeal* that profusely castigated white America for its blatant hypocrisy in professing to be religious Christians all the while brutalizing and holding black people in abject and perpetual slavery and servitude.[25] Jesus was the central figure of revolution in this formative black theology of liberation. Nat Turner launched an insurrection that he insisted was the inspiration of the Holy Spirit linked with Jesus. Doing anything but rebelling against the illegitimacy and irreligiosity of slavery was tantamount to "wasting the Holy Spirit!" in his words.[26]

That nineteenth-century revolutionary religious fervor was transported into the twentieth century, most visibly during the epoch of civil rights (1955–66) and Black Power (1966–mid 1970s). Albert Cleage, minister at the Shrine of the Black Madonna in Detroit, went on to elaborate the revolutionary Jesus in his book, *The Black Messiah*, in the early 1960s.[27] It was then, too, that the pioneer of the black theology movement of the 1960s, James Cone, came to formally launch the black theology liberation movement with the publication of *Black Theology and Black Power*, in which Cone argued that to be Christian in the United States was to be black, and that Christian faith was synonymous with the philosophy of Black Power that sought the well-being and liberation of black people from the clutches of an inhuman, racist white society. Cone argued:

> If the gospel is a gospel of liberation for the oppressed, then Jesus is where the oppressed are and continues his work of liberation there. Jesus is not safely confined in the first century. He is our contemporary, proclaiming release to the captives and rebelling against all who silently accept the structures of injustice. If he is not in the ghetto, if he is not where men are living at the brink of existence, but is, rather, in the easy life of the suburbs, then the gospel is a lie. The opposite, however, is the case. Christianity is not alien to Black Power; it is Black Power.[28]

Cone argued convincingly that Jesus was black because, as the Liberator, he was already involved in the liberation struggles of poor and oppressed black communities.

On the African continent, Jesus came to be viewed as an ancestor, a brother. In *Toward an African Theology*, John Pobee frames Jesus as the ancestor within the Akan tradition of Ghana.[29] Mercy Oduyoye, a feminist African theologian, describes Jesus as a redeemer and savior, similar to the view of the Judeo-Christian tradition. In the Fanti tradition of Ghana, the term *Ponfo Kese* (savior) is used.[30] Charles Nyamiti from Tanzania likens Jesus to an ancestral figure bound in sacred communication with believers: son, logos, descendant, ancestor.[31] Black theology and African theology became inextricably interwoven in the confluence of the liberation struggle by black South Africans (Azanians) against the colonial system of apartheid in South Africa, best concretized in former Archbishop Desmond Tutu's view:

Black Theology arises in context of black suffering at the hands of rampant white racism. And consequently Black Theology is much concerned to make sense theologically out of the black experience whose main ingredient is the suffering in and the light of God's revelation of Himself in the man, Jesus Christ. It is concerned with the significance of black existence, with liberation, with a meaning of reconciliation, with humanization, with forgiveness.[32]

During the evolution of black theology in the 1970s and 1980s, the subject of Jesus became paramount in discourses on black theology. Black women theologians such as Jacquelyn Grant and Katie Cannon wrote extensively on the need for women's affirmation in black theological formulation. Jacquelyn Grant, for instance, penned a book that specifically addressed the divergence of the subject of Jesus in black and white communities, entitled *White Women's Christ and Black Women's Jesus: Feminist Christology and Womanist Response* and Katie Cannon published *Katie's Canon: Womanism and the Soul of the Black Community*. Renita Weems came out with *Just a Sister Away* in 1988 and in 1993 Delores Williams published *Sisters in the Wilderness* (surfacing the themes of survival and quality of life in addition to liberation). Kelly Brown Douglas published *The Black Christ*, which configured Jesus as manifest in the struggles of poor black women, critiquing structures of patriarchy, racism, and classism in her work.[33] The significance of these texts was the way that they critiqued structures of patriarchy in theological reflection and demanded that black male theologians pay particular attention to the experiences of women, especially poor black women. The role of Jesus as liberator that encompassed the struggles of black women whose voices had generally been silenced by a racist and sexist United States society marked a watershed for black liberation theology as propounded by James Cone in the 1960s.

With the approach of the twenty-first century, other creative conceptualizations of Jesus have emerged from black theologians and teachers. Theologizing from the black British context, Robert Beckford, a teacher and minister, described Jesus in ways that harmonized with the Rastafarian community: Jesus is Dread. Beckford asserts:

A Dread Christ equips Black folk to face and destroy all structures of oppression – being Dread, for the Black church, is to engage in the struggle for Black freedom. Furthermore, to say that Christ is Dread is to unveil a Christ of Black upliftment, Black empowerment and Black progress. Similarly, a Dread Christ tells Black British people that the Jesus of history is with them as they

protest, fight, boycott, celebrate and progress. In short, a Dread
Christ is a Black Christ participating in Black lives and Black
struggles. In the context of Britain, a Dread Christ is the focus of
our socio-political struggle and the source of joy for our resurrected
lives.[34]

Beckford repudiates traditional European Enlightenment figures as additional sources for the Dread theology of liberation, by proposing the
reappropriation of black historical figures who resisted slavery and
oppression: "Nanny of the Maroons, Paul Bogel and William George
Gordon of the Morant Bay Rebellion (1865), the rebellion of Samuel Sharp
(Jamaica, 1832) and the politics and spirituality of the nineteenth-century
Jamaican Baptist mystic, Anthony Bedward."[35] He includes Amy Jacques
and Marcus Garvey and Pan-African thinker and activist E. W. Blyden as
additional historical sources in the propounding of a black theology of
liberation relevant to the black community in Britain.

THE BLACK JESUS IN THE TWENTY-FIRST CENTURY

In the twenty-first century, given the environmental devastation
suffered by Mother Earth and her children, including the human beings,
four-leggeds, birds, trees, mountains, seas, oceans, rivers and streams,
and all creatures that move on their bellies on the face of Mother
Earth, the black Jesus must be viewed in terms of restoring harmoni-
ous relations with our original mother, Earth.[36] Both the tenacity and
the impending collapse of Western imperialism and the accompanying
capitalist system (that we behold now through the daily plummeting
of the credit-based housing market in the United States, which constitutes almost half of the country's gross domestic product, along with
the real shortage of oil supplies and skyrocketing oil prices, and the profound impact of global warming that has dried historical water supplies
for human, animal, and plant consumption) have resulted in environmental catastrophes from which human beings particularly may never
recover.

Climate change is an integral part of our cultural landscape today.
The polar ice caps and glacial sheets are melting as the result of global warming. The human impact on the disharmony of the environment has different results. The cyclone in Myanmar, the 9.0-magnitude
earthquake and subsequent tsunami in Japan, the tragedy of Hurricane
Katrina in August 2005 in the southern United States of America,[37]
the dust-bowl effect in the southwestern part of the United States and

in southern Africa, and the destruction of the Amazon rainforest (the lungs of the planet, where one-fifth of the fresh water on the planet is found and where 13,000 acres of forest are erased each day or an area the size of eight football fields per minute) have all caused widespread suffering of humans, and animal and plant life. Most disturbing is the fact that in this modern era "the normal trickle of extinction has become a gushing hemorrhage as 100 species or more disappear every day."[38] A 2009 study, *The US State of the Birds*, revealed that over a third of the nation's bird species are under serious threat and in deep decline.[39] The astronomical rise in prices of basic food products such as corn and soybeans are as a result of clearing forests and fields for soy for ethanol consumption by the United States, in particular, resulting in food riots in thirty countries. Black theology must become involved in these indigenous struggles to heal Mother Earth so that she in turn can heal all of us and the next seven generations. Can we add something about Jesus from a black environmental theology of liberation?

For African people in the United States, in Africa, and the rest of the African diaspora, in fact for all of the colored peoples and working-class peoples of the world, the black Jesus of the twenty-first century is the symbol of the indigenous Liberator and transformer, who resists Western globalization and insists on returning to the paths of the African ancestors who had struggled for countless generations to live in harmony with the rhythm of Mother Earth and in sync with her cycles and seasons. The pulverization of poor black life in the United States, with almost a million poor black women and men serving long jail terms,[40] the decimation of poor black youth by the capitalist drug economy, the collapse of public school systems and rampant illiteracy that characterizes so much of youth culture, and the social fragmentation that results in over 50 percent of black children being born in single-mother homes, often mired in poverty, are all testimony of the fundamentally morally bankrupt nature of the elite, US white ruling-class capitalism. Its appetite for profits is limitless as it engages in senseless wars against Mother Earth and her children. The result? Poverty, annihilation, and genocide in its wake.

The irruption of the AIDS epidemic, where half of all infections are now suffered by black women,[41] is another index of the social cancer of a rapacious capitalism that spends hundreds of billions on research by profit-greedy pharmaceutical corporations that have no positive antidotal effect on those afflicted by the HIV virus. So, too, US imperialist invasions of countries in the underdeveloped world such as Iraq and Afghanistan, and the corresponding expenditure of hundreds of billions of dollars on weapons of mass destruction and death of the poor in these nations are all indications of the pathology of Western colonialism that has never come to grips with and reversed course from its early warring against Mother Earth and the rest of the natural world from the tenth century.[42]

The black Jesus of the twenty-first century is a healer of the earth and all the children of the earth, particularly the black oppressed. Jesus is indigenous, black, female, economically impoverished, but culturally powerful in resisting the edifice of Western neocolonialism, capitalism, globalization, sexism, and environmental annihilation. In the book *The Healers*, Elder Ayi Kwei Armah reminds us of the steps we need for our own individual and collective spiritual, physical, and mental health, principles that can empower black workers across the African diaspora as they struggle for independence, justice, freedom, human rights, food, a relevant education, health care, and family stability. These principles are vital for the establishment of Pan-African worker solidarity because of their grounding in positive revolutionary culture:

(1) The healer does not drink or smoke intoxicants.
(2) The healer does no violence against human beings. She or he does not fight.
(3) The healer should never call upon her or his god to destroy anyone.
(4) The healer does not go to the king's court and avoids going to any place where people go to seek power over other people. Healers work to create power based on respect.
(5) The healer does not gossip, or talk ill about others, and nor must she or he quarrel.
(6) The healer does not waste the night. "She or he spends the time of early night thinking over the work she's or he's done for the day, and about what she or he will do on the morrow. The remainder of the night she or he sleeps, to rise early as her or his spirit awakes."
(7) The healer respects those older than herself or himself.[43]

For Christians, the black Jesus of the twenty-first century is the revolutionary healer, par excellence.

Black theology must strive and struggle to embody the revolutionary praxis of humility, self-discipline, sobriety, and respect for the earth and all her children, so that the next seven generations of black families can be prepared and preserved for a future underlined by incessant struggle that ultimately culminates in a spiritual reunion with Mother Earth, harmony with the ancestral world, and an appreciation of Jesus in the world of human beings.

CONCLUSION

The black Jesus today recognizes the limitations and ephemeral character of all human economic and political systems, including Western socialism. The black Jesus is thus spiritually anchored and epistemologically moored in the Original Spirit that birthed all life and that surpasses all physical life in that it has always been and always will be. The black Jesus is not politically apathetic or reactionary, but realizes the historical contradictions of the Western European world that have defined all economic and political philosophies for the past thousand years, which are rooted in a supercilious attitude toward Mother Earth and view her as an inanimate being to be conquered and commodified. It is no coincidence that Western (white Christianity) in many quarters is a dying religious tradition today as European-origin populations age in many countries while youth of color globally grow exponentially in number with an estimated 487 million Christians in Africa alone.[44] For instance, there are more Protestant Lutherans in Tanzania than in Germany or the United States with the membership of the Evangelical Lutheran Church in America dropping by 15 percent since 1987.[45] The black Jesus of today is a revolutionary figure whose indomitable spiritual power empowers the oppressed to fight to defend the earth against the ceaseless violation of her being by Western industrialism, realizing that all systems that wage war against the earth are assured of eternal destruction. Ultimately, the black Jesus of the twenty-first century is the ancestor that reaches back millennia, perhaps even millions of years, whose existence is not defined by linear Western time, but by the cycles and circles of the universe of which we are all an integral part, female and male, oppressed and oppressor alike.

Notes

1   Cain Hope Felder, *Troubling Biblical Waters: Race, Class, and Family* (Maryknoll, NY: Orbis Books, 1989); Cain Hope Felder (ed.), *Stony the Road We Trod: African American Biblical Interpretation* (Minneapolis, MN: Fortress Press, 1991); Robert E. Hood, *Must God Remain Greek? Afro-Cultures and God-Talk* (Minneapolis, MN: Fortress Press, 1990); Joerg Rieger, *Christ and Empire: From Paul to Postcolonial Times* (Minneapolis, MN: Fortress Press, 2007).
2   Henry Green, "The Socio-Economic Background of Christianity in Egypt," in Birger A. Pearson and James E. Goehring (eds.), *The Roots*

of Egyptian Christianity (Philadelphia, PA: Fortress Press, 1986), pp. 100–14, is one example. Otto Meinardus, also a historian, is another, evident in his work, *Christian Egypt: Ancient and Modern* (Cairo: Cahiers d'Histoire Egyptienne, 1965).

3 Gustavo Gutierrez, *The Power of the Poor in History* (Maryknoll, NY: Orbis Books, 1983), p. 201. Guttierrez uses this expression from the Brazilian theologian Leonard Boff's work, *Teologia do cativerio eda libertação* (Lisbon: Multinova, 1976).

4 Juan Luis Rivera, *A Violent Evangelism: Christian Conquest of the Americas* (Knoxville, TN: Westminster Press, 1995).

5 See William Mosley, *What Color Was Jesus?* (Chicago, IL: African American Images, 1987), p. 7. Mosley is quoting from Ben Ammi's *God, the Black Man, and Truth* (Chicago, IL: Communicators Press, 1982), p. 7. Jeremiah A. Wright, Jr., "Introduction," in Mosley, *What Color Was Jesus?*, p. viii. For more on the rivers and location of Eden, see Prince Vuyani Ntintili's "The Presence and Role of Africans in the Bible," in *Holy Bible: The African American Jubilee Edition, Contemporary English Version*, ed. Jubilee Bible Project (New York: American Bible Society, 1999), pp. 100–01; David T. Adamo, *Africa and the Africans in the Old Testament* (Eugene, OR: Wipf and Stock Publishers, 1998), pp. 24–25, 59; Modupe Oduyoye, *The Sons of the Gods and the Daughters of Men* (Ibadan, Nigeria: Sefer Books, Ltd., 1998 [first published by Daystar Press in Ibadan, Nigeria and Orbis Books in Maryknoll, NY, 1984]), p. 42; Spencer Wells, *The Journey of Man: A Genetic Odyssey* (Princeton University Press, 2003); Cain Hope Felder, *Troubling Biblical Waters*, p. 37; Charles B. Copher, *Black Biblical Studies: Biblical and Theological Issues on the Black Presence in the Bible* (Chicago, IL: Black Light Fellowship, 1993), pp. 12, 37; Cheikh Anta Diop, *The African Origin of Civilization: Myth or Reality*, ed. and trans. Mercer Cook (New York: Lawrence Hill & Company, 1974). Also see Laurenti Magesa, *African Religion: The Moral Traditions of Abundant Life* (Maryknoll, NY: Orbis Books, 1997), pp. 26–27; Cain Hope Felder, "The Presence of Blacks in Biblical Antiquity," in *Holy Bible: The African American Jubilee Edition*, p. 121 (the entire piece documents black reality in the New Testament); and Walter Arthur McCray, *The Black Presence in the Bible* (Chicago, IL: Black Light Fellowship, 1990), pp. 125–28.

6 John Lame Deer and Richard Erdoes, *Lame Deer: Seeker of Visions* (New York: Pocket Books, 1994), p. 168.

7 See Theophile Obenga's classic work, *African Philosophy: the Pharaonic period, 2780-330 B.C.* (Popenguine, Senegal: Per Ankh, the African Publishing Cooperative, 2004), for an illumination of the continuity of the ancient Egyptian language, *Mdw Ntr*, and concepts of philosophy, theology, astronomy, science, and medicine, with the rest of Africa.

8 E. A. Wallis Budge, *Osiris and the Egyptian Resurrection*, vol. II (New York: Dover Publications, 1973), p. 136.

9 Julian Baldick, *Black God: The Afro-Asiatic Roots of Jewish, Christian, and Muslim Religions* (London and New York: I. B. Tauris Publishers,

1997), p. 61. On the Egyptian influence on ancient Greek thought: see Wim van den Dungen, "Hermes the Egyptian: The Impact of Ancient Egypt on Greek Philosophy," www.maat.sofiatopia.org/hermes1.htm; Philip Coppens, "Egypt: Origin of the Greek Culture," *Frontier Magazine* 5(3) (May–June 1999), also amended online at: www.philipcoppens.com/egyptgreece.html; Richard Hooker, "Greek Philosophy," www.wsu.edu/~dee/GREECE/PRESOC.HTM; George G. M. James, *Stolen Legacy: Greek Philosophy Is Stolen Egyptian Philosophy* (Trenton, NJ: African World Press, 1993); Marshall Clagett, *Ancient Egyptian Science, a Source Book*, vol. III, *Ancient Egyptian Mathematics. Memoirs* of the American Philosophical Society (Philadelphia, PA: American Philosophical Society, 1999); Ian Hodder and Scott Hutson, *Reading the Past: Current Approaches to Interpretation in Archaeology* (Cambridge University Press, 2004); John Gardner Wilkinson, *The Ancient Egyptians*, vol. 1 (Chestnut Hill, MA: Adamant Media Corporation, 2001; first published London: John Murray, 1854); and Innocent C. Onyewuenyi, *The African Origin of Greek Philosophy* (Charleston, SC: BookSurge Publishing, 2005).

10   Bojana Mojsov, *Osiris: Death and Afterlife of a God* (Malden, MA, and Oxford: Blackwell Publishing, 2005), p. 90.

11   Ibid., p. 91.

12   Omar Ayyad, "The Ancient Egyptian Roots of Coptic Christianity," *Coptic Review* 9(4) (Winter 1988): 105–14.

13   Theophile Obenga, *African Philosophy during the Period of the Pharaohs* (London: Karnak House Publishers, 2006).

14   Marimba Ani, *Yurugu: An African-Centered Critique of European Cultural Thought and Behavior* (Trenton, NJ: African World Press, 1994).

15   Hood, *Must God Remain Greek?*, p. 5.

16   See for instance, the cardinal texts by John Mbiti, *Concepts of God in Africa* (New York: Praeger, 1970) and Bolaji Idowu, *Olódùmarè: God in Yoruba Belief* (London: Longman, 1962) on this subject.

17   See for instance, Joseph Inikori, *Africans and the Industrial Revolution in England: A Study in International Trade and Economic Development* (Cambridge and New York: Cambridge University Press, 2002); John Hope Franklin, *From Slavery to Freedom: A History of Negro Americans* (New York: Knopf, 1988); W. E. B. DuBois, *The World and Africa: An Inquiry into the Part Which Africa Has Played in World History* (New York: Viking Press, 1947); John Jackson, *Introduction to African Civilizations* (New York: Citadel Press, 1995); Charles Johnson and Patricia Smith, *Africans in America: America's Journey through Slavery* (New York: Harcourt, Brace and Company, 1998) on the subject of the holocaust of enslavement of Africans in Europe and the Americas.

18   Dwight N. Hopkins, *Down, Up, and Over: Slave Religion and Black Theology* (Minneapolis, MN: Fortress Press, 1999); Gayraud S. Wilmore, *Black Religion and Black Radicalism: An Interpretation of the Religious History of African Americans* (Maryknoll, NY: Orbis

Books, 1998); Vincent Harding, *There Is a River: The Black Struggle for Freedom in America* (Orlando, FL: Mariner Books, 1993).

19 Albert Raboteau, *Slave Religion: The "Invisible Institution" in the Antebellum South* (New York: Oxford University Press, 1978).

20 See especially "Muslims in a Strange Land: African Muslim Slaves in America," in Richard Brent Turner, *Islam in the African American Experience* (Bloomington, IN: Indiana University Press, 2004), ch. 1.

21 Kelly Brown Douglas, *The Black Christ* (Maryknoll, NY: Orbis Books, 1994).

22 James H. Cone, *The Spirituals and the Blues: An Interpretation* (Maryknoll, NY: Orbis Books, 1992); Wyatt Tee Walker, *"Somebody's Callin' My Name": Black Sacred Music and Social Change* (Valley Forge, PA: Judson Press, 1983); James Weldon Johnson and J. Rosamond Johnson, *The Books of the American Negro Spirituals* (Jackson, TN: Da Capo Press, 2002).

23 Obery M. Hendricks, *The Politics of Jesus: Rediscovering the True Revolutionary Nature of Jesus' Teachings and How They Have Been Corrupted* (New York: Three Leaves, 2007).

24 Richard Allen, *The Life, Experience, and Gospel Labours of the Rt. Rev. Richard Allen* (Philadelphia, PA: Martin & Boden Printers, 1833). Richard S. Newman, *Freedom's Prophet: Bishop Richard Allen, the AME Church, and the Founding Fathers* (New York University Press, 2009).

25 David Walker and Henry Highland Garnet, *Walker's Appeal, with a Brief Sketch of His Life and also Garnet's Address to the Slaves of the United States of America* (Amazon's Kindle Edition: Public Domain Books, 2006).

26 See Nat Turner, *The Confessions of Nat Turner*, ed. Thomas Gray (Miami, FL: Mnemosyne Publishing Co., 1969), for an elucidation of Turner's account of being inspired by the "Holy Spirit" toward rebellion and insurrection.

27 Albert B. Cleage, Jr., *The Black Messiah* (New York: Sheed and Ward, 1968).

28 James H. Cone, *Black Theology and Black Power* (Maryknoll, NY: Orbis Books, 2001), p. 38.

29 John Pobee, *Toward an African Theology* (Nashville, TN: Abingdon Press, 1979).

30 Mercy Amba Oduyoye, *Hearing and Knowing: Theological Reflections on Christianity in Africa* (Maryknoll, NY: Orbis Books, 1986), p. 102.

31 Charles Nyamiti, *Christ as Our Ancestor: Christology from an African Perspective* (Gweru, Zimbabwe: Mambo Press, 1984), p. 20.

32 Desmond Tutu, "Black Theology/African Theology: Soul Mates or Antagonists?" in James H. Cone and Gayraud S. Wilmore (eds.), *Black Theology: A Documentary History*, vol. 1, *1966–1979* (Maryknoll, NY: Orbis Books, 1979), p. 489.

33 See Jacquelyn Grant's *White Women's Christ and Black Women's Jesus: Feminist Christology and Womanist Response* (Atlanta, GA: Scholars Press, 1989); Katie Cannon's *Katie's Canon: Womanism and the Soul of*

the *Black Community* (New York: Continuum, 1995); Renita Weems' *Just a Sister Away: A Womanist Vision of Women's Relationships in the Bible* (San Diego, CA: LuraMedia, 1988); Delores Williams' *Sisters in the Wilderness: The Challenge of Womanist God-Talk* (Maryknoll, NY: Orbis Books, 1993); and Kelly Brown Douglas' *The Black Christ* for an exposition of black womanist theology and the redefining of Christology in terms of the experiences of black women, particularly the poor.

34 Robert Beckford, *Jesus is Dread: Black Theology and Black Culture in Britain* (London: Darton, Longman and Todd, 1998), pp. 146–47.

35 See his analysis, ibid.

36 See Dianne D. Glave, "Black Environmental Liberation Theology," in Dwight N. Hopkins *et al.* (eds.), *Walk Together Children: Black and Womanist Theologies, Church and Theological Education* (Eugene, OR: Cascade Books, 2010). James H. Cone, "Whose Earth Is It Anyway? 1998," in Cone, *Risks of Faith: The Emergence of a Black Theology of Liberation, 1968–1998* (Boston, MA: Beacon Press, 1999); Dwight N. Hopkins, "Holistic Health and Healing: Environmental Racism and Ecological Justice," *Currents in Theology and Mission* 36(1) (February 2009).

37 Cheryl A. Kirk-Duggan (ed.), *The Sky Is Crying: Race, Class, and Natural Disaster* (Nashville, TN: Abingdon Press, 2006).

38 Franz J. Broswimmer, *Ecocide: A Short History of the Mass Extinction of Species* (London and Sterling, VA: Pluto Press, 2002).

39 Cornelia Dean, "One-Third of U.S. Bird Species Endangered, Survey Finds," *New York Times*, March 20, 2009.

40 Mark Lewis Taylor, *The Executed God: The Way of the Cross in Lockdown America* (Minneapolis, MN: Fortress Press, 2001).

41 Kristal Brent Zook, *Black Women's Lives: Stories of Pain and Power* (New York: Nation Books, 2006); Quinn Gentry, *Black Women's Risk for HIV: Rough Living* (New York: Routledge, 2008); Dorie J. Gilbert and Ednita M. Wright, *African American Women Living with AIDS: Critical Responses for the New Millennium* (New York: Praeger, 2003); Dorie J. Gilbert and Ednita M. Wright (eds.), *African American Women and HIV/AIDS: Critical Responses* (New York: Praeger, 2002).

42 See Kirkpatrick Sale, *The Conquest of Paradise: Christopher Columbus and the Columbian Legacy* (New York: Plume, 1991), pp. 82–84, for a detailed treatment of the early cultures of medieval Europe that devastated the ecological environment of countries in Western Europe.

43 These principles are derived from Ayi Kwei Armah's book, *The Healers: A Novel* (Popenguine, Senegal: Per Ankh, the African Publishing Cooperative, 2000), pp. 108-113, using inclusive gender language for reference to the healer.

44 George Weigel, "Christian number-crunching" at http://thebostonpilot.com/article.asp?ID=12941.

45 See the *LSTC Epistle*, Winter 2012, Magazine of the Lutheran School of Theology, p. 12.

8 Black theology and the Holy Spirit

GARTH BAKER-FLETCHER

At the dawning of the era of slavery, captured West African peoples in the New World (of North and Latin America and the Caribbean) joined their voices in shouts, moans, and deep groaning of their inner spirit. Calling on God's Spirit to manifest itself, they looked for a release from captivity and bondage.[1] What W. E. B. DuBois called the "spiritual strivings" of black folk were uttered before the master in whispers, subvocalizations of agony, or in the times of gathered worship in what were called "hush harbors." The hush harbors were the secret places where enslaved black folk could experience the Holy Spirit as an enlivening, wondrous, and overwhelming experience. Outside of the seeming omnipresence of the master's ears, these enslaved African peoples forged a relationship with God through their experience of the Holy Spirit. Following DuBois' instructive musings, these enslaved people allowed the Spirit to whip them into the utterly primal, emotional, and effervescent experience of what DuBois called "the Frenzy."[2]

This Spirit-induced Frenzy was not always welcomed by all black folk, especially in the early nineteenth century. Eminent Christian physician Martin Delaney derided many black churches for what he believed to be their spirituality of excessive otherworldliness and crude imitation of white church moralism.[3] Episcopal pastor Alexander Crummell sought to de-emphasize what he considered to be the overly zealous spirituality in black churches – calling instead for a *this*-worldly, tough-minded, and politically activist, theologically informed spirituality.[4] Presbyterian pastor Edward Blyden posited such terms as "uplift" and "Elevation" to describe a very rationalistic and systematic understanding of Christian faith. Such a faith was radically black nationalist and emphasized a "doctrine of divine providence that could account for suffering as a preparation for a great work."[5] All three black men were more interested in African Americans learning how to be active social justice agents rather than validating their spiritual propensities.

Skipping to the mid twentieth century, we come to a tremendously influential and controversial essay, "Are American Negro Churches Christian?" by Joseph R. Washington, Jr.

Answering the question negatively, Washington portrayed the worship of Negro churches as being too inclined to "release and an occasion for class identification" rather than authentically Christian.[6] While roundly criticizing the white church for its perversion of Christian doctrine by racism, Washington invariably implied that the segregated religion of the Negro church was, in some manner, sub-Christian.

It was not until the seminal works of James H. Cone and J. Deotis Roberts that we find a positive systematic exposition of the Holy Spirit. In his first book, *Black Theology and Black Power*, we find Cone's Christocentric elaboration of the person and work of the Holy Spirit. He notes that the Holy Spirit is traditionally understood to be the third Person of the Trinity – God the Father, God the Son, and God the Holy Spirit. For his purpose, Cone claims that "God's manifestation as Spirit is indispensable for a total picture of the Christian God."[7] Thus the manifestation of the Holy Spirit is, in fact, the Spirit of God [the Creator] and the Spirit of Christ.

Cone characterizes the Holy Spirit as: "the power of God at work in the world effecting in the life of his people his intended purposes."[8] Thus the power that is the Holy Spirit is an "active power," the very "personal activity of God's will."[9]

Moreover, while the blessing of the Holy Spirit was "rare" in the Old Testament, because of Christ's death and resurrection, the Spirit can be manifested in "all who respond to God's act in Christ."[10] Therefore the Spirit is "the power of Christ himself at work in the life of the believer." For Cone, the "modern church" has been wrong in turning the manifestation of the Holy Spirit into a privatized ecstatic experience, of a life of "individual purification from sin," sin being counted as "ritual pollutants" such as alcohol and tobacco.[11] In fact, he takes such views as being "hopelessly impoverished."[12]

This rather traditional way of writing about the Holy Spirit quickly turns into a potent message of black liberation for Cone. For example, the person of the Spirit does not get bogged down with theological abstractions, but acts with the passion of a John Brown, saying "Racism is evil, kill it!"[13] The person of the Holy Spirit takes no time out for small talk, but engages in rigorous social critique of the "fact" of evil that is racism. Those who follow this Spirit are spiritually impelled to take the side of the sufferer of racism. Such taking sides – seeing the event of racism as an evil to be eradicated – is a radical act of "obedience unto death" for the Spirit-filled believer. Such radical obedience is an adequate determination of whether one is "possessed" of the Spirit or not.[14]

Cone does not stop here. For him, the Spirit can act upon people and their actions even if they are nonbelievers. As God used Cyrus of Persia (Isa. 45), God can also use modern people who are committed to fighting suffering. Exegeting the famous parable of the last judgment (Matt. 25:31ff.), Cone describes people's divisions to the left or right of the throne of judgment in accordance with their response to the need of the neighbor. Jesus grants a new life to those on the right because they practiced compassion and liberation for the oppressed and poor. To help the least in society is helping Jesus. Those on the left receive eternal banishment because they turned their backs on the poor and the oppressed and, consequently, acted contrary to Jesus.

Both sides are surprised by the outcomes of new life and eternal banishment, the ones on the right because they were not consciously trying to help Jesus, but rather to "help those in trouble."[15] The ones on the left wanted to excuse themselves from acting because they were convinced that "they would have been prepared to love their neighbor only if in meeting him they had unmistakably met Christ himself."[16] Cone says of such persons that they "want only to use the neighbor as a means to achieve a private, selfish end."[17] Thus the person living in accordance with the Spirit is someone whose *will* has been transformed into God's will and whose actions have "become God's action."[18]

Cone now makes a critical pivot in his thinking. He mentions that Black Power, while not "consciously seeking to be Christian, seems to be where there is trouble."[19] To the extent that Black Power shows both its concern and desire to meet the needs of the oppressed folk, so it fulfills the aim of doing and being the "work of God's Spirit."[20] Criticizing Christians for using the poor as a means of attaining one's own salvation, Cone affirms that one becomes poor in and through "the Spirit of Christ."[21]

Thus one can be certain that one is possessed of God's Spirit through the "subjective certainty" that one is in touch with that experience that is "Real."[22] Cone posits that "the experience is its own evidence, the ultimate datum."[23] To try to find some "higher evidence," whether it is in the Bible, the Church Fathers, or even in the church, is to look for something more authentic, more "real than the encounter itself."[24] It really comes down to a "relationship" with the Spirit of Christ. Such a relationship, for Cone, is proof in itself.[25]

However, J. Deotis Roberts considers his work to be *black church theology* rather than the *black liberation theology* of James Cone.

Roberts wants to investigate the relationship between the doctrine of the Holy Spirit and human liberation, and the connection between the *charismata* and personal and social transformation.[26] Roberts describes black church theology by assuming an interpenetration between the social and the personal, and the physical and the spiritual – something that Western theology tends to divide.

Calling thinking about the Holy Spirit a "cardinal doctrine of the Christian faith," Roberts wants to correct the silence of liberation theologians on the Holy Spirit.[27] For him, the worship of most blacks is "satiated with the presence of the Holy Spirit"; on the other hand, the "worship of more cultured and educated blacks often suffers from the Spirit's absence."[28] Roberts finds both sides in need of more information and understanding. Both turn away from a concern for the "social, economic, and political aspects of liberation" that is so critical to genuine black church theology.[29]

Beginning with the doctrine of the Holy Spirit, Roberts explains the etymology of the word "spirit," which comes from *ruach* in Hebrew and *pneuma* in Greek. Both words mean "breath," "wind," "storm," and "breeze." Metaphorically, they mean "principle of life" and "vitality."[30] While human beings and animals possess *ruach*, God *is* preeminently *ruach*; so wherever God acts, we become aware of the "presence and power of *ruach*."[31] This is true for the Old Testament (*ruach*), and the New Testament (*pneuma*). In fact, in the New Testament, the *pneuma* refers to the "dynamic principle of life" while the word *nous* refers to the "mind" and "intellect." From both words, we can surmise that "Spirit means that God is a vital, acting God" who "grants life and vitality to creation."[32]

Roberts, like Cone before him, posits an intimate relationship between Christology and pneumatology. He notes that the early Church Fathers such as Ignatius, Second Clement, and Shepherd of Hermas posited a *pneumatic Christology* that presented Jesus as both "bearer" and "sender" of the Holy Spirit.[33]

> Jesus is conceived by the Spirit, guided by the Spirit, filled with the Holy Spirit. The Spirit rests on Jesus, and goes out from Jesus. The one on whom the Spirit remains baptizes with the Holy Spirit.[34]

Unfortunately, by the middle of the second century, Christians such as Titianus began to conflate *ruach* with *dabar* (word); or in Greek, *pneuma* with *logos*. Since *logos* was a popular Greek philosophical concept at the time, it was picked up as the favored way to talk about Jesus Christ. Thus *logos Christology* displaced the older *pneumatic*

Christology. It was an unfortunate move because it made Christology rely more on Hellenistic categories than on the resources of the Old Testament and the three synoptic Gospels. Roberts sees this as both distorting and impoverishing the biblical basis of Christology. Therefore, Roberts strives to go back to a *pneumatic Christology* in order to create a "sound doctrine of the Holy Spirit."[35]

One of the larger Holy Spirit movements in black American churches is Pentecostalism. Yet Roberts questions whether modern Pentecostalism (with the Holy Spirit as a cardinal principle) provides the same experience of the outpouring of the Spirit that occurred in the New Testament. Is baptism in the Holy Spirit a distinct "second blessing" from that of conversion? After a full theological discussion, Roberts tends toward calling the baptism of the Holy Spirit a "supplement to faith."[36] He sees a danger between a supplementary experience and establishing what is "faith's center."[37] Roberts notes that despite Pentecostalism's emphasis on "moral perfection," its virtues are often "negative and private."[38] Further, Pentecostalism ignores social transformation because it is short on social conscience and commitment to social justice. Thus, Roberts concludes with a firm disagreement with the ethical foundations and practices of Pentecostalism.

Roberts resumed his critique of Pentecostalism, particularly in its problems with (1) explaining how the power of God can meet people's needs and (2) depicting racism in its historical and theological manifestation. Like James S. Tinney, Roberts notes that had racism not been a part of early Pentecostalism, then its social consciousness might have also been different.

Racism, according to Tinney and Roberts, is *historical* within the experience of Pentecostalism. Many whites ignored the seminal event of the Azusa Street revival in Los Angeles in the first decade of the twentieth century, preferring to document the *glossolalia* experience of the white American Charles Parham as having been the *first* such Pentecostal experience. The earlier Azusa Street revival comprised mainly people of color. Whites have also negated black American W. J. Seymour's authenticity as a leader, noting that he was a "disciple" of Parham. All this led to a radical split within the Pentecostal movement along racial lines from the first years of its formation.

Racism also affected the *theology* of Pentecostalism. Whites were quite content to hold to the doctrine that stated that "scriptural revelation is final and without error." Black Pentecostals, on the other hand, held an open view of the scriptural canon, insisting upon the "new revelation" available through various prophecies, oracles, and other manifestations of the *charismatic gifts*. Such revelations have had an institutional impact, often basing the founding of new groups on such revelation. The black Pentecostal movement has therefore rejected the traditional fundamentalist-evangelical theology of white Pentecostals and, thus, trusted in "oral traditions, African cultural retentions, and the like."[39]

Roberts goes on to describe the racism within Pentecostalism as having an *institutional* impact. White superiority is promoted in several ways: segregated organizations and alliances, white flight from the inner cities, congregations secured under white control, and blacks relegated to subordinate roles.[40] Theologically, racism is seen in the exclusive images of a white Jesus, and of an all-white biblical cast in Sunday school literature. Roberts also examines a tendency of white Pentecostals to be "anti-Third World," as well.[41]

Moving back to the first point about the lack of social consciousness in Pentecostal churches, despite approbations of spiritual power, Roberts sees positive signs. In fact, quoting James Forbes, Roberts appreciates black Pentecostal leaders' willingness to look beyond an individualistic grasp of the power of the Holy Spirit. He notes that Forbes subscribes to a "progressive Pentecostalism" that embraces both personal experience and the fight against sources of social evil.[42]

It restores a sense of worth, identity, and God-relatedness to persons who come out of loneliness, lostness, meaninglessness, and a crisis of identity. Persons experience joy, peace, healing, and personal freedom when exposed to the Spirit's influence. But there will also be the expectation of spiritual gifts by which one can fight the forces of evil and promote the cause of the kingdom. Forbes goes even further. He asserts that the church, under the inspiration of the Holy Spirit, will offer counseling for personal healing and, at the same time, will seek the aid of agencies for social welfare.[43]

Roberts develops the implications of a "progressive Pentecostalism," saying that it "goes beyond institutional or denominational narrowness." Such a Pentecostalism does not narrowly construe the activity and implications of the presence of the Holy Spirit – limiting the Spirit's impact to one or two personal appropriations. Rather, the progressive Pentecostal movement embraces a theology that affirms that "Every human or divine activity that serves the realization of the kingdom of God is the concern of the Holy Spirit."[44] This means that the Holy Spirit works both outside as well as inside the four walls of the churches. It is not limited to the spiritual perfection of individual souls only, but sees the Spirit's work as anything "that affects our attainment of an abundant life and social freedom."[45] As such, the Spirit is that force that moves us beyond the past toward an "open and new future."[46]

Finally, Roberts considers the role of the Holy Spirit in the church. He notes that the church is the creation of the Spirit, both institutionally and as a community.[47] As an institution, we are talking about structures, "established relationships and patterns of historical and social order." As a *community*, we are speaking of the *event* that occurs within and between persons. Roberts insists that there is an interrelationship between the institution and the event of the church. The event of the church points us to the spontaneous, energizing human response to the activity of the Holy Spirit, as well as "the character of the community's life of grace."[48]

The black church is both an event and an institution. In its worship, the black church gathers as an event. Yet the event occurs within the reliable, stable framework of the institutionalized organization called "church."[49] The Spirit is one who heals, comforts, renews, and empowers in the context of meaningful worship. It is something that occurs not only *inside* of persons, but *between* persons. For Roberts, the Holy Spirit is that presence and power that is more interested in relationships between human beings than within them. Such emphasis on relationships may be scripturally cited in the Beatitudes of Matthew 5 and the "fruit of the Spirit" in Galatians 5.[50]

In conclusion, Roberts asserts that the Spirit not only heals, but it empowers us for liberation. One experiences the power of the Holy Spirit not only as a dove, but as wind and fire that helps us to envision the Comforter as the *Strengthener*. Thus, *justice* within the social order, just as much as love, peace, and joy within individual hearts, is the necessary "evidence" that the Spirit has been present in power.

Dwight Hopkins' *Down, Up, and Over: Slave Religion and Black Theology* offers a creative Trinitarian look at the Spirit. For Hopkins, black theology is built upon the threefold structure: God as the Spirit *for* us; Jesus Christ as the Spirit *with* us; and human purpose as the Spirit *within* us.[51] All things in this book are built from the agonistic struggle for selfhood that African Americans have experienced, beginning with enslavement.

The Spirit of God *for* us is the "Spirit of total liberation." It is the Hebrew *ruach*, breathing into us for our benefit. Such a Spirit of total liberation is, in fact, the ethical "divine face of freedom ... the ongoing process of embedded transcendent ethics of holistic spiritual and material humanity."[52] God for us has a social location, and that is "with the poor communities on this earth."[53] To deny this social location is to break with the "original covenant of the Spirit's presence for broken humanity." Thus God *for* us is the "fundamental act," the ethical doing of God acting for our benefit.[54]

Hopkins defines God ontologically as the "emancipating being for the oppressed of the earth." This being is a total, holistic, and ongoing process. This Spirit is dynamic without beginning or end, the great self-naming of God in Exodus, "I AM that I AM."[55] God is present, for us now, and forever. This very naming of God is *inclusive* of gender; aligning itself against gender asymmetry, it appears as both mother and father.[56]

Divine revelation is the epistemological demonstration of the emancipated being known as the Spirit of liberation. It may be found in the biblical verification of "the original intent of equality among and non-privileging of skin colors,"[57] an equality that cuts across all nations and humanity. Further, the epistemological demonstration of the Spirit of liberation may be found in the creation of the earth itself. All humanity is created out of divine breath deposited into the earth's dirt, according to the Genesis account. The very ground reveals the divine intent for all peoples to be dispersed with equality and freedom.

The Spirit for us elects the poor not to make of poverty a sacred thing, but to identify poverty as demonic. In fact, so pervasive is the nonliberating dynamic that sometimes the poor work against their own interests. Yet and still, it is the very will of the Spirit of liberation for persons to reach their highest "divine creativity."[58] Thus, the Spirit of total liberation works for all those (black folk and otherwise) who suffer "underneath the heel of victimization, through the interplay of God's glory and unity, righteousness and omnipresence, constancy and eternity, omnipotence and mercy, grace and holiness, wisdom and patience."[59]

The Spirit *with* us is the fulfillment of the Spirit of liberation. This fulfillment, for Dwight Hopkins, is Jesus, "the decisive revelation of God with us."[60] Jesus understood His purpose as the "continuation" of the literal and spiritual meaning of Isaiah 61:1–3; as He attested in Luke 4:18–19. This was Jesus' calling.

Jesus, for Hopkins, announced a "freedom calendar."[61] Such a "calendar" is not a facile rendering of peace, but is the product of the "judgment day, the day of vengeance." Such a day is a "historical juncture" wherein peoples of all nationalities and colors will be able to "submit their lives to an accounting." Yet Hopkins is careful to note that this day will be a time of comfort for the victims of unjust injuries. In his own words, it will be the divine spirit of liberation acting as both "mother and father who elevates and clothes the downcast spirits with a 'garment of praise'."[62] Thus the day of vengeance will be a joyful and comforting one for those who have suffered.

Jesus offers the paradigm of servanthood for the outcast. Such a servanthood is a different kind of model of leadership and power, a model in which power is for healing and not destruction. Such a power Jesus chooses to share with us because such a sharing fulfills the "mandate" of service to and for others.[63]

In Hopkins' thought, the sole criterion of the coming "Common Wealth" inaugurated by Jesus is "justice for the poor and weak in society." As Matthew 25:31–46 indicates, the bar of justice and final judgment is Jesus' end-time goal. Thus all will be asked whether they had aided the establishment of the Common Wealth on earth – giving food to the hungry, reallocating the resources of wealth, giving water to the poor, welcoming the stranger, clothing the naked, and visiting prisoners, all of whom are the poorest of the poor.[64]

Jesus' goal, therefore, is to be *with* us. So doing, according to Hopkins, He will bring all humanity to the bar of judgment and guide humanity successfully through the various tests of judgment. This goal empties out as false the values of the world such as "the monopolization of wealth, the best educational credentials, [and] long membership in a church."[65]

Ultimately, for Hopkins, the Spirit that is Jesus frees us in conversion. We experience a freedom from fear of any body, situation, or thing. It works on the inside of human beings, creating a "full self and full voice to the downtrodden."[66] Such a conversion dynamic generates both corporal and spiritual transformation, a new way of feeling, perceiving, and understanding truth. We continually ask what choice we will pursue – "Will it be 'the devil', or Jesus the Spirit with us?"[67] Thus, the Spirit *accompanies* the poor as they struggle along life's difficult journey endowed with new gifts and new power.[68]

Finally, the Spirit is *in* us, embedded in the relationship between the Spirit and oppressed and poor humanity.[69] It manifests in the movement human beings make for the "establishment of the new self and new Common Wealth on earth."[70] Yet such an establishment cannot come to its potential full flowering because we human beings are "broken vessels." We "fall short of what God, the Spirit of liberation for us, has for us on the other side of Jordan." Only in death will there be a "complete liberation" of the equality of all people. Here, Hopkins' theology of the Holy Spirit redefines the meaning of "death."[71] He calls it the drive we have for "home," home being both a place *on* the earth and a place after death. It is a consciousness of freedom wherein one is freed from the limitations of the "capabilities and powers of this earth." For Hopkins, this is the "transcendence of the Spirit for us."[72]

Only after death (that is, the complete defeat of human selfishness and private monopolization of God's wealth) will all people be equal in the state of complete liberation.[73]

Home cannot be limited to "heaven" because that would deny "the Spirit in us that empowers us to struggle for liberation and practice freedom on earth even in our fallible state as broken human vessels."[74]

The Spirit in us has a vocational obligation to all spheres of life, including the communal. The communal includes issues of "arranging ownership and control of God's wealth and resources."[75]

In Hopkins' work, the Spirit manifests itself in both *macro* and *micro* levels of existence. The *macro* level engages us in "a direct engagement with the larger structures of political economic power"; whereas the *micro* level "comprises instances of the Spirit's presence revealed on smaller everyday experiences of liberation beliefs and practices."[76] The aim of both levels is bringing together the exigencies of the micro-personal with the "macro pictures of political economy."[77] The Spirit of liberation is the juncture of the two, the norm of the least and lost in society. What this means is that Hopkins posits what he calls "full spiritual and material humanity" as the reflection of the "fullness of God's gift of liberation from creation," which, by its nature, "must include all aspects of what it means to be human."[78]

In his discussion of things necessary for being fully human Hopkins has an interesting section on the need for the expression of the Spirit within as the ability to "make fun of the oppressor." This ability to joke functions as a leveling device between the poor and the so-called "omnipotence of the monopolizers of divine creation."[79] He says that just participating in laughter reduces the level of an exploiter to that of any other human being, and alleviates the "insanity of being victimized by abuse."[80]

Furthermore, the Spirit within us affirms, particularly for poor and black people, the ability to liberate themselves "from the chains of self-hatred, misinformation, and subservience to whiteness as normative."[81] Self-liberation breaks the unhealthy longing to become white themselves that often accompanies the poor and blacks. Thus, the Spirit of liberation within "calls" poor black folk to be "black" unashamedly. Self-affirmation overturns the normativity of whiteness with a "healthy, sacred love of the black self."[82] Such a resounding "yes" to liberated black selfhood leads poor black folk to reclaim the biblical indications of black presence in the Bible itself. This reclamation is particularly important in seeing Jesus as an African-Asiatic Jew with curled hair and bronze skin coloring.[83]

In conclusion, Hopkins affirms his basic belief in the incarnational qualities of the Spirit of liberation. It manifests itself throughout several realms of human interaction, particularly in the macro, micro, language, and racial-cultural identity spheres. These four important spheres flow directly from the very substance of the Spirit of liberation. A belief in these "foundational" processes incarnates the Spirit. These four "disciplines of creativity" work with us to co-constitute the new self and the new "Common Wealth," despite the presence of negative internal "demons" who attempt to weaken our bonds with the Spirit of liberation. Based on the biblical witness, the traditions of black churches, and ongoing attempts toward full spiritual and material humanity within the black community, Hopkins strongly asserts that the "good news" must begin at the bottom of society. The Spirit of liberation helps the vast majority, the poor and the blacks, to overcome all obstacles that hold them back from the fulfillment and wealth of God's Common Wealth.[84]

Complementing and further deepening black theology, womanist theology, particularly the Trinitarian writings of Karen Baker-Fletcher, provides a rich articulation of what the Holy Spirit means for black women and men. Baker-Fletcher begins with the simple basic theological affirmation that God *is Spirit*. She goes on to affirm that while the entire Trinity is a Spirit, the Holy Spirit is one of the Greek *hypostases* or *relations* of the Trinity. The Holy Spirit is the "life-inspiring" relation, the very "breath of God."[85] The Hebrew *ruach* or Spirit was present at creation, thus making the entire Trinity present at creation, breathing life into both the rest of nature and human beings. It is that breath that makes us "alive, lively and dynamic."[86] It enables us to live in loving community with creation, serve as stewards for creation, and love creation with God's compassion and reason.[87] The Spirit infuses life into everything, even down to the molecular activity of rocks and earth itself.

Resonating with the process theology of Alfred North Whitehead and Charles Hartshorne, Baker-Fletcher notes that God "feels" the world's joys and sorrows through the agency of the Holy Spirit. God "feels" the world because God is the "feeling of the world's feeling." In other words, God is compassion. God's compassion guides creaturely existence by the guiding power of the Spirit of Christ, the second relation of the Spirit that is God in Trinity.

In process thought, movement occurs through the process of becoming and perishing. Growth occurs through the positively destructive becoming and perishing that is the "power of dynamic movement." A vivid aspect of this dynamic movement is the process of sanctification, which is the process wherein the Holy Spirit justifies and redeems the human self.[88]

Jesus is the one who is "dust and Spirit." He combines the aspects of "matter and divine energy, body/soul and Spirit." As such, he is able to "prehend" our joys and sorrows, both our feelings of well-being and sufferings, as well. Thus, we understand that through this creature of dust and Spirit, God is passionately with us because God *is* compassion. God's compassion is *with* us, therefore God "feels" with us as we go about our everyday tasks.[89]

The Spirit, for Baker-Fletcher, is omnipresent. It is the "power that brings life out of death."[90] Quoting Psalm 139:7–12, Baker-Fletcher affirms that there is no place anywhere that we can hide from God or fail to find God. The Spirit is therefore present in both the First and New Testaments as that power which is creative, prophetic, and renewing.[91] The famous acts within the Bible, whether it is David dancing before the ark of the covenant, prophetic speeches and acts, or the deeds of the early apostles, all occur *in the Spirit*. The very resurrection of Jesus as Christ is an act of the Holy Spirit. People recognize and receive the promise of Jesus as Christ through the agency of the Holy Spirit.

In Baker-Fletcher's thought, we first meet the *Holy* Spirit through Mary. It is in the first story of the New Testament, in Matthew, that Mary encounters the Holy Spirit as that power which creates Christ's conception and makes incarnation possible. How this is done, the Bible does not say specifically, but we do know that through the agency of the Holy Spirit Christ comes as a gift to both Mary and to the world.[92]

Ultimately for Baker-Fletcher, theology requires a strong doctrine of the Holy Spirit because it is the power of healing and resurrection. Such a doctrine affirms the power of healing and resurrection both in eternal and temporal time.[93] Yet the Holy Spirit does not manifest itself as a "genie in a bottle," popping up automatically at our command. Rather, those who believe in the miraculous power that is the Holy Spirit experience a "something," what William James calls "the More."[94] This "More" transforms suffering, illness, pain, and disability into what Baker-Fletcher calls the evidence of "sustaining grace."[95] Such evidence does not come with condescension or bitterness, but with respect and joy. For Baker-Fletcher, our response to the Holy Spirit is one of thankfulness for the abundant life God has granted.[96]

In conclusion, it is important to note how central the doctrine of the Holy Spirit is for such black and womanist theologians as Cone, Roberts, Hopkins, and Baker-Fletcher. It is not peripheral to their theological concerns, but emerges front and center. From the West African genealogy of Spirit presence, across the Atlantic slave trade into the Americas, from the slavery period (1619–1865) in North America through the subsequent centuries until today, the motivating power of black religion and black theology has been a spirit of survival and ultimately liberation.

Notes

1 In 1441, a group of Portuguese sailors captured and took back several Africans from the West Coast of Africa to the Christian monarch of Portugal. This marks, in a sense, the beginning of the European Christian slave trade in black bodies from, primarily, West Africa. However, it is in the seventeenth and eighteenth centuries where we find the increase of European Christians stealing West African peoples.

2 W. E. B. DuBois, *The Souls of Black Folk* (New York: The Modern Library, 2003; originally published in 1903).

3 Gayraud S. Wilmore, *Black Religion and Black Radicalism: An Interpretation of the Religious History of African Americans*, 3rd edn. (Maryknoll, NY: Orbis Books, 1998), p. 136.

4 Ibid., pp. 140–41.

5 Ibid., p. 145.

6 Joseph R. Washington, Jr., "Are American Negro Churches Christian?" In James H. Cone and Gayraud S. Wilmore (eds.), *Black Theology: A Documentary History*, vol. 1, *1966–1979* (Maryknoll, NY: Orbis Books, 1979), p. 97.

7 James H. Cone, *Black Theology and Black Power* (New York: Seabury Press, 1969), p. 57.

8 Ibid.

9 Cone quotes Eduard Schweitzer here from *Bible Key Words*, vol. III (New York: Harper & Brothers, 1960), p. 2.

10 Cone, *Black Theology and Black Power*, p. 57.

11 Ibid., p. 58.

12 Ibid.

13 W. E. B. DuBois, *John Brown* (Charleston, SC: Nabu Press, 2010).

14 Cone, *Black Theology and Black Power*, p. 59.

15 Ibid.

16 Ibid.

17 Ibid.

18 Ibid.

19 Ibid., p. 60.

20 Ibid.

21 Ibid.

22   Ibid.
23   Ibid.
24   Ibid.
25   Ibid., p. 61.
26   J. Deotis Roberts, *Black Theology in Dialogue* (Philadelphia, PA: Westminster Press, 1987), ch. 5, "The Holy Spirit and Liberation," p. 53.
27   Ibid.
28   Ibid., p. 54.
29   Ibid.
30   Ibid.
31   Ibid., pp. 54–55.
32   Ibid., p. 55.
33   Ibid., p. 56.
34   Ibid.
35   Ibid.
36   Ibid., pp. 57–58.
37   Ibid., p. 58.
38   Ibid.
39   Ibid.
40   Ibid., pp. 60–61.
41   Ibid., p. 61.
42   Ibid., referring to James A. Forbes, Jr., "Shall We Call This Dream Progressive Pentecostalism?" *Spirit* 1(1) (1977): 13–16.
43   Roberts, *Black Theology in Dialogue*, p. 61.
44   Ibid.
45   Ibid.
46   Ibid.
47   Ibid., p. 62.
48   Ibid.
49   Ibid., p. 63.
50   Ibid., pp. 63–64.
51   Dwight N. Hopkins, *Down, Up, and Over: Slave Religion and Black Theology* (Minneapolis, MN: Fortress Press, 1999), p. 158.
52   Ibid.
53   Ibid.
54   Ibid., pp. 159–69.
55   Ibid., pp. 162–63.
56   Ibid., p. 164.
57   Ibid., p. 167.
58   Ibid., p. 169.
59   Ibid., p. 189.
60   Ibid., p. 193.
61   Ibid., p. 194.
62   Ibid., p. 195.
63   Ibid., p. 196.
64   Ibid., p. 197.
65   Ibid., p. 198.

66 Ibid., p. 229.
67 Ibid.
68 Ibid., p. 231.
69 Ibid., p. 238.
70 Ibid., p. 239.
71 Ibid., p. 248.
72 Ibid.
73 Ibid.
74 Ibid.
75 Ibid., p. 251.
76 Ibid., p. 254.
77 Ibid.
78 Ibid.
79 Ibid., p. 255.
80 Ibid.
81 Ibid., p. 262.
82 Ibid.
83 Ibid., p. 263.
84 Ibid., p. 275.
85 Karen Baker-Fletcher, *Dancing with God: The Trinity in Womanist Perspective* (St. Louis, MO: Chalice Press, 2006), p. 62.
86 Ibid.
87 Ibid.
88 Ibid.
89 Ibid.
90 Ibid., p. 146.
91 Ibid., p. 148.
92 Ibid.
93 Ibid., p. 156.
94 Ibid., pp. 156–57.
95 Ibid., p. 158.
96 Ibid., p. 159.

9 Black theology and human purpose

RIGGINS R. EARL, JR.

In black theology, the notion of human purpose is closely tied to a perception of Jesus. In this sense, human purpose (or theological anthropology) is connected to Christology (or the life and import of Jesus the Christ). It is the human being, Jesus, who models human purpose. Therefore, in this chapter, I draw on Christological lessons in order to surface the human purpose themes of self-denial, agency, identity, and liberation. To highlight the lessons of Jesus for human purpose, I compare and contrast the relationship between black American theology and African theology. In fact, since the majority of black Americans' lineage goes back to Africa, it helps to put into conversation these two understandings of human purpose.

Theologians Josiah Young and Dwight Hopkins have contributed to informative studies demarcating the similarities and dissimilarities of black and African theologies.[1] Their fine works respectively implicate the need for liberation theology to address the complex ethical challenge of generic (nonspecific) self-denial. The generic character in the biblical Jesus' call to discipleship in several of the Gospel narratives is rather transparent: "If any man would come after me, let him deny himself, take up his cross daily and follow me" (Luke 9:23; Mark 8:34). This is human purpose. Jesus' biblical command of generic self-denial as a voluntary optional response to his requirement of Cross-bearing discipleship presents its own theological and ethical challenge to the oppressed. It presupposes that the colonized and the colonizer of Jesus' day will encounter the command through their own respective experiences.

I contend in this study that the generic character of the biblical Jesus' command of self-denial is potentially both problematic and liberative. Jesus' command to voluntarily deny one's self and take up one's cross, which is viewed as the optional initial mandatory prerequisite to discipleship, challenges the oppressed to rethink their agential identity and worth. It raises questions about human purpose. It also challenges the oppressed to rethink their Christology, that is, specifically the question of Jesus as their liberator and model of human purpose. Philosophically and socially, the idea of self-denial must be viewed as the primal ethical act that is foundational to the self's developmental sense of agential identity and accountability. An understanding of agential identity and accountability is derived from a social encounter with the other. The biblical Jesus' command of generic self-denial is challenging, at face value, in that it appears to force racial and cultural self-abdication. This provokes the question: What is the difference between the biblical Jesus' command of generic self-denial and the oppressor's forced racial and cultural self-denial?

On close inspection, one difference is that the biblical Jesus gives the hearer the option of denying his/her self and following him. A second difference between the command of the oppressor and that of Jesus is: (1) the oppressor's reward for forced racial and cultural self-denial is temporal servile identity survival while (2) Jesus' reward for generic self-denial, as a result of free choice, is an eternal life identity role of exalted dignity with God: "For whoever will save his life shall lose it: but whoever will lose his life for my sake, the same shall save it" (Luke 9:24). Here human purpose is to be with God and liberated from oppression. Biblically, generic self-denial is the prerequisite qualification for membership in Jesus' Cross-bearing fellowship, the union card for eternal life. Black liberation theologians and ethicists have been slow to address the challenging ethical aspect of Jesus' command of generic self-denial as the prerequisite for discipleship.[2]

The remainder of this chapter will show that "black and African cousins of liberation theology" must critically engage the complex Christological ethical challenge of generic self-denial for the oppressed. Jesus Christ challenges the human purpose of the oppressed person. These theological cousins must do this in the light of their unequivocal commitment to such concepts as racial and cultural *self-recognition, self-worth,* and *self-care.*[3] Black and African "distant cousins" must address the generic self-denial's implications for liberation. They must respond to it as the primal ethical response to Jesus' chain of serial commands, explicit in the discipleship formula, such as: "come unto me"; "take up my cross"; "and follow me daily." Liberation theology has merely attended to the Cross-bearing requirement of Jesus' call to generic self-denial for discipleship. Human purpose is to follow Jesus. But what are the implications of pursuing this path?

This study will show that the self-denial phase of Jesus' call to discipleship requires that victims of colonialism and slavery, in particular, critically engage it afresh. Such a study is necessary primarily because oppressed black people first heard Jesus' call to self-denial secondhand, via the mouths of their enslavers and colonizers. Given this fact, black theology must ask the following questions about human purpose: what amounts to black self-denial in the context of such experiences as slavery, colonialism, and classism? What is the human purpose for the black self of colonialism, slavery, and classism? How do experiences of these "isms" obscure or make transparent Jesus' command for self-denial as the prerequisite to responding to the call of discipleship? These are three of the critical questions that drive this study of black theology and human purpose.[4]

SELF-DENIAL AND THE OPPRESSED

Issues of race, ethnicity, slavery, and colonialism obviously have not been of major concern for modern white theologians. It certainly did not seem to be the case for such contemporary thinkers in Reformed theology as Karl Barth and Paul Tillich or for Karl Rahner.[5] Self-denial unto martyrdom in the writings of the theologian and martyr Dietrich Bonhoeffer seems to be an anomaly. Imprisoned by the German Nazi regime under Adolph Hitler, Bonhoeffer's serious commitment to Jesus' generic self-denial discipleship provoked him to raise the haunting theological, anthropological and ontological question: "Who am I?" Bonhoeffer provides the answer himself that implicates a need to transcend race and culture: "Whoever I am, Thou knowest, O God. I am thine!"[6] The biblical teaching is that God requires unconditional self-denial as the prerequisite for fulfilling his will. Bonhoeffer declared:

> Self-denial is never just a series of isolated acts of mortification or asceticism. It is not suicide, for there is an element of self-will even in that. To deny oneself is to be aware only of Christ and no more of self, to see only him who goes before and no more the road which is too hard for us. Once more all that self-denial can say is: "He leads the way, keep close to him."[7]

For the oppressed, the complex ethical challenge arises where the act of self-valuing conflicts with that of being valued (or countervalued) by the other – that is, in this case, Jesus being the ultimate Other. Inherent in this conflict, arising out of valuing and being countervalued, is the society's skewing of the self's worth for socioeconomic exploitation. Systemic oppression demands that oppressed individuals falsely value themselves instrumentally, if not intrinsically, through the eyes of their oppressors and vice versa. Invariably, oppressed persons are required to see themselves as being of inferior instrumental or extrinsic worth. This certainly was the case in Jesus' day. It is no less the case for the "distant cousins" of black and African theologies.

Dietrich Bonhoeffer understood that this summons of Christ demanded ultimate sacrifice. The basic point here is that Jesus' call to generic self-denial, when processed through the experiences of slavery, colonialism, and classism, complicates it for the victimized. It exacerbates the hearer's dialectical sense of instrumental and intrinsic worth. Can the potential disciple deny his/her cultural sense of particular self-worth without denying their intrinsic worth? For instance, did not Jesus of the scriptures value Peter, James, and John's instrumental usefulness as fishermen for ministry in the kingdom? The Gospels portray Jesus as valuing both the individual's intrinsic and extrinsic value (e.g., the woman caught in adultery; the Samaritan woman at Jacob's well).[8] Recovering the biblical Jesus' method of valuing has been (and still is) no less the aim of black and African theologies. Informed by this biblical portrait of Jesus as liberator, black and African theologies have countered slavery and colonialism in their struggle for a transformative view of generic self-denial as Jesus' means to liberative discipleship. A critical engagement of generic self-denial, slavery, and the Christological challenge is necessary at this point.

BLACK AMERICAN SLAVERY, CHRISTOLOGY, AND GENERIC SELF-DENIAL

The Christological challenge of self-denial is at the heart of black Americans' slave experience. What is the inherent ethical tension between blacks' experience of American slavery and the Christological call to self-denial? What has been liberation theologies' contribution to this problematic for blacks? Slavers, on the one hand, declared in the name of Jesus that blacks, other than instrumentally, were of no recognizable agential value in "the white man's Christian civilization." Jesus was presented as the only one who could change the spiritual worth of the African. These rulers, on the other hand, declared that Jesus could whiten and eternally save blacks' souls for heaven. Undoubtedly, this skewed view affected blacks' interpretation of Jesus' call to generic self-denial. Slavers preached to their slaves the notion of servile Christianity, the belief that God would reward them in heaven for obedience to their earthly masters.[9] Exhorting slaves to be humble like Jesus was the common practice of the slave master. The language of the slave conversion stories speaks more in terms of the impotence of the slave self in the face of both the determinative power of sin and the awesome power of God. The idea of being aware of free will, prior to conversion, is not one that frequently occurs in the slave narratives. Slaves believed that, as taught by their masters, their disobedience to God, manifested in such conduct as "drinking, dancing, and smoking," was caused by some outside force, that is, generally that of the devil. In the light of this fact, slaves dramatically characterized conversion to God in such vivid metaphorical phrases as: "God struck me dead"; "my dungeon shook and my chains fell off." Being rendered totally impotent in the presence of God is a common idea that runs through the slave conversion narratives. Following such a dramatic conversion episode, the convert was expected to express daily commitment, under the aegis of the spirit, to a life of self-denial for Christ. For this reason, the convert, as a free agent, makes the act of self-denial, which consummates in the Cross-bearing life of following Christ, the heart of his/her testimony.[10]

Black preachers' sermonic moral exhortations of puritanical self-compromise in the face of racial insult constitute a rich repository in black church culture from slavery to the 1950s and the 1960s civil rights movement. Scholars have often viewed this as the politics of race and character.[11] As one trend in black religion, black preachers' puritanical belief in racial self-compromise for Christ enabled them and their followers to survive "the nadir" of slavery and racial oppression. It therapeutically prepared black Americans for the inevitable assertion of militant political theology. It must be viewed as the antecedent to Martin L. King, Jr.'s leadership of the civil rights movement and James Cone's academic version of black liberation theology.[12] Many leading black preachers of America, prior to the modern civil rights movement under Martin L. King, Jr., were the precursors of such puritanical preachments of self-denial. King himself was a part of that heritage. Puritanical racial self-compromise preachments were thought to be the necessary moral means of blacks coping with the white racist society's dehumanization of them. Racial self-compromise was viewed as necessary for blacks to pave the road with their deeds of compromise in the face of white power (Booker T. Washington was the chief apostle of this belief). Slavery and racism in America forced many blacks to maintain one trend in black religion: pursuing a servile virtue of puritanical racial self-compromise by making themselves go the second mile to placate whites and their Christ.

James Cone's *Black Theology and Black Power* and Delores Williams' *Sisters in the Wilderness* provoked a challenging discussion about black puritanical self-denial and racial self-compromise for Jesus

Christ.[13] Cone did this by demanding that Jesus be seen as the black Messiah who liberates black people. Williams countered Cone's assumption by critiquing the salvific presupposition of Jesus' atonement on the Cross for black people. These different approaches to Christology and the challenge of generic self-denial demanded that academics appreciate the dialectical nature of black religion. It required that blacks critically affirm the inherent tension between the therapeutic and the political dimensions of black religion. James Cone and Delores Williams have made unique contributions to the Christological challenge of the ethics of self-denial in human purpose.

James Cone's black Messiah and the ethical challenge of racial self-denial

Drawing on the trend of black slave religion, Cone substitutes self-actualization for self-denial in his argument for black liberation. He redefines liberation as "(1) relationship with God, (2) self-actualization, (3) protest and struggle for freedom, and (4) hope."[14] Frederick L. Ware's commentary on Cone's understanding of self-actualization illuminates our premise:

> With respect to self-actualization, liberation means the freedom to be the self that God has created one to be. For both the oppressed and oppressors, this freedom is from distorted conceptions of the self and hindrances to actualizing each person's potential. Protest and struggle for freedom are indicative of freedom in the form of God's immediate presence among the oppressed to resist evil and live.[15]

Unlike the traditional preachers of the black church tradition, James Cone dared to make blackness an inherent part of Christology. It is for this reason that Cone defines racism as being the cardinal sin for which black people need a black Messiah for their deliverance from the oppression of whiteness. Cone's version of Christology raises at least one critical question in the light of the above argument on racial self-denial and Cross-bearing: If the Messiah is black, what does it mean for a black person to have to deny one's self? What does Christological blackness suggest for human purpose?

Countering the criticism of white racism, Cone purports that his black Messiah is existentially symbolic rather than literal.[16] He did this to counter Albert Cleage's call for a literal black Messiah.[17] Cone's symbolic view of the black Messiah drew J. Deotis Robert's counterresponse.

Roberts, trying to avoid Cleage's literal black Messiah trap, argues that oppressed people must see the black Messiah as the means to the "Christ of faith." He concludes that "the black Messiah must ultimately point to and give way to a colorless Christ." Because he sees the ultimate goal as reconciliation, Robert's states, "The black Messiah liberates the black man. The universal Christ reconciles the black man with the rest of mankind."[18]

Cone's notion of the black Messiah presents a different challenge for thinking theologically and ethically about racial self-denial as a cornerstone in black theology's understanding of human purpose. In the light of Jesus' challenge to choose generic self-denial, we must ask: What must black people deny if Jesus is black? For Cone, they must obviously deny the false white Messiah who is incarnate in themselves. This provokes the question: What is the relationship between Jesus as the white Messiah and Jesus as the black Messiah? Where was the black Messiah when the enslavement of blacks took place?

Delores Williams' Christology and the generic self-denial challenge

Williams' Christology has no place for the idea of generic, gender, or racial self-denial for Jesus. She fits more into what I would call the type of the self-care ethical response to the biblical Jesus' commandment of generic self-denial and to the enslavers' Jesus demand for racial self-denial. I risk this assertion because Williams rejects the atonement doctrine that believers have traditionally held about Jesus Christ. The traditional doctrine is that human beings are redeemed through Jesus having innocently suffered violence, abuse, and death at the hands of wicked men. Williams thinks that the atonement idea places too much emphasis on Jesus' suffering and not enough on his visionary teachings. For her, the biblical Jesus' command of self-denial for fulfilling Cross-bearing expectations is absurd. For Williams, humankind is redeemed through Jesus' ministerial vision of life. She says:

> Nothing is divine in the blood of the cross ... Jesus did not come to be a surrogate. Jesus came for life, to show humans a perfect vision of ministerial relation that humans had very little knowledge of. As Christians, black women cannot forget the cross, but neither can they glorify it. To do so is to glorify suffering and to render their exploitation sacred.[19]

Williams' rejection of the atonement theory places her in direct opposition to the core belief of most black liberation theologians, who posit
Jesus' victimization on the Cross and resurrection as the liberation
model for the oppressed.[20] It is Williams' belief that the idea of Jesus'
atonement death on the Cross does not motivate the oppressed to overcome their sufferings. In it, they see suffering glorified in Jesus Christ,
as it was his suffering alone that results in redemption.

If consistent, Williams must reject the theory of generic self-denial
for the ultimate redemption of the other. In light of this: To what degree
does Williams believe in redemptive suffering? Williams is addressing
the side of the story of Hagar's involuntary suffering for her child (in the
Book of Genesis). How do we explain those Hagars and Sarahs who suffer, for reasons that are not always related to the oppressor, willingly for
their children, as well as humanity-at-large in the name of Christ and
count it a joy (e.g., Mother Theresa)?

Delores Williams posits two African American traditions of biblical
hermeneutics for understanding God's activity among the oppressed.
The first Williams calls "the liberation tradition of African American
biblical appropriation."[21] The second Williams calls "the survival/qual-
ity-of-life tradition of African American biblical appropriations."[22]

The critical question is: How does black Americans' view of Jesus'
call to generic and racial self-denial compare with the way that Africans
have heard it via the acoustical grids of colonialism and neocolonialism?
Does Jesus' accent on self-denial suggest a human purpose differently
when that accent is understood by the oppressed in different contexts?

To further distinguish between black and womanist theologies' debate over human purpose, we globalize it with an African
comparison.

AFRICAN COLONIALISM, CHRISTOLOGY, AND GENERIC SELF-DENIAL

The colonizers' Jesus of cultural self-denial is at the core of Africans'
colonial and neocolonial experiences. In the case of Africans, it seems
to be less explicit because African theologians have often crafted their
need to respond to Jesus differently from black liberation theologians
in America. We ask: How has the contemporary theologian of African
liberation theology responded to this in the face of the Christological
ethical challenge of the peasants of Africa's need for self-care? The key
question here is: In what way did colonialism impact Africans' hearing of Jesus' generic self-denial Cross-bearing commandment? What did

this mean for the colonized African whose sense of self was undoubtedly shaped by a tie to such primal cultural structures as land and kinship? What does it mean in a colonial and neocolonial theology that
makes *ancestors* and the *creation* itself, rather than individual *conversion*, the point of departure? Theologian Josiah Young notes that blacks
and whites are responsible for bringing the colonized Jesus to Africa. In
a most helpful categorization, Young characterizes the colonial period
of African theology as the third phase:

> The Christianity of the third phase took root and flourished in
> West Africa largely because Africans themselves played a seminal
> role in the planting of Christianity there. These Christians,
> ancestors of African theology, include Samuel Crowther, James
> Holy Johnson and Edward W. Blyden. Discussion of them requires
> an appreciation of Great Britain and the rise of the Industrial
> Revolution, which made slavery a less viable economic mode – a
> fact that facilitated the abolitionism that burgeoned there.[23]

Young's analysis shows that the first black missionaries such as Blyden
and Crowther struggled with the issue of Christianity and European
culture and that of indigenous African culture. The missionaries' Christ
of European culture demanded that Africans deny having any good of
themselves in order to become his disciples. Likewise, in this view,
Christ demanded that black Africans borrow their humanity from him.
White missionaries who could embrace indigenous African culture
were faced with a different kind of question about what constituted
self-denial.

For colonial missionaries, Jesus Christ incarnate in European culture demanded absolute cultural self-denial on the part of those of indigenous African culture. It was this that informed blacks' and whites'
missionary attempts to be bearers of the Gospel of Jesus Christ to colonial Africa in the eighteenth century. Their attempts highlight the
genesis of Jesus' ethical challenge of generic self-denial in the mind
of Africans. Africans of the different countries on the continent were
being confronted by former black slaves from America to accept Jesus'
ethical challenge of generic self-denial. Ironically, some of the former
slaves who had become Christians were caught between the African's
need for a generic self-denial response to Jesus' call and a self-care one.
They seemed to sense intuitively what became a "Christ and culture"
dilemma. This dilemma takes place between those absolutely intoler-
ant of African traditions (i.e., white missionaries) and the mixed views
of blacks' response.

Blacks' mixed views of African traditions and Jesus' command of generic self-denial

Black leaders settled in Africa to do missionary work in significant numbers. Some of these people were sponsored by white missionary organizations, whether British or adherents of America's immigration and colonization movement.[24]

Pivotal theological insight is to be had from a history-making event of slavery and Christianization that took place in Freetown on the West African coast during the eighteenth century. Lamin Sanneh notes that Freetown became a center for the Christianization of thousands of Africans rescued by the British antislavery patrols operating in West African coastal waters. Josiah Young's most important point for our purposes here is that recaptives, as with slaves in the Americas, found points of continuity between their traditional religion and Christianity there.[25] Young's observation about the fundamental difference between Africans as recaptives in Freetown and Africans enslaved in North America is even more pertinent for our discussion. He thinks the difference

> is that Africans enslaved in North America were mostly Christianized as slaves. Many Africans, however, particularly outside South Africa, in this period were Christianized after being rescued from slavery. Notable among these recaptives was Bishop Samuel Crowther, a significant exponent of indigenization.[26]

Crowther's moderate African affirmation of indigenization was distressing for missionaries who believed unconditionally in Jesus' command of self-denial. It raises the question of missionaries' abilities to value the African's worth through the lens of his/her traditional religions. Such an interpretation of Jesus' call for self-denial challenges the value of Africans' status as human beings based on their religion and culture.

Black American missionaries to Africa such as Alexander Crummell and Edward Blyden embody the making of the conflict between the value of Christian culture and that of indigenous African culture. Josiah Young's summary of the differences and similarities between the two leaders is helpful:

> Whereas Crummell sought to discard African traditional culture, Blyden envisioned the retention of traditional African values in an African civilization critical of the enlightenment. Resisting certain modernizing forces, Blyden appreciated how African traditional values could benefit blacks in the postmodern age. If Crummell

thought modern science should immediately replace "heathen superstition," Blyden had a more critical view of Western science.[27]

Young appreciates Blyden's affirmation of the redemptive values of African culture as a providential legacy:

> Your first duty is to be yourself ... You need to be told constantly that you are Africans, not Europeans – black men not white men – that you were created with the physical qualities which distinguish you for the glory of the Creator, and for the happiness and perfection of humanity; and that in your endeavors to make yourselves something else, you are not only spoiling your nature and turning aside from your destiny, but you are robbing humanity of the part you ought to contribute to its complete development and welfare, and you become as salt which has lost its savor – good for nothing – but to be cast out and trodden down by others.[28]

Since widespread independence, neocolonial Africa has given birth to a new guard of liberation theologians such as Mercy Oduyoye and Jean-Marc Ela. These thinkers are challenging blacks to struggle with the ethic of self-denial in the light of the Africans' need for self-care and self-actualization. Ela writes: "A time of challenge is beginning for Christians who have discovered Jesus Christ through the theology of the 'salvation of souls.' It requires us never again to accept the living Gospel in a condition of dependence. Our churches will no longer be able to sit at the tables of the rich in order to bring back only crumbs to 'poor blacks.'"[29] Mercy Oduyoye challenges African theologians further to deny the oppressive patriarchy and embrace a Christology that is liberating of African women. Along with Elizabeth Amoah, Oduyoye explores African women's Christology. She does this with the acknowledgement that African men's Christologies, despite their sexism, have recognized that Western paradigms are too otherworldly for Africans, whose traditional memory has been shaped by values that emphasize health and wholeness now.[30] These theologians argue against a Christian self-denial that points to African human purpose as dependence on abstract idealism.

Whites' single-minded view of traditional African culture and Jesus' command of generic self-denial

From colonialism to neocolonialism, this conflict between the human purpose manifest in traditional African culture and Jesus' instructions of self-denial has been marked by the Christian missionaries' (white and black) diligent efforts to erase African traditions. Most missionaries believed that eradicating African traditions was the prerequisite for the Africans to correctly respond, via the missionaries' forceful hand, to the colonizer Jesus' command of cultural self-denial. Scholars have asserted that missionaries deemed the African way of life thoroughly uncivilized and irredeemably heathen. Desmond Tutu notes that "the missionary [attempted to demolish the African] past."[31] Colonial missionaries projected onto Africa a white imperialistic image of Jesus, which, if embraced, would have a devastating impact on human purpose.

For instance, in the realm of philosophical anthropology, whites who saw Africans through Immanuel Kant's lens of the eighteenth-century European Enlightenment concluded that they were naturally moral deficient and for this reason lacked character. Critics of Africa applied Kant's idea of man being the creator of his own worth and dignity to prove that the African was subhuman. According to Kant, superior moral capacity accounted for the European's superiority. He reasoned that while the non-European may have "value," it is not certain that he or she has true worth. Kant proceeded to say:

> Everything has either value or a worth. What has value has a substitute which can replace it as its equivalent; but whatever is, on the other hand, exalted above all values, and thus lacks an equivalent ... has no merely relative value, that is a price, but rather an inner worth, that is dignity ... Hence morality, and humanity, in so far as it is capable of morality, can alone possess dignity.[32]

Kant's rational way of declaring blacks inferior impacted the way that leaders of the Christian church saw and related to the darker-skinned people of the world. It reinforced the white missionaries' belief in the need for their imperialistic white Jesus to hold the African hostage to the colonizers' culture of self-deprecation.[33]

RETHINKING HUMAN PURPOSE AS SELF-DENIAL AND LIBERATION

Above, we have posited that this Christological challenge of the biblical Jesus' generic self-denial command demands a critical theological and ethical investigation. This Christology had direct impact on human purpose in black theology and African theology. If human purpose is to be disciples of what Jesus calls humans to be, then we need to broaden a human purpose of self-denial to include additional perspectives. Blacks' and Africans' critical reflections upon the ethical and theological challenges of Jesus' generic self-denial command stand to enrich the plethora of existing scholarly literature. Their discourses on generic self-denial make transparent the need for rethinking the biblical Jesus' command in the face of the history of colonialism and slavery.

This essay enables the reader to see the need to weigh the idea of Jesus' generic self-denial command over against the oppressor's mandatory culture of self-deprecation imposed upon the oppressed. Self-denial as an optional response to Jesus' discipleship call must be heard in relationship to other such psychological constructs as *self-actualization*, *self-control*, and *self-care*. In black theology, this broadens our understanding of human purpose.

The conflicting moral requirement of *self-denial* in the face of self-deprecation continues to haunt oppressed people of all races and cultures. It forces the oppressed to try to live creatively between human purpose as a voluntary optional response to Jesus' command of self-denial and the oppressor's forced definition of human purpose as a requirement of self-abdication. However, during his lifetime, Martin L. King, Jr. demonstrated that the voluntary optional response to Jesus' command of self-denial provides the window for the oppressed to liberate themselves and their oppressors.[34] King's civil disobedience leadership, as a form of human purpose, is a model example of one choosing Jesus' voluntary self-denial optional response to suffer for justice over the oppressor's forced unjust servitude. James Cone correctly saw that, especially as embodied in King, obedience to the way of the Cross of Jesus, which symbolizes self-denial, leads to self-actualization.[35] For King and Cone, self-denial commanded by Jesus empowers the oppressed to assert human purpose in a nonpassive, self-agential manner.

Some black American liberation theologians have found it difficult to hang the identity of black people on Jesus' principle of optional self-denial that leads to bearing one's Cross for him. Delores Williams, who is a primary representative of this camp of thinkers, has denounced this perspective as oppressive for an already oppressed people. At face value, Williams seems to be on point in her analysis. Yet she overlooks, it seems, the fact that the hearer's response to Jesus' command of self-denial is optional. It is Jesus' gift of choice that makes the Cross bearable. When the oppressed hears Jesus' call through the grid of the oppressor, Jesus' gift of the freedom of choice is truncated. This is the case because the oppressor demands self-denial on the part of the oppressed and Cross-bearing as the means for making a humble slave, a contented sufferer.

The conflicting moral needs of self-denial, self-control, and self-care collectively and individually have been no less haunting for would-be black Christians on the African continent. Colonial whites eliminated for the African the voluntary option of responding to Jesus' command of self-denial by voiding it of all political meaning. They did this through the controlling ideology of colonialism, which demanded that African blacks deprecate their cultural identity in becoming followers of Jesus. Contemporary scholars note that this contributes to the devastating economic, political, and social devastation of the African continent.[36]

Contemporary African theologians such as Jean-Marc Ela, Mercy Oduyoye, and Laurenti Magesa have all contributed to the needs of African Christians to struggle for the liberation of Africa. A common fact is that the black continent's oppressors have been within and without its borders. The common call of contemporary black African theologians is for a holistic Christian Gospel in Africa. That is to say, to follow Jesus includes a human purpose of liberation on earth. The Catholic theologian Jean-Marc Ela thinks that such a Gospel must be prophetic and priestly.[37]

Black liberation theologians, like their African cousins, are confronted with the human purpose challenge of hearing afresh Jesus' call to generic self-denial. That is to say, both are embracing the Jesus command of discipleship through their own heritages of slavery and colonialism. They are challenged to see it as a gift of choice rather than that of necessity. Blacks and Africans might stand to benefit from a conference that would make Jesus' call to self-denial for Cross-bearing discipleship the thematic focus for human purpose.

Notes

1   Josiah U. Young III, *Black and African Theologies: Siblings and Distant Cousins* (Maryknoll, NY: Orbis Books, 1986), p. 107.

Both descendants of black Americans and Africans have had their identity and sense of worth shaped by their enslavers' and colonizers' teachings of Jesus Christ as savior and Lord. Black theologian Josiah Young notes that white slavers' and colonizers' Christology impacted Africans and black Americans in similar and dissimilar ways. Young boldly concluded over a decade ago that black and African experiences of enslavers' and colonizers' versions of Christianity made them "distant cousins" rather than "siblings." For Young this has mainly had to do with the fact that "the principal exponents of African theology stress their distance from black American theology, the two streams of theology are now only distant cousins." See also Dwight N. Hopkins, *Black Theology*

USA and South Africa: Politics, Culture, and Liberation (Maryknoll, NY: Orbis Books, 1989). James Cone has correctly noted about Hopkins' *Black Theology USA and South Africa*: "Black theology continually poses a challenge to Christian witness and faith. Through a critical analysis of leading religious thinkers, Dwight N. Hopkins explores the fundamental differences and similarities between black theology in the United States and black theology in South Africa and asks: What is the common denominator between the two?" See Hopkins' *Black Theology USA and South Africa* promotional statement.

2   Peter Paris, *Virtues and Values: The African and African American Experience* (Minneapolis, MN: Fortress Press, 2004). This has probably had to do more with the fact that the Christological focus of black liberation theology has been primarily on liberation and reconciliation. This has been the case for black liberation theologians in Africa and America. Peter Paris' comparative analysis of virtue ethics between blacks and Africans is instructive. See Paris' *The Spirituality of African Peoples: The Search for a Common Moral Discourse* (Minneapolis, MN: Fortress Press, 1995).

3   Michele Foucault, *The History of Sexuality: The Care of the Self* (New York: Vintage, 1998); Beverly Eileen Mitchell, *Black Abolitionism: A Quest for Black Dignity* (Maryknoll, NY: Orbis Books, 2005); and Lee H. Butler, *Liberating Our Dignity: Saving Our Souls* (St. Louis, MO: Chalice Press, 2006).

4   Dwight N. Hopkins, *Introducing Black Theology of Liberation* (Maryknoll, NY: Orbis Books, 1999); Delores S. Williams, *Sisters in the Wilderness: The Challenge of Womanist God-Talk* (Maryknoll, NY: Orbis Books, 1993); and James H. Cone, *God of the Oppressed* (San Francisco, CA: Harper & Row, 1975). The works of these theologians have shaped my way of reading Christology from the problematic of oppression.

5   For a Catholic theologian's perspective of self-denial and holiness see Karl Rahner, *Encyclopedia of Theology: A Concise Sacramentum Mundi* (New York: Continuum International Publishing Group, 1975). For Karl Barth, Paul Tillich, and Søren Kierkegaard, see Jonathan Edwards' sermon "Undergoing Suffering a Duty to Christ," in *The Works of Jonathan Edwards*, vol. VIII, *Ethical Writings*, ed. Paul Ramsay (New Haven, CT: Yale University Press, 1989), pp. 318–19.

6   Dietrich Bonhoeffer, *Letters and Papers from Prison*, abridged edn. (London: SCM Press, 1953), p. 126.

7   Dietrich Bonhoeffer, *The Cost of Discipleship*, abridged edn. (New York: Macmillan, 1959).

8   Both stories can be found in the Gospel of John. See John 4 as well as John 8.

9   See Dwight N. Hopkins, *Down, Up, and Over: Slave Religion and Black Theology* (Minneapolis, MN: Fortress Press 1999).

10 Clifton H. Johnson, *God Struck Me Dead: Religious Conversion Experiences and Autobiographies of Ex-Slaves* (Philadelphia, PA: Pilgrim Press, 1969).

11 For a classic example of the black Puritan version of self-denial see *The Works of Francis J. Grimke*, vols. I, II, and III, ed. Carter G. Woodson (Washington, DC: Associated Press Inc., 1942).

12 See Joseph H. Jackson, *Unholy Shadows and Freedom's Holy Light* (Nashville, TN: Townsend Press, 1967); Jacquelyn Grant, *White Women's Christ and Black Women's Jesus: Feminist Christology and Womanist Response* (Atlanta, GA: Scholars Press, 1989); Ella Mitchell, *Those Preachin' Women* (Valley Forge, PA: Judson Press, c. 1985–96); Adam Clayton Powell, *Adam by Adam: The Autobiography of Adam Clayton Powell, Jr.* (New York: Dial Press, 1971).

13 James H. Cone, *Black Theology and Black Power* (New York: Seabury Press, 1969), and Williams, *Sisters in the Wilderness*.

14 Cone, *Black Theology and Black Power*, pp. 141–62; see also Frederick L. Ware's summary in *Methodologies of Black Theology* (Cleveland, OH: Pilgrim Press), p. 38.

15 Ware, *Methodologies of Black Theology*, p. 38.

16 Cone, *Black Theology and Black Power*, pp. 133–37.

17 See Albert B. Cleage, Jr., *The Black Messiah* (Trenton, NJ: Africa World Press, 1989).

18 J. Deotis Roberts, *Liberation and Reconciliation: A Black Theology* (Maryknoll, NY: Orbis Books, 1994), pp. 130–40.

19 Williams, *Sisters in the Wilderness*, p. 167.

20 See theologians Latta Thomas, *Biblical Faith and the Black American* (Valley Forge, PA: Judson Press, 1976) and *The Biblical God and Human Suffering* (Elgin, IL: Progressive National Baptist Publishing House, 1987), and Olin P. Moyd, *Redemption in Black Theology* (Valley Forge, PA: Judson Press, 1979).

21 Williams, *Sisters in the Wilderness*, pp. 2, 5–6.

22 Ware's summary of Williams, *Sisters in the Wilderness*, in *Methodologies of Black Theology*, pp. 37, 38, 53–54.

23 Josiah U. Young III, *African Theology: A Critical Analysis and Annotated Bibliography* (Westport, CN: Greenwood Press, 1993), pp. 9–10.

24 Scholars have noted the differences and similarities in the unique perspectives of early black missionaries to Africa such as Edward Blyden and Alexander Crummell. Their responses to the value of African culture demand a different assessment of Jesus' challenge for the colonialized African to deny him/her self.

25 Lamin O. Sanneh, *West African Christianity: The Religious Impact* (Maryknoll, NY: Orbis Books, 1983), pp. 83–89.

26 Young, *Black and African Theologies*, p. 11.

27 Josiah U. Young III, *A Pan-African Theology: Providence and the Legacies of the Ancestors* (Trenton, NJ: Africa World Press, 1992), p. 55.

28 Quoted in Hollis Lynch, *Edward Wilmot Blyden: Pan-Negro Patriot, 1832–1912* (New York: Oxford University Press, 1970), p. 215.

29 Jean-Marc Ela, *My Faith as an African* (Maryknoll, NY: Orbis Books, 1988), p. 126.

30 See Elizabeth Amoah and Mercy Amba Oduyoye, "The Christ for African Women," in Virginia Fabella and Mercy Oduyoye (eds.), *With Passion*

and *Compassion: Third World Women Doing Theology* (Maryknoll, NY: Orbis Books, 1989), pp. 35–46.

31 Edward Fashole-Luke, Richard Gray, Adrian Hastings, and Godwin Tasie (eds.), *Christianity in Independent Africa* (London: Rex Collins, 1978), p. 365.

32 See Emmanuel Chukwudi Eze, "The Color of Reason: The Idea of Race in Kant's Anthropology," in Eze (ed.), *Postcolonial African Philosophy: A Critical Reader* (Cambridge, MA: Blackwell Publishing, 1997), p. 121.

33 See Emmanuel Chukwudi Eze (ed.), *Race and the Enlightenment: A Reader* (Hoboken, NJ: Wiley-Blackwell, 2008).

34 Martin Luther King, Jr., *Stride toward Freedom: The Montgomery Story* (New York: HarperCollins, 1987), and *Strength to Love* (Minneapolis, MN: Fortress Press, 2010).

35 James H. Cone, *Martin and Malcolm and America: A Dream or a Nightmare?* (Maryknoll, NY: Orbis Books, 1991).

36 Walter Rodney, *How Europe Underdeveloped Africa* (Washington, DC: Howard University Press, 1981).

37 Jean-Marc Ela, *African Cry* (Eugene, OR: Wipf and Stock, 2005), and *My Faith as an African*.

10 Theology's great sin: silence in the face of white supremacy

JAMES H. CONE

Dietrich Bonhoeffer and Martin Luther King, Jr. were two of the most outspoken Christian theologians against injustice and suffering in the twentieth century. Bonhoeffer, a German Lutheran, was hanged in a Nazi prison at Flossenburg in Bavaria, on April 9, 1945. King, an African American Baptist, was assassinated while fighting for garbage workers in Memphis, Tennessee, on April 4, 1968. Both were 39 years old at the time of their deaths. What distinguished Bonhoeffer and King from most theologians was their refusal to keep silent about the great moral issues of their time and situation, and their courage to fight social and political evils in their societies that challenged religious meaning. They opposed Nazi and American racism fiercely – knowing that it would probably lead to their deaths. "When Christ calls a man," Bonhoeffer said, "he bids him come and die."[1] King was just as prophetic and courageous: "If physical death is the price I must pay to free my white brothers and sisters from the permanent death of the spirit, then nothing could be more redemptive."[2] The lives and writings of Bonhoeffer and King tell us far more about what it means to be a Christian and a theologian than all the great tomes in the history of theology. Their martyrdom placed Christian identity at the foot of the Cross of Jesus and in the midst of oppressed people fighting for justice and freedom.

We need more theologians like Bonhoeffer and King – more scholars in religion with the courage to speak out against wrong, especially the evil of white supremacy. No one can deny that racism is a major killer in the modern world. Yet there has been considerable resistance to seeing it as a profound problem for the religion of Christianity. During the course of five centuries, Europeans and white North Americans system-atically confiscated lands and committed genocide against untold numbers of indigenous people around the world. When whites "discovered" something they wanted, whether land or labor, they took it with very little thought of the consequences for the lives of the people already there.

"Can any nation ... discover what belonged to someone else?" asked the seventeenth-century Dutch jurist Hugo Grotius (1583–1645).[3] Few Europeans asked such questions but instead exploited lands and peoples unhindered by philosophy, religion, or ethics. In fact, these disciplines assisted them in justifying their violence as they viewed themselves as God's chosen people to subdue indigenous people and their land. Author Eduardo Galeano claims that 150 years of Spanish and Portuguese colonization in Central and South America reduced the indigenous population from 90 million to 3.3 million.[4] During the twenty-three-year reign of terror of Leopold II of Belgium in the Congo (1885–1908), scholarly estimates suggest that approximately 10 million Congolese met unnatural deaths – "fully half of the territory's population."[5] Then, in one brief moment, the Nazis committed an unspeakable racist crime: the industrialized mass murder of 6 million Jews in Europe.

Physical death is only one aspect of racism that raises serious theological questions. Spiritual death is another, and it is just as destructive, if not more so, for it destroys the soul of both the racists and their victims. Racism is hatred run amok. It is violence against one's spiritual self. Through cultural and religious imperialism, Europeans imposed their racist value system on people of color and thereby forced them to think that the only way to be human and civilized was to be white and Christian. It not only makes the oppressed want to be something other than they are but also to become like their oppressors. Malcolm X called it self-hate – the worst mental sickness imaginable. The poison of white supremacy is so widespread and deeply internalized by its victims that many are unaware of their illness and others often do not have the cultural and intellectual resources to heal their wounded spirits. In my travels around the world, I am amazed at how much people of color want to be white. They want to look like whites, talk like whites, and even pray like whites. Many are still worshipping a white God and a blond-haired, blue-eyed Jesus – still singing, "Wash me and I will be whiter than snow." As James Baldwin put it: "It is a terrible, an inexorable, law that one cannot deny the humanity of another without diminishing one's own: in the face of one's victim, one sees oneself."[6]

We are all bound together, inseparably linked to a common humanity. What we do to one another, we do to ourselves. That was why Martin King was committed absolutely to nonviolence. Anything less, he believed, was self-inflicted violence against one's soul. "Through violence you may murder the hater, but you do not murder hate. In fact, violence increases hate ... It [begets] what it seeks to destroy."[7] King struggled mightily to redeem the soul of America so that people of all colors and religious orientations could create the beloved community.

Racism is particularly alive and well in America. It is America's original sin, and as it is institutionalized at all levels of society, it is its most persistent and intractable evil. Though racism inflicts massive suffering, few American theologians have even bothered to address white supremacy as a moral evil and as a radical contradiction of our humanity and religious identities. White theologians and philosophers write numerous articles and books on theodicy, asking why God permits massive suffering, but they hardly ever mention the horrendous crimes whites have committed against people of color in the modern world. Why do white theologians ignore racism? This is a haunting question – especially since a few white scholars in other disciplines (such as sociology, literature, history, and anthropology) do engage racism. Why not theologians? Shouldn't they be the first to attack this evil?

When I began writing about racism in American theology, the churches, and the society more than forty years ago, I really thought that, after being confronted with the sin of their silence, white theologians would repent and then proceed to incorporate a radical race critique in their theological and religious reflections. Most were sympathetic with the civil rights movement and some even participated in the marches led by Martin Luther King, Jr. Whenever King asked for help, white ministers vacated their pulpits and even a few theologians suspended classes or cut short summer vacations and joined him in the fight for racial justice. Also, the rise of Latin American liberation and feminist theologies and the deepening of the Jewish–Christian dialogue on the Holocaust created a liberating theological atmosphere for a serious and sustained engagement of racism. Some dialogue did occur on race and gender between white feminist and womanist and mujerista theologians. There were also spirited dialogues on race and class among white Latin Americans and people of color in the Ecumenical Association of Third World Theologians (EATWOT). We are all familiar with the many heated exchanges in white churches in the 1960s as blacks created caucuses and called for Black Power and white church people wondered why their black brothers and sisters felt so powerless and angry after the breakdown of segregation in God's house. It took some while for whites to realize that blacks and other people of color did not want to be integrated out of power with a few white-selected colored tokens as window dressing. Even Martin King called for a period of "temporary segregation in order to get to the integrated society."[8]

In contrast to these small but important efforts in the churches and other contexts, white North American and European male theologians hardly ever mentioned the sin of racism in their public lectures and writings during the 1960s and 1970s. They wrote mostly about the "death of God" controversy and the secular spirit that created it. It was as if they were intellectually blind and could not see that white supremacy was America's central *theological* problem. They engaged Latin Americans on class contradictions, talked to feminists about gender issues, and dialogued with Jews about Christianity and anti-Semitism. However, when the time came to talk about theology and racism, they initially could not believe that we had the audacity to engage them in a serious intellectual discussion about theology and its task. What could blacks possibly know about theology? When we refused to be intimidated by their intellectual arrogance, they tried to convince us that race was of secondary importance to class and would be automatically eliminated when justice is achieved in the political economy. When we rejected that view as faulty and racist, they walked away as if we were too emotional and not intelligent enough to understand their sophisticated, theoretical analysis.

Of course, not all white theologians were silent about white supremacy. The late Fred Herzog of Duke University was a prominent exception, and it was not easy for him to critique racism in the white theological establishment. He spoke to me many times about the pain of his isolation and the rejection by his white male colleagues. When Herzog switched his theological focus from race to class, concentrating on Latin American liberation theology, as others such as Robert McAfee Brown and Harvey Cox did, his white colleagues became much more open to engaging his discourse about liberation theology. As long as liberation-talk ignores racial oppression, white religion scholars are much more inclined to take it seriously.

I believe that there are white religion scholars today who are aware that all is not well on the racial front. They know that white supremacy is a horrendous evil that must be destroyed before humanity can create a world free of white arrogance. We may debate strategies for fighting white supremacy but there can be no debate about whether the anti-racist struggle is a worthy and necessary calling for a religious institution and its theology.

Before I get into strategies, it is important to make a distinction between personal prejudices and structural racism. Dealing with people's personal prejudices should not be the major concern. It is emotionally too exhausting and achieves very little in dismantling racism.

I am not very concerned what people think about me as long as their personal prejudices are not institutionalized. The issue is always structural. While I may not get people to like me, it is important that the law prevent them from harming me on the basis of their prejudices.

Before we can get whites to confront racism, we need to know why they avoid it. Why don't white religion scholars write and speak about racism? This is a complex and difficult question because the reasons vary among individuals and groups in different parts of the country. There are probably as many reasons as there are people. I will advance my perspective on this issue and invite whites and people of color to participate with me in an exploration of white silence on racism. We all have some insight into this problem. My reflections focus mainly on white theologians, ministers, and the churches. Hopefully what we say will have meaning for people in other institutions as well.

(1) Most importantly, whites do not talk about racism because they do not have to talk about it. They have most of the power in the world – economic, political, social, cultural, intellectual, and religious. There is little that blacks and other people of color can do to change the power relations in the churches, seminaries, universities, and society. Powerful people do not talk, except on their own terms and almost never at the behest of others. All the powerless can do is to disrupt – make life uncomfortable for the ruling elites. That was why Martin King called the urban riots and the rise of Black Power the "language of the unheard." The quality of white life is hardly ever affected by what blacks think or do. The reverse is not the case. Everything whites think and do impacts profoundly on the lives of blacks on a daily basis. We can never escape white power and its cruelty. That is why blacks are usually open to talking to whites in the hope of relieving their pain but the latter seldom offer a like response, because they perceive little or nothing to gain.

Power corrupts, and as, Lord Acton said, "absolute power corrupts absolutely." When this idea is applied to the relations between whites as a group and people of color, it is possible to get a glimpse of how deeply white supremacy is embedded in the American way of life. "The sinfulness of man," wrote Reinhold Niebuhr, "makes it inevitable that a dominant class, group, and sex [and race should be added here] should seek to define a relationship, which guarantees its dominance, as permanently normative."[9]

How can we destroy white supremacy and create a more just society when whites as a group hold most of the power? The rise of Black Power during the 1960s and 1970s in white churches and other institutions was profoundly alienating, gut-wrenching, and divisive in every segment of our communities. How do whites avoid arbitrary group power or condescending patronage? How do blacks avoid racial essentialism, talking and acting as if biology alone defines truth? Again I quote Niebuhr, but this time on the blindness of the oppressed: "Every victim of injustice makes the mistake of supposing that the sin from which he suffers is a peculiar vice of his oppressor."[10]

That the oppressed are sinners too is a very important point to make but often hard to hear, especially when it is made by the oppressor. The ever-present violence in poor communities is at least partly due to the sins of the oppressed. We must never assume that God is on the side of the oppressed because they are sinless but rather because of God's solidarity with weakness and hurt – the inability of poor people to defend themselves against violent oppressors.

When black liberation theology first appeared the few white theologians who addressed it often quoted Niebuhr to us about the sins of the oppressed. Because I questioned their motives, I quoted Niebuhr back at them. "Socio-economic conditions," wrote Niebuhr, "actually determine to a large degree that some men are tempted to pride and injustice, while others are encouraged to humility. The biblical analysis agrees to the known facts of history. Capitalists are not greater sinners than poor laborers by any natural depravity. But it is a fact that those who hold great economic and political power are more guilty of pride against God and of injustice against the weak than those who lack power and prestige ... White men sin against Negroes in Africa and America more than Negroes sin against white men."[11]

(2) White theologians avoid racial dialogue because talk about white supremacy arouses deep feelings of guilt. Guilt is a heavy burden to bear. Most Americans have at least a general idea of the terrible history of white supremacy, and that alone can create a profound guilt when blacks and others tell their stories of suffering and pain. Whites know that they have reaped the material harvest of white domination in the modern world. The material wealth of Europe and North America was acquired and enhanced through the systematic exploitation of lands and peoples in Africa, Asia, and North and South America. A critical exploration of the theological meaning of slavery, colonialism, segregation, lynching, and genocide can create a terrible guilt. As Reinhold Niebuhr said: "If ... the white man were to expiate his sins committed against the darker races, few white men would have the right to live."[12]

Whites do not like to think of themselves as evil people or that their place in the world is due to the colonization of Indians, the enslavement of blacks, and the exploitation of people of color here and around the world. Whites like to think of themselves as hard-working, honorable, decent and fair-minded people. They resent being labeled thieves, murderers, slaveholders, and racists. There are whites who say that they do not owe blacks anything because they did not enslave anybody, did not segregate or lynch anybody, and are not white supremacists. They claim to be color-blind and thus treat everybody alike. At an individual level, there is some commonsense truth about that observation. But if you benefit from the past and present injustices committed against blacks, you are partly and indirectly accountable as an American citizen and as a member of the institutions that perpetuate racism. We cannot just embrace what is good about America and ignore the bad. We must accept the responsibility to do everything we can to correct America's past and present wrongs.

(3) Another reason why whites avoid race topics with African Americans is because they do not want to engage black rage. Whites do not mind talking as long as blacks don't get too emotional, too carried away with their stories of hurt. I must admit that it is hard to talk about the legacies of white supremacy and not speak with passion and anger about the long history of black suffering. It is not a pleasant thing to talk about, especially for people of color who have experienced white cruelty. I would not recommend race as a topic of conversation during a relaxed social evening of blacks and whites. Things could get a little heated and spoil a fun evening.

Whites who talk with me about white supremacy need to be informed and sensitive to the common humanity we all share. All I ask of whites is to put themselves in black people's place in this society and the world, and then ask themselves what they would say or do if they were in black people's place. Would you be angry about 246 years of slavery and 100 years of lynching and segregation? What would you say about the incarceration of 1 million of your people in prisons – one half of the penal population – while your people represents only 12 percent of the US census? Would you get angry if your racial group used 13 percent of the drugs but did 74 percent of the prison time for simple possession?[13] Would you caution the oppressed in your community to speak about their pain with calm and patience? What would you say about your sons who are shot dead by the police because their color alone makes them prime criminal suspects? What would you say about ministers and theologians who preach and teach about justice and love but ignore the sociopolitical oppression of your people? Black anger upsets only whites who choose to ignore catastrophic black suffering.

But even whites who acknowledge black suffering often insist that we talk about our pain with appropriate civility and restrained emotions. That was why they preferred Martin King to Malcolm X. Malcolm spoke with too much rage for their social taste. He made whites feel uncomfortable because he confronted them with their terrible crimes against black humanity. Addressing the question about whether he spoke with too much emotion, Malcolm responded:

> When a man is hanging on a tree and he cries out, should he cry out unemotionally? When a man is sitting on a hot stove and he tells you how it feels to be there, is he supposed to speak without emotions? This is what you tell black people in this country when they begin to cry out against the injustices they're suffering. As long as they describe these injustices in a way that makes you believe you have another 100 years to rectify the situation, then you don't call that emotion. But when a man is on a hot stove, he says, "I'm coming up. I'm getting up. Violently or nonviolently doesn't even enter the picture – I'm coming up you understand."[14]

Malcolm called his style telling the "naked truth" about the white man. He knew whites did not like to hear blunt truth. "I love to talk about them," he proclaimed to a Harlem rally. "Talk about them like dogs. And they should be able to take it. Now they know how we feel. Why, when I was a little boy they called me nigger so much I thought that was my name."[15] Malcolm believed that whites needed to know how blacks really felt, and he did not think that civil rights leaders like King were forthcoming in this regard. They were too compromising. They sugarcoated the truth so whites would not feel so bad about what they did to us. When Malcolm felt that black leaders were letting whites off the hook, he turned his anger on them and accused them of making it easy for whites because they cared more about white emotional comfort than the suffering of the black poor.

Because the spirit and language of black liberation theology was closer to Malcolm than Martin, white theologians were reluctant to engage us. They got nervous and made their way for the exit every time a militant black theologian came near them. I must admit I was pretty hard on them and that partly accounts for their silence. But I was not going to pamper privileged whites. How could our relationship be comfortable and easygoing, lovey-dovey, when black people were dying in the streets? They still are!

Blacks invoking the race card also make whites uncomfortable. I must admit that blacks sometimes play the race card in inappropriate times and places. It is a quick conversation stopper. But whites should remember that blacks have the race card to play because America dealt it to them. It is not a card that we wanted.

When blacks play the race card, it is often a desperate attempt to get whites to listen to them and to take their suffering seriously. Racism is a highly charged subject for blacks – similar to the strong reactions anti-Semitism generates among Jews. White Americans have some empathy for Jewish suffering. That is why the USA supports Israel and built a huge Holocaust Museum in Washington, DC. Whites do not have a similar empathy for black suffering, even though our suffering is much closer to home. That is why there is no slavery museum in Washington and no reparations forthcoming for two and a half centuries of slavery and a century of Jim Crow segregation and lynching. Such thoughts are anathema to most white Americans. When America is forced to consider black suffering, whites advance all kinds of technical and legal reasons to dismiss doing anything about the crimes committed against black people.

Consider the insightful comment of Pamela A. Hairston of Washington, DC, responding in a letter to the *Christian Century* on the issue of reparations for African Americans:

> With the Homestead Act of 1862, Congress gave away more than 270 million acres of land to more than 2 million white Americans – 160 acres per person or family, free. This was enacted on January 1, 1863, the same day President Lincoln signed the Emancipation Proclamation. Another such act, the Southern Homestead Act, granted ex-slaves or freed men 40 acres, and some ex-slaves did receive a few acres, which were later given back to the Confederates. The ex-slaves were evicted. America preferred to keep the ex-slaves as sharecroppers.
>
> After 200-plus years of inhumane slavery and hard free labor they gave my ancestors nothing but 100-plus more years of hate, black codes, Jim Crow laws, the Klan, lynchings, poverty, oppression, segregation, and fear. Wouldn't black America – no, America as a whole – be a better nation if they had given the 40 acres as promised? Right now, I'd take an acre and a chicken.[16]

With this terrible history, why is it so difficult to get white people to acknowledge what America owes to black people?

We all benefit and suffer from what happened in the past and we owe it to ourselves to learn from the good and to correct the bad. We cannot survive as a nation with huge economic divisions between rich and poor, deep social alienation between whites and people of color. We are one people. What happens to one happens to all. So, even if we are not directly responsible for past injustices, we are responsible for the present exploitation. It is our responsibility to create a new future for all. We need to ask what kind of society we want. Do we want a society that puts more blacks in prisons than in colleges? We are all responsible for this world, and as human beings, we will have to give an account of what we said and didn't say, what we did and didn't do about justice for all.

Whites and blacks must learn to work together. Our future depends on it. But that can never happen creatively until whites truly believe that their humanity is at stake in the struggle for racial justice. Speaking on behalf of Jews, Rabbi Joachim Prinz, then President of American Jewish Congress, expressed this point eloquently at the 1963 March on Washington: "It is not merely sympathy and compassion for the black people of America that motivates us, it is above all and beyond all such sympathies and emotions a sense of complete identification and solidarity born of our own painful historic experiences."[17] There are few whites who really know how to express that sort of solidarity.

(4) Whites do not say much about racial justice because they are not prepared for a radical redistribution of wealth and power. No group gives up power freely. Power must be taken against the will of those who have it. Fighting white supremacy means dismantling white privilege in the society, the churches, and in theology. Progressive whites do not mind talking as long as it doesn't cost much, as long as the structures of power remain intact.

Although white Christians and other religious communities acknowledge their sinful condition and that their inordinate power as a group makes them more prone toward injustice in relation to other minority groups, they find it nearly impossible to do anything to relinquish their advantage. Individuals are often self-critical but groups are inevitably selfish and proud. No theologian has been more insightful on this point than Reinhold Niebuhr: "The group is more arrogant, hypocritical, self-centered and more ruthless in the pursuit of its ends than the individual ... If we did for ourselves what we do for our country, what rascals we would be."[18]

When and how should whites break their silence? There are many whites who want to effect change but do not know when and how to do it. There are a few white theologians who want to break silence and do something about bringing more justice and love in America and the world.

I urge white theologians, ministers, and other morally concerned persons to break their silence immediately and continuously. It is immoral to see evil and not fight it. As Rabbi Prinz put it: "Bigotry and hatred are not the most urgent problems. The most urgent, the most disgraceful, the most shameful and most tragic problem is silence." Theologians and ministers, churches, synagogues, and associations must not remain onlookers, – that is, "silent in the face of hate, in the face of brutality, and in the face of mass murder."[19] We must speak out loud and clear against the evil of racism, not for the sake of the black poor but for ourselves, for our churches and theologies, for America and the world, and most of all for humanity.

Talking about how to destroy white supremacy is a daily task and not just for consultations and conferences. If we only talk about white supremacy at special occasions set aside for that, the problem will never be solved. Blacks do not have the luxury of just dealing with racism in church meetings or academic settings. If that were true, it would not be so bad. No day passes in which blacks don't have to deal with white supremacy. It is found everywhere – in the churches, seminaries, publishing houses, in government, and all around the world. There is no escape. If whites get tired of talking about race, just imagine how exhausted people of color must feel.

The development of a hard-hitting antiracist theology by white religion scholars is long overdue. What would an antiracist theology look like? It would be first a theology that comes out of an antiracist political struggle. Talk is cheap if there is no action to back it up. We must do something concrete about dismantling white supremacy. I know this task is not easy, but a very difficult endeavor. Yet, do not be discouraged. Despair only supports the enemy. Working together with each other and with the Great Spirit of the universe, we can accomplish more than we ever dreamed. I want to commend people who are fighting structural racism. Keep working at it, "don't get weary," as the black spiritual says, "there is a great camp meeting in the Promised Land." That song is not primarily about the geography of heaven but rather a message of hope in dire circumstances. Blacks, with their backs against the wall of slavery, were saying that evil will not have the last word about their humanity. We have a future not made with white hands.

Begin the antiracist struggle where you are. If you are in the churches, get together with other committed persons and analyze ecclesiastical structures and disclose how they reinforce racism. If you are in a seminary, university, or college, start there and connect your struggle with others. If you are in a publishing house, start talking with those who are interested in making it more inclusive of people of color. While it is useful to bring in outside resource persons to assist you, there is no substitution for hard work. Work at a pace as if you were going to do it for the rest of your life. There is joy in justice work because it enhances your humanity. Justice work in any situation is the most satisfying activity one can do. I just love it and would not take anything for the opportunity to be involved in it. If you do not love racial justice work, then do not do it. We need and want people who are human beings first – which means taking the same risks for the stranger that they take for their own kind.

One of the most important things whites can do in fighting white supremacy is to support black empowerment in society, church, and theology. Black empowerment is blacks thinking, speaking, and doing for themselves. The black church and black liberation theology are black empowerment in religion.

To create an antiracist theology, white theologians must engage the histories, cultures, and theologies of people of color. It is not enough to condemn white supremacy. The voices of people of color must be found in your theology. You do not have to agree with their perspectives but you do have to understand them and incorporate their meanings in your theological discourse. This is what white theologians almost never do. There are almost no references to black scholars or other people of color in any of the writings of major white male theologians. Even when white theologians talk about race, as Reinhold Niebuhr did occasionally throughout his career, there are no citations from black intellectuals who informed his thinking. How can anybody write about race in an informed way and not engage the writings of W. E. B. DuBois, Zora Neale Hurston, Ida B. Wells-Barnett, Richard Wright, James Baldwin, and Howard Thurman?

In America, we have a lot of racist theologies. Let us hope that white theologians, ministers, and other concerned human beings will end their silence about the evil consequences of racism so they can join people of color in their fight against white supremacy and connect the struggles in the USA with the fight for justice around the world. "What we all want," proclaimed W. E. B. DuBois, "is a decent world, where a [person] does not have to have a white skin to be recognized as a [human being]."[20]

Notes

1   Dietrich Bonhoeffer, *The Cost of Christian Discipleship*, 2nd edn. (New York: Macmillan, 1959), p. 79.

2 Cited in James H. Cone, *Martin and Malcolm and America: A Dream or a Nightmare?* (Maryknoll, NY: Orbis Books, 1991), p. 315.
3 Cited in Peter Linebaugh and Marcus Rediker, *The Many-Headed Hydra: Sailors, Slaves, Commoners, and the Hidden History of the Revolutionary Atlantic* (Boston, MA: Beacon, 2000), p. 17.
4 Eduardo Galeano, *Open Veins of Latin America: Five Centuries of the Pillage of a Continent* (London: Monthly Review Press, 1973), p. 50.
5 See Adam Hochschild, "Hearts of Darkness: Adventures of the Slave Trade," *San Francisco Examiner Magazine*, August 16, 1998, p. 13. This essay is an excerpt from his excellent book, *King Leopold's Ghosts: A Story of Greed, Terror, and Heroism in Colonial Africa* (New York: Houghton Mifflin, 1998). Louis Turner estimates that 5 to 8 million were killed in the Congo. See his *Multinational Companies and the Third World* (New York: Hill and Wang, 1973), p. 27.
6 James Baldwin, *Nobody Knows My Name* (New York: Dell, 1967), p. 66.
7 Martin Luther King, Jr., *Where Do We Go from Here? Chaos or Community* (Boston, MA: Beacon, 1967), p. 62.
8 Martin Luther King, Jr., "Conversation with Martin Luther King," *Conservative Judaism* 22(3) (Spring 1968): 8.
9 Reinhold Niebuhr, *The Nature and Destiny of Man: A Christian Interpretation*, vol. 1 (New York: Charles Scribner's Sons, 1941), p. 282.
10 Ibid., p. 226.
11 Ibid., pp. 225, 226.
12 Reinhold Niebuhr, "The Assurance of Grace," in *The Essential Reinhold Niebuhr: Selected Essays and Addresses*, ed. Robert M. Brown (New Haven, CT: Yale University Press, 1986), p. 65.
13 See *World: The Journal of the Unitarian Universalist Association* 14(2) (March/April 2000): 61.
14 Cited in Peter Goldman, "Malcolm X: Witness for the Prosecution," in John Hope Franklin and August Meier (eds.), *Black Leaders of the Twentieth Century* (Urbana, IL: University of Illinois Press, 1982), p. 315.
15 Malcolm X, "Unity Rally Speech," Harlem, NY, August 10, 1963.
16 See "Letters: Acts of Reparation," *Christian Century* (December 6, 2000): 1283.
17 Rabbi Joachim Prinz at the March on Washington, cited in *New York Times* (August 29, 1963): 21.
18 Niebuhr, *Nature and Destiny of Man*, pp. 208, 209.
19 Cited in *New York Times* (August 29, 1963): 21.
20 Cited in David Levering Lewis, *W. E. B. DuBois: The Fight for Equality and the American Century, 1919–1963* (New York: Henry Holt & Co., 2000), p. 543.

11 Theodicy: "De Lawd knowed how it was." Black theology and black suffering

ALLAN A. BOESAK

RAISING THE QUESTION IN ENCOUNTER

For black theology it was never just the colossal reality of evil that constituted the problem of theodicy. It was always the fact that the reality of suffering and evil challenged the faith affirmation that God is liberating the oppressed from human captivity.[1] All of the questions ensuing from this fact remain centered on this assumption. In black theology, the point of departure is never a philosophical, theoretical debate – it is always the hard, bitter reality of suffering in the lives of black people, and the belief in God as the God of liberation. The questions, as to whether God is omnipotent and unlimited in goodness, and why God does not destroy the powers of evil through the establishment of righteousness, are never questions that stand on their own. They are always contextualized and followed by the question: "If God is the One who liberated Israel from Egyptian slavery, who appeared to Jesus as the healer of the sick and the helper of the poor, and who is present today as the Holy Spirit of liberation, then why are black people still living in wretched conditions without the economic and political power to determine their historical destiny?"[2] This is the question that characterizes and particularizes the theodicy issue in black theology.

The Western theological tradition, Cone observes, has approached the question in a way that locates "the problem of suffering either in the logical structure of the rational mind or in the interior depths of the human heart, and thereby negates the praxis of freedom against the structures of injustice and oppression."[3] In contrast to this "spectator approach," the black religious perspective on suffering was created "in the context of the human struggle against slavery and segregation."[4] In the (South) African context one would include colonialism, land dispossession, and apartheid.

The intensity of the question arises not so much in the context of natural disasters such as floods or drought; for people whose ancient religious beliefs were rooted in an unbreakable bond with the earth and the cycles of nature, these mysteries did not make them question God. Illness, infirmities, and death were understood as unavoidable in the passage of life. Such suffering was part of being human in the world, "but it is not the ideal will of God for us."[5] It is the unjust and unjustifiable suffering caused by human cruelty, hatred, and rapaciousness that mystified understanding and nullified acceptance. It is within *that* context that the question about God and suffering was raised. It is within *that* context that people wrestled so intensely with God. It is within *that* context that the biblical stories of slavery, the exodus and the wilderness, the cries for justice in the prophets and the psalms, and the stories of Jesus of Nazareth and his suffering on the Cross made so much sense and caused them to respond with so much faith. As in the Bible, for black Christians it is not a context of intellectual concern about the content of divine justice; it is a context of *encounter* with injustice, violence, and unjustifiable suffering. And it is in *encounter* with God's struggle against injustice and oppression that the answer is sought, and given.[6]

SEEKING RESPONSE IN ENCOUNTER

Black Christian faith does not deny the reality of the presence of evil. Martin Luther King, Jr.'s question is at once rhetorical and paradigmatic: "Is anything more obvious than the presence of evil in the universe?"[7] For King, the question is truly universal; he understands evil "in all its evil dimensions": in truth sacrificed for political self-interest, in "imperialistic nations" crushing other nations with social injustice, in colonialism, racial oppression, and in "calamitous wars."[8] Black theologians from the United States have insisted more upon the specificity of suffering within the context of racist oppression in America.

Understandably, King's more inclusive approach would readily find more appreciation in the black world outside the USA. Black South African theologians too, within the context of apartheid, emphasized the particularity of blackness and black suffering.[9] For black theology as contextual theology this is both unavoidable and necessary. However, inasmuch as black theology claims that justice for black people is necessary "so that justice can be realized for all"[10] and that black people are elected to be Yahweh's "Suffering Servant [who] are called to suffer with and for God in the liberation of humanity,"[11] it claims a universal salvific moment that is crucial and, in my view, entirely legitimate. That means that black theology will have to hold on to these realities: the particularity of black suffering, the recognition of the universal nature of evil, and the universality of the redemption black suffering and struggle with and for God offer the world. Surely Cone cannot mean that this salvific moment is tied to blacks in the USA only. As womanist theology has also made clear, the transnational, transgender and ecumenical reality of black theology demands an inclusionary particularity.

It is true that the question has not been uniformly answered. For some, the answer has long been the accommodation to pain and suffering through acceptance of a theology of passivity as a sign of "subjection to God's will" and proof of "Christian piety," so central and necessary to the world-wide European Christian missionary enterprise during the nineteenth century. But that is exactly the kind of theological understanding that black theology has unmasked, resisted, and replaced, ever since the times of slavery and colonization.

This resistance was not simply resistance to theological constructs. It was a resistance to socioeconomic exploitation, political oppression, human degradation, cultural destruction, to the loss of land, the denial of human rights, and to genocide. But it was also resistance to a concept of God that allowed oppression to continue *in God's name*. The examples from the United States abound[12] – David Walker, Bishop Daniel Payne, Bishop Nathaniel Paul, and so many others – but from South Africa they are less plentiful, more hidden, one reason being the fact that we have very little direct witness in writing from the slaves and the colonized. One has to deduce from court records (where they always appeared as accused, never as witnesses) and the writings of white missionaries or historians of the time, interpreting their words and deeds. The same is true of the Khoi-Khoi and the San, the first nations of South Africa, overrun by European colonizers since 1652 and subjected to genocide and cultural annihilation.

Yet we know that by the end of the eighteenth century Khoi-Khoi preachers, despite sometimes severe persecution, traveled far and wide preaching against slavery and against its acceptance as God's will. They believed that white slave owners did not "own" the Gospel as they claimed, but rather that God was on the side of the oppressed.[13]

Consequently the Khoi-Khoi Christians who followed the prophet and millenarian Khoi leader Jan Paerl into conflict with colonists in resistance to dispossession, exclusion, and oppression,[14] did so consciously, even though they must have known that the odds were enormous, adding "a new dimension to Khoi-Khoi defiance of colonial rule."[15] They, like their spiritual ancestors in the Bible and their counterparts in slave-holding America, sought and found their response to their anguished questions in the encounter with suffering and resistance.

They had not the luxury of or the inclination for metaphysics, contrasting the "goodness" of God with the "reality" of evil, testing the "ability" or "willingness" of God to abolish evil, in the end drawing conclusions about whether God is "not perfectly good" or not "unlimitedly powerful."[16] Their struggle with God arose within a context of total devastation, total mercilessness, visited upon them by representatives of a totally omnipotent white God. Knox represents this mercilessness well, in asking "Who cares particularly for the Negro, or Hottentot or the Kaffir?" Then, sadly, Knox continues, "Destined by the nature of their race to run, like animals, a certain limited course of existence, it matters little how their extinction is brought about."[17] It is in the encounter with this reality that the question of black suffering and God's justice was raised, as it would be during more than three centuries of colonialism and apartheid. For them too, as for the people of Israel, suffering is real and contradicts the ways in which the people of Israel understand God. And as with Israel, their appeal to God is marked by the painful contradiction that faces all monotheism: it is an appeal to God against God, calling God to account in God's name (see Jer. 15:18; Gen. 18:25; Job 29:12, 14). It is protesting with Job against the doctrine that suffering was the result of sin, punishment for disobedience. After all, the premise of the Job story was that Job was "blameless and upright, one who feared God" (1:1). God knew this. Job knew it too and did not hesitate to remind God of it.

Those of the black Christian faith understood that these words came from people who could stand before God because they stood up for justice and righteousness with God in the world. They cried out, and they *knew* that their cries were not only heard, but were *implanted* by Yahweh, and believed that God heard God's own voice when they called for justice and liberation.

These examples from scripture imply a boldness that can only come from faith, an intimacy that can only come from awe, a strength that can only come from knowing both the depth of immeasurable suffering and of divine commitment to love and justice. What speaks here is not certitude but conviction, conceived not in theoretical speculations but forged in the fires of encounter. It is the essence of black religious experience. So despite suffering and this contradiction, biblical faith continued to insist on the sovereignty of Yahweh's justice and the divine will to establish the divine righteousness in human history.[18]

Black faith has always known that nothing here is taken for granted, as Bishop Daniel Payne has taught us: "I began to question the existence of the Almighty, and to say, if indeed there is a God, does he deal justly? Is he a just God? Is he a holy Being? If so why does he allow a handful of dying men to oppress us?"[19] Similarly, we were taught by John Ntsikana, South Africa's nineteenth-century blind and gifted poet, catechist, and the first African on the subcontinent to compose Christian hymns in African languages:

> Some thoughts till now never spoken
> Make shreds of my innermost being
> And the cares and fortunes of my kin
> still journey with me to the grave.
> I turn my back on the many shams
> that I see from day to day;
> It seems we march to our very grave
> encircled by a smiling Gospel.
> For what is this Gospel?
> And what salvation?
> The shade of a fabulous ghost
> that we try to embrace in vain.[20]

Black people knew all about the struggle with "the shade" of that "fabulous ghost" cast upon us by humiliation, suffering, and death caused by the sinfulness of those who used a "smiling gospel" to justify our pain. The graves Ntsikana speaks of are not metaphorical. He lived and worked during the "Hundred Year War" between the white settlers and the Xhosa. The "shreds" of his "innermost being" are the echoes of the cries of the Psalmist: "How long, O Lord?" (Ps. 13) and "Out of the depths I cry!" (Ps. 130). The "Gospel" Ntsikana had heard was one from which he could derive no understanding, no sharing of the pain, no comfort for his tortured soul, no strength for his standing up against the evil that led his people to their grave. This white Gospel was "the many shams" he saw "from day to day." He knew too that the Gospel he had heard was not real – it was only the "shade" of the real Gospel in which he believed, as he wrote all those wonderful hymns and continued to inspire his followers till the time of his death, suggesting that one is to "Keep a firm hold on the Word of God. Should a rope be thrown round your neck, or a spear pierce your body, or should you be beaten by sticks or struck with stones, don't give way."[21]

Throughout, black Christianity held on to the faith expressed in 1916 by one of South Africa's greatest sons, Sol Plaatjie: "The only thing that stands between us and despair is the thought that Heaven has not yet failed us."[22] The Revd. James Calata, leader of the Cape African Congress in 1938, told his people to hold on to the belief that "the handle that turns the wheels of the universe is in the hand of God" and because of that hand "a new world is about to be begotten."[23] And Chief Albert Luthuli, that greatest of Christian struggle leaders in South Africa, wrote "My own urge, because I am a Christian is to get into the thick of the struggle with other Christians, taking my Christianity with me."[24] Luthuli understood that finding God was to find God in the encounter of suffering and struggle. That understanding was the deepest essence of the legacy he left his people: "The road to freedom is via the Cross."[25]

Three points need to be summarized here. First, the question of suffering, oppression, and divine justice and deliverance was a fundamental question in the black religious experience everywhere. How much the Khoi-Khoi wrestled with the God of their ancestors (whom they called *Tsui//Goab*), we might never know. It is certain, however, that they did wrestle with the God of Jesus Christ whom they came to know through the biblical story. Second, the belief that God is not the cause of their suffering. Suffering is caused by sinful human beings, who, in their oppression of blacks, rebelled against God, and hence lost their claim upon God and denied the very nature of God as a God of justice, love, and liberation. Within their understanding, *they* became the representatives of God in the world. White people did not "own" the Gospel, even as they now owned the land and the people. Third, in contrast with much of Western theology, the question of suffering and the divine response never arose within a philosophical, theoretical framework, but always in encounter with unearned suffering and resistance to injustice and oppression, and therefore in encounter with God's liberating work on behalf of the oppressed.

SUFFERING, DIVINE LOVE, AND DIVINE POWER

Still, for others, William Jones foremost among them, our question has to do with God's unwillingness or inability to deliver the oppressed from injustice and to end their suffering.[26] But, Cone insists, "It is a violation of black faith to weaken either divine love or divine power."[27] However, neither black theology nor womanist theology makes this statement from the view of those in positions of dominance, power, and control. The issue here is not whether the idea of God's omnipotence should be discarded, for the slaves never doubted the power of God even though they understood the presence of evil.[28] They believed that God's presence sustained them in bondage, in the midst of evil. God's sustaining power is known – encountered – in resistance to evil.[29] God's power is shown in God's ability and willingness to share in solidarity of love with the victims of oppression. Blacks remain strong in suffering because God is powerful, and suffered with them. In the words of Zora Neal Hurston's Nanny, "But nuthin' never hurt me, 'cause de Lawd knowed how it was."[30] The Lord knew not just *what* it was, but *how* it was, in solidarity, in grieving, in struggle and resistance.

Black theology makes a distinction between "oppressive" and "redemptive" suffering. Oppressive suffering is not only the suffering inflicted upon blacks, it is the resignation to that suffering without resisting and hence rising above it. Otherwise, suffering becomes "a god … a cult, idolatry … and cannot be endured."[31] Redemptive suffering is suffering for the sake of liberation, for humanity.[32] If suffering makes us stronger, it is not a strength to endure, but to resist.

But it is not just a matter of God's standing in solidarity with us in our suffering and struggle against oppression. It is also, as Dietrich Bonhoeffer teaches us, our "standing with God in the hour of God's grieving."[33] In the pain and suffering of humanity, God is "overcome by grief." It is a grief that makes God "bear all sin and pain and death," as Bonhoeffer writes in the poem where he first raises this idea.[34] God is overcome by the pain sinful human beings inflict on each other. In their hurt, God is hurt. God is suffering at the hands of a hostile world. The grieving of God is not in the pain of God for God, but in the pain of God in the suffering of humanity. "Grieving with God" – that is the sign of our faith, for this is what it means to be "caught up in the way of Jesus Christ." That means, black theology argues, making choices, not just for the oppressed in their suffering, but also for the oppressed in their struggle against oppression, and that is discipleship. When we fail to stand with those who suffer, we fail to stand with God, because that is precisely where, and *how*, God stands, not just in front of the oppressed, in protection of them; not just alongside in solidarity with their struggle, but in identification with them in their struggle for liberation.

JESUS, THE CROSS, AND THE RESURRECTION

The Cross of Jesus is central to the black Christian understanding of suffering. "On the cross," Cone states, "God's identity with the suffering of the world was complete … The cross of Jesus reveals the extent of God's involvement with the suffering of the weak."[35] Hence, "to Africans, the crucified Jesus is irresistible."[36] Other South Africans agree, as Gerhard Cloete notes, "The cross is the ultimate test of Jesus' love for the oppressed."[37] In the Cross, Tokatso Mofokeng asserts, black people see the identification of Jesus with themselves, between his suffering and theirs, as they relive his painful narrative at the hands of "white evil forces."[38]

Mofokeng echoes that hauntingly beautiful, mournful song sung at funeral after funeral during the struggle against apartheid, "*Senzenina*": "What have we done ... what have we done ... Our only sin is the colour of our skin." For this reason, Mofokeng argues, the resurrection is more distant for black believers, it "falls outside the sphere of life experience of the average black Christian who takes concrete life seriously and would not want to escape out of it into pietism ... [hence] this event remains a vague and illusive scriptural information and article of the apostolic faith."[39] In fact, "the following of Jesus and his history by the mind ends in paralysis on the cross at Golgotha."[40] Similarly, for Buthelezi, "There are many for whom the whole of life seems to be a long Good Friday."[41] Desmond Tutu, however, reminds us of the significance of the resurrection, as it is there that we can have hope, for "Nothing can be more hopeless than Good Friday; but then Sunday happens."[42]

Desmond Tutu is right, but this is not a flight into pietism as Mofokeng fears. It begins with the acknowledgement of the reality of Good Friday and the overwhelming presence of the *mysterium iniquitatis* – "our bewilderments" – and ends with the recognition of the power and empowering reality of the resurrection. The resurrection of Christ is God's insurrection, God's *apanastasia*, God's rebellion against all sin, inhumanity, death, and destruction. It is God's rebellion against our resignation, our need for compromise with evil, and our tendency toward despair and hopelessness, against our willingness to sell God's dreams for God's people to the highest bidder in the name of "realism." To this point, as I have written elsewhere, "The open tomb is the surest guarantee against the enclosure of our soul, against the imprisonment of our spirit, against the interment of our hopes which, if they remain in the grave of our own lost-ness, will surely and irrevocably be lost."[43] Hence Cone can say that the oppressed mustn't worry over suffering, because of the Cross.[44] The Cross is not the sign of God's violence to Jesus, it is violence visited upon Jesus by the evil powers of this world, who could not abide his challenging, healing, liberating presence in the world. Jesus' death on the Cross was a punishment not from God, but from those in power in the Roman Empire who divined precisely the threat Jesus of Nazareth posed to the empire.[45] This is what Pilate knew as he faced Jesus, as John the Apostle explains (John 18 and 19). The man before Pilate is condemned, yet he is king, albeit unlike all the kings of the world. He is a king without armies and weapons, without the instruments, propaganda, and ritualized deceit without which the emperor could not exist, without the trappings and pretensions of power in order to maintain his hold over others. He is a king, as I have noted in another context, "out of whose sacrificial defencelessness emerges a strength that is the most consistent challenge to the powers of this world."[46] So we are left, now, with the challenge to reconcile the two seemingly disparate events of Cross and resurrection.

It is not necessary to dichotomize the Cross and the resurrection. As it is in Jesus' life, so it is in his death. Jesus "empties himself" into the form of a slave, and it is before the slave that every knee shall bow (Phil. 2:6–11). The Apocalypse understands this well. John sees Jesus as the "lamb that was slain," and it is as the "slain lamb" that Jesus is found worthy to open the scroll (Rev. 5:5), not the Caesar, even though his court poets address him as *princeps principium, summe ducum.* "Worthy" only is the Lamb. He stands "as though slain" but he *stands;* slain, but yet he is Lord. He is Lord in his suffering, not in spite of it. As suffering Lord he is victor over his enemies, and the enemies of the little ones with whom he has identified himself, for he carries their wounds in his body. In their afflictions he is afflicted. In their oppression, he is oppressed. He is risen, but that does not remove him from his people. John recognizes how he still bleeds for and with his people.[47] It is for these reasons that black faith explodes with joy, not of escapism, but through encountering the liberating power of God in the midst of suffering.[48] Their suffering is for the sake of freedom and justice, for the sake of humanity, for the sake of God. In the apartheid struggle we sang not only *Senzenina,* "What have we done," as we mourned, but also *Thuma mina, Nkosi yam'!,* "Send me, Lord!," and therefore we could sing *Akanamandla uSatani!:* "It is broken, the power of Satan is broken, Hallelujah!," as we struggled and went to prison.

BEYOND THE WHITE, RACIST GOD

Finally, in posing and answering our question, Africans cannot simply ask whether God is "a white racist." The devastating presence of evil in Rwanda and Burundi, the Central African Republic, Uganda, and Zimbabwe, for example, has forced the question beyond white racism. It goes beyond the counting of the dead – in a shorter time more than the Jewish dead in the Holocaust.[49] It even goes beyond the mercenary, the merciless soldier, or the power-hungry dictator. It is also about a "soft-spoken, fatherly figure," an "eminent bishop of the church," who provided guns to the soldiers to kill the Tutsi women and children who had taken refuge in the sanctuary of his church after he had lured them in with promises of protection. That was the day, said Father Celestin Hategekimana of Rwanda, "When Satan wore a collar."⁵⁰

In light of these African realities the presence of evil cannot simply be located in God's "white racism." Here, too, we are called to "grieve with God" in the "countless sacrifices by way of the unspeakable suffering imposed on [African people] by their inhuman overlords."⁵¹ These sacrifices have been in vain, says Nigerian theologian Gabriel Abe, benefiting only the Western world and its servants, "the corrupt local rulers supported by the multi-national corporations," but perhaps we could be persuaded "that no more human sacrifices may be tolerated" by a turn to "a remembrance of, and identification with Jesus, the innocent slave, the altruistic priest-diviner, the Suffering Servant."

Notes

1 See, e.g., James H. Cone, *God of the Oppressed*, rev. edn. (Maryknoll, NY: Orbis Books, 1997), p. 150; also Cone, *The Spirituals and the Blues* (New York: Seabury Press, 1972), ch. 4. In this foundational matter, as in others, it is James Cone's brilliance that has led the way in modern black theological thinking.
2 Cone, *God of the Oppressed*, p. 150.
3 Ibid., pp. 163, 164.
4 Ibid., p. 169.
5 See M. M. Makhaye, quoted in Gerrit Brand, *Speaking of a Fabulous Ghost: In Search of Theological Criteria, with Special Reference to the Debate on Salvation in African Christian Theology* (Frankfurt am Main: Peter Lang, 2002), p. 165.
6 Cone, *Spirituals and the Blues*, p. 61.
7 Martin Luther King, Jr., *Strength to Love* (Philadelphia, PA: Fortress Press, 1981; 1st edn. 1963), p. 77.
8 Ibid., pp. 77, 78, 80, 110–11.
9 See, e.g., Basil Moore (ed.), *The Challenge of Black Theology in South Africa* (Atlanta, GA: John Knox Press, 1974); Allan Aubrey Boesak, *Farewell to Innocence: A Socio-Ethical Study on Black Theology and Black Power* (Maryknoll, NY: Orbis Books, 1977); Tokatso Mofokeng, *The Crucified among the Cross-Bearers: Towards a Black Christology* (Kampen: Kok, 1983).
10 Cone, *God of the Oppressed*, p. 159.
11 Ibid., p. 178.
12 Ibid., pp. 169–78 ("Suffering in the Black Religious Tradition"), and especially the references to Benjamin E. Mays, *The Negro's God* (Boston, MA: Chapman and Grimes, 1938), and Carter G. Woodson,

Negro Orators and Their Orations (New York: Russell and Russell, 1969).

13 Raymond Beddy, *Inleiding tot die Geskiedenis van die Khoikhoi en San as Afrikane, vanaf die evolusionere ontstaan in Noord-Afrika tot die hede in Suid Afrika* (Bloemfontein, South Africa: Handisa Media, 2007), p. 48.

14 Russel Viljoen, *Jan Paerl, a Khoikhoi in Cape Colonial Society 1761–1851* (Leiden: Brill, 2006), pp. 42–47.

15 Ibid., p. 45.

16 Cf. John Hick, *Evil and the God of Love* (New York: Harper & Row, 1996), p. 5, quoted in Cone, *God of the Oppressed*, p. 165

17 See the nineteenth-century British scientist Robert Knox, *The Races of Mankind: A Philosophical Inquiry into the Influence of Race over the Destinies of Nations*, quoted in Bernard Magubane, "The African Renaissance in Historical Perspective," in Malegapuru William Makgoba (ed.), *African Renaissance* (Cape Town, South Africa: Tafelberg; Sandton, South Africa: Mafube Publishing, 1992), p. 26.

18 Cone, *God of the Oppressed*, p. 153.

19 Ibid., p. 173.

20 Quoted in Allan Boesak, *The Tenderness of Conscience: African Renaissance and the Spirituality of Politics* (Stellenbosch, South Africa: Sun Press, 2005), p. 136.

21 Cited in *The Dictionary of African Christian Biography*, from Frederick Quinn, *African Saints: Saints, Martyrs and Holy People* (New York: Crossroad, 2002), www.dacb.org/storiessouthafrica/ntsikana.

22 See Tom Karis and Gwendolyn M. Carter (eds.), *From Protest to Challenge: A Documentary History of African Politics in South Africa*, vol. i, *1882–1934* (Stanford University Press, 1972), p. 137, quoted in Boesak, *Tenderness of Conscience*, pp. 126, 127.

23 Tom Karis and Gwendolyn M. Carter (eds.), *From Protest to Challenge: A Documentary History of African Politics in South Africa*, vol. ii, *1935–1952* (Stanford University Press, 1973), p. 332; Boesak, *Tenderness of Conscience*, p. 131.

24 Albert Luthuli, *Let My People Go! The Autobiography of Albert Luthuli* (Cape Town, South Africa: Tafelberg; Sandton, South Africa: Mafube Publishing, 2004; 1st edn. 1960), p. 148; see Boesak, *Tenderness of Conscience*, pp. 111, 112.

25 See Karis and Carter (eds.), *Protest to Challenge*, vol. ii, p. 488; Boesak, *Tenderness of Conscience*, p. 111.

26 See, e.g., William Jones, *Is God a White Racist?* (Garden City, NY: Anchor Books/Doubleday, 1973); Anthony B. Pinn, *Why, Lord? Suffering and Evil in Black Theology* (New York: Continuum, 1995). Space does not allow us to enter into Jones' important argument. Readers are referred to his writings and Cone's response in *God of the Oppressed*.

27 Cone, *God of the Oppressed*, p. 150.

28 Cf., e.g., Julie Hopkins, on the "mystery" of God's "abdication" of power in "sharing with the victim (on the Cross) in solidarity of suffering and grief." *Towards a Feminist Christology: Jesus of Nazareth, European*

Women, and the Christological Crisis (Grand Rapids, MI: Eerdmans, 1995), quoted in J. Denny Weaver, *The Nonviolent Atonement* (Grand Rapids, MI: Eerdmans, 2001), pp. 134–37. See also Catherine Keller, in a different context but making the same point, "Omnipotence and Preemption," in David Ray Griffin, John B. Cobb, Richard A. Falk, and Catherine Keller (eds.), *The American Empire and the Commonwealth of God: A Political, Economic, Religious Statement* (Louisville, MO: Westminster John Knox Press, 2006), pp. 123–36. "A womanist ethic rejects suffering as God's will and believes that it is an outrage that there is suffering at all ... A womanist ethic must be dedicated to eliminating suffering on the grounds that its removal is God's redeeming purpose;" see Emilie M. Townes, "Living in the New Jerusalem," in Townes (ed.), *A Troubling in My Soul: Womanist Perspectives on Evil and Suffering* (Maryknoll, NY: Orbis Books, 1993), pp. 83, 84.

29   See Weaver, *Nonviolent Atonement*, pp. 168–70.

30   See Katie G. Cannon, *Black Womanist Ethics* (Eugene, OR: Wipf and Stock, 1988), p. 133.

31   Cf. Manas Buthelezi, "Daring to Live for Christ," *Journal of Theology for Southern Africa* 11 (July 1975): 7–10.

32   Ibid. See also Cone, *God of the Oppressed*, and Mofokeng, *Crucified among the Cross-Bearers*. There is no contradiction, in my view, with Martin Luther King, Jr.'s idea of "redemptive suffering." For him, too, "redemptive" suffering is "unearned suffering," but that suffering is suffering in the cause of justice, inflicted while resisting the forces of evil.

33   *Dietrich Bonhoeffer Werke*, vol. VIII (Gütersloh: Kaiser, 1998), pp. 515–16. See also Allan Boesak, "To Stand Where God Stands: Reflections on the Confession of Belhar after 25 Years," *Studia Historiae Ecclesiasticae* 34(1) (July 2008): 161–62.

34   *Bonhoeffer Werke*, VIII, pp. 515–16; see also "Christians Stand by God," in John W. Matthews, *Anxious Souls Will Ask ...: The Christ-Centered Spirituality of Dietrich Bonhoeffer* (Grand Rapids, MI: Eerdmans, 2005), p. 17.

35   Cone, *God of the Oppressed*, p. 161.

36   Gabriel M. Setiloane, "I Am an African," *Risk* 9(3).

37   G. D. Cloete, *Hemelse Solidariteit* (Kampen: Kok, 1981), p. 91.

38   Mofokeng, *Crucified among the Cross-Bearers*, p. 28.

39   Ibid., p. 29.

40   Ibid.

41   Manas Buthelezi, "Violence and the Cross in South Africa," *Journal of Theology for Southern Africa* 29 (December 1979): 51–55, at p. 52, quoted by Mofokeng, *Crucified among the Cross-Bearers*, p. 41. One can question whether Buthelezi really supports Mofokeng's contention. Buthelezi is addressing the Cross in the context of violence in South Africa, asking whether the Cross either justifies or permits the violence done to blacks, from whom it seems to be expected to believe this through their faith in Jesus and the meaning of his death: "It is not the violence of the cross that saved us," Buthelezi argues here, "but the love

of God that endured it [i.e., the violence]": "Violence and the Cross," p. 52.

42 Quoted in Jim Wallis and Joyce Hollyday (eds.), *Crucible of Fire: The Church Confronts Apartheid* (Maryknoll, NY: Orbis Books, 1989). See also Boesak, *Tenderness of Conscience*, pp. 128, 129. On the *mysterium iniquitatis* see also Allan Aubrey Boesak, *Comfort and Protest: The Apocalypse from a South African Perspective* (Philadelphia, PA: Westminster Press, 1987), pp. 117ff.; on the resurrection, see p. 58.

43 Boesak, *Tenderness of Conscience*, p. 129.

44 Cone, *God of the Oppressed*, p. 161.

45 See Boesak, *Comfort and Protest*, 1987. See also, e.g., Joerg Rieger, *Christ and Empire: From Paul to Postcolonial Times* (Minneapolis, MN: Fortress Press, 2007); Carter Warren, *Matthew and Empire: Initial Explorations* (Harrisburg, PA: Trinity International Press, 2001); Richard Horsley (ed.), *Paul and Empire: Religion and Power in Roman Imperial Society* (Harrisburg, PA: Trinity International Press, 1997); Richard Horsley (ed.), *Paul and Politics: Ekklesia, Israel, Imperium, Interpretation* (Harrisburg, PA: Trinity International Press, 2000).

46 Boesak, *Comfort and Protest*, p. 57.

47 Ibid., pp. 58, 59.

48 On the joy of the oppressed in their suffering, see Cone, *God of the Oppressed*, pp. 165f., and Cone, *Spirituals and the Blues*, ch. 4.

49 "The most efficient mass killing since Hiroshima and Nagasaki," says Philip Gourevitch, quoted in Jacques Pauw, *Dances with Devils: A Journalist's Search for Truth* (Cape Town, South Africa: Zebra Press, 2006), p. 65. This is not to ignore the point of William R. Jones' book nor his argument about the "three essential elements" of black suffering, namely its "maldistribution," its "enormity," and its "trans-generational" nature. See William R. Jones, "Theodicy: The Controlling Category for Black Theology," quoted by Clarice J. Martin, "Black Women's Spiritual Autobiography," in Townes (ed.), *Troubling in My Soul*, p. 22. It is simply to caution against either linking this to God's "racism" or ignoring the destructiveness of human sinfulness wherever or in whomever it may exhibit itself. Evil does not always wear a white face. Locating the atrocities and suffering visited upon African people across the continent over the last thirty years or so in God's "racism" would as surely disempower Africans to resist the evil in their midst and change the conditions of their ongoing oppression.

50 Pauw, *Dances with Devils*, p. 105. The accounts of Pauw and Immaculée Ilibagiza, *Left to Tell: Discerning God amidst the Rwandan Holocaust* (Carlsbad, CA: Hay House Inc., 2006) make devastating reading.

51 Gabriel Abe, "Redemption, Reconciliation, Propitiation: Salvation Terms in an African Milieu," *Journal of Theology for Southern Africa* 95 (1996): 3–12, quoted in Brand, *Speaking of a Fabulous Ghost*, p. 179.

12 Black theology and the Bible

MICHAEL JOSEPH BROWN

BLACK THEOLOGY'S DOCTRINE OF SCRIPTURE

Black theology views the biblical witness as one of its sources. By this it means that the Bible provides access to the divine revelation; but black theology does not equate the Bible with full divine self-disclosure. Rather it focuses on those themes within the biblical corpus that promote liberation and affirm the personhood of individuals of African descent. Thus, any notion of plenary verbal inspiration in connection with this theological perspective is misguided. In other words, black theology has never claimed to accept the entirety of scripture with its periodically contradictory statements, perspectives, and practices. This allows black theology to avoid some of the thornier issues raised by biblical scholars (and others) regarding the particulars of passages as well as entire books within the canon (e.g., the endorsement of slavery in Eph. 6; Col. 3; and 1 Pet. 2).

Following Karl Barth and the so-called neoorthodox position, black theology has adopted in large measure the perspective that the Bible is a powerful and important *witness* to the divine revelation, but that full divine self-disclosure has only occurred in the incarnation of Jesus Christ. Thus, black theology appropriates the biblical corpus in a selective, if not entirely critical, manner.

Using Jesus' sermon in Luke 4:18–19 as its normative hermeneutical lens, black theology advances a reading of scripture that places it in conversation with the contemporary experience of *blackness* among persons of African descent. Of course, it is true that the exodus narrative has functioned centrally in the black theological enterprise. Drawing primarily on the experience of slaves, the exodus narrative forms the symbolic core of much of black theology's eschatological vision. Still, Jesus' sermon in Luke 4 carries functional, if not logical, priority over the exodus narrative when it comes to evaluating, for example, other biblical passages. This is the case, especially since in its classic articulation, black theology (a) places significant emphasis on Jesus as God's embodied self-revelation, and (b) restricts the exodus narrative to the singular theme of liberation.[1] Other texts have been influential as well; most notably, Psalm 68:32 and the theme of exile (see, e.g., Ps. 137).

Since the ministry of Jesus is at the core of black theology's orientation, it may be helpful to "flesh" out how this frame of reference influences this theological perspective, generally, and its appropriation of the Bible, specifically. In contrast to much of traditional evangelical theology, black theology reclaims the full humanity of Jesus – a process Joseph Johnson has dubbed "detheologizing."[2] As he says, "Detheologizing demands that we recover the humanity of Jesus in all of its depth, length, breadth, and height. Jesus was born in a barn, wrapped in a blanket used for sick cattle, and placed in a stall. He died on a city dump outside Jerusalem."[3] Allan Boesak added, "[Jesus] knew what it was to live like a hunted animal."[4] The reason Jesus' humanity needs to be recaptured in its fullness has to do with the theological and, more importantly, social function of the decidedly divinized Jesus of traditional evangelical theology, at least as commonly understood. As Johnson and other black theologians argue, the theologically constructed Jesus of evangelical Christianity is something other than an appropriately historically situated Jesus. The evangelical Jesus is a Janus figure, promoting a positive and empowering pattern of identity formation for Anglo-Americans while simultaneously promoting a negative and subservient pattern of identity formation for African Americans. In this ideological construct, what is noble and courageous about Christian existence is the domain of the white person. What is long-suffering, self-effacing, and meek is the preserve of the black person. Indeed, black theologians recognized the importance of social location in the theological enterprise long before its contemporary prominence.

Detheologizing makes real "the offense of the incarnation."[5] The historical Jesus, black theologians argue, is not the figure portrayed in the popular rhetoric of evangelical Christian preaching and teaching. The historical Jesus was poor. As Boesak poetically argues, "He belonged to a poor dispossessed people, without rights in [his] own land, subjected daily to countless humiliations by foreign oppressors."[6] James Cone points to four characteristics of Jesus' life and ministry that form the historical kernel of the Gospel accounts and demonstrate Jesus' solidarity with the poor and oppressed: (1) the conditions of his birth, (2) his solidarity with sinners through his baptism and his solidarity with God through his temptation, (3) his ministry directed to the poor, and

(4) his death and resurrection as the fulfillment of his campaign for the poor.[7] In short, what black theologians argue is that the historical Jesus was someone intimately acquainted with the symbolic experience of blackness.[8]

Having recontextualized Jesus, the task of interpretation in the mode of black theology is to determine the appropriate hermeneutical prism through which to adjudicate the various canonical texts. Cone makes this approach explicit in his groundbreaking "Biblical Revelation and Social Existence," when he writes, "The hermeneutical principle for an exegesis of the scriptures is the revelation of God in Christ as the liberator of the oppressed from social oppression and to political struggle, wherein the poor recognize that their fight against poverty and injustice is not only consistent with the Gospel but is the Gospel of Jesus Christ."[9] Although this hermeneutical orientation contradicts much of the enterprise of biblical scholarship, as Robert Bennett's essay "Biblical Theology and Black Theology" makes clear, it would be too presumptive to dismiss entirely such an interpretive strategy without appropriate appreciation and scrutiny.[10]

The claims of black theology are not universal, nor are they meant to be. As Cone has argued, the claims of black theology (as with all other theological expressions) are the product(s) of cultural conditions. As such, it is interested language. The same is true of any interpretive claims black theology makes of the Bible. Central to the limited or contextual nature of this theology's assertions is the contingent nature of the experience from which it speaks. Although black theology sees freedom as a strict necessity in metaphysical terms, liberation struggle as a response to oppression is only a conditional necessity. In other words, oppression is the deprivation of freedom. It is not the same as conflict, which is arguably "an inescapable feature of life."[11] By contrast, oppression is metaphysically unnecessary and conditional. It is not a strictly necessary component of the human experience as such. It is rather an artifice, a construct of certain individual and communal patterns of past and repeated behavior that when taken together deprive some in the polity of their ability to self-express in an authentic fashion. The only legitimate and inevitable response to oppression is liberation struggle. In this sense, struggle is a metaphysical necessity because it is a response to the deprivation or compression of freedom. Yet it is not a strict necessity in metaphysical terms, since the elimination of oppression would remove the need for liberation struggle. In short, struggle is necessary only as long as oppression continues to exist.[12] By analogy, the hermeneutical principle of black theology – that the Gospel of liberation *is* the

Gospel of Jesus Christ – is a conditional necessity insofar as it responds to the experience of oppression. It is not a claim to universal truth as commonly understood.

Black theology's approach to reading the Bible is not to wrestle with the text on its own terms (i.e., in the sense of traditional historical-critical biblical scholarship), but to distill from the text that message of liberation that will assist contemporary persons of African descent in their struggle for freedom and experience of blackness. Such a hermeneutical stance is questionable if argued in the context of some European Enlightenment notion of truth. If, however, one takes seriously the recognition, even among contemporary biblical scholars, that disinterestedness in the interpretive enterprise is an epistemological fallacy – that is, the social location of the interpreter does influence her role in the hermeneutical process – then there is a strategic legitimacy to the black theological hermeneutic. In fact, the recognition among biblical scholars that it matters who is asking the questions is consistent with Cone's contextual-dialectical method in that the identity of the interpreter-theologian is of fundamental and exceptional importance when it comes to reading the Bible.[13]

A WOMANIST DOCTRINE OF SCRIPTURE

Black theology is an organic enterprise.[14] It has grown and expanded over time, increasingly including perspectives absent in its initial articulation. The womanist theological perspective represents one of the ways in which this theological orientation has grown. I resisted incorporating it into the above discussion of black theology's doctrine of scripture because I deem them sufficiently different in their approaches and aims to necessitate separate treatment. Others might disagree.

Layli Phillips defines womanism broadly in this fashion:

Womanism is a social change perspective rooted in Black women's and other women of color's everyday experiences and everyday methods of problem solving in everyday spaces, extended to the problem of ending all forms of oppression for all people, restoring the balance between people and the environment/nature, and reconciling human life with the spiritual dimension.[15]

Although womanism is not exclusively gender-based, at least according to Phillips, its connection to gender is the fact that the historically produced matrix characteristic of African American womanhood (race/class/gender) serves as a point of origin for a social perspective that addresses multiple topics and problems. What distinguishes it most from the classic black theological perspective is that womanism aims at the universal. As outlined above, classic black theology posited its statements as contextual, even in the hermeneutical enterprise. By contrast, beginning solidly with herself, "the womanist expands her area of concern into a universal arc of political concern, empathy, and activism."[16] In other words, the womanist voice arises from a concrete appreciation of oneself as a culturally situated being while simultaneously recognizing oneself as part of a common humanness.

In association with the classic black theological perspective, womanism is anti-oppressionist and identifies with liberationist projects of all sorts, supporting the liberation of all human beings from all forms of oppression. Yet it is not as ideologically driven as classical black theology in that it seeks to promote liberation through its appeal to what it calls the vernacular. By this it means "the everyday" – everyday people, living everyday lives, with everyday concerns. It is not only solidarity with non-elites, but, more importantly, a grounded trust in them to envision and accomplish liberation. In two respects it serves as an advancement upon the traditional, largely academic orientation of black theology. First, it recognizes an "underestimated genius for problem solving" among non-elites.[17] Second, it highlights an innate resistance among non-elites to succumb to the structures and strictures of institutions that would and do oppress them.

The goal of womanist social change is commonweal, the state of collective well-being, which, in turn, influences its understanding and use of scripture. Its methods of social transformation cohere around the activities of harmonizing and coordinating, balancing, and healing. Undeniably, relationship is at the center of womanist concerns. Nevertheless, there is in womanist thought the idea that in order to secure and promote the good of all we must first establish our own well-being, a component of healthy individualism largely absent from classic black theology.

Dialogue is at the center of womanist engagement, a form of interaction analogous to the biblical study communities organized in South America and Africa.[18] Here a key metaphor for the enterprise is the kitchen table. It is "an informal woman-centered space where all are welcome and all can participate."[19] At the kitchen table, differences are arbitrated, existential equality is realized and valued, and the reshaping of reality occurs. The goal of such dialogue is not to vanquish or eliminate those who disagree with the (arguably) dominant perspective. It is rather to facilitate authentic life pursuit within the context of commonweal. In this respect it does not advocate or attempt to create "unity." Far too often such attempts and appeals simply meant the suppression or neutralization of difference, an anemic form of political rhetoric whose only appeal is that of expediency.

The kitchen table as a metaphorical location for dialogue in womanism is influenced by the concomitant appeal to the practice of hospitality, a religious praxis that runs throughout the biblical witness. Guests at the table are welcomed and treated in ways that respect their personhood. In fact, hospitality is central to the womanist's ability to manage difference. "Hospitality is a way of acknowledging dignity, offering nurturance, promoting amity, and providing pleasure to foster positive intra- and intergroup relations."[20]

In the kitchen-table metaphor, womanist thinkers draw together several strands of their social-change perspective. The metaphor uniquely represents the womanist concern for commonweal. It is at the kitchen table where we exercise our concern for common nourishment. Resonances can be found here with the Eucharistic table, where not only is everyone fed but also where everyone receives an equal portion. Something similar can be said for how the metaphor incorporates the practice of hospitality.

Likewise, the kitchen table is anti-oppressionist in its basic conception. It brings individuals together around common concerns, such as food, recognizing that all (the privileged and the oppressed) require vital material and immaterial elements, if human flourishing is to occur. Finally, the employment of the kitchen-table metaphor highlights the anti-institutional orientation of the womanist perspective, by which I mean political (i.e., governmental) and corporate (i.e., business) institutions as commonly understood. In many respects, African American women and men have never sat idly by waiting for institutions to provide recognition and assistance in the face of a pressing problem to solve. More importantly, this anti-institutional bias reflects the recognition on the part of womanists that what is at the core of almost all problems is not an institutional structure as much as it is a psychological and/or spiritual one. This yields an approach to biblical interpretation that is universal in the best sense of the term.

The interpretive approach that informs biblical interpretation in the womanist mode is in one sense contextual, although its true aim is universal. It begins with the social location of black women, a hermeneutical move that is decisively contextual. Womanist theologians and biblical scholars extract the values and traditions inherited from their social location as an existentially grounded source for interpretive reflection. This allows them to adopt a critical posture toward the biblical text. From this perspective, they address a world made up of multiple forms of oppression that work simultaneously to marginalize them as well as others. They seek not only to uncover the historical meaning and context of the Bible, but also to name the specific agendas, cultural biases, ideological motivations, and political influences that brought forth the texts in their final form. By unmasking a variety of oppressive structures, including their interrelationships, womanists seek to understand and address the experience of all humanity, most particularly those who are marginalized.

Such an inclusive analysis makes this approach universal in a way that the classic black theology approach to interpretation, as well as others, is not. A womanist reading of scripture allows for a multidimensional engagement and appropriation of the Bible. By ultimately bringing everyone to the kitchen table, it privileges existential concerns, allowing for an interpretive outcome that speaks multidimensionally and yet open-endedly. In doing so, it places the biblical witness in its proper theological context, not privileging the Bible at the expense of human and nonhuman life (the typical evangelical Protestant move), nor disregarding the Bible whenever its statements become "inconvenient" (a move typical of many inside and outside the academy). In solidarity with the classic black theology approach to scripture, the womanist hermeneutic maintains that the social location of the interpreter is of fundamental and exceptional importance, while simultaneously arguing that by bringing everyone to the kitchen table we can develop a theological reading of scripture that speaks "nourishingly" to our common human experience.

PURSUING A LIBERATING HERMENEUTIC

Black theology's pursuit of a liberated and liberating hermeneutic goes back to the beginning of the discipline. It is probably fair to say that while black theology has made considerable use of the African American tradition as a source for its claims, it has been not nearly as effective in using the Bible for the same purposes. Historically, two problems confronted black theologians in their attempts to wed scripture and theological perspective. First, there has been a widespread lack of interest in such liberatory and contextually grounded theologies among mainstream American biblical scholars. Although conceptually based on the Barthian understanding of scripture, which is undeniably conversant with the biblical witness, early black theologians struggled to find confirmation for their perspective in mainstream biblical scholarship. James Cone's "Biblical Revelation and Social Existence" (mentioned above) was a constructive attempt to merge the two. Second, until recently, African American biblical scholars were nearly nonexistent.[21] For black theology, the absence of African American scholars trained in the discipline of biblical interpretation was a critical handicap. Combined, these dual deficiencies denied black theology critical reflection on one of the traditional sources for all Christian theology, the Bible.

With the marked rise in the number of African American biblical scholars over the last half of the twentieth century, black theology has experienced the fruits of a burgeoning wealth of critical biblical interpretation. In its initial phase, the project of African American biblical interpreters was corrective historiography. Looking at the biblical texts through new eyes, these scholars attempted to reclaim the lands and peoples of the Bible for Africa. Relying on an almost distinctively American notion of race, African American biblical scholars challenged the implicit, but dominant, idea that the world of the Bible was a virtual extension of Europe. And although some of their claims were overreaching, these scholars did accomplish the task of "othering" the biblical world. Also of importance to this initial phase of biblical interpretation was its employment of the concept of Afrocentricity, the idea of placing Africa as an ideological construct at the center of biblical investigation. In this initial phase, biblical interpreters served black theology well, providing it with much-needed historical grounding and analysis. In subsequent phases, African American biblical interpreters would challenge black theology's assertion that the Bible is a document consistently advocating liberation.

Subsequent phases of African American biblical interpretation would move away from corrective historiography toward other forms of interpretive engagement. Most notably, biblical interpreters began to focus on the individual reading of the text as a constructor of meaning. This is most evident in the work of scholars published in the last two decades of the twentieth century, as well as the beginning of the twenty-first. The assertion that accompanied such a move among these interpreters was the recognition that any attempt at proposing a liberated and liberating hermeneutic rested more with the reader than with the contents of the Bible itself. By itself, the Bible is a complicated collection of documents lacking one consistent message. This is especially true when it comes to the project of liberation. Certain texts might advocate a concern for the marginalized (i.e., epistemological privilege), but many others do not.

Further, influenced by engagement with biblical scholars from other ethnic backgrounds (e.g., Asian, Latino, African)[22] and the womanist theological project, African American biblical scholars argued increasingly that any form of interpretation amounted to adopting an advocacy position and that any interpretation seeking legitimacy must take into account the pluralistic environment of the United States.

The shift in interpretive engagement from historiography to the social location of the reader, including the recognition that the Bible is inconsistent on the subject of liberation, prompted subversive readings of scripture. Many questioned the religious structures and rhetoric of the Old and New Testaments. Although these scholars remain committed to the task of promoting the liberation and well-being of the marginalized, they consistently advocate caution in the ways readers engage biblical texts. The most radical aspect of this new engagement with scripture, at least for the largest part of African American biblical scholarship, has been its understanding of scripture. Many appear to reject the idea that scripture is *both* authoritative and normative for Christian social existence, at least directly.[23] They question frequently the degree to which the Bible's statements and orientations are to be accepted as normative. In their most recent statements, African American biblical scholars appear to value the Bible as an authoritative document, but they reserve the right to repudiate its normative declarations as well as attempts to force (theological) conformity to a hermeneutical lens, even when that lens is black theology itself.

What African American biblical scholars have accomplished in the closing decades of the last century, as well as in the current one, has been nothing less than remarkable. Not only have they initiated an entirely new hermeneutical program, but they also have ignited a conversation regarding the nature of hermeneutics itself. Although they have successfully challenged much of mainstream biblical scholarship's claim to disinterested interpretation, considerable work remains to be done in this burgeoning field of cultural hermeneutics. Likewise, if these biblical interpreters desire to continue the enterprise of black theology, then much constructive work needs to be accomplished on both sides.

First, African American biblical scholars have yet to provide a coherent account of the type of scholarship they seek to overturn. Although it is clear that these scholars seek to challenge an uncritical acceptance of the historical-critical method (and much of its accompanying theology) as it has been taught in the majority of educational institutions, they have not been clear as to whether there is anything salvageable in the method at all. Second and related, African American hermeneutics appears to be in need of stronger theoretical grounding. The residual reliance of such scholars on the historical-critical perspective highlights the absence of any viable alternative theory of textual interpretation in the enterprise. These scholars have typically ignored black theology's understanding of scripture because, until recently, it was largely anemic (if spoken of at all). Both, it appears, have left almost unexamined the theological categories and orientations that support their inquiries.

Third, African American biblical scholars must revisit the topic of Africans in the biblical world. Such biblical scholarship has moved quickly from corrective historiography to a form of cultural hermeneutics that has virtually ignored the presence of Africans in the text. Africans are depicted in various parts of the Bible, especially the Old Testament, and this alone should stimulate African American scholars to analyze further the ways in which Africans have been portrayed. These scholars have been largely reluctant to offer critique, along with valorization, of the Egyptians and Ethiopians who appear in the biblical narratives. The most noteworthy example from the perspective of black theology may be the exodus narrative. What does it mean for black theology to appropriate as one of its central images of liberation a narrative in which an African people, or at the very least its leader, is portrayed as the enemy of God?

Finally, African American biblical scholars have largely ignored the perspectives of the people at the heart of black theology's concern, marginalized African Americans. Of course, African American biblical interpreters have been and continue to be concerned about the liberation of their people as well as others. Nevertheless, scholarship in this mode has too often been on behalf of individuals in need of liberation rather than from or in conversation with them.[24] A similar critique has been leveled against at least some expressions of black theology as well. Engaging actual communities of interpretation (i.e., churches and so forth) would go a long way toward advancing a liberating hermeneutic, one that stands in stark contrast to the largely fundamentalist and evangelical readings that predominate in many African American religious communities.

BLACK THEOLOGY IN THE WAKE OF THE PURSUIT OF A LIBERATING HERMENEUTIC

Having taken up the gauntlet laid down by black theology, African American interpreters have pursued the liberatory potential available in the scriptures. To the chagrin of its earliest theological advocates, an African American reading of scripture has served to complicate the idea that the Bible is a consistent and reliable source for human liberation. In partial response, black theology has undergone a great deal of internal scrutiny, launching a nearly divisive argument among its proponents.

By destabilizing black theology's initial (and largely uncritical) employment of scripture, African American hermeneutics contributed to a nearly debilitating question that pervades contemporary black theology: What does it mean to be black and Christian?[25] The relationship between the two categories – black and Christian – was simply assumed in the early days of black theology. More recently, black theologians and religious thinkers have placed such a relationship under critical scrutiny. Beginning, arguably, with the work of Charles H. Long, an increasing number of African American religious scholars have challenged the traditionally Christian aspects of the black theological enterprise, including its reliance upon scripture, in favor of exploring in greater depth the "racial-cultural" side.[26] Thinkers such as William Jones,[27] Cornel West,[28] Victor Anderson,[29] Anthony Pinn,[30] Will Coleman,[31] and others have sought to disengage black theology from its moorings in traditional Christian categories and sources, arguing that a thorough grounding in the black religious experience can yield a more authentic account of the Christianity appropriated and maintained by persons of African descent in North America.[32] In fact, Pinn would disengage African Americans from Christianity altogether.

Black theology's relationship to conventional Christianity's sources and traditions has not withered away entirely. Dwight Hopkins has relentlessly sought to answer the question at the center of contemporary black theological reflection. Despite the work of African American biblical scholars, Hopkins defines black theology as "the interplay between the pain of oppression and the promise of liberation found in the Bible, on the one hand, and a similar existence experienced by African Americans and poor people today."[33] In his decision to hold in creative tension the dual tasks of black theology (i.e., the black religious experience and the witness of scripture), Hopkins is followed by David Goatley, whose work brings together the testimony of enslaved blacks and the "Godforsakenness" of the Markan Jesus.[34] J. Kameron Carter argues for an even more explicit connection between black theology and traditional Christian theological reasoning.[35] In other words, the idea that black theology can distill a liberatory hermeneutic from the biblical witness remains a pursuit for many.

Black theology's future understanding and use of scripture may depend largely on its ability to negotiate the American Protestantism from which it was born. Black Catholic theology, for example, has many resources to offer its Protestant counterpart, including a doctrine of scripture that is not beholden to the caricatured and privileged position of *sola scriptura* that pervades a great deal of African American Protestant theological reasoning.[36] African American biblical scholarship can assist in this project by first attending to the issues outlined above. Biblical scholars can further assist in the black theological project by providing these theologians with critical readings of previously unexamined texts that may yield some liberatory content.[37] At present, black theology's use of scripture has been chastened by African American biblical scholarship as well as by criticisms from within its own ranks. For its future, black theologians must take up the challenge to employ scripture in a more sophisticated fashion and defend its use against those who would argue scripture's virtual theological irrelevance to the African American Christian experience.

Notes

1   For a critique of this restricted understanding of the exodus narrative, see Cheryl A. Kirk-Duggan, "Let My People Go! Threads of Exodus in African American Narratives," in Randall C. Bailey (ed.), *Yet with a Steady Beat: Contemporary U. S. Afrocentric Biblical Interpretation*, Society of Biblical Literature, Semeia Studies 42 (Atlanta, GA: Society of Biblical Literature, 2003), pp. 123–43.
2   Joseph A. Johnson, "Jesus, the Liberator," in James H. Cone and Gayraud S. Wilmore (eds.), *Black Theology: A Documentary History*, vol. I, *1966–1979*, 2nd edn. (Maryknoll, NY: Orbis Books, 1993), pp. 203–13, at p. 208.
3   Ibid.
4   Allan Boesak, "The Courage to be Black," in Cone and Wilmore (eds.), *Black Theology: A Documentary History*, vol. I, pp. 193–202, at p. 197.
5   Johnson, "Jesus, the Liberator," p. 209.
6   Boesak, "The Courage to be Black," p. 197.
7   James H. Cone, *A Black Theology of Liberation: Twentieth Anniversary Edition* (Maryknoll, NY: Orbis Books, 1990), p. 210; and outlined in Edward Antonio, "Black Theology," in Christopher Rowland (ed.), *The Cambridge Companion to Liberation Theology* (Cambridge University Press, 1999), pp. 63–88, at p. 82.
8   For a critique of ontological blackness, see Victor Anderson, *Beyond Ontological Blackness: An Essay on African American Religious and Cultural Criticism* (New York: Continuum, 1995).
9   James H. Cone, "Biblical Revelation and Social Existence," in Cone and Wilmore (eds.), *Black Theology: A Documentary History*, vol. I, pp. 159–76, at p. 174.

10 See Robert A. Bennett, "Biblical Theology and Black Theology," in Cone and Wilmore (eds.), *Black Theology: A Documentary History*, vol. 1, pp. 177–92.

11 Theodore Walker, Jr., *Mothership Connections: A Black Atlantic Synthesis of Neoclassical Metaphysics and Black Theology*, ed. David Ray Griffin. SUNY Series in Constructive Postmodern Thought (Albany, NY: State University of New York Press, 2004), p. 49.

12 In my articulation of black theology's understanding of liberation struggle, I am indebted to and draw heavily upon the work of Theodore Walker, Jr. See his *Mothership Connections*, pp. 48–51.

13 For an interesting discussion of James Cone's "hermeneutic of language" and how it influences the black theological reading of scripture, see Diana L. Hayes, "James Cone's Hermeneutic of Language and Black Theology," *Theological Studies* 61 (2000): 609–31.

14 As will become apparent in the following discussion, I resisted entitling this section "The Womanist Doctrine of Scripture" because of the decidedly nonideological character of the enterprise. Since womanist thought works hard to overcome rigid lines of intellectual demarcation (e.g., through the kitchen-table metaphor mentioned in the following section), it appeared misrepresentative to me to portray this section as the definitive statement on womanist biblical interpretation.

15 Layli Phillips, "Introduction," in Phillips (ed.), *The Womanist Reader* (New York: Routledge, 2006), p. xx. In framing my discussion of womanism, I draw deeply upon the articulation of the enterprise advanced by Phillips. Her work in this area has been instructive to me, and I believe her general overview of the enterprise grounds the discussion, even in its theological expression, appropriately. An article from a womanist theologian addressing a scriptural passage one may want to consider is Jacquelyn Grant, "Womanist Jesus and the Mutual Struggle for Liberation and on Containing God (Matthew 17:1–5 with special emphasis on Matthew 17:4)," *Journal of the Interdenominational Theological Center* 31 (2003–4): 3–33.

16 Phillips, "Introduction," p. xxiii.

17 Ibid., p. xxix.

18 For more information on these communities and their engagement with the Bible, see Michael Joseph Brown, *Blackening of the Bible: The Aims of African American Biblical Scholarship*. African American Religious Thought and Life (Harrisburg, PA: Trinity International Press, 2004), pp. 7–16.

19 Phillips, "Introduction," p. xxvii.

20 Ibid., p. xxviii.

21 This is not to suggest to the reader that the number of African American biblical scholars approaches anything similar to, say, their proportion of the overall American population. However, positive change has occurred. See Brown, *Blackening of the Bible*, pp. 19–20, for further discussion of this issue.

22 Fernando F. Segovia, *Decolonizing Biblical Studies: A View from the Margins* (Maryknoll, NY: Orbis Books, 2000); Tat-Siong Benny Liew,

What Is Asian American Biblical Hermeneutics: Reading the New Testament (Honolulu, HI: University of Hawaii Press, 2008).

23   See Brown, *Blackening of the Bible*, especially pp. 120–52.

24   A clear exception to this statement is the recent publication of Brian K. Blount, Cain Hope Felder, Clarice J. Martin, and Emerson B. Powery (eds.), *True to Our Native Land: An African American New Testament Commentary* (Minneapolis, MN: Fortress Press, 2007). At the time of this writing, the book has only been out for less than a year, and it is still difficult to determine its effect among African American religious communities.

25   This is the question pursued by Dwight N. Hopkins in three of his latest works, *Introducing Black Theology of Liberation* (Maryknoll, NY: Orbis Books, 1999); *Down, Up, and Over: Slave Religion and Black Theology* (Minneapolis, MN: Fortress Press, 1999); and *Heart and Head: Black Theology – Past, Present, and Future* (New York: Palgrave Macmillan, 2002). Hopkins' work in these books is outlined and critiqued in an article by J. Kameron Carter, "Contemporary Black Theology: A Review Essay," *Modern Theology* 19 (2003): 117–38. For another overview of the contemporary state of black theology, see Dwight N. Hopkins and Linda E. Thomas, "Black Theology U.S.A. Revisited," *Journal of Theology for Southern Africa* 100 (1998): 61–85.

26   Carter, "Contemporary Black Theology," p. 121. For an exploration of the importance of culture to the black theological enterprise with an attempt at conceptual clarity, see Dwight N. Hopkins, "Black Theology: The Notion of Culture Revisited," *Journal of Theology for Southern Africa* 123 (2005): 74–83.

27   William R. Jones, *Is God a White Racist? A Preamble to Black Theology* (Boston, MA: Beacon, 1998).

28   See Cornel West, *Prophesy Deliverance! An Afro-American Revolutionary Christianity* (Philadelphia, PA: Westminster, 1982); *The American Evasion of Philosophy: A Genealogy of Pragmatism*, ed. Frank Lentricchia (Madison, WI: University of Wisconsin Press, 1989); *The Ethical Dimensions of Marxist Thought* (New York: Monthly Review, 1991).

29   See Anderson, *Beyond Ontological Blackness*; Victor Anderson, *Creative Exchange: A Constructive Theology of African American Religious Experience* (Minneapolis, MN: Fortress Press, 2008).

30   Anthony B. Pinn, "Rethinking the Nature and Tasks of African American Theology: A Pragmatic Perspective," *American Journal of Theology and Philosophy* 19(2) (1998): 191–208; *Why, Lord? Suffering and Evil in Black Theology* (New York: Continuum, 1995); *Varieties of African American Religious Experience* (Minneapolis, MN: Fortress Press, 1998).

31   Will Coleman, *Tribal Talk: Black Theology, Hermeneutics, and African/American Ways of "Telling the Story"* (University Park, PA: Pennsylvania State University Press, 2000).

32   See, e.g., the work of William D. Hart, *Edward Said and the Religious Effects of Culture* (Cambridge University Press, 2000); Eddie S. Glaude,

Jr., "Pragmatic Historicism and 'The Problem of History' in Black Theology," *American Journal of Theology and Philosophy* 19(2) (1998): 173–90; *Exodus! Religion, Race, and Nation in Early Nineteenth-Century Black America* (University of Chicago Press, 2000).

33 Hopkins, *Heart and Head*, p. 7.

34 David Emmanuel Goatley, *Were You There: Godforsakenness in Slave Religion* (Maryknoll, NY: Orbis Books, 1996).

35 See Carter, "Contemporary Black Theology," especially pp. 133–37.

36 See, e.g., Cyprian Davis, "Black Catholic Theology: A Historical Perspective," *Theological Studies* 61 (2000): 656–71; Jamie T. Phelps, "Communion Ecclesiology and Black Liberation Theology," *Theological Studies* 61 (2000): 672–99.

37 This is the promise of *True to Our Native Land* mentioned above, as well as a companion project recently undertaken by Old Testament/ Hebrew Bible scholars.

13 Protestant ecclesiology

JEREMIAH A. WRIGHT, JR.

I offer my observations on Protestant ecclesiology both as an academically trained historian of religions and as the pastor of a black congregation for thirty-six years. My studies and my experience have taught me that when it comes to "black theology" there is a major difference between black liberation theology and theology that grows out of the black religious experience. At times the two are synonymous and at times they are dichotomous. One of the reasons that is true is because there is no such thing as a monolithic black religious experience.

On a global scale, black Protestant churches continue to grow at an amazingly rapid pace, from the Anglican/Episcopalian members to the Evangelical and Pentecostal members of the black religious experience. Before beginning any discussion of contemporary manifestations of the highly diverse black Protestant church, however, I have found it helpful both as a seminary professor and as pastor to differentiate between what I call black theology prior to the systematized articulation of that reality, by scholars such as James H. Cone, the father of black theology in the modern era, and the black theology that was current in the black religious experience of Africans in the diaspora from the 1600s to 1966.

Black theology in the North American African diaspora from the days of the transatlantic slave trade and through the twentieth century was a powerful and exciting mixture of West African religious beliefs, religious beliefs picked up in the Caribbean during the "seasoning process," and a mixture of religious beliefs brought to the United States because of the nature of the triangular slave trade.

At one end of the spectrum, there were the outright, adamant, and radical protestations of the "folk" whose theology would not allow them to see themselves as slaves. Dr. Na'im Akbar of the Association of Black Psychologists says that in order for slavery to be slavery, the slave has to give psychological assent to the enslaver in order for the enslaver to place that individual in slavery.[1] Millions of enslaved Africans never gave that psychological assent.

There is a major difference between being in bondage and being in slavery. Many of the enslaved Africans were in bondage in that their bodies were in chains; but they were never in slavery, because their minds and their spirits were adamantly free. Their spiritual, "Oh Freedom," is one of many proofs of that reality. One line from that spiritual, "Before I'd be a slave, I'd be buried in my grave and go home to my God and be free," attests to their resistance to the notion of allowing an enslaver to have psychological power over them.

The spirituals, the folklore, the sermons, and the testimonies from the period of the transatlantic slave trade provide a wealth of additional evidence of psychological resistance to slavery and the Africans' absolute refusal to give that kind of power to those who called themselves "slaveholders" or "slave owners." The spiritual "I told Jesus it would be alright if He changed my name" stands in direct and defiant opposition to the notion that a European slaveholder had the right to change an African's name.

That kind of defiance produced slave rebellion after slave rebellion, slave revolt after slave revolt, and it brought into existence the phenomenon of the creation of alternative communities that we have come to know as the Maroons (Africans of Spanish and Portuguese ancestry), the *palenques* (Mexicans of African ancestry) and the *quilombos* (Brazilians of African ancestry). The theology undergirding these rebellions, revolts, and creation of alternative communities was black liberation theology long before any systematic academic understanding or explication of the meanings and the themes running through the religious thought of the enslaved Africans who brought these phenomena into existence was undertaken.

The combination of Christian beliefs and African religious beliefs (not to mention the African Christianity that was brought to the "New World" by Africans who were already Christians before slavery) produced the theology that undergirded Toussaint L'Ouverture and Dessalines' revolt in Haiti. The implication for black Haitian Christians who were still alive during the transatlantic slave trade and the black Haitians today in the Anglican churches both in the United States and in Haiti are classic examples of a black theology that is not consistent with what is considered "normative" North American theology.

The theology that undergirded the black church's active involvement in the revolts of the Revd. Gabriel Prosser (1800), the Revd. Denmark Vesey (1822), the writings of David Walker (a steward in the AME Church in 1828), and the revolt that shook the Western hemisphere, the revolt of the Revd. Nathaniel Turner in 1831, are classic examples of a black theology that was foundational for the Africans who refused to be enslaved.

The theology of the Revd. Harriet Tubman – one of the most famous conductors on the Underground Railroad – is yet another example of a defiant theology that refused to be compliant when it came to the issue of slavery or "giving psychological assent" to those who sought to hold others in bondage. The Revd. Tubman's famous summation of her work further illustrates the point made by Dr. Akbar and the Association of Black Psychologists. Harriet said when asked about her nineteen return trips back into the bowels of the slave-holding South to free a total of over 300 Africans, "I could have freed more if they had only wanted to be free." Those who did not *want* to be free were the Africans who had given "psychological assent" to their enslavers.

Beginning with that radical stance of a black theology that understood that faith in God was more than worship services, a study of black Protestant ecclesiology proceeds along a lengthy spectrum with many varieties of black theology when looking at the Protestant church in North America.

In the late eighteenth century, Africans in the Baptist churches and in the Methodist Episcopal churches started pulling away from white denominations to form their own independent churches. The white denominations practiced segregation, and to African Christians that was dichotomous to the teachings of Jesus Christ. Rather than revolution and fighting to the death as their approach or response to the issue of segregation and slavery, however, the Africans who started those churches felt that establishing independent congregations and inviting whites to join their congregations would be "a more perfect way" (1 Cor. 12) to show their white brothers and sisters, and to show the world what it meant to be the church *in* this world, but not *of* this world.

Richard Allen and Absalom Jones in 1787 are two examples of this aspect of the many varieties of black theology found along its lengthy spectrum. Their being dragged out of St. George's Methodist Episcopal Church in Philadelphia, Pennsylvania and starting the Free African Society is one manifestation of a black theology that refused to bow at the altar of segregation.

Absalom Jones' becoming the first rector ordained by the Anglican Church to be the pastor of the first African Episcopal Church in Philadelphia in 1791 is an example of black theology where coexisting in the same denomination with the whites who held slaves was one option. Black Anglicans who were free blacks, black Anglicans who were still enslaved, and white Anglicans who were against slavery and/

or who were themselves slaveholders all professed to be worshipping the same God.

Richard Allen's founding of Bethel African Methodist Episcopal Church – a congregation for Africans, but welcoming all others – is an additional instance of a black theology that saw itself coexisting with whites who were racist in practice, but who were still offered the opportunity for repentance and for forgiveness. James Varrick's African Methodist Episcopal Zion Church (the first church in 1796) is yet another example cut from cloth of the "peaceful coexistence" kind of black theology that refused to give up its African origins while refusing to bow at the altar of segregation.

Six years before, Denmark Vesey was leading his insurrection in Charleston, South Carolina, the African Methodist Episcopal church held its first general conference and elected Richard Allen to be its first bishop. Vesey's desire to be free and Richard Allen's belief in emigration and the establishment of a colony in Haiti are further manifestations of a black theology, which refused to give up Christ in spite of white racist Christians who sought to crush hope and to define Africans as less than human.

The spectrum of diversity in the black religious experience and in representations of black theology, however, does not stop with "moderates" such as Richard Allen, Jarena Lee (the first black woman preacher in the AME Church), or Absalom Jones. There were within African Methodism strong advocates for an African-centered theology such as Bishop Henry McNeil Turner and Edward Wilmot Blyden. There were also strong advocates for emigration to Africa such as Monroe Trotter, the Revd. Lott Carey (Liberia), and believers who gave up on the notion of America ever being a "Christian country" and living up to the principles and practices of the inclusive Christ whose name white racists claimed.

There were also African American Christians who believed firmly in the notion of second-class citizenship. One would be dishonest not to at least mention the "black theology" of the Christians who opposed (and told on!) Gabriel Prosser, Denmark Vesey, Nat Turner, and Harriet Tubman. The theology that came out of that "accommodationist" side of the black religious experience became one of the reasons so many Africans in the nineteenth and twentieth centuries gave up on Christianity and left the church.

The black theology of the late nineteenth and early twentieth centuries brought an additional dimension to the table – a dimension that should not be overlooked and one that is not easily nuanced. A confluence of factors from the 1870s through the turn of the century started a theological and psychological avalanche that is still reverberating over 120 years later.

The formation of schools for the "freedmen" in the 1870s brought missionaries from New England and from white denominations into the South in the thousands. Along with the education that they brought to freedmen who could not read or write, they, however, also brought the notion of their "white" culture being synonymous with Christianity. And that caused problems with which the black Protestant church still wrestles in the twenty-first century.

The missionaries who were trained at white schools and the black clergy who were also trained in white schools tried to teach the students at the black mission schools (which later became black colleges and universities, now known as "historically black colleges and universities" or HBCUs) that black music was not "cultured." They taught the Africans that their music was not sacred. They taught the Africans that their music was pagan and heathen; and they taught them that the use of their African bodies and the African style of singing, dancing, and expressions of joy in their worship services were "of the devil."

Some students at the HBCUs bought into that kind of racist teaching, and their theological positions are a part of the family of traditions that make up that wide and lengthy spectrum of black theological thought in the Protestant church. Other Africans, however, resisted the white supremacist teaching and saw it as not of God. Bishop Daniel Alexander Payne of the AME Church (trained in a Lutheran seminary) told a presiding elder from the sea-coast islands of South Carolina where the Gullah people had settled in large numbers that they had to stop singing those "fist and heel" ditties from slavery. He wanted to stamp out that kind of African singing. The presiding elder's statement to Bishop Alexander became a "mantra" that is still being used in black theology and in the black church in the twenty-first century. The presiding elder said to Bishop Payne: "Bishop, without the beat, the spirit don't come!"

That understanding of African rhythms, African music, African ways of worship, and African expressions of faith was not limited to the South Carolina and Georgia sea-coast islands, moreover. It swept throughout the African Christian community in the New World and became one of the "battlegrounds" in terms of understanding what it meant to be a black Christian as opposed to what it meant to be a white Christian in blackface.

The theology of the Holiness Church, which embraced African music, the theology of a Charles Albert Tindley, a black pastor and hymnodist who fought the racism in the Methodist Episcopal denomination that refused to ordain him, even when he had taught himself Hebrew and Greek, crystallized a form of black theology that was in resistance to and stood over and against the white racism that passed itself off as "universal theology" in the North American Protestant communion.

The Holiness Church and its music in the late nineteenth century also provided the fertile ground from which sprang the Azusa Street revival and the birth of Pentecostalism in the United States of America. The theology of the black Pentecostal churches is yet another form of black theology that cannot be overlooked.

Not as widely known as the Church of God in Christ or the other predominantly black Pentecostal denominations, moreover, is what Hans Baer writes about in his *Black Spiritual Movement* – and that is the Spiritual Church in North America.[2] The Metropolitan Spiritual churches of America and all of their sister denominations have a form of black theology that is closely akin to what Dr. Ogbu Kalu writes about in his book, *African Pentecostalism*.[3]

Those churches have a black theology that is a combination of the spiritual, cultural and/or religious practices brought into the United States by African Christians from Haiti (*vodun*), Cuba (*santeria*), Brazil (*candomblé*), Jamaica (*cumina* and *obeah*), Belize (*garifuna*), and Trinidad and Tobago (*shangò*). Those religious traditions mixed with the Protestant theology of the Metropolitan Spiritual churches to form a branch of black theology that is woefully understudied. The belief, on the part of these African Christians in the North American diaspora, in being able to enlist the aid of God (or the gods) in bringing down the strongholds of racism is a form of black theology that must not be overlooked.

In all of these forms of religious practice, the Africans in the diaspora drew and draw deeply from a well of experience that says that being "the church" means a whole lot more than worshipping on Sunday. It means a whole lot more than the preachments and pronouncements of those who are called "the faithful." It means addressing after worship the sinful practices of a government, a culture, or a society that defines one part of God's creation (the black part) as being inferior to some other part of God's creation (the white part).

Even the African spiritual "I Got Shoes" pokes fun at both white Christians and black Christians who "talk the talk" of being a Christian, but whose "walk" makes them seem more like children of the devil. In that spiritual they sing, "Everybody talking 'bout Heaven ain't going there!"

The notion of "church" for the Africans in America was like their understanding of "church" back home in Africa. In West Africa, there is no such thing as just one day a week where God and matters of the divine take precedence. In African culture, God and the things of God (the divine) are infused throughout an individual and a community's life from birth through death and into life after death.

There are high feast days, there are holy days, and there are special days of worship; but for the African, church is more than worship. "Church" has to do with everything from birth to the passage from this life into the afterlife – the life of the Elders.[4] It is with that understanding of "religion" that Africans shaped and formed the black theology that came to be a part of the Protestant church in the United States of America.

That understanding meant that worship of God was one thing. Worship was necessary. Worship was essential. Worship was crucial if one wanted to keep one's mind intact. What Africans did after worship, however, to make this world in which they lived a more livable world was just as important as what took place in the worship services.

One's belief in God, one's embrace of the Holy and one's being embraced by the Holy meant liberation. It meant a healing that was communal and not just individual. It is that part of the black theology of the Protestant church of America that must be understood as the fertile ground from which you find the brilliant mind, musings, and methodology of James H. Cone.

One major (and often overlooked) aspect of black theology in the early years of the twentieth century can be understood from reading *Black Apostles: Afro-American Clergy Confront the Twentieth Century*.[5] Unsung heroes and sheroes such as Gordon Blaine Hancock taught that black theology meant the "double duty dollar." It meant not spending your money where you are disrespected. It did not just mean worship on Sunday. It had to do with where you worked and how you spent the earnings from where you worked the other six days of the week.

William Seymour, another giant lifted up in the book *Black Apostles*, was the father of Pentecostalism in the United States of America. He taught that the true test of the Holy Ghost (and this is black theology at its finest) was not whether one could speak in tongues; rather the true test was where one stood on the issue of race. It is that thinking and that kind of black theology that shaped black Pentecostalism in North America.

The theology of Adam Clayton Powell, Sr. (charismatic preacher, former pastor of the Abyssinian Baptist Church, activist, theologian, and one of the founders of the National Urban League), the theology that undergirded the work of the Legal Defense Fund of the National Association for the Advancement of Colored People, and the theology that pulled together in the mid 1950s the Montgomery bus boycott and the subsequent formation of the Southern Christian Leadership Council, is the black theology that "on the ground" was the same black theology that James Cone wrote about for the academy.

In the late 1960s, James H. Cone's challenging works (augmented by and buttressed by the writings of J. Deotis Roberts, Gayraud Wilmore, and others) shook American Christianity to its foundations. The racist assumptions upon which white supremacist theology had been constructed since the founding of the country, which declared "all men equal" while holding Africans in slavery, was exposed for just what it was and is. It is Dr. Cone's writings and those of his colleagues that I call the "systematized theology" of black liberation theology.

The writings of Cone, Wilmore, and J. Deotis Roberts, and those of their students (Jacquelyn Grant, Katie Cannon, J. W. Kinney, Dwight Hopkins, Linda Thomas, Kelly Brown Douglas, Dennis Wiley, and others) provided the theological, theoretical, epistemological, hermeneutical, and philosophical basis for understanding the black revolution of the 1960s and the black church after Carter G. Woodson.[6]

My reading of the apparent "rupture" between the academy and the congregation, however, offers what I believe is a very helpful set of observations for understanding what has taken place within the black Protestant church over the past forty years.

First of all, to many members of the black congregations (and unfortunately far too many of their pastors), the writings of Cone, his colleagues, and his students were "for the academy." Black pastors and black parishioners felt that the writings of the black academicians were not intended for them. It was an analysis of what the academicians were doing, but it was not meant for them, the "ordinary" people in the pew. That perception, unfortunately, was undergirded (from my perspective) by a series of things:

(1) Most black pastors in the United States of America are not seminary-trained.
(2) Most black pastors, therefore, had not read, still have not read, and many *cannot* read the profoundly insightful works of Cone (or Cornel West and Michael Eric Dyson, for that matter).
(3) Many of the theologians in Cone's age group – Dwight Hopkins calls them the "first generation of Black theologians"[7] – did not "do

church." They did not and do not belong to church. They did not and do not attend church regularly. They were upset with the "other-worldly" focus of far too many black churches. They resented those black pastors who did not stand with Dr. King or with the National Committee of Black Churchmen and those who put together the Black Manifesto; and as a result they cut themselves off from the very congregations for whom and to whom they should have been writing.

(4) Black parishioners were not aware of Cone's work and saw no evidence of his findings in their local congregations.

(5) There were far too few churches in the African American church tradition that were trying to implement the principles embraced by Cone and as a result, "black theology" became, over a forty-year period, a mere discussion that was held on the academic level by black scholars of religion, but not a reality put into practice at the black congregational level.

I offer those observations as one who is intimately familiar with both sides of the issue, one who is a seminary-trained preacher and pastor, one who is a black theologian, one who is a seminary professor, and as one who is the retired pastor of a large black church who served a black congregation for over three decades of my life.

Dr. Dale Andrews addresses this "rupture" between the academy and the parish in *Practical Theology for Black Churches: Bridging Black Theology and African American Folk Religion.*[8] Dr. Andrews writes as a professor of homiletics and pastoral theology. I write, however, as a pastor. I refused (and still refuse) to buy into what I call the North Atlantic model of theological education. I was a student of that "first generation" of black theologians and I was constantly put down and "beat up" because I would not give up my relationship with a local congregation. I preferred to believe, however, that one's theology had to make contact with the people one was serving otherwise it was a meaningless academic exercise.

I came to that belief, first of all, because of the environment in which I was raised. At Virginia Union University (where I studied), we had PhDs who taught theology while pastoring churches. I had my belief strengthened, moreover, when as a member of the board of directors of the Black Theology Project I heard one of the professors at the seminary in Matanzas (in Cuba) say that they refused to allow anyone to teach in their seminary who was not actively involved in or engaged in the work of a local congregation. The Black Theology Project was one of several "projects" that made up the Theology in the Americas movement of the 1960s and 1970s in which theologians, religious scholars, and church persons from all three Americas met together to dialogue and strategize from their own particularities as they tried to be faithful to the Gospel of Jesus Christ from their own experiences of living under oppression and white supremacy.

Cuban theologians, who had lived through the Batista years (Rubén Fulgencio Batista Zaldívar was a military man who was well liked by American interests and took over the Cuban government in 1933) and the years of the American blockade, firmly believed that the theology of the people in the pew had to be informed by academicians who worshipped in those same pews with them fifty-two weeks a year!

To see the rich theology of James Cone and Jacquelyn Grant, the powerful insights of John Kinney and Katie Cannon, and the challenging concepts of Delores Williams and Gayraud Wilmore ignored by local pastors and unheard of by congregation members was anathema to me. My friends in the academy were writing about what my friends in the local church were doing. Many of them had been trying to do black theology, and much of their work was not being seen, appreciated, or lifted up as the work of the church that refused to bow at the altar of white supremacy.

I had seen in practice what I had learned both in the academy and in the congregation of believers. I had seen black theology as a part of the prophetic tradition of the black church. I had been taught that the black theology of Africans had three primary themes running throughout its history – liberation, transformation, and reconciliation.

Black theology had its roots in the sixty-first chapter of Isaiah, where God says the prophet is to preach the Gospel to the poor and to set at liberty those who are held captive. Liberation was one of three primary themes that ran throughout the history of the black church in North America, whether it was the institutional church or the "underground" church (or the Invisible Institution). Liberating the captives, I was taught, also liberates those who are holding them captive.

Liberation frees the captive and it also frees the captors. It frees the oppressed and it simultaneously frees the oppressor. The prophetic theology of the black church during the days of chattel slavery had been a theology of liberation. It was preached to set free those who were held in bondage spiritually, psychologically, and physically; and it was not only preached. It was also practiced. It was practiced to set the slaveholders free from the notion that they could define other human beings or confine a soul that had been set free by the power of the Gospel.

The black church taught me that transformation was God's desire for positive, meaningful, and permanent change. God does not want one people seeing themselves as superior to other people. God does not want the powerless masses (the poor, the widows, the marginalized, and those underserved by the powerful few) to stay locked into sick systems that treat some in the society as being "more equal" than others in the same society. God's desire is for positive change or true transformation; real change, not cosmetic change; radical change or a change that makes a permanent difference in the lives of people and in the societies in which they live each day.

The church tradition in which I grew up taught that transformation was God's desire for changed lives, changed minds, changed laws, changed social orders, and changed hearts in a changed world. That is why God sent God's son to this world, and that principle of transformation was and is at the heart of the prophetic theology of the black church. What I had been taught and what I had learned from the lives of Gabriel Prosser, Denmark Vesey, Ida B. Wells, Harriet Tubman, Nat Turner, and Bishop Henry McNeil Turner, and what James Cone was writing about were one and the same.

The black theology that was created in the holds of slave ships, during the Middle Passage, in the slave quarters in Jamaica and Georgia, and in the Maroon communities from Bahia to Birmingham had as its foundational basis liberation, transformation, and reconciliation. The black church's role in the fight for equality and justice in North America from the 1700s up through the twenty-first century had always had at its core the nonnegotiable doctrine of reconciliation. Dr. Samuel DeWitt Proctor (pastor emeritus of the Abyssinian Baptist Church, college dean, theologian, professor, humanitarian, and mentor of this author) used to always point out in his lectures and in his preaching that blacks in North America were the only people in human history who were called on after their slavery was ended to share the same real estate with those who had once enslaved them and to do so without killing their former enslavers.

Dr. Proctor taught that the only way that was possible was through the hard work of reconciliation. As I experienced it in the black church, reconciliation began with the children of God *repenting* for past sins against each other. Jim Wallis says America's greatest sin (i.e., racism) has never been confessed, much less repented for, and that was and is a blockage to true reconciliation. Black theology stated, however, that repenting for past sins and being reconciled to one another was God's desire for God's people, who were all made in the image of God and who were all equally loved by God. The theology of the church in which I had grown up and the theology being articulated by important scholars such as James Cone, J. Deotis Roberts, Dwight Hopkins, and Gayraud Wilmore were one and the same.

Seeing the crucial insights of Cone and his colleagues ignored in the black church was incredible to me, and I was determined as a pastor that I was not going to let that happen. I tried for thirty-six years to implement the principles of black liberation theology in the church where I served. I am happy to report that I was not alone.

Second- (and third-) generation theologians/practitioners of black liberation theology are proving what I believed on a daily basis. Dwight Hopkins and Linda Thomas received their PhD and MDiv degrees, respectively, under James Cone. For over a decade while I served as the pastor of Trinity United Church of Christ, they were active members of that congregation – working in the academy, teaching seminarians, and working in the church teaching parishioners the powerful principles of black liberation theology.

Dr. John W. Kinney, who also received his PhD under Dr. Cone, never gave up his pastorate of the Ebenezer Baptist Church in Beaver Dam, Virginia. While president of the Accreditation Committee of the Association of Theological Schools, Dr. Kinney maintained a level of academic excellence while pastoring with the same excellence the people where God placed him.

Dennis Wiley (also a Cone PhD) has pastored the Covenant Baptist Church of Washington, DC, for a quarter of a century. Kelly Brown Douglas (a former Cone PhD advisee) served an Anglican church in Washington, DC, the nation's capitol. And Frederick Douglas Haynes, III has implemented the principles of black liberation theology at the Friendship West Baptist Church in Dallas, Texas, for over twenty-nine years as of this writing. More clergymen and clergywomen can be added to this list.

Returning to the opening theme of this chapter about there being no monolithic church, however, one must take note of the widely disparate understandings of what it means to be a black Christian. Just a cursory examination of the black Anglican Church gives a glimpse of how diverse that understanding can be. The question "What does it mean to be an Anglican, a black Anglican, and a part of the Episcopalian Church in this world as an African or an African American?" is a complex one. The Anglican Church in the United States of America first split over the notion of ordaining women as priests – the equality of clergywomen is one of the tenets of black theology. The Anglican Church in America has further split over the issue of ordaining gay, lesbian, bisexual, and transgendered persons.

The Anglican Church in Africa is also split over the issue of gender and gender-identity. Black theology embraces inclusivity. Many black Anglicans also embrace inclusivity and many others do not. Archbishop Desmond Tutu of the Anglican Church of South Africa embraces inclusivity, but his brothers in the Anglican Church in Nigeria (and several of his brothers in South Africa) take serious issue with including any but heterosexual persons in their communion. The Anglican Church is threatening a split over that very issue, and all of them call themselves a part of the black church embracing black theology.

Dr. Ogbu Kalu's work likewise points out the differences in Protestant ecclesiology on the continent of Africa. His book *African Pentecostalism* shows the widely disparate understandings of what it means to be a Pentecostal in West Africa, in East Africa, in Southern Africa, and in South Africa.

The field of Protestant ecclesiology in the African church both on the continent and in the diaspora is an exciting, diverse, and fascinating one. It is one that deserves a study period by period (from the slave era, through colonialism, through twentieth-century racism, to this so-called "post-racial" era), and it is a field that helps those who wish to know how God has moved among God's people of color.

The foregoing offers a rich and vast perspective, yet is a mere glimpse at what this tantalizing field of study can offer. Time and space will not permit the kind of discussion that this subject deserves. I therefore encourage further study, and I encourage an even deeper examination of the black church in the North American diaspora.

Notes

1   Na'im Akbar, *Breaking the Chains of Psychological Slavery*, rev. edn. (Tallahassee, FL: Mind Productions and Associates, 1996).

2   Hans Baer, *The Black Spiritual Movement: A Religious Response to Racism*, 2nd edn. (Knoxville, TN: University of Tennessee Press, 2001).

3   Ogbu Kalu, *African Pentecostalism: An Introduction* (Oxford University Press, 2008).

4   See John S. Mbiti's *Introduction to African Religion* (Portsmouth, NH: Heinemann, 1991) and *African Religions and Philosophy* (Portsmouth, NH: Heinemann, 1992).

5   Randall K. Burkett and Richard Newman (eds.), *Black Apostles: Afro-American Clergy Confront the Twentieth Century* (Boston, MA: G. K. Hall & Co., 1978).

6 See C. Eric Lincoln, *The Black Church since Frazier* (New York: Schocken Books, 1974).

7 Dwight N. Hopkins, *Introducing Black Theology of Liberation* (Maryknoll, NY: Orbis Books, 1999).

8 Dale Andrews, *Practical Theology for Black Churches: Bridging Black Theology and African American Folk Religion* (Louisville, KY: Westminster John Knox Press, 2002).

14 Roman Catholic ecclesiology

CYPRIAN DAVIS, OSB

In his commentary on the Song of Songs, Origen spoke of the church as a black woman. One of the first Church Fathers, Origen (c. 184– c. 253), born in Alexandria, was a teacher in the catechetical school, a theologian, biblical scholar, and, later in life, a priest. He wrote a commentary on almost all of the books of the Old Testament and on some of those that would be found in the New Testament. Like most early church writers, Origen moved from the literal meaning of the text to the allegorical meaning of the scriptural passage. When writing on the Song of Songs, Origen saw this text as the love song of Solomon and the Queen of Sheba (Ethiopia). Origen saw Solomon as Christ and the Queen of Sheba as the Church. It is she who in the first chapter of the Song of Songs says, "I am black and beautiful, O daughters of Jerusalem" (Song of Songs 1:5, Septuagint version).[1] Origen wrote:

> This queen came, then, and, in fulfillment of her type, the Church comes also from the Gentiles to hear the wisdom of the true Solomon, and the true Peace-Lover, Our Lord Jesus Christ.[2]

He lists the black figures of the Old Testament, all of whom in some way are examples of the Church: "Now ... since we are on the subject of the Church that comes of the Gentiles and calls herself black and yet beautiful." He mentions the Ethiopian woman who became the wife of Moses, and he writes "Moses himself was never so highly praised by God as on this occasion when he took the Ethiopian wife."[3] In the same passage, Origen refers to Ebed-melech the Kushite who saved the life of Jeremiah by drawing him up from the abandoned cistern where he had been lowered into the miry mud and left to die.[4] For Origen, not only the Queen of Sheba, black and beautiful, but also the wife of Moses and Ebed-Melech the Kushite, protector of the prophet – all of these are figures of the Church of the Gentiles.

[The Queen of Sheba] came to Jerusalem, then, to the Vision of Peace with a great following and in great array; for she came not with a single nation, as did the Synagogue before that had the Hebrews only, but with the races of the whole world.[5]

Origen lived in the most cosmopolitan and multiethnic metropolis in the late Roman Empire. He saw the church in the context of universality. After the peace of Constantine, in the fourth and fifth centuries, the African kingdom of Ethiopia became Christian and the kings of Ethiopia would trace their lineage back to Solomon and the Queen of Sheba. It was in the sixth century that Nubia (present-day Sudan) would become Christian under the influence of Justinian (d.565) and his wife Theodora (d.548).

African American Catholics traced their spiritual lineage back to the church of Africa. They developed their own vision of what the Catholic Church was and what it should be. This ecclesiology was the result of their own faith and fears, and the expression of their own hopes and history.

THE FOURTH BLACK CONGRESS OF 1893

In 1893, black Catholics assembled in the Fourth Black Catholic Lay Congress as part of the Columbian Exposition in Chicago. The members of the Black Catholic Congress drew up an address to their fellow Catholics and to the black community.

They began with a profession of love and loyalty to the Catholic Church and to the See of Rome:

The colored Catholics of the United States, through their representatives to the fourth congress in convention assembled ... with the approbation of His Grace, Archbishop Feehan [of Chicago], invoke the blessing of God, the prayers of the Holy Church, and the good-will of mankind in issuing their fourth address ... We first renew our profession of love and loyalty to the Holy Church and our submission to the See at Rome.[6]

These black Catholics "proclaim" their faith in what the church is and what it does. The church does not err in proclaiming the "rights of man." The church's mission is to teach the "doctrine of love and not of hate [and] to raise up the downtrodden." That mission is to make it known everywhere that "we all have stamped on our immortal souls the image of God." We are thereby the brothers and sisters of Christ and heirs of heaven.

These Catholics proclaim that "the Church has laboured to break down the walls of race prejudice." The address goes on to say that only virtue truly elevates a man and only vice degrades him. They deplore that there are those among the clergy who have given in to racial prejudice in the USA. As a result, they have an obligation not only to black Catholics but also to the church to denounce the racist practices that are clearly violations of canon law and Catholic practice. "If we would have our rights, we must demand them."

This address refers to a brief report given to the fourth congress from a committee of grievances, which was formed in the previous black lay congress to document racist practices and discrimination in the various dioceses of the United States. At this lay Catholic congress held in Philadelphia in 1892, it was decided to send out a questionnaire to all the heads of dioceses in the United States. In 1892, there were eighty-two dioceses and four vicariates (a territory not fully formed into a diocese). The questions asked whether the diocese had mandatory segregation for blacks in its churches and in other Catholic institutions. For example, were blacks forced to assist at mass from the balcony or in some other restricted area; whether black students had access to the same schools and colleges as whites; whether blacks were admitted into Catholic hospitals? If there was racial discrimination, the question was asked: Who was responsible for these restrictions? Out of the eighty-six questionnaires sent, sixty-seven bishops replied. This kind of questioning of the Catholic bishops by laypersons was unheard of in this period. It is even more surprising that over two-thirds of the bishops took the time to reply. Most, to be sure, did not agree that there was discrimination mandated by the diocese. Most claimed that any discrimination was the practice of individual parishes. Nevertheless, in the fourth congress it was determined that the results of the questionnaire would be sent to Rome.[7] Examples of discrimination were published in both the daily press and the Catholic press. A copy of the questionnaire with the covering letter is to be found in the files of the Apostolic Delegation now in the Vatican archives. Although there seems to be no specific mention of this report from the grievance committee, there was a letter from the Congregation of the Propaganda Fide in 1904 to the Apostolic Delegate, Archbishop Diomede Falconio, OFM, concerning information given to the curia affirming that the situation of the "Catholic Negroes ... is very humiliating and entirely different from that of the whites."[8] This rather terse and peremptory letter was one example among many of Rome's intervention, often behind the scenes, on behalf of black Catholics.

The high point of this congress of 1893 is their admission of what the church is. "We know that the Roman Church, as she is One and Apostolic, is also Catholic and Holy. With ... confidence in the rectitude of our course[,] in the enduring love of Mother Church, and the consciousness of our priesthood, we show our devotion to the Church, our jealousy of her and our love for her history." As a result, they had the duty to call attention to the racist actions of some members of the Catholic clergy. Despite their love of the church and pride in its history, they recognize the harm done to the Catholic Church by those who have given in to prejudice and race hate. "Those who have departed from the teachings of the Church we would see reclaimed, and those of our own people ... opened to the light of God." The authors of this address used the phrase "consciousness of our priesthood." Although not contrary to Catholic teaching – by baptism all are made a priestly people – it would have a Protestant ring in the ears of Catholics after the Council of Trent. In the Catholic theology of that time, the sacrament of holy orders was to be seen as totally different from the sacrament of baptism.

The end of the nineteenth century was the high point of European immigration of Catholics into the United States. These immigrants brought with them their patron saints, such as Boniface, Patrick, Louis the King, and Francis of Assisi. On the other hand, in this document black Catholics look back to the African saints of the early church. "[W]e rejoice that our Church, the Church of our love ... has not failed to stand by its historic record ... did not the Holy Church canonize Augustine and Monica, Benedict the Moor, Cyprian, and Cyril, Perpetua, and Felicity." The list is slightly erroneous. Benedict the Moor (d.1589) lived in Sicily, a contemporary of Martin Luther. African slavery had been introduced into such Mediterranean countries as Sicily, Portugal, and Spain by the fifteenth century. Benedict was born into the African slave community imported into Sicily. Becoming a Franciscan friar after being freed, he was hailed by all for his holiness and spiritual counsel. Canonized in 1807 by Pius VII, he was a popular saint for both white and black. His canonization was to be an example that a black slave could be raised to the altar. The Cyril in the list is St. Cyril, patriarch of Alexandria, who died in 444, theologian and early church writer. Perpetua and Felicity, both from North Africa, probably Carthage, Perpetua the Roman matron, Felicity the slave, were both martyred. Their names with that of Cyprian, bishop of Carthage, are still mentioned in the mass. These Catholics turned their devotion not to European piety but to the tradition of the early church.

Finally, the address turns to the question of black priests. Although the practice of ordaining native clergy as soon as the candidates were ready was Catholic Church practice, the American bishops found it difficult to accept the ordination of black men to the priesthood.[9] They presumed that the respect given to the white Catholic priest would be unacceptable for white Catholics to give to a black priest. The first recognized African American priest was Augustus Tolton. A student at the Urban College in Rome – established to train missionary clergy – he was ordained in Rome in 1886. For the African American Catholic community, the ordination of Augustus Tolton as priest was a source of pride and jubilation. Charles R. Uncles, the second black priest (ordained in 1891), was the first to be ordained a priest in the United States.[10] For black Catholics in the 1890s, this was the recognition in America that one of their own had reached the dignity of the priesthood. In the words of the address: "[E]very fraternal greeting extended the priests of our race, are in our opinion so many more proofs of the Divine truth of Catholic religion."

The address ended with a hope and an expectation. The day would come when the "whole colored race ... will be knocking at [the Catholic Church's] doors for admittance" once the church "teaches everywhere that truth of Catholic doctrine which knows no distinction of races or previous condition."

Given the beautiful words of loyalty and promise, one might have wished for a more powerful ending. The writers of the text chose their words with sincerity but also with circumspection. Nevertheless, the address sets forth three statements of faith from a people who were only recently freed from slavery and were deeply conscious of mirroring the image of Christ. Their vision of the church was of an organization that taught love and not hate, that as part of the church they bore the image of God, and that social justice is the enduring mark of the universal church.

THE CHURCH IS THE LAITY

The organization of black lay Catholics was the work of a former slave named Daniel Rudd, born in Bardstown, Kentucky in 1854. Daniel Rudd was raised a Catholic. Both of his parents were slaves. An older brother had gone to Springfield, Ohio, after the Civil War. Rudd later followed him to Ohio where he finished high school. Early on he became editor of a black weekly newspaper, which quickly became a black Catholic weekly newspaper. In 1888, it became known as the *American Catholic Tribune*. Rudd had two basic beliefs. The first was that the Catholic Church would raise up the black race in America. This is what the Church had done for all peoples and would now do for the black race. Rudd lectured all over the United States, insisting that "there is no leadership quite so capable as that of the Catholic Church ... up to this time, [she] has been the only successful leader of men of all the other races." "The Catholic Church alone can break the color line. Our people should help her to do it."[11]

Rudd's second major belief was that the African American Catholics should unite. As a result, Rudd began to speak about a nationwide congress of black Catholics. He wanted them to come together and confer, "to have our people realize the Church's extent among them. Let us stand forth and look at one another."[12] A man of unlimited optimism and initiative, he brought about the first congress of black Catholic laypersons in Washington, DC, at St. Augustine's Church. The congress was held from January 1 to January 4, 1889. It was the first time that black Catholics had ever come together to deliberate and to discuss as a body. It was a huge success.

They finished the congress with a visit to President Grover Cleveland in the White House, a little more than a mile away, and a cablegram from the Holy See. In a final address to their fellow Catholics, they expressed their concerns and cares. They wished the church to know the issues that concerned them as a community and a people. They called for more parochial schools, for trade schools to train more skilled workers, for better housing, for better labor opportunities, the need for "orphanages, hospitals and asylums"; and they expressed the hope "that our Catholic brethren throughout the land will generously help us by their sympathy and fellowship in the ... work ... of our entire people."[13] Social justice concerns would be the concern of all of the black Catholic congresses; education, both academic and vocational, would always head the list. Admission to labor unions and access to full employment was in next place. The social issues are the church issues.

The congress of 1889 would be followed by four others: in Cincinnati, 1890; in Philadelphia, 1892; in Chicago, 1893, whose statement of belief we saw earlier; and the last in Baltimore in 1894. These congresses had two results: they brought together black Catholic lay leaders from every part of the country and they created a type of black Catholic consciousness. Perhaps few were as sanguine as Daniel Rudd, but they were as forthright in demanding their place in the Catholicism of the United States because the Catholic Church was expected to have a place for them. Unlike many other ethnic groups within American Catholicism, these Catholics did not have the clergy to speak for them. Black Catholics revered Augustus Tolton; but they could not have him as a leader. In their midst, however, they did have professional leaders and political activists.

As early as 1853, a black woman named Harriet Thompson wrote a letter addressed to the Most Holy Father, Visible Head of the Church of Jesus Christ. The letter is to be found in the Propaganda archives in Rome. The pope to whom it was addressed was Pius IX (1846–78). A note in the archives indicates that the letter reached his desk. Harriett Thompson wanted the pope to know the situation of black Catholics.

"I humbly write these lines to beseech your Holiness in the name of the same Saviour if you will provide for the salvation of the black race in the United States." She was very articulate, grammatical errors notwithstanding. She wanted the pope to know that it is a mistake to think that the Church "watched with equal care over every race and color, for how can it be said they teach all nations when they will not let the black race mix with the white." She pointed out the difficulties that existed between the Irish and the blacks in New York City. She pointed out that they would not admit their black children into the Catholic schools. She pointed out that in New York the public school teachers were Protestants and that they ridiculed Catholicism before their children, made fun of the Eucharist, and said that confession was only to make money. Harriet Thompson does not hold back her feelings at the way she sees black children being treated. She names names. She points out the fact that her archbishop, John J. Hughes, did not consider black Catholics as part of his diocese – she was correct, Hughes was indifferent to black Catholics. On the other hand, she lists the priests who were open to the needs of black Catholics. She wanted the pope to alert Archbishop Gaetano Bedini, who was in the United States, to investigate the needs of black Catholics. Harriet Thompson ended her letter, "I hope if it is the will of God for the black race to be saved something will soon take place for the better." Twenty-eight men and women signed the letter.[14]

BLACK CATHOLIC LIBERATION

Thomas Wyatt Turner was born a sharecropper's son in 1877 in southern Maryland. He died in 1978. This is the land of black Catholics, descendants of slaves, who were owned and evangelized by the Jesuits.

Turner was a Catholic all of his life. He fought for a church that he sincerely loved and fiercely contested. Very poor, Turner was given the opportunity to win a scholarship to Lincoln University in Pennsylvania if he became an Episcopalian. On the advice of a friend, he decided to remain a Catholic. This choice was to determine his whole life. Turner attended the Catholic University of America until he ran out of funds.[15] Shortly thereafter, the Catholic University of America closed its doors to blacks as did all of the other institutions of higher learning in the nation's capital until after World War II. Turner finished his studies in biology from Howard University. He would obtain his doctorate from Cornell University in 1921. With the administration of Woodrow Wilson, the District of Columbia slowly reverted to Southern mores and practice, and slowly racial segregation in government and public life appeared. Turner supported the NAACP both in Baltimore and in Washington. In World War I, he was responsible for aid and assistance to black Catholic soldiers who had previously been neglected. By 1919, he had organized a committee of twenty-five members known as the Committee for the Advancement of Colored Catholics. It soon became an action committee and a pressure group to work for an end of racism within the Catholic Church. He then began in 1924 Federated Colored Catholics as an organization that would increase understanding between black Catholics and would "educate and motivate" black Catholics, working to bring about change and not just discuss it. In a letter to the American hierarchy in 1932, he calls on the bishops to institute a program for racial justice. He asks them to see that in their respective dioceses they will seek to prevent any practices that do not offer equal opportunities to African Americans as well as to whites; that every bishop shall see that in his diocese no institution of higher learning, no hospital, no orphanage is closed to black Catholics "because of the color of their skin." The hierarchy are asked to carry out a campaign of education "to instill in all, the true Catholic attitude toward the colored people." Bishops are asked to see that those who hear confessions urge their penitents to correct their sins of prejudice and to encourage vocations among black youths to the priesthood and religious life.

Turner believed that African American Catholics should take the initiative to work for an end to the manifold ways blacks were treated differently from white Catholics. The organization he founded was to seize every opportunity to call attention to the racial situation of blacks in all parts of the church. Turner welcomed the assistance and the support of white priests and laypeople; but he insisted that a black layman should be in charge. This brought about a conflict between him and such outstanding Jesuit priests as John LaFarge, SJ, and William Markoe, SJ, who had lent their talents and their publications for an end to racial prejudice and discrimination. These men sincerely believed that Turner, in his insistence on a black-led, activist organization, was guilty of racial discrimination. LaFarge, for instance, had begun the Catholic Interracial Councils, which brought African American Catholics in dialogue with white Catholics in discussion groups and joint religious retreats. Turner in his turn believed that these activities were good, but he wanted an organization with blacks in control, ready to denounce prejudice everywhere and promote all measures to defeat it.[16] The disagreement eventually brought about the dissolution of the Federated Colored Catholics in about 1952.

BLACK CATHOLIC THEOLOGY

In some respects, the African American Catholic community was not in the first ranks of the civil rights movement. The leadership of Martin Luther King, Jr., the Southern Christian Leadership Committee, and CORE, or the Congress of Racial Equality, arose within the black Protestant churches in the South. Catholics, black and white, began to participate only gradually. Yet black Catholics such as Alexander Pierre Tureaud (d. 1972) in New Orleans and Earl Johnson (d. 1988) in Jacksonville, Florida, both lawyers, were doing in their respective states what Thurgood Marshall was accomplishing on a national level. In fact, the Roman Catholic, French-speaking, southeastern Louisiana and New Orleans people of color never accepted racial segregation. Tureaud was a young man studying law at Howard University when Homer Plessy of *Plessy* v. *Ferguson* – "separate but equal" – fame died in 1925.

The Catholic Church became a participant in the civil rights movement when priests and nuns (in full religious habit), black and white, went to Selma, Alabama, in the spring of 1965 at the invitation of Martin Luther King, Jr. Selma was a turning point in American Catholic history. For the first time, priests and religious sisters had officially demonstrated openly for an end to racial segregation in American public life. The critical point for black priests and religious sisters came a little later.

In April of 1968, Martin Luther King, Jr. was assassinated in Memphis, Tennessee. Rioting broke out in the major cities of the North. A meeting of the Catholic Clergy Conference on the Interracial Apostolate was to be held at the Sheraton-Cadillac hotel in Detroit later in the month. The conference brought together white priests working in black parishes and African American priests and religious brothers. In the wake of the rioting, Mayor Daley of Chicago had given the order to "Shoot to kill" for looters. The vice-president of the conference, a black priest, sent letters to all black priests to come one day early for a caucus meeting to decide how black priests should respond. It was the first time that black priests had ever come together in such numbers. It was a time of self-reflection and heightened consciousness. Many shared their pain and suffering. There was, however, a great variety in each one's experience and not everyone was in agreement, nor was everyone speaking in the same terms.

After much discussion, it was determined that a statement, practically a manifesto, should be delivered to the American bishops in the light of the current crisis and the general feeling of African Americans. The statement began:

> The Catholic Church in the United States, primarily a white racist institution, has addressed itself primarily to white society and is definitely a part of that society. On the contrary, we feel that her primary, though not exclusive work, should be in the area of ... societal change.[17]

The statement went on to say that the church needed to listen to the black community and "to consult the black members of the Church, clerical, religious and lay." It called for the presence of "black priests in decision-making positions on the diocesan level," it called for efforts to be made to recruit black men for the priesthood and the permanent diaconate, and it asked that white priests working in the black community be more attuned to the thinking, feelings, and culture of African American men and women.[18]

This meeting in 1968 resulted in the creation of the National Office of Black Catholics, the National Black Sisters' Conference, a seminarians' association, and an office of lay leaders.

The events of 1968 were somewhat similar to, yet different from the address of black Catholics in the Fourth Congress of 1893. In 1893, laymen called for the church to become a home for justice, social concern, and openness to black people. The atmosphere was irenic. In 1968, the atmosphere was one of anger, impatience, and foreboding from priests toward their bishops and for the future in the inner city. These questions, however, led to the maturing of African American Catholic theologians.

Meeting in the motherhouse of the Oblate Sisters of Providence in Baltimore in 1978, a little over thirty black Catholic theologians, priests, sisters, brothers, and seminarians came together for what was to be the Black Catholic Theological Symposium. The main topic was black theology and Catholic theology. In the preface to the proceedings, Thaddeus Posey, OFM Cap. wrote:

> The Black approach to theology is rooted in a positive identification and creation. It is positive because we affirm ourselves, our history and our destiny in the Faith. These are God's gifts. Until recently, the [Catholic] Church has not encouraged this ... identification among Black Catholics.

He goes on to say, however, that the Church had always expressed her faith within diverse cultural heritages and diverse racial groups without a loss of unity and rootedness in tradition.[19] This is what black Catholic theology means: to talk about God, to talk about the church within the culture and the experience of black Catholic people.

CONCLUSION

In the Dogmatic Constitution on the Church, promulgated by the Second Vatican Council, the church is called a mystery and the "Sacrament of Salvation."

The Catholic people are "the People of God." Origen spoke of the church as the Queen of Sheba, a black-skinned Queen of Ethiopia. The African American Catholic community always saw itself as an essential part of this mystery. They fought for their faith in their own household. They refused to eat only the crumbs from the table.

Like the Three Kings, they have brought their own rich treasures and their special gifts.

Notes

1   The Greek Septuagint was the text used by all the ancient churches.
2   Origen, *The Song of Songs. Commentary and Homilies*, trans. R. P. Lawson (London and Westminster, MD: Newman Press, 1957), pp. 92–98; *Origène. Commentaire sur le Cantique des Cantiques*, trans. Luc Bressard, OCSO and Henri Crouzel, SJ, Sources Chrétiennes 375 (Paris: Editions du Cerf, 1991), p. 277.
3   Origen, *Song of Songs*, p. 97. Present-day scriptural scholars would not agree that Moses had married a Kushite or Ethiopian woman.
4   Jeremiah 38, 39.
5   Origen, *Song*, pp. 98–99 (*Origène. Commentaire*, p. 277).
6   The original text is in the archives of the University of Notre Dame, Papers of William J. Onahan, Box IX-1-0. The printed text is in

Cyprian Davis, OSB, "Two Sides of a Coin: The Black Presence in the History of the Catholic Church in America," in Secretariat for Black Catholics, National Conference of Catholic Bishops, *Many Rains Ago. A Historical and Theological Reflection on the Role of the Episcopate in the Evangelization of African American Catholics* (Washington, DC: United States Catholic Conference, Inc., 1990), pp. 49–62; for the address, see pp. 57–58. See also "The Black Catholic Lay Congresses, 1889, 1893," in Cyprian Davis, OSB and Jamie Phelps, OP (eds.), *"Stamped With the Image of God": African Americans as God's Image in Black* (Maryknoll, NY: Orbis Books, 2003), pp. 79–83.

7 Robert Wood to Archbishop Satolli, August 14, 1894, Del. Ap. U.S.A. xiii (Società) no. 8, Congresso dei Cattolici di Colore (1893–94), Vatican Archives. See Cyprian Davis, OSB, *The History of Black Catholics in the United States* (New York: Crossroad, 1990), pp. 190–91. "The Treatment of Colored Catholics by the Church. Surprising Assertions as to Race Discrimination – A Protest to go to Rome," *New York Sun*, Friday, June 29, 1894, Letters to the Editors. Robert Wood wrote: "As Chairman of the Grievance Committee, I received sixty-seven letters from Catholic Bishops, some good, some not. One blamed the timidity of colored people for tolerating these outrages. Many blamed public opinion ... I tell every Bishop or priest who discriminates or permits discrimination against colored Catholics in his diocese or church, that he is either vicious or a coward."

8 Cardinal Gotti to Mgr. Falconio, January 18, 1904, Del. Ap. U.S.A., ii, no. 60b. Condizione dei negri, 1904, Vatican Archives. See Davis, *History*, pp. 195–96, 306.

9 See Stephen Ochs, *Desegregating the Altar. The Josephites and the Struggle for Black Priests, 1871–1960* (Baton Rouge, LA: Louisiana State University Press, 1990).

10 Tolton was not the first black priest. The three Healy brothers, James Augustine Healy, Patrick Francis Healy, and Alexander Sherwood Healy, were the sons of Michael Morris Healy, a native of Ireland, who came to Georgia, established a plantation, never married but had nine children by Mary Eliza, his slave. Morris' children were legally slaves but Michael Healy had been able to send them North. James Augustine Healy became bishop of Portland, Maine, as the first black bishop in the United States; Patrick Francis Healy, SJ became the first president of Georgetown University in Washington, DC (he was accepted as white); Alexander Sherwood, known to be black, was secretary to the bishop of Boston, John Williams, and accompanied him to the First Vatican Council. He died young. They were born slaves and known to be black by some of their peers, but they did not identify themselves as black nor seemingly did they accept themselves as black.

11 *American Catholic Tribune*, January 3, 1891; April 18, 1891.

12 Ibid., May 4, 1888.

13 Davis, *History*, pp. 173–75. See Congress of Colored Catholics of the United States, *Three Catholic Afro-American Congresses* (New York: Arno Press, 1978).

14 Congregation of the Propaganda archives, Scritture Riferite nei Congressi: America Centrale, vol. xvi, fols. 770v–775r, University of Notre Dame, microfilm. Davis and Phelps (eds.), *"Stamped with the Image of God,"* p. 30.

15 See unpublished memoirs in the Moorland-Spingarn Research Center, Manuscript Division, Thomas Wyatt Turner, Box 153–8, Folder 3, Memoirs, Washington, DC: Howard University.

16 This disagreement and its results are related in Marilyn Nickels, *Black Catholic Protest and the Federated Colored Catholics 1917–1933: Three Perspectives on Racial Justice* (New York: Garland Publishing, 1988). See also Cyprian Davis, OSB, "Black Catholics in the Civil Rights Movement in the Southern United States: A. P. Tureaud, Thomas Wyatt Turner, and Earl Johnson," *U.S. Catholic Historian* 24(2006): 69–81.

17 Davis, *"Stamped with the Image of God,"* pp. 111–12. "A Statement of the Black Catholic Clergy Caucus," in James H. Cone and Gayraud S. Wilmore (eds.), *Black Theology. A Documentary History*, vol. i, *1966–1979*, 2nd edn. (Maryknoll, NY: Orbis Books, 1993), pp. 230–32.

18 Ibid.

19 Thaddeus J. Posey, OFM Cap. (ed.), *Theology: A Portrait in Black.* Black Catholic Theological Symposium i (Pittsburgh, PA: Capuchin Press, 1980), Preface, p. 3.

15 Dignity and destiny: black reflections on eschatology

J. DEOTIS ROBERTS

INTRODUCTION

In this chapter, I will attempt to present my version of the meaning of eschatology. The views presented here are personal. They are, at the same time, the reflections of a person who has been in the black context for several decades. My witness in the church and the academy has been universal. Here, my focus is from the black experience; it is therefore delimited. I also speak from my development of a program of black theology.

The study of my life is forthcoming in a work titled, *Seasons of Life*.[1] What I have to say here is a brief account.

I was born in the southern United States (in North Carolina, 1927), and my education (up to the Bachelor of Divinity degree) was obtained in this state. This is likewise the state where I pastored my first church. Educated at Johnson C. University (BA) and Shaw University (BD), I led the Union Baptist Congregation at Tarboro, North Carolina.

My next challenge was as assistant pastor of the Union Baptist Church in Hartford, Connecticut, where I obtained the STM (or Master of Sacred Theology degree) in philosophy of religion. During the Hartford period I was a part-time migrant minister to black, Jamaican, and Puerto Rican migrants.

One year was spent in Macon, Georgia, as Dean of Religion at Georgia Baptist College. During 1952–53, I was married to Elizabeth Caldwell of Landis, North Carolina. We moved to Shaw University in the fall of 1953, when I was to be college minister and Professor of Bible and Ethics.

From 1955 to 1957, on leave from Shaw University, I was in Scotland in pursuit of the PhD in philosophical theology. While working on a dissertation on the Cambridge Platonists, I spent a spring term in Cambridge. Much time was also spent in London. I continued writing in

Edinburgh, but led the congregation of the Radnor Park Congregational Church in Glasgow, Scotland, as interim pastor.

My return to the USA took place in 1958 (late spring). I was greeted by my wife and a one-year-old daughter, Edin Charmaine. We lived in Raleigh, North Carolina, and I resumed my duties at Shaw University. I received my PhD *in absentia* in the fall of 1957. In the fall of 1958, I was appointed as theologian at Howard University's Divinity School. A newborn son, J. Deotis Roberts, Jr., was born in 1958. The family of four then moved to Washington, DC, where I was to remain until 1980.

At Howard University, I was to teach many courses in World Religions, Philosophy of Religion, Ethics, and Ecumenics, along with Systematic Theology. For a period of two years, I supervised the ministry of student pastors in Washington, DC, and Baltimore, Maryland. The reader will recall, I had already been pastor at several places. Thus my work for several years at Howard University had been interdisciplinary, ecumenical, and inter-religious. My study and travel had taken me to Asia, the Middle East, North Africa, and Europe. This wide experience was used in my teaching at Howard and my ministry at churches.

There was also an involvement in the civil rights movement. It was this movement that led me back to the USA upon completing my work at Edinburgh. I had studied Law and Theology at Duke University (in a special summer program, led by Professor Waldo Beach). Since Howard law professors had led in this struggle, I joined Spottswood Robinson, then dean of the Law School, in setting up a course at Howard to meet current trends.

In the late 1960s, the message of black ministers, the urban racial unrest, and the crisis of black consciousness at Howard reached me and "aroused my dogmatic slumber." While being involved in Law, Asian Studies, and African Studies, among other things as theologian, I was summoned by circumstance to bring theology into a conversation with Black Power and black consciousness.

I will leave my life story at this point, and move to black theology. It was the reflection of Albert Cleague, as pastor, and James H. Cone, as theologian, that led me into this concern. One cannot overlook all that I had been concerned about earlier, nor the context at Howard or in urban America, especially among my people, as a means to my theological reflections. My role as minister and theologian, at Howard Divinity School, must be considered.

This phase of my Introduction is brief. Before turning to the constructive phase of my essay, I would like to pose a question. This discussion should be considered as a partial answer. Why is eschatology such an important concern for theology, especially black theology?

First, there is a strong focus on the end of time and the world beyond. While the general reflection on the return of Christ and the end of time seems to mark fundamentalism, the stress of black theology seems to relate to the concerns of the present and the future, after the present has been experienced. Or again, how the present is connected to the hereafter as one great development.

Second, the Bible holds such belief as an important focus in black belief and the Bible seems to have so much to say about eschatology. Thus there is a great interest in the subject.[2]

Third, eschatology is of much interest because it is so personal. For black people, it concerns persons-in-community.

Fourth, we are interested in how the concern for the future is reflected in the present life.

Fifth, with so much emphasis upon the relation of faith to prosperity, blacks are asking about faith and poverty and other ills.

Sixth, blacks want to know about the relation between faith and nurture of persons for the present and the future. Education and health are being discussed.

Seventh, black theology places so much stress on heaven as a place. The real meaning of heaven as a state is missed. How does our relationship to God and humanity impact the meaning of eschatology?

These are just some of the issues raised in black theology. The reader should note how the author's project is related to the past. It will be evident that what I have to say on the subject reflects both experience and context.

BLACK ESCHATOLOGICAL REFLECTIONS ON DIGNITY

We now enter the constructive phase of our thoughts on eschatology. Usually such reflections refer only to the second coming of Christ, the apocalypse, the end of time, or heaven-future. However, for the black theologian, there is a strong emphasis upon the *nowness* of faith. This embraces all concerns for the kingdom of God, as well as personal faith. Personal societal interests are thus embraced.

We ask: How does our faith in God, through Christ and the power of the Holy Spirit, make life more human? What this implies is a need to look again at creation. We have a concern for the environment, but our focus, as a result of the oppression of blacks, places a great emphasis on the human.

There is a comingling of creation with redemption and all ethics with reference to the kingdom of God.

The dignity of the human entity is foundational to everything in our reflection.[3] The understanding of our creation implies that all human life is sacred. It was created. This means that human life is valuable as God initiated it. Its dignity is God-given and not humanly bestowed. The discussion of black theology upon this is constant. From historical and sociological perspectives, in the United States of America, Christians, among others, have treated blacks as if they were nonhuman. The creation and spread of black theology became a sheer necessity to set the Christian record straight.

The examination of the dignity of the human, as created by God, leads black theologians to discuss the "I–You" relationship between all humans. The nature of the relation between whites and blacks emerged as a proper subject. Whites were considered as superior and blacks were viewed as inferior. Our task is to continue a conversation to bring about change.

The formula of "I–You" comes out of my Bonhoeffer reflections, as I compared Bonhoeffer with M. L. King, Jr., in another discussion. According to Bonhoeffer, it is a different reference to relate to God (as "I–Thou") than it is to relate to other human beings in the "I–You" context. Though this insight came to Bonhoeffer during Hitler's reign, it symbolizes the relations between whites and blacks for many years. This emphasis of whites over blacks has been present constantly and has given rise to the black church and the black theology it informs.

Many illustrations from the late 1960s come to mind. As a young adult, I was walking with my father-in-law downtown in a Southern town in the 1960s. We were greeted by the cordial remarks of a local white Christian gentleman. He remarked: "How are you boys today?" He meant well and there were afterthoughts in his mind. It was OK to be Christian and consider blacks as inferior or even as nonhuman. The "I–Thou" relation (a relation reserved for God) did not have anything to do with an "I–It" relation to black people. The point is made. All of theology needed to be restructured. This meant the Bible needed to be "reread" and all the doctrines of the Christian faith needed to be "rethought" in light of the black experience.

My task, in view of experiences, nationwide and global, was to bring what I knew from the past to present attention. Therefore, I stressed liberation and reconciliation. Liberation was a given. However, reconciliation was never "cheap grace." The person was always understood to be in relation to others, individually and socially.

Dignity was always to reside in a social and public context. My trip to the heart of Africa, as well as family studies, gave force to these convictions. Involvement in the black churches, colleges, and communities enhanced my eschatological reflections. The enrichment of different views on the Christian faith strengthened my theological understanding of the future, beyond life and death, and was a part of all my theological writing, teaching, and activities. As theologian, I was anxious to pass on the notion that both the individual and the system had to change. Justice and love must now be brought together in theological reflection and action.

Whereas I had participated with white religious scholars and pastors in apologetics (both interfaith and ecumenical) thought and action, black theology required a careful examination of the context of thought and action. This meant that black theology had to be rooted in the black experience.

In the quest for the *dignity* of being black and human in the 1960s, there arose a new consciousness around the assumption that "black is beautiful." In this new consciousness there was to be an emergence of the humane use of power, a new self-respect and recognition, individual, social, and total.[4]

BLACK ESCHATOLOGICAL THOUGHTS ON DESTINY

"Destiny" refers to a predetermination and/or purpose. This implies that an assignment or dedication is made in advance. It is quite obvious that this is true of human life both as an individual and as a collective experience. But the issues are how this can be and how this is to be determined.

At the outset, we made it clear that this discussion is delimited. We do not address such topics as dispensationalism or apocalypticism in this study. The usual matters of biblical interpretation, based on division or time of zones, are not the issues for black theology. Neither is our main concern the end of time and the second coming of Christ. We are mainly concerned with how we can move forward, as a person and as a people, in the present life. We are interested in the relation between the best we can know and be in the present time, and the approach to our everlastingness in the presence of God.

While we have addressed the how and the why of the nadir period of black theology, it is almost an embarrassment to note that between the late 1960s and the present, little has changed in white–black relations. The black struggle to overcome oppression continues. It has taken a different shape and it is now confronted by the claims of diversity. We must be aware of the issues we face at present and will confront in the future.

Life is fundamental to all that we know now. Life is the controlling category. Our preoccupation is with life, and not death. While some Christians are preoccupied with death, black theologians must focus on life. We are aware that life continues beyond the demise of the present body. However, what we are concerned about is a holistic notion of the present life and how this completeness of life will continue beyond physical death in relation to our understanding of God.

Black theology views the *end* as the beginning. The relation of creation to eschatology is evident in our reflection on the doctrine of the last things. When we consider the dignity of life, as we have done, we are led directly to how life began for all humans. We do not have creation bestowed upon us by other humans. The value of nature and all creation is a gift from God, the author of creation.

When I was asked by the editors of this volume to write on eschatology, it came to my attention that the doctrine of creation is just as precious to me as any consideration of the last things. It was, likewise, valuable to look at eschatology, after the living and blessing of a long life, on the assumption of heaven as a future reality. The alpha and the omega of life is a unity to be sought.[5]

Life is given in creation. It is not based upon social or historical facts. Life is inherently valuable. This harks back to God. The mistreatment of any human is undesirable and should be opposed, especially through laws. Love, justice, and the humane use of power support the verdict that life is good and that life is sacred; color, race, class, or any other description does not alter the stamp of value, which God or the Creator has placed upon life.

As we reflect upon this givenness of value of life, we are led directly to *diversity*. Black theology has always placed a proper emphasis upon diversity. However, we must be aware that diversity builds upon the fact that all life is of equal value. We are also reminded that diversity does not replace dignity. In fact diversity is rooted in the awareness that all humans have been created equal.

There is much to be said about diversity. However, this is a subject given much attention now. When black theology emerged, our concern was primarily with whites oppressing blacks. Diversity now, as well as then, should come to the fore as one considers what it means to be black in the society of the United States. Here, I recall a recent conversation with Alexander Haley, son of the famous Alex Haley. This Haley had concluded, after several instances of US states making apologies for black slavery, that it is important to hold a perspective on slavery after being a slave. All decent people can denounce slavery from the top down on moral and rational grounds. To view slavery from the inside is basic. The similar view can be applied to diversity.

Thus black theologians have constantly referred to diversity, from their experience of being black. Other persons of color and different genders enter future conservations from the present. Nevertheless, the consideration of blackness from the inside has been with us constantly.

Multiculturalism may be more to the point, as black theologians attempt to describe where they were and are at present. There were a number of religious and ideological issues afloat in the 1960s and 1970s. We were abreast of all those issues. However, our approach was from inside and consistent with our anchor in the black heritage. Our concern was not to put others down, but to promote the power and consciousness of the masses of the black oppressed.

Much of my life as a theologian, from the late 1950s, had been given to dialogue, at home and abroad. My entrance into the theological and churchly concerns of the black theology movement was based upon discussions of black theology in the social contexts of its engagements. There were social, historical, political, ideological, ecumenical, and inter-religious issues to be confronted. It was in facing this reality that I as a black theologian had my say in dialogue with others. Civil rights, black nationalism, Black Power and consciousness, Vietnam, as well as other issues faced us at home. Abroad, there was also the demise of colonialism and the emergence of Zionism, Minjung, and the Latin American liberation theologians. For black theology, there is the now of eschatology as well as the then or future of the doctrine of the last things. There is a timelessness inherent in black theological reflection. In it the past, present, and the future greet each other. Due to my emersion in classical Christian Platonism as well as the quest for a rational place to stand in the examination of faith, I was not dogmatic in the approach to blackness. I was always open to dialogue. However, I also knew how to stand firm when it was obviously needed. In this stance, the knowledge of the world of ideas, other cultures and ethnic backgrounds, as well as races, aided the process of dialogue to forge a place to stand.[6]

As we look at the black view of destiny, it is obvious that the relation between our suffering and future must be considered. Much suffering is based upon poverty and the lack of resources to fund a decent life. Meagre inheritance resources, lack of employment, and cheap labor confront any reflection upon the destiny of black people.

Much pain stems from the absence of health care. Blacks encounter all the ills of mortal life, often without the intellectual and financial needs to overcome such pain. The pain has been endured, as a given. Much pain has been absorbed in view of heaven-future.

At this point, I can remember the comments of my mother, when I was a young boy. My mother could observe much poverty and social brutality due to her race in the South of the USA. She would long for heaven-future and say: "If you miss heaven, you miss everything." At every funeral, she would receive a vivid description of the beauty and blessings of the future life. There was no deliverance from the suffering experienced in her view. And yet her faith would be present in the faith, which followed. "Son, pursue a good education, and prepare yourself for a good life." Her faith led her to expect the "unseen." This I call "Hope against hope!"

Much later, as a black theologian, I could understand why black believers could see a relation between the present and the future, beyond physical death. At this juncture, I could envisage something else. It seemed to me that the future life could motivate life-present as an end. One could view the future, as breaking in the present. This view also enriched and gave power to the present life.[7]

It was helpful, in doing theology, to meet and work with the Revd. Leon H. Sullivan, the founder of Opportunities Industrialization Center (OIC), who was inspired by M. L King, Jr., and the civil rights efforts to lift up what he called economic, social, and political "alternatives to despair." Blacks could live a hopeful or positive existence. He turned to lives of self-help and people-uplift.

What Sullivan found in his ministry, Dr. Howard Thurman discovered in his thought-reflection. Thurman saw the pursuit of a good life as being continuous beyond physical endeavor. In fact, the living of a good life could be both a motivation and prelude to heaven-future. A college professor of religious education often remarked that if one lives a good life, going to heaven-future will take care of itself.

This section has treated just a few reflections of mine upon eschatology as a destiny. We move now to a concluding statement.

CONCLUSION: ALPHA AND OMEGA AS A BLACK THEOLOGICAL REFLECTION

A lot of our thinking on the emergence and continuation of black theology centers upon eschatology. However, we are concerned about what I would describe as realized eschatology – in which the beginning looks toward the end as an everlastingness at the time, while the end harks back through history to the creation. God is the real consummation of the eschaton. The continuity of life is a part of this continuum.[8]

Much thinking upon eschatology is related to how we understand the kingdom of God. Is it totally futuristic, or does it involve the transformation of the present in love, justice, and power? Black theology asserts that both the future and the present are involved in the understanding of the kingdom. "Thy kingdom come on earth as it is in heaven" is our constant plea (Matt. 6:10). The kingdom is present wherever the will of God is being done, individually and socially in *ethics* and *faith*.

Furthermore, the Christian tradition, incorporated in black theology, asserts that both the individual's redemption and social conditions are contexts in which God's work is to be done. Although I have spent years perfecting the Western views in theology, philosophy, and ethics, I have also been reflecting in Asia, Africa, Australia, and Latin America. I studied in Britain and Germany, extensively, and agree with Tutu, that the Western tradition is *apologetic* while the Eastern and Southern traditions are *synthetic*. My views bring these threads together. I also focus on the history and reflection of an oppressed community in the United States.

My theology considers the kingdom of God (in all times and places) as well as heaven-future. Black theology interprets what happens now and it is based upon the entire Bible: social justice, the ministry of Jesus, the witness of the people of God, and not the Book of Revelation only.

Thus human destiny, dialogue of thought, cultures and faith, the context of decision, and more, is to be explored as a challenge to black theology.

We do not know what the future holds but we know who holds the future. The author of nature is the giver of grace and will be with us always. In the end, God!

Notes

1   J. Deotis Roberts, *Seasons of Life: By Grace, with Gratitude – A Memoir* (Largo, MD: Charp Communications, forthcoming).
2   J. Deotis Roberts, *Christian Beliefs* (Atlanta, GA: John Colton and Associates, 1981), pp. 72–74. The civil rights movement, the encounter with Malcolm X, the Black Power event, etc. are among the things that first aroused my interest in black theology.
3   J. Deotis Roberts, *Liberation and Reconciliation: A Black Theology* (Philadelphia, PA: Westminster John Knox Press, 1971), pp. 76–99.

4   J. Deotis Roberts, "Black Consciousness in Theological Perspective," in J. J. Gardner and J. D. Roberts (eds.), *Quest for a Black Theology* (Philadelphia, PA: Pilgrim Press, 1971), pp. 62–81.

5   J. Deotis Roberts, *A Black Political Theology* (Philadelphia, PA: Westminster John Knox Press, 1974), ch. 8, pp. 188–89.

6   J. Deotis Roberts, *Black Theology in Dialogue* (Philadelphia, PA: Westminster John Knox Press, 1987); see pp. 11–19. Here I discuss contextualization as a theological method. See also David Emmanuel Goatley (ed.), *Black Religion, Black Theology: The Collected Essays of J. Deotis Roberts* (Harrisburg, PA: Trinity Press International, 2003), pp. 1–10.

7   J. Deotis Roberts, *The Prophethood of Black Believers* (Louisville, KY: Westminster John Knox Press, 1994).

8   Roberts, *A Black Political Theology*, pp. 178–89.

Part III

Global expressions of black theology

16 The history of black theology in South Africa

MOKGETHI MOTLHABI

The history and evolution of black theology in South Africa (BTSA) may be roughly divided into five phases. These phases include the following:

(1) the establishment of the Black Theology Project;
(2) the broadening of the debate on the subject of black theology, including the participation of black university students, black church and other organizations, and some white academics, among others;
(3) the renewal of black theological activity, by the second generation of black theologians;
(4) the revival of the hitherto defunct Black Theology Project;
(5) a final, still undetermined phase that is the result of general confusion regarding the new direction that theological activity should take in the country following the demise of apartheid and the relative success of the black liberation struggle.

This chapter begins with a close examination of these five phases of BTSA, followed by a look at the relationships it had with some of the theologies closest to it in its earlier days.

THE FIVE PHASES OF BLACK THEOLOGY (SA)

Phase one
The Black Theology Project (BTP) operated and campaigned through the organization of seminars in various parts of the country. Among the venues at which the earliest seminars were held is the Wilgespruit Fellowship Centre, originally a Lutheran mission, located in Roodepoort near Johannesburg. The first seminars were organized under the aegis of the University Christian Movement (UCM) directorate of Theological Concerns, headed by Dr. Basil Moore, an ordained Methodist minister. Later, a student intern from the Federal Theological Seminary, Sabelo

Ntwasa, was appointed the first director of the BTP. He was subsequently ordained a priest of the Church of the Province of South Africa (CPSA), commonly referred to as the Anglican Church (in American terms, Episcopalian).

Some of the early participants of the first black theology seminars included figures such as Dr. Manas Buthelezi, Bishops Alpheus Zulu and Lawrence Zulu, the Revd. B.N.B. Ngidi, the Revd. Clive McBride, and the Revd. Bonganjalo Goba, among others. Buthelezi later became bishop of the Lutheran Church in Johannesburg, after serving briefly in the Christian Institute of Southern Africa (CI) and being one of the respondents to the Schlebusch Commission of Enquiry.[1] Goba also acquired a doctorate in Chicago and later became professor at a number of institutions in South Africa and the USA. Basil Moore was forced into exile after being confined to house arrest by a government banning order, later becoming a professor in Australia.

Less familiar in BTSA's first phase is the communication that went on at the beginning between the officials of the UCM and black theologians in the United States, especially James Cone. As it was promulgated by the UCM, the early BTSA followed developments in the USA closely at the time, and especially the publication of Cone's first two books, *Black Theology and Black Power* and *A Black Theology of Liberation*.[2] As a result of these books, the UCM engaged in ongoing communication with American black theologians and tried to learn as much as possible from them regarding this new method of theology and its vision of human liberation seen from a theological perspective. This communication, which included visits to the USA by individuals from the UCM, is well substantiated by Basil Moore.[3]

Most of the writings that came from this first phase of BTSA were of an exploratory nature.[4] While a few of them reflected some keen theological insight, many were quite superficial and consisted largely of authors' outpourings regarding suffering under apartheid and its evil policies. Theological response to this state of affairs consisted of arguing that it was not intended by God and citing biblical texts, such as the Exodus story and Luke 4:18, to prove that God was on the side of the oppressed. This aspect of the early approaches to BTSA has recently come under severe criticism from Alistair Kee.[5]

Phase two

The second phase of BTSA may perhaps be called the engagement and response phase. During this phase, some new participants entered the challenge and debate, including university students, some individual ministers of religion, black church organizations, and some white theology academics. Most prominent among these groups was perhaps the South African Students' Organization (SASO). SASO subscribed to the philosophy of black consciousness and saw black theology as a natural ally to its cause of "conscientization." The reason for this was that, to quote from an article by one of its leaders, "Black people are notoriously religious."[6] Because of this assumed religiosity of black people, it seemed natural to conclude that one of the ways to work for their liberation was through inculcating a proper understanding of the theological underpinnings – from a black perspective – of the teachings of the church. For this reason, SASO established a special commission on black theology to conduct research into its socioreligious significance.

The commission established contacts with black clergy and their organizations, and also worked closely with UCM's BTP. It also worked closely with another organization, the Black Community Programmes (BCP). This organization was responsible for a number of research projects in the black community, including the publication of an important annual survey, *Black Review*, and a black analysis of events in the country, *Black Viewpoint*. The SASO BTSA commission reported annually to SASO's General Students' Council (GSC), where black theology occupied an important spot on the agenda, often accommodating lively debates regarding the teachings of the Bible, the role of the church, white theology, and the response of black theology in general. In one of his seminal essays, "Black Consciousness and the Quest for a True Humanity," Steve Biko devotes special attention to black religion as originally practiced in South Africa and to the anticipated reorienting role of black theology.[7]

During this phase of BTSA there was a special campaign to "conscientize" individual ministers of religion in the approach of black theology and to organize them into black ministers' caucuses. This was in order to encourage them to fight collectively against racism and discrimination in the church; to contextualize their religious services and preaching by taking account of the people's needs and struggles here and now, rather than orienting them toward a future "kingdom come"; and also to remain ever alert to the general sociopolitical and economic conditions in the country. While both SASO and the BTP were equally involved in this campaign of organizing black ministers, perhaps SASO was much more successful than the BTP. The BCP was also involved in its own way in dealings with black clergy. These three establishments also took their mission to church organizations such as IDAMASA

(Inter-Denominational African Ministers' Association of South Africa), AICA (African Independent Churches' Association), and others. Of particular interest during this phase of BTSA was the involvement of white academics in both trying to understand the significance of black theology and to explain it to white Christians, and their involvement in the debate on some of the positions advanced by black theology. These activities were undertaken not only in writing for academic publications, but also in the form of national conferences and academic seminars. A prominent conference in this regard was held at the Lutheran Theological Seminary in Mapumulo, Natal (now Kwa-Zulu Natal), on the theme "Toward a Relevant Theology for Africa."[8] From this conference, it was obvious that one of its chief aims was to evaluate black theology and its implications for the church in South Africa. The broad range of papers presented included topics on African traditional religion, African theology, black theology, and white theology. Its final recommendations were for some hybrid kind of theology that acknowledged some of the charges made by BTSA but also wanted to accommodate other theological perspectives prevalent in the continent, specifically in South Africa.

Around this time black theology was no longer the concern of black theologians only. White academics also read about it and engaged critically with it. One of the leading scholars among these was the late David Bosch, a University of South Africa professor and world-renowned missiologist. Bosch advanced the position that there were five trends in BTSA. The first of these trends, according to him, followed the "American model." Its emphasis was on contextualization, concerned with bread-and-butter issues, and it focused on the struggle for black liberation. The second trend almost equated BTSA to African Theology (AT) in the sense of "soul mates"[9] as defined by Desmond Tutu. The third trend was accommodative of African traditional religion; and the fourth saw the original struggles of the African Independent Churches (AICs) as early expressions of BTSA. The fifth trend discussed by Bosch is perhaps best illustrated by Emmanuel Martey's depiction of a "wholesome" AT,[10] involving both liberation and inculturation.[11]

Phase three

The third phase of BTSA manifests itself in two ways in the country. First, it manifests itself in the form of a lull in activity in black theology, especially between the mid 1970s and the early 1980s. It is reported, however, that some activities on the subject did take place on a smaller scale through the efforts of another black organization, the Black Renaissance Convention (BRC). It was headed by Dr. Smangaliso Mkhatshwa, a Catholic priest, later to become also the Deputy Minister of Education and Executive Mayor of Tshwane (Pretoria). The BRC organized the last black theology conference of this phase in Maseru, Lesotho, in 1978.[12]

The second manifestation of this phase of BTSA was in the form of a retreat and a period of academic formation by a group of young clergy who may be referred to as the second generation of black theologians. During this period these young ministers, including lay theology enthusiasts, independently undertook study for higher degrees in different fields of theology, mostly in Europe and the USA. Their studies later resulted in publications of their doctoral theses in their various fields, approached from the perspective of black theology. Notable among these theses were: Allan Boesak, *Farewell to Innocence* (1976); Bonganjalo Goba, *An Agenda for Black Theology* (1988); Takatso Mofokeng, *The Crucified among the Cross-Bearers* (1983); Clement Mokoka, *Black Experience and Black Theology* (1984); Itumeleng Mosala, *Biblical Hermeneutics and Black Theology in South Africa* (1989); and Cecil Ngcokovane, *Demons of Apartheid* (1989), among others.

This second generation of black theologians, including others whose theses were not directly focused on black theology, returned to South Africa in the early 1980s. Some of them joined academic institutions, which still had an almost exclusively white orientation in their curricula and were not readily amenable to giving special attention to black theology. Thus, although these new black academics had great ideas about implementing what they had learned abroad, their impact was limited to where this was possible at all. This partly accounts for the fact that BTSA never really developed a full presence as an academic discipline. Others from this generation of black theologians became involved in other fields of work, including the church and nongovernmental organizations. Prominent among them was Allan Boesak, whose work in his church and his political activism led to his election as president of the World Alliance of Reformed Churches.

Phase four

The third phase of BTSA leads directly to the fourth. In this phase the new doctors of theology regrouped in the hope of reviving the old campaign of BTSA, but now with more vigour accompanied by strong backgrounds in academic education in their respective fields.

They reconstituted and restructured the then defunct BTP and also founded the *Journal of Black Theology in South Africa*.[13] Their activities coincided with the establishment of a new theological organization in the country, called the Institute for Contextual Theology (ICT). Although the ICT's aims were broader than those of the old BTP, it was keen to accommodate a black theological perspective in order for its work to be relevant to the black majority of South Africa. For this reason, members of the BTP were invited for discussions and consultations by the Institute. These culminated in the establishment of the Black Theology Reflection Group (BTRG), a group that subsequently met on a monthly basis to reflect theologically on the situation in the country.

Theological reflections in the ICT led to new developments in the approach of black theology in the country. These developments involved a paradigm shift from the original sole focus on race as being responsible for black oppression and the many distortions in the Christian teaching that were responsible for its perpetuation. The shift was toward the inclusion of class and gender analyses in theological reflection as means of addressing other prominent forms of injustice in the country. It meant that poverty and economic forms of exploitation as well as various forms of discrimination against women were to be taken seriously and given special focus by black theology.

Hitherto these two avenues of concern were considered to be the concerns of Latin American liberation theology and feminist/womanist theology. It was made clear in the debate on their inclusion for special focus by BTSA, however, that a "general black theology" that did not pay special attention to issues of poverty and the gender concerns of black women could not be considered to be fully representative in its liberation struggle. Indeed, black women were part of the oppressed majority; yet they were oppressed not only as black, but also as women – even at the very hands of black men themselves. The poor majority in South Africa were also black people; yet even here the poor blacks experienced more deprivation and oppression than the black elite, who were also part of the problem for the poor in the country. BTSA, therefore, had to be explicit and specific in its advocacy of liberation of black women and the black poor as well, in particular. Although there was vigorous debate on this issue, as explained by the then ICT general secretary, Frank Chikane,[14] debate that threatened to divide black theologians into three separate camps, there was ultimate concurrence that the struggle was one, although many-faceted.

Most of these debates took place in the context of a number of conferences on BTSA, organized by the ICT. Two of these conferences,

one held in Johannesburg and the other in Cape Town, led to the publication of a collection of essays, *The Unquestionable Right to Be
Free.*[15] This publication was followed by another, compiled independently by the BTP in honor of Archbishop Desmond Tutu. It was given
the title *Hammering Swords into Ploughshares: Essays in Honour of
Archbishop Desmond Mpilo Tutu.*[16] Other publications of this phase,
not falling under the organization of the ICT, included Tutu's *Hope and
Suffering* (1983); Boesak's *Black and Reformed* (1984); Simon Maimela
and Dwight Hopkins' *We Are One Voice* (1989), among others.

The BTP also organized its own conferences independently of the
ICT. Venues for these conferences included Pretoria; Johannesburg;
Midrand, near Johannesburg; and Gaborone, Botswana. At the Midrand
conference, in 1992, a proposal was made for the establishment of a membership structure in order to encourage broader participation in black
theology activities. The name given to this structure was Community
of Black and African Theologians (COMBAT). This structure, however,
did not succeed in getting off the ground, partly because of the lack of
human power and partly because of the lack of immediate funding. The
last conference organized by the BTP during this phase took place at the
University of South Africa in 1995.

Phase five

The fifth and last phase of BTSA, at this point in time, is quite
elusive, perhaps even nonexistent. It is not clear whether this is only a
temporary lull in theological activity, a temporary retreat for the sake
of recovery or the end mistakenly implied by the title of Kee's book.[17]
It is not only black theology, however, that is currently in a state of
disarray in South Africa, but also the entire organizational theological
enterprise, especially outside the academic sphere. Even in academic
institutions, however, many theological departments have been forced
to close down during the past decade, with more and more attention
now diverted to religious studies. The blame for this particular state
of affairs is laid at the door of the post-apartheid government's policy
on education, which emphasizes equal treatment of all religions. Since
theology is largely associated with Christian teachings, it is viewed as
exclusive of other religions, compared to religious studies, which is
inclusive.

The current disarray in the theological enterprise is, paradoxically,
largely perceived as the outcome of the relative success of the liberation
struggle and the fall of apartheid. During the days of apartheid, all efforts,

even in the church's struggle for justice, were largely focused on the elimination of the injustices of apartheid. The government of the day, therefore, was viewed as the personification of this evil and was, consequently, seen as the concrete adversary of the struggle for change. From the perspective of theology, it was viewed as the beast in Revelation, the intolerable leviathan. With the beast defeated, there now seems to be nothing more to fight except for the minor manifestations of social evil that will never completely disappear. However, no government system can be perfect and there is always need to work for positive change. In view of this, there is a need for a new approach toward bringing about this change through addressing present-day problems, which are of a different nature from those of apartheid times. In other words, there is a need for a new theological paradigm, which will be more congruent with the needs of the current situation in the country.

It is this need for a new paradigm that is dumbfounding to black theologians. A recent attempt at a fresh start in the form of so-called theology of reconstruction does not seem to have had much appeal in the country and is now hardly heard about. From the side of BTSA, the dumbfounding seems to be almost absolute except for an occasional lone voice.[18] Regrettably, this impression seems to have provided justification to those of its opponents who originally accused it of being a reactionary type of theology. There have always been questions such as: What agenda will BTSA have after apartheid? In order for BTSA to shrug off this kind of charge, it will have to develop a new paradigm – a paradigm that will address itself to the multiple present-day evils, such as ongoing poverty, slum-dwelling, the inadequate social services still prevalent in many black communities, and many other types of issue.

THE RELATIONSHIP BETWEEN BTSA AND AFRICAN THEOLOGY

The relationship between BTSA and AT received its classic representations from Manas Buthelezi and Desmond Tutu. Buthelezi rejected the idea of any kind of relationship between the two theologies, while Tutu supported and affirmed the significance of such a relationship. In rejecting the relationship, Buthelezi approached the idea in exclusivist terms of having to choose between the two. This necessity of choice was reflected by the title of an article he wrote on the subject, stated in the form of a question: "An African Theology or a Black Theology?"[19]

He compared the two theologies in terms of their approaches, which for him determined the choice to be made. According to this comparison, African theology followed the ethnographical approach, while BTSA followed the anthropological approach. Buthelezi identified BTSA with the anthropological approach and saw it as a more suitable theology for South Africa than AT, which he identified with the ethnographical approach. His main suspicion of the latter arose from the perception that it based its point of departure on misconceived "elements of the traditional African worldview." Such a worldview, however, he argued, was not based on reality but was, instead, "an ethnographical reconstruction." This was because ethnography is mainly concerned with the cultures of nonliterate peoples whose past customs can be accessed mainly through some form of reconstruction. It was doubtful according to Buthelezi, therefore, whether a worldview based on such a reconstruction of reality could be considered a "valid postulate" for AT.[20]

Buthelezi was further concerned that such a preoccupation with a reconstructed past would lead to distractive fantasies about some golden age instead of encouraging concentration on present-day realities. These realities, for black people, naturally had to do with experiences of oppression and suffering under white racism, exploitation, and contempt. Since BTSA had a clear focus on such present-day concerns, it obviously deserved to be chosen as the more relevant theology for South Africa, while AT had no place in the country at all – at least in its current form.

In contrast, Tutu's interpretation of the relationship between BTSA and AT was inclusive. To the question whether they were soul mates or antagonists, he instead affirmed their oneness by seeing BTSA as part of AT. He illustrated this by seeing BTSA as "the inner and smaller in a series of concentric circles."[21] He referred to their different starting points in terms of their contextual origins, AT being originally from independent Africa at the time, while BTSA arose from a situation of oppression and racism; hence BTSA's concern with liberation. While Tutu welcomed the fact that AT helped to affirm "African religious consciousness," he regretted its tendency to remain disengaged from the concrete problems of people in Africa. For this reason he was more critical toward it than toward BTSA. In contrast, BTSA was seen as "more thoroughly and explicitly political than AT."[22] However, though it was equally guilty of the opposite extreme of failing to give proper recognition to African culture and traditional religious practices, Tutu failed to take it to task for this failure, thus showing his own bias toward BTSA.

Tutu's position on the relationship between BTSA and AT was obviously identical to Martey's later representation of AT as incorporating the two aspects of liberation and inculturation. This obviously refers to the "new" AT, since "traditional" AT was solely focused on inculturation in the form of "indigenization" and related concepts. In Tutu's terms, this relationship means that BTSA and AT are two sides of the same coin, which, in Martey's analysis, is African theology. In the final analysis, it would appear that "a BTSA or an AT" (*pace* Buthelezi) that did not reflect the two sides of liberation and inculturation remained one-sided and incomplete. Consequently, it can be concluded that in today's South Africa, BT is AT and AT is BT.

Notes

1   This was a government-appointed commission to investigate the activities of the UCM, the Christian Institute of South Africa, and the Wilgespruit Fellowship Centre.
2   James H. Cone, *Black Theology and Black Power* (New York: Seabury Press, 1969); *A Black Theology of Liberation* (Philadelphia, PA: J. B. Lippincott, 1970).
3   Basil Scott Moore, "Black Theology: In the Beginning," *Journal for the Study of Religion* 4(2) (September 1991): 25.
4   The first collection of essays, *Essays on Black Theology*, ed. Mokgethi Motlhabi (Johannesburg, South Africa: University Christian Movement), appeared in 1972. It was subsequently edited for English and American editions by Basil Moore. The true editor of the 1972 edition was, in fact, Sabelo Ntwasa. However, because of a government banning order imposed upon him before the publication of the book, his name was replaced by that of Motlhabi.
5   Alistair Kee, *The Rise and Demise of Black Theology* (Aldershot, UK; Burlington, VT: Ashgate, 2006).
6   N. Barney Pityana, "What Is Black Consciousness?" in Basil Moore (ed.), *The Challenge of Black Theology in South Africa* (Atlanta, GA: John Knox Press, 1974), pp. 58–63, at p. 58.
7   Steve Biko, "Black Consciousness and the Quest for a True Humanity," in Moore (ed.), *Challenge of Black Theology*, pp. 36–47.
8   See H. J. Becken, *Relevant Theology for Africa* (Durban, South Africa: Lutheran Publishing House, 1973).
9   See note 21, below.
10   Emmanuel Martey, *African Theology: Inculturation and Liberation* (Maryknoll, NY: Orbis Books, 1993).
11   See David Bosch, "Currents and Crosscurrents," in James H. Cone and Gayraud S. Wilmore (eds.), *Black Theology: A Documentary History*, vol. 1, *1966–1979*, 2nd edn. (Maryknoll, NY: Orbis Books, 1993), pp. 220–37.

12 See Frank Chikane, "Foreword," in Itumeleng J. Mosala and Buti Tlhagale (eds.), *The Unquestionable Right to Be Free: Black Theology from South Africa* (Johannesburg, South Africa: Skotaville; Maryknoll, NY: Orbis Books, 1986), p. xiv.

13 The last issue of this journal was, unfortunately, in 1998.

14 Chikane, "Foreword," p. xv.

15 Mosala and Tlhagale (eds.), *The Unquestionable Right to Be Free.*

16 Buti Tlhagale and Itumeleng Mosala (eds.), *Hammering Swords into Ploughshares: Essays in Honour of Archbishop Desmond Mpilo Tutu* (Johannesburg, South Africa: Skotaville, 1986).

17 While Kee is clearly critical of black theology in many of its manifestations, he states that his reasons for writing the book are not to encourage black theologians to give up their task, but to "move on, for the sake of the black poor of America, Africa and the third world." *Rise and Demise of Black Theology*, p. x.

18 See Tinyiko Maluleke, "Black Theology Lives! In a Permanent Crisis," *Journal of Black Theology in South Africa* 9(1) (May 1996): 1–30.

19 Manas Buthelezi, "An African Theology or a Black Theology?" in Moore (ed.), *Challenge of Black Theology*, pp. 29–35, at p. 29.

20 Ibid., pp. 31–33.

21 Desmond Tutu, "African Theology/Black Theology: Soul Mates or Antagonists?" in D. W. Ferm (ed.), *Third World Liberation Theologies: A Reader* (Maryknoll, NY: Orbis Books, 1986), pp. 256–64, at p. 262.

22 Ibid.

17 Black theology in Britain
ANTHONY REDDIE

One of the overarching difficulties in seeking to articulate the defin-
itional intent and ideological positionality of black theology in Britain is
that of seeking to construct a working "mythology" in which to locate
one's epistemological work. In the US context, for instance (from which
black British theology has derived much of its inspiration and nurturing),[1] there remains a potent and visceral narrative of African American
identity and positionality within the body politic of that nation. The
legacy of chattel slavery as depicted by Dwight Hopkins,[2] Anthony
Pinn,[3] and others has outlined the historical and theological features
that underscore black existence in the American continent. For many
of "us," black British life is best understood in terms of the mass migration of black people from the Caribbean islands of the British Empire to
the United Kingdom between 1948 and 1965.[4]

A helpful means of deciphering this ongoing problem is to investigate the thorny question of acceptable nomenclatures for being black in
Britain. For most black Americans, the designation *African American* is
a straightforward descriptor for what it means to be a person of African
descent living in the United States of America. In Britain, many black
people, such as myself, will describe themselves as *African Caribbean*.
This descriptor is indicative of one's heritage and ethnicity, but tells us
nothing about one's nationality. In using the term *African Caribbean* I
am identifying myself with the diasporan African "Roots" and "Routes"
(in the British context, both words are pronounced the same, hence the
alacrity with which we use such terms as an alliterative heuristic) of
my heritage, but in sociopolitical terms, I remain loath to confirm my
connection with a context in which black people continue to be denied
the full rights of sociocultural belonging.[5]

So what can this subjective, experiential, and discursive entrée tell
us about the nature and intent of black theology in Britain? Namely,
that black theology in Britain is a heterogeneous and plural term, discipline, and form of contextual praxis. The author of this chapter is

a black British-born subject of Caribbean roots. My parents were part of the most significant migratory movements in contemporary British history. The mass migratory movement of black people from Africa and the Caribbean in the years following the end of World War II has often been termed the *Windrush*.[6] The postwar presence of black people within British inner cities and churches is a phenomenon that has been described by a great many sociologists and historians.[7] This influx is perceived as commencing with the arrival of 492 Jamaicans at Tilbury docks on the ship SS *Empire Windrush*, June 22, 1948. While there has been a black presence in Britain since the times of the Romans, the birth of Britain's black communities,[8] for the most part, dates from the influx of Caribbean migrants in the post-World War II epoch.

DEFINING BLACK THEOLOGY IN BRITAIN

When speaking of black theology in Britain, I am speaking of the specific self-named enterprise of reinterpreting the meaning of God as revealed in Christ, in light of existential black experience in Britain. This approach to engaging with the Christian tradition is not unlike black theology in differing arenas such as the USA or South Africa, where one's point of departure is the existential and ontological reality of blackness and the black experience, in dialogue with "Holy Scripture."

Black theology in Britain is governed by the necessity of ortho-praxis rather than orthodoxy. In using this statement, what I mean is that one's starting point in talking about God is governed by the necessity to find a basis for acting in response to the existential struggles and vicissitudes of life, which impinge upon one's daily operations in the attempt to be a human being. The need for a response to the realities of life as it is in postcolonial Britain is one that has challenged many black British Christians to seek in God a means of making sense of situations that seem inherently senseless.[9]

British black theology has been inspired by the work of, predominantly, North American scholars, most notably James Cone,[10] Delores Williams,[11] and Jackie Grant.[12] In the British context, the framework for a black hermeneutics has been eloquently articulated by Robert Beckford.[13]

In defining black theology in Britain, I acknowledge my own limited viewpoint at this juncture. For while there is a growing wealth of literature that has explored black theology from within other religious paradigms, including Rastafarianism,[14] Hinduism,[15] and traditional African religions,[16] black theology in Britain has been dominated by

Christianity. I write as a Christian practical black liberation theologian who is based at a church-sponsored theological college.

WHAT IS THE "BLACK" IN BLACK THEOLOGY IN BRITAIN?

Black theology in Britain, much like the development of black identities, can be viewed as plural, hybrid, and dynamic, thus eschewing any simplistic attempt to essentialize or to reify identities.[17] The term "black" has to be understood within the context of Britain with all its peculiarities and inconsistencies. The use of the term "black" does not simply describe one's epidermis, but is rather a political statement relating to one's sense of marginalization within the contested space that is Britain. The term is used to identify one as a socially constructed "other," juxtaposed with the prevailing Eurocentric discourses that dominate the normative gaze and trajectory of what it means to be *authentically British*. While black theology in Britain has been dominated by black people of African and Caribbean descent, Asian scholars of the ilk of Inderjit Bhogal[18] and Mukti Barton[19] have made an impressive and much-needed contribution to the development and refining of this theological discipline and transformative model of contextual praxis.

A SHORT CONTEMPORARY HISTORY OF BLACK THEOLOGY IN BRITAIN

One can argue that the birth of black theology in Britain occurred when enslaved Africans such as Mary Prince,[20] Olaudah Equiano,[21] and Ignatius Sancho[22] began to write their memoirs in the eighteenth century. The more contemporary development of black theology in Britain emerges from a generation of black pastors and ministers, predominantly in the Anglican and Methodist churches, who, while in the throes of reflecting on their ministerial practice, began to speculate on the possibility of creating a black British theology of liberation. Religious practitioners such as Gus John, Robinson Milwood, David Moore, and Wesley Daniel,[23] who were either in pastoral ministry or college or seminary students, remain the early pioneers in the development of black theology in Britain. Black theology, then, as a literary form in Britain, is less than thirty years old.[24]

These indefatigable stalwarts did not occupy academic positions, nor were they afforded luxurious reflective space in which they could concentrate solely on their work in this regard. Essentially, many of them had to earn their living undertaking the daily labors of pastoral ministry and formative educational training.

BLACK THEOLOGY IN BRITAIN AND
THE BLACK CHURCH

Black theology in Britain does not exist in a vacuum. In many different contexts, the church in general and the "black church" in particular have proved to be the most durable of locations from which and in which the nascent practices of black theology in Britain has flourished. The ongoing development of black theology in Britain has operated largely within the parameters of the black church as opposed to the formal structures and scholarly hinterland of the academy. At the moment, only three academic institutions are presently teaching black theology in the curriculum.[25]

In using the term "black church," I want to suggest two differing ecclesial configurations for locating an operative center for the practice and theorizing of black theology in Britain. The first configuration, and by far the most visible, is that of black-led Pentecostal churches. These churches owe their origins to black migrants traveling from the Caribbean in the postwar mass movement of the last century. The first churches were offshoots of predominantly white Pentecostal denominations in the Southern States of the USA. These churches were first planted in the UK in the early 1950s. The largest and most established of these churches are the New Testament Church of God and the Church of God of Prophecy.[26] The second strand is black majority churches in white historical denominations.[27] These churches are demographically determined, as their black majority membership has grown out of black migrants moving into inner-city urban contexts, coupled with the flight of the white middle class.[28]

Within the literature of black religious studies, particular emphasis is placed on the role of the black church as the major (in some respects, the only) institution that has affirmed and conferred dignity upon the assaulted personhood of black people.[29]

CLASSICAL BLACK BRITISH PENTECOSTALISM
AND BLACK THEOLOGY

While some adherents of British Pentecostal churches came as communicant members of historical (white) denominations,[30] many of these individuals, however, arrived as members of established Pentecostal denominations in the Caribbean. For many, their arrival in the UK was born of an intense missionary desire to plant and establish their own churches in this new cultural and social context. A detailed history of this largely untold narrative can be found in the work of black British scholars such as Joe Aldred,[31] Mark Sturge,[32] and Doreen McCalla.[33]

There is no doubting the important contribution black British Pentecostalism has made to the development of black theology in Britain. In the works of such individuals as Joe Aldred and Robert Beckford, black British Pentecostalism has been able to assert the importance of religio-cultural aesthetics and codified forms of sanctified worship, highlighting the emotive power of black worship as a countercultural phenomenon in order to counter racism.[34]

The weakness in black British Pentecostalism as a conduit for the development and sustenance of black theology in Britain can be detected in its seeming inability to engage explicitly with the central tenets of black hermeneutical thought, particularly in terms of interrogating the Bible. This weakness has been highlighted in comparatively recent work.[35] This perceived weakness of black majority Pentecostal churches in Britain rests upon the historical relationship between these churches and white Southern American fundamentalist Christianity. The two leading Pentecostal churches in Britain, the New Testament Church of God and the Church of God of Prophecy, both have their roots and formative development in the South of the United States of America.

One of the defining characteristics of black Pentecostal churches is their worship style, which draws upon a range of black diasporan (and continental) African traditions, some of which are African American in style. The invocation of the spirit within black Pentecostal worship, for example, is fused with an expressive, informal liturgy; this has been one of the defining hallmarks of black religiosity. Robert Beckford offers a carefully constructed black British Pentecostal perspective on this creative dynamic in which participation and movement is an important means by which the liberative impulse of black life is expressed.[36]

BLACK THEOLOGY AND WHITE MAJORITY CHURCHES IN BRITAIN

The second ecclesial configuration is that of black churches in white majority historical churches in Britain. The majority of the black members in such churches in Britain can trace their roots to Africa and the

Caribbean. The greater number of these church adherents attend black majority churches in predominantly inner-city urban contexts.[37] These churches operate, in effect, as black enclaves within the overall white majority structure of the church as a whole. Among the most significant churches in this category are Walworth Road Methodist Church (in South London) and Holy Trinity Birchfield Church of England (Birmingham).

The development of black theology within these white majority historical bodies has emerged as a result of demographic changes in inner-city areas within the larger cities and towns in Britain. This development has not occurred through a self-conscious separation along the lines of "race," as has been the case in the USA. Recent research by Peter Brierley has shown that the majority of black Christians in Britain belong to white majority historical churches (by a factor of almost two to one).[38] Black theology in Britain, then, has developed most markedly from within the white historical churches. The work of Barton (Anglican), Jagessar (United Reformed), and myself (Methodist), all based at the Queen's Foundation for Theological Education, has been most notable for the long-held commitment to black theology. This work has taken expression in books, essays, and in the monthly National Black Theology Forum.

The black theology in Britain that has emerged from white historical churches is notable for its commitment to challenging racism and white ethnocentric sociocultural norms. Whether in Barton's work on critiquing Anglican ecclesiological practices[39] or in my own context of the challenging of Eurocentric epistemological frameworks for Christian learning,[40] black theologians whose work arises from within the white historical tradition have gained an important measure of respect for their ongoing commitment to black theology.

The weakness of the historical churches as a site for the development of black theology rests on their ongoing relationship to the hinterland of postcolonial cultural norms. In short, black people in these Christian traditions have to negotiate with an alternative form of theo-psycho schizophrenia, operating as black enclaves within white-dominated contexts. This necessitates a form of double vision that can be psychologically destructive. While British Pentecostalism provides the emotional and liturgically cathartic space in which the black self can seek repose in experiential worship and African Caribbean religio-cultural aesthetics,[41] the theological underpinning in such settings remains studiously wedded to white Euro-American fundamentalism. Conversely, black theology that emerges from within white historical churches (e.g., Anglican, Methodist, or United Reformed) possesses a greater readiness to engage with deconstructive and radically prophetic models of hermeneutics. The gains of these traditions, however, sit in dialectical tension with the unreconstructed whiteness and colonially informed norms of inherited ecclesial practices and liturgical formations. In terms of the latter, one only has to witness in these settings the formal operations of pre-modern white European worship traditions along with the sense of cultural dissonance felt by black people, in order to gain some sense of the weakness of these ecclesial paradigms in offering an effective platform for the development and practice of black theology in Britain.[42]

THE WORK OF ROBERT BECKFORD

As the most recognized black theologian in Britain, Robert Beckford's work remains hugely important to the visibility and direction of this discipline and practice in the British context. His work has always contained a strong investment in black Caribbean popular culture, particularly that which emanates from within the wider frameworks provided by reggae aesthetics. In many respects, this new direction is shown in sharp relief by his latest work, *Jesus Dub*.[43] In this text, Beckford continues in his radical juxtapositioning of black religion (African Caribbean Pentecostal Christianity) and black popular culture. *Jesus Dub* juxtaposes the "church hall" and the "dance hall" in order to rework the theo-political dimensions of black aesthetics, space, and religio-cultural positionality in terms of black people's postcolonial subjectivities and identities in twenty-first century Britain.

Beckford's central thesis is that "Dub is an act of deconstruction, where a reggae musician takes apart the key elements of a music track, and repositions them, transforming the original, thereby enabling new ways of hearing and understanding."[44] He argues that throughout diasporan African history, black working-class people have constantly used music and faith as constructs by which they might resist racialized oppression. This work represents the continuing exploration of black theology and popular culture in Britain.

MY OWN WORK

Alongside Robert Beckford, the other major black theological undertaking in Britain, certainly in terms of scholarly output, has been my own work. If you will pardon the immodesty, I want to look at aspects of my own developing approach to black theology in order to discern an alternative direction in which this discipline is moving in this country.

My own training has been in the area of practical theology: specializing in the juxtaposing of black theological content with the educational concerns for conscientization and formation among ordinary black people. This approach to "doing black theology" is one that I have termed practical black liberation theology. Practical black liberation theology in Britain is predicated on the notion of Christian believers engaging in what I call "performative action." Performative action requires that we creatively engage with the "other" in a specified space (what one might term "ecclesia" or "communities of faithful practice"⁴⁵) in which the rules of engagement are constantly being defined and redefined.⁴⁶

In order to provide an embodied reality for the practice of performative action, I have created a number of experiential exercises in which adult participants can explore the dynamics of encounter and transformation in a personal, collective, and corporate sense within safe learning environments. The thrust for this work has emerged from a previous piece of research.⁴⁷ This approach to undertaking black theology in Britain, which is based upon my own idiosyncratic interests in experiential learning and Christian formation, draws upon the central tenets of black theology as a means of creating new ways of engaging in this discipline and practice. My work is eclectic and interdisciplinary and, like Beckford's, is not doctrinal or systematic, nor is it located purely within the academy for the benefit solely of other scholars. In both Beckford's and my own work (which many would deem the most significant black British theology today) one can witness two alternative (and yet complementary) tributaries for the flow and progress of black theology in Britain.

CONCLUSION

In conclusion, then, black theology in Britain, like her many counterparts in of the rest of the world, is committed to a radical appropriation of the Gospel in order that those who are the "least of these" (Matt. 25:31–46) might live, and have that life in all its fullness (John 10:10). This ongoing work is grounded in a praxis that is not mindful of either doctrinal purity or Biblical literalism. As such, black theology in Britain continues to challenge normative black Christian faith that has for far too long drunk rather too deeply from the well of "evangelical post-Reformation theology," which has largely muted Christianity's embodied radical intent. Instead, black theology in Britain continues to offer a radical form of thinking and contextual praxis that simultaneously seeks to empower marginalized and disenfranchised black people alongside the need to challenge and inspire white power to see and act differently.

Notes

1 See Anthony G. Reddie, *Black Theology in Transatlantic Dialogue* (New York: Palgrave Macmillan, 2006).
2 See Dwight N. Hopkins, *Down, Up, and Over: Slave Religion and Black Theology* (Minneapolis, MN: Fortress Press, 1999).
3 Anthony B. Pinn, *Terror and Triumph: The Nature of Black Religion* (Minneapolis, MN: Fortress Press, 2003)
4 See Anthony G. Reddie, *Faith, Stories and the Experience of Black Elders: Singing the Lord's Song in a Strange Land* (London: Jessica Kingsley, 2001).
5 See Paul Gilroy, *"There Ain't No Black in the Union Jack": The Cultural Politics of Race and Nation* (London: Hutchinson, 1987) and also *The Black Atlantic: Modernity and Double Consciousness* (London: Verso, 1993).
6 This term originates from a pivotal event on June 22, 1948, when 492 Jamaicans arrived at Tilbury docks on the SS *Empire Windrush*. These postwar pioneers ushered in a wave of black migration to Britain from the Caribbean, which (for the most part) forms the basis for black African and Caribbean communities in Britain. For further information see Mike Phillips and Trevor Phillips, *Windrush: The Irresistible Rise of Multi-Racial Britain* (London: HarperCollins, 1999).
7 Selective literature includes R. B. Davidson, *Black British* (Oxford University Press, 1966); R. A. Easterlin, *Immigration* (Cambridge, MA: Belknap Press of Harvard University Press, 1982); Paul Hartman and Charles Hubbard, *Immigration and the Mass Media* (London: Davis-Poynter, 1974); Edward Scobie, *Black Britannia: A History of Blacks in Britain* (Chicago, IL: Johnson Publishing Co., 1972); Ken Pryce, *Endless Pressure* (Bristol, UK: Classical Press, 1979); and Winston James and Clive Harris, *Migration, Racism and Identity* (London: Verso, 1993).
8 See Gretchen Gerzina, *Black England: Life before Emancipation* (London: John Murray, 1995).
9 These themes are explored to great effect by Robert Beckford in *God of the Rahtid* (London: Darton, Longman and Todd, 2003), pp. 1–30.
10 See James H. Cone, *A Black Theology of Liberation* (Maryknoll, NY: Orbis Books, 1986).
11 See Delores S. Williams, *Sisters in the Wilderness: The Challenge of Womanist God-Talk* (Maryknoll, NY: Orbis Books, 1993).
12 See Jacquelyn Grant, *White Women's Christ and Black Women's Jesus: Feminist Christology and Womanist Response* (Atlanta, GA: Scholars Press, 1989)

13 See Robert Beckford, *Dread and Pentecostal* (London: SPCK, 2000).

14 See William David Spencer, *Dread Jesus* (London: SPCK, 1999).

15 Michael N. Jagessar, "Liberating Cricket: Through the Optic of Ashutosh Gowariker's Lagaan," *Black Theology: An International Journal* 2(2) (July 2004): 239–49.

16 Kampta Karran, "Changing Kali: From India to Guyana to Britain," *Black Theology in Britain: A Journal of Contextual Praxis* 4(1) (November 2001): 90–102.

17 See Paul Gilroy, *Between Camps: Nations, Cultures and the Allure of Race* (London: Allen Lane, The Penguin Press, 2000).

18 See Inderjit S. Bhogal, "Citizenship," in Anthony G. Reddie (ed.), *Legacy: Anthology in Memory of Jillian Brown* (Peterborough, UK: Methodist Publishing House, 2000), pp. 137–41, and Inderjit S. Bhogal, *On the Hoof: Theology in Transit* (Sheffield, UK: Penistone Publications 2001).

19 Mukti Barton, *Rejection, Resistance and Resurrection: Speaking Out on Racism in the Church* (London: Darton, Longman and Todd, 2005).

20 Mary Prince was a nineteenth-century black slave woman who published her autobiography in 1831 detailing her experiences of hardship, struggle, and emancipation. Her book was entitled *The History of Mary Prince, a West Indian Slave. Related by Herself. With a Supplement by the Editor. To Which Is Added, the Narrative of Asa-Asa, a Captured African* (London: F. Westley and A. H. Davis, 1831). It was a key text in the abolitionary movement of the nineteenth century.

21 See Vincent Caretta (ed.), *Olaudah Equiano: The Interesting Narrative and Other Writings* (New York and London: Penguin Books, 1995).

22 See Vincent Caretta (ed.), *Letters of the Late Ignatius Sancho, an African* (New York and London: Penguin Books, 1998).

23 See Reddie, *Black Theology in Transatlantic Dialogue*, pp. 26–32, for further information on this important narrative.

24 For more on the history of black theology in Britain, see ibid., pp. 143–66.

25 At the time of writing, these are Oxford Brookes University, The Queen's Foundation for Ecumenical Theological Education, and the University of Birmingham.

26 See Joe Aldred, *Respect: A Caribbean British Contextual Theology* (Peterborough, UK: Epworth Press, 2006).

27 These denominations include the Church of England (the Anglican Church), the Roman Catholic Church, the Methodist Church, the Baptist Church, and the United Reformed Church.

28 See John L. Wilkinson, *Church in Black and White. The Black Christian Tradition in "Mainstream" Churches in England: A White Response and Testimony* (Edinburgh: St Andrew Press, 1993).

29 See C. Eric Lincoln and Lawrence H. Mamiya, *The Black Church in the African American Experience* (Durham, NC, and London: Duke University Press, 1990) and Peter J. Paris, *The Social Teaching of the Black Churches* (Minneapolis, MN: Fortress Press, 1985). See also Anne H. Pinn and Anthony B. Pinn, *Black Church History* (Minneapolis,

MN: Fortress Press, 2002) for a brief selection of an extensive literature in this area of black theological work.

30 See Wilkinson, *Church in Black and White.*

31 See also Joe D. Aldred, "Respect: A Caribbean British Theology" (unpublished PhD thesis, Department of Biblical Studies, University of Sheffield, 2004).

32 See Aldred *Respect* and Mark Sturge, *Look What the Lord Has Done! An Exploration of Black Christian Faith in Britain* (London: Scripture Union, 2005).

33 See also Doreen McCalla, "Black Churches and Voluntary Action: Their Social Engagement with the Wider Society," *Black Theology: An International Journal* 3(2) (July 2004).

34 See Beckford, *Dread and Pentecostal.* See also Aldred, *Respect.*

35 See Reddie, *Black Theology in Transatlantic Dialogue,* pp.67–70.

36 Beckford, *Dread and Pentecostal,* pp.176–82.

37 See M. Byron, *Post-War Caribbean Migration to Britain: The Unfinished Cycle* (Aldershot, UK: Avebury, 1994). See also R. B. Davidson, *West Indian Migrants* (London: Oxford University Press, 1962) and R. Glass (assisted by Harold Pollins), *Newcomers: The West Indians in London* (London: George Allen and Unwin. 1960).

38 Peter Brierley, *The Tide Is Running Out: What the English Church Attendance Survey Reveals* (London: Christian Research, 2000), p. 136.

39 See Barton, *Rejection, Resistance and Resurrection.*

40 See Anthony G. Reddie, *Nobodies to Somebodies* (Peterborough, UK: Epworth Press, 2003).

41 See Robert Beckford, *Jesus Dub* (London: Routledge, 2006).

42 See Reddie, *Nobodies to Somebodies,* pp.105–6.

43 See Beckford, *Jesus Dub.*

44 Ibid., p.1.

45 See Commission on Urban Life and Faith, *Faithful Cities: A Call for Celebration, Vision and Justice* (London: Church Publishing and the Methodist Publishing House, 2005).

46 See Jose Irizarry, "The Religious Educator as Cultural Spec-Actor: Researching Self in Intercultural Pedagogy," *Religious Education* 98(3) (Summer 2003): 365–81. See also Clark C. Apt, *Serious Games* (New York: Viking Press, 1970).

47 See Anthony G. Reddie, *Acting in Solidarity: Reflections in Critical Christianity* (London: Darton, Longman and Todd, 2005).

18 Slave religion and black theology in Brazil

WALTER PASSOS

INTRODUCTION

I write about black theology in a country where the universities, theological seminaries, and churches do not get involved with the black population and its ethnic-racial questions, nor do they get involved with how this black population originally lived and interpreted their experiences with God.

I start with the question of how the black population lived and understood its experiences of God. However, to start with such a question presents itself as a paradox, because while the black community is full of faith, rejects atheism, and is represented in significantly large numbers in the various Christian denominations whose structures are exclusive, racist, and Eurocentric, they don't understand that the racism practiced in these denominations and in which they participate is the complete negation of the message of Yahoshua and the absolute negation of the sovereignty of YHWH.

THEOLOGY AND THE HISTORY OF SLAVERY

Brazil has the third largest population of blacks in the world, India being the first, because of its great contingent of Dalits, followed by Nigeria.[1] Brazil is also, indisputably, the country with the largest number of Catholics in the world. Thus, it is worrisome that a black Christian population of such importance has not developed, in its theological thinking, ways of effectively resisting centuries of oppression and racism. Brazil is a country with a great Latin-rite Catholic influence. José Carlos Gentili has shown in *The Church and the Slaves* how the Catholic Church promoted the exploitation of the enslaved African workforce as well the catechization of Indians.[2] Catholic ideology involved extreme exploitation of African workers and the radical breaking of their cultural and religious traditions, and was supported by pro-slavery priests such as Jorge Benci, who affirmed that slavery was the result of original sin.

It was necessary to inculcate in the African and his descendants that their religious-cultural values were wrong, that they were pagans and worshiped the devil. This was confirmed by the attempt to humanize Africans with baptism in African prisons before their kidnapping (slavery) to Brazil or on arrival there. If the psychological meaning of baptism for the enslaved was the breaking of his ancestral traditions and, for the master, the evangelization of the slave, an "act of goodwill", to take the "Good News" to the indigenous and predestined people became exploitation by the will of God.

Protestants, in their flight from the religious wars in Europe, came to Brazil in the hope of recreating places where they could live out their religion in peace. The first experiences of colonizing Protestants in Brazil were those of the French Huguenots in the two invasions of the Portuguese colony, and those of the Dutch Reformed in the Dutch invasions in Bahia and Pernambuco. The French as well as the Dutch followed the Calvinistic faith. In 1557, the French sent two pastors, one of whom was Pierre Richier, and a group of religious followers of John Calvin. Among them was the cobbler Jean de Léry, who returned to Europe to study theology at the Geneva Academy in Switzerland and wrote a narrative, *History of a Journey to the Land of Brazil*, published in France in 1578. During the time the French were in Brazil, a controversy with Nicolau Durand Villegaignon, leader of the colonizing expedition, over the Calvinist sacrament resulted, in 1558, in the first defense of the Protestant faith in Brazil: the Confession of Faith of Guanabara.

Like Catholics, Calvinistic Protestants enslaved the blacks and waged war against the quilombos of Palmares.[3] Two groups, the Huguenots and the Reformed, defended the slavery of African blacks and their descendants.

Racist whites of the Southern United States, during and at the close of the Civil War, came to Brazil and brought social intolerance marked by religious, cultural, and ethnic concepts of white superiority. Addressing only the national elite, they preached two things – salvation and perdition, heaven or hell, the wide way and the narrow way – and the idea of superiority and contempt for other religions. They framed this in terms of a great battle against liberalism and the religious practices of the new colonialism. Thus when they did not find liberalism to confront, they turned against Catholicism, which they considered ignorant and idolatrous, a victim of the influence of Afro-Brazilian cultures. The majority of Catholics already practiced syncretism and religious parallelism. The attack against Catholicism was also transformed into a frontal attack against those of African descent who practiced popular Catholicism.

Racist missionaries allied themselves with the new white Brazilian converts from the interior of the states of Rio de Janeiro, Minas Gerais, São Paulo, and states to the south of the country, who lived in a system inclined to slavery. Brazilian Protestants and their missionaries took no part whatsoever in the fight against slavery in Brazil. The Protestantism that was established in Brazil was conservative in all senses and became one of the most reactionary forms, based on theological fundamentalism and committed to preaching a moralist and racist Gospel, cultural superiority, and pietistic practices. It adapted very well to the well-established slave-owning Brazilian agricultural middle class that was a direct descendant of the masters of the enslaved, which found in the fundamentalist preaching the ideas of natural selection and the doctrine of predestination and election. The imported Protestantism taught that poverty was a fruit of sin and a sign of rejection by the divine and that African descendants (blacks and mestizos) were outside of the plan of evangelization and did not deserve the respect of Christians.

The social and cultural superiority of Protestants was reinforced by the need for Protestantism to impose itself as a model for the formation of intellectuals from the agricultural middle class, and it thus became the predominant factor in the elitist investment in education. We note the marked presence of pastors of the historical churches with English, North American, and German last names, excluding African descendants, educated according to the North American-inspired educational model. In some Brazilian states, schools were founded that adhered to the racist Protestant educational project. Mission Protestantism would affect cultural Afro-Brazilian patterns within its sphere of influence, because, in spite of the repudiation of African descendants, more and more of these would be "converted to the new religion," accepting the deformed biblical teaching and becoming "believers." One new project was put into practice, "the ideology of whitening," with various forms of cultural denial, including the prohibition of musical instruments of African origin, which were considered "demonic." Even in the most remote parts of the country, foreign evangelists introduced into the services the piano, organ, and other instruments that were strange to the blacks and the rural white population.

Using professors from the USA, theological institutions invested in the training and formation of new leaders to continue the missionary work. Many families from the interior of Brazil sent their children for pastoral training based on the biblical and cultural interpretation of the missionaries. The new pastors gained the contempt of the blacks who were already adherents of the new religion (attending Sunday schools, for instance), whose identities were themselves rejected by fundamentalist teaching.

As far as Catholicism is concerned, it should be noted that its first act concerning slavery was to "liberate" slaves from the African "curse" by administering baptism. This is the act of washing, cleansing, bathing, purifying, and making the candidate reject all of his religious history and forcing him to assimilate elements of faith in a relationship with an inaccessible, white, distant, and oppressive God. The curse, it was thought, arrived from the continent of Africa by means of the enslaved. Likewise, Protestantism made parallelism and syncretism impossible within the religious faith of the Africans. Their descendants became the target of violent attacks, and the act of being baptized was the beginning of the process of purification that led to acceptance of the situation of slavery, ceasing to be a "beast" and becoming a "human being," and walking in a life of submission in order to inherit paradise. The new concept of curse was predicated on a genetic relationship between the African and his ancestors, as well as a relationship to the past of his or her parents, grandparents, and great-grandparents, who worshipped a different and ancient God, resulting in affliction throughout Brazil. The "curse" was supposed to affect generations of one's family as well as one's financial situation, employment, and other domestic and personal arrangements.

In this way slavery in Brazil affected Africans spiritually, destroyed and separated families, created traumas and fears. Slavery affected Africans and their descendants genetically, and with the abolition of slavery the black ceased to be enslaved and had to confront new situations that were imposed upon him. The majority were illiterate, unemployed, and today must fight for a piece of the pie of the Brazilian economy. Blacks are among Brazil's major nation-builders but receive only crumbs, make up the majority of the unemployed, are frequently homeless, are victims of alcoholism, which was a habit already initiated in slavery by slavers as a part of the diet, and suffer many other emotional problems so that they are not concerned with the so-called "encostos"[4] so spread by these religious groups. Black people deal more with the concrete materiality of their oppression rather than a singular focus on invisible spiritual demons. What such groups should say is that YHWH is just and he does not agree with social injustice, whether committed by whites, mestizos, or blacks.

The ideological diffusion of the concept of curse is being carried out by evangelists and others working with those of African descent because they believe that once they were cursed and are now actually free from that curse. I knew a black pastor named Albert who said that he had a mission from God to preach the Gospel in Bahia after spending some time evangelizing on the African continent, and that the great problems of the blacks can be summed up in the concept of "encostos." He said the map of Curuzu Street in Liberty,[5] Salvador, Bahia, was shaped like the head of the devil. Despite suffering racial discrimination and his claims that he knew what he was doing, that black pastor tried to organize a church formed by blacks and taught the ideology of the curse.

The principal doctrine of these churches is the expulsion of the "encostos" that is the hereditary curse of those of African descent, and it is only with exorcism that the congregants or anyone else can receive divine blessings, become prosperous, healthy, and happy. The discourse of the curse created and developed by Western slavers and reformulated today has already been accepted and honored by the black majority in all the churches, including those that say they reject the ideology.

My paternal ancestors were priests of African "cults," and when I was six years old my mother became a Presbyterian. Because of this, I spent a good part of my life in Calvinism and even became a Presbyterian minister and defended Calvinistic theology. Today I do not think like a Calvinist because Calvinism has nothing to do with the African population or Afro-diaspora.

In many cases familial influences determine our conception of faith, our cosmogonies, and the various discourses and analyses of reality. The black Brazilian population accepts these familial influences with large memory lapses, linearly deformed or spoiled. We can understand this process as one of alienation from one's roots.

Furthermore, Protestant mission hymnology contributed to the denial of the culture and freedom of those of African descent by using an inaccessible language that was reactionary, racist, overemphasized life after death, and encouraged indifference toward social questions of oppression and racism, as if everything was predestined according to the will of God. The hymns, the pastoral messages, and the biblical teaching are based on the dichotomy of body and spirit.

Even today black religious musical expression is still considered pagan and demonic by various Protestant denominations.[6] The music within the black community is ancient; African and African American services possess in their musicality one of the best expressions of their

religiosity. In the Afro-Brazilian religious services the songs are fundamental to the connection of the human being with spiritual forces. The
black Brazilian population has an ancestral cultural foundation based
on oral expression; music is a teaching form capable of transmitting
effective religious knowledge. It is troubling that music is manipu-
lated by churches to entice and dominate the poorest and most needy
black classes and to serve as an escape valve for the rich and dominant
classes.

THEOLOGY AND INCULTURATION

Inculturation consists of the process of introducing one culture into
another, and this is almost always imposed. This process became very
common in dynamic Brazilian theology. Meanwhile, it was developed
by means of two dialectic processes.

The first of these takes the form of religious syncretism between
the Afro-Brazilian religions and their perspectives of faith, and Roman
Catholicism. It is interesting to note that in spite of apparently peaceful interaction, there is no mention of inculturation, because there was
no birth of a new religion. But there was an attempt to hide the racial
and ethnocentric process of religious domination hatched in African
slavery, in which, as shown earlier, various techniques were utilized by
the slavers to maintain domination, among which was the breaking up
of racial groups in the slave quarters and the imposition of white religion. However, these impositions did not completely erase indigenous
African spirituality. In fact, a religious parallelism existed. The imposed
religion of the white slave owner was forced onto the enslaved, while,
at the same time, the enslaved Africans maintained their sacred worldview. For instance, the enslaved pretended to worship Catholic saints
when, in fact, they were worshipping African divinities with dances,
choruses, and parties. From this came a fomenting of religious syncretism, and the practices of religious parallelism maintained by those of
African descent and, today, these practices make up intrinsic elements
of their faith, explicitly reconfiguring the partial consequences of cultural domination.

The other process of inculturation consists in the attempt by some
to Africanize the rites of Christianity. This process, in fact, is configured as a forced inculturation by the churches. Various Catholic leaders
hold so-called Afro-masses, where the essence of theology suffers no
modification, creating moments of catharsis and fraud for the faithful.
The so-called Afro-masses of black Catholic pastors and of the agents

of pastoral blacks are the only masses and meetings allowed by white priests and bishops, who monitor them and analyze as much as they can in order to make sure that the established order is maintained. Besides, whatever is white, European, Western, and colonizing was always considered positive in religion and whatever is black, African, and derived from slavery became a synonym for negativity.

One of Brazil's most important black Catholic organizations is Pastoral Agents for Blacks (APNs). Between 1979 and 1982, the first meetings of black men and women motivated by faith to address black issues took place. Their goal was to develop resources for the situation of Afro-Brazilians. From this particular context APNs was born, on March 14, 1983, in the city of São Paulo. However, these pastoral agents for blacks and other pastoral Catholics who discuss the racial question do not have proposals for theological change; they accept the Catholic catechism like children and teach it, and they act as mere representatives of Roman Catholic authority and its maintenance of oppression. They are organizations that spread white Western Christianity and are permitted by white Western Christianity while they masquerade as African.

In the case of the historical Protestant churches, a little questioning or discrimination in its sphere of influence takes place, but it is in these churches that the process of inculturation is most pernicious because they are immersed in the racism of the theology of prosperity. According to BIRS data,[7] there are about 15 million black Protestants throughout Brazil. This portion of the population has the most acculturated theology, because it not only abdicates its ethnic identity, but also becomes a symbol of satanism, fighting every ethno-racial and African manifestation or anything of African origin. In this context various interpretations crop up, giving rise to extreme equivocations, including among them those that integrate the so-called black evangelical movement, whose best-known contemporary figure is Pastor Batista Marco Davi. Pastor Marco Davi, in his book *The Blackest Religion of Brazil*, announces vehemently that Pentecostalism is the largest black Brazilian religion. However, it is widely acknowledged that the major religion by number of black followers is Catholicism. The truth, however, is that the blackest religion in Brazil and the one that preserves the values that identify Africans and their descendants is, in fact, the folk religion, Candomblé, because it seeks to preserve the African values of life, culture, and spirituality in their wholeness.

Pentecostalism, despite the majority of its members being blacks, does nothing to fight racial discrimination and maintains a process of aid to the forces of racism. The Pentecostal leadership is made up largely of white pastors who lead the black majority. It is important to reemphasize the function of the Sunday school in the historical and Pentecostal churches in the formation of church members. The Sunday school is a school with whitening as its objective, because it leads black people, from infancy, to the denial of their origins, reinforcing prejudice, machismo, and low self-esteem. Black Christians in Brazil have blindfolds over their eyes and fear the hell taught by the whites. Pastors of various denominations and leaders who know about the racial discrimination remain quiet; thus they are coparticipants and feed the lies.

There are some groups in Brazil within "evangelical" churches, which we understand to include all manifestations of Protestantism, whether historical or not, that try to discuss the racial question. Some emerging leaders are immediately dismissed by the denominations and large ecumenical organizations or are needed for the implementation of social projects elsewhere.

In 2008, Hernani Francisco da Silva, leader of the Society of Cultural Missions Quilombo and director of Cenacora and other organizations, published a document entitled "Pardon: The 120 Years of the Unfinished Abolition and the Historical Churches."[8] This article, though well argued, did not impress the black pastors and believers within the large Protestant denominations who are led by whites, and the whites did not take the discussion to their councils and assemblies. The black Protestant movements have not managed to form a black theology, because when they do so they will have to leave their structured churches and the black people of these churches will not follow them. The cry of the black Protestants in the white churches is stifled, because it is not founded in radical changes of exegesis and biblical hermeneutics. They are not prophetic voices accusing the Brazilian churches of being the synagogues of Satan and demanding a clear departure from this racist and oppressive structure. There is a lack of courage in the leadership because they do not yet have the prophetic discourse of freedom.

THEOLOGY AND AFROCENTRICITY

The black Christian in Brazil has serious problems of identity; he lacks the joy of belonging; he does not have an African memory; he feels lost and seeks to mirror European traditions and ways of thinking. He becomes a defender of European practices because he modified and solidified these practices, giving as a motive the need to feel a part of a promised future of equality in outer space (heaven) after his death.

The black Christian has no identity because at every moment he needs to feel included in the religion of his ex-masters in the slave quarters, and the current owners of his thinking. Conversion and baptism were forced upon him. Therefore, he puts forth the effort to create inculturation in the services and masses in order to feel, for a few moments, "free" from the heavy load of carrying the identity of another. These are the moments of "freedom": the drumming and dances permitted in the slave quarters of the white man. Christianity is European, be it Catholic or Protestant; it is not the original religion of the black people. The only black religion in Brazil is Candomblé, and for this reason it is the most persecuted by black Christians. People are also appearing in Brazil who are associated with the Hebrew Israelites and beginning to disclose that the blacks are the original Hebrews. They are beginning to disclose a theology based on the exegesis, hermeneutics, and history of the plan of YHWH for the true Israelites who came to be enslaved on the West African coast.

There is still much to be studied about the presence of the Hebrews in the Americas, coming from the continent of Africa, victims of slavery. Various scholars and members of the Afro-diasporic community have begun to realize the importance of understanding inherited rites and traditions: the necessity to understand and revise the diasporas; the Hebrew Israelites at different points in the invasions of Israel and when they went to the African continent; the formation of the Hebrew kingdoms in Africa; place names still extant throughout Africa; the rituals of the African population and religions in the Americas, "coincidentally" like the rituals of the Hebrews that are dealt with in the Torah; the so-called "coincidences" of Dan, one of the most important voodoo entities, and Dan the son of Israel, both related to the serpent; the words in the Hebrew language that live in many African languages of the slaves who came to the Americas; and in addition, the innumerable "coincidences" that are still very explicit in African American traditions. All these historical proofs need to be studied without fear or prejudice to rediscover our true identity. The experience of African and Afro-diasporic societies makes it necessary that we use our Afro-centered methodologies to respond to the sciences that try to destroy us.

Since the emergence of so-called North American black theology in the 1960s, it has seemed that there would be a radical change in theological thought, but it has turned out to be a theology of the moment without the philosophical or biblical structure to maintain it. It got its answers for racist oppression in that moment of American society and became enslaved by the lack of a Pan-African and Afrocentric practice, and lost itself in its weak concept of liberation. It had a good response because of the existence of the black established churches, unlike in Brazil, which never had black churches, and it can, in certain moments, provoke a discussion of economic and social oppression, but has otherwise shown itself to be unable to influence theologies and theologians in America. The great error of black theology was the lack of an Afrocentric base, and because of this its discourse, like other theologies of liberation, could not maintain a hope for black people.

The impoverishment of Africans and Afro-diasporas, the changes in diet, the increase of illnesses such as Ebola and AIDS, the destruction of agricultural areas, transformations in traditional forms of religious practice, the growing lack of respect for elders, and the lack of trust in the power of women, have resulted in the intensification of the pursuit of money and the unrestrained desire to acquire material goods, influenced by widespread theologies of prosperity (capitalist ideology under the guise of religiosity). In this process the traditions have become progressively despised and ignored. Africans and Afro-diasporas became easier targets for control and domination, because when we doubt our traditions and despise our ancestry we are committing spiritual and physical suicide that curses the ancestral legacy and creates a corrupt generation that is ashamed of who it is. Afro-centered theology is the hope for all humanity, starting with black people.

Theology arises with the first black civilizations and thus it is necessary to review the presuppositions of denial of this legacy story. The black in and of himself is a theological being, the first human being created in the image and likeness of YHWH, who first understood his design, who questioned and learned of his desires, and who first was interested in his message of hope. There is no other way of doing theology if the contemplation of Afro-Asia is denied. There must be an understanding of the geography, history, and philosophy of these first civilizations. The epithelial color of the theologian is not important. He has to look at Afro-Asia and understand why YHWH in his eternal wisdom chose the black civilizations as participants of his great project of the reconciliation of humanity with the Creator.

Notes

1   It is generally estimated that Brazil is second in contingent population of blacks, Nigeria's being greater.

2   José Carlos Gentili, *The Church and the Slaves* (Natal, RN, Brazil: RN Economico, 2006), pp. 64–65.

3   Editors' note: quilombos are descendants of slaves who escaped slave plantations to live in the mountains and other hiding places.

4   A term used by the Universal Church of the Reign of God to designate demonical possessions among their faithful.

5   Considered the largest black neighborhood in Latin America.

6   www.executivaipb.com.br/Emails/emails.asp (accessed January 27, 2004).

7   Brazilian Institute of Research and Statistics, a branch of the federal government responsible for research and censuses.

8   Available at http://perdaopovonegro.blogspot.com/2008/05/o-perdo-os-120-anos-da-abolio-inacabada.html.

19 Black theology in Cuba

RAÚL SUÁREZ RAMOS

The missionary work of white North American Protestants lacked understanding of the African presence in Cuba, especially in a nation with such profound roots. Everything in Cuba (the sense of national identity, the essence and expressions of Cuban culture, its revolutionary thought, its struggle for the abolition of bondage, for independence, liberation, and national sovereignty) is influenced by the considerable presence of male and female Africans who arrived in a colonized land into which they were brought as slaves. United States Protestant Southern mission boards arose in the 1880s, and for the next decade, and until 1898, they contributed financial aid, advice, and, in some sense, even respect for the Cubaness that the first church founders infused into the incipient Protestantism on the island.

Evangelical and Protestant work in Cuba at the end of the nineteenth and the beginning of the twentieth centuries began with the labor of patriot pastors.[1] This period was characterized by the participation of the Protestant religious movement in the struggle for the country's independence and its social progress, among other things. These individuals were able to combine the Gospel and their passion for independence from a foreign yoke without any contradiction. In responding to an authentic identity and compromise, the people called their congregations "churches of the Cubans," whereas a process of disillusionment had led to the Catholic churches being characterized as the "churches of the Spaniards." These churches grew and developed a leadership with a deep Christian sense and a strong patriotism.

Beginning in 1898, events turned in the opposite direction. This formidable group of Cuban patriots who led their churches was progressively subordinated and displaced. The ecclesial leadership that they had developed and organized was replaced by the missionaries who were sent by the mission boards during the first American military intervention in Cuba.[2] Generally, these missionaries came from churches in the South, and their influence extended to the churches in Cuba called

Home Mission Boards, which suggests a strong annexationist stance, obviously inspired by the doctrine of Manifest Destiny. For them, Cuba was a domestic territory.

As the Revd. Pablo Odén Marichal has rightly stated, a summary of the events would suggest that idea. Duarte, one of the main leaders of the Episcopal Church of Cuba, had to resign due to the false accusations of two North American missionaries. They withdrew all necessary resources for Someillán, who was the founder of Cuban Methodism, including support for his family and for evangelical work; he finally had to leave his denomination. Alberto J. Díaz, who was the initiator of Baptist work in Cuba, was replaced by an American missionary, and his congregation at the Teatro Janet (Janet Theater) was expelled. Collazo was not honored as a founder of his Presbyterian Church – this distinction was attributed to an American man – and he was relegated to rural projects. Deulofeu was marginalized and was destined to serve in small towns for declaring himself a socialist. As a result of these neocolonized politics, de-Cubanization began to take place in evangelical churches and a type of transplanted North American congregation was being created in the Southern style not only in cultural terms, but also in terms of structural, liturgical, and doctrinal foundations.

BLACK PASTORS WITHIN THE PROTESTANT CHURCHES

One of the consequences of the dominance in Cuban churches of North American Home Mission Boards was the exclusion of black Cuban pastors; a radical politics that did not allow ministerial candidates to enroll in theological educational institutions. Extensive research in other denominations has not been completed, but in the case of the Baptist Convention of Western Cuba, sponsored by the Southern Baptist Convention, this consequence could be seen at work.

Among the Cuban pioneers of the ecclesial work who were converted in this convention there were at least two black pastors: the Revd. J. J. Negrín and another pastor whose last name was Carbonell. They disappeared without leaving a trace of the full performance of their ministry. The reasons they did not continue beyond the year 1902 are unknown. This is the year when the first American intervention was finalized. As the Baptist Convention of Western Cuba "North Americanized" their leadership, their "whitening" was made absolute. This explains, among other things, the almost generalized failure of the black Cuban population's evangelization. Other historical churches had similar experiences, extending even to the absence of black students in their colleges, generally directed by American missionaries.

Some theological seminaries were practically closed to aspirant black or mestizo students. Even up until 1959, the Seminario Teológico de la Habana (Havana Theological Seminary) did not enroll any black students. We know of only two students who registered, but they did not continue past the second academic year. The autobiography of black Baptist pastor Antonio Hernández Loyola provides appropriate evidence. For over twenty-five years, Hernández Loyola did his best to gain admission to the Seminario Bautista de la Habana (Havana Baptist Seminary). He held on to the letter sent by the superintendent of the Home Mission Board of the Southern Baptist Convention in Cuba, who was also the seminary's rector. That letter explained why his petition was denied. In spite of this decision, he was ordained to the ministry later because of the excellent pastoral work he had carried out. Attempting to justify this refusal, based on the fact that the churches would not tolerate a black pastor, would constitute a pretext to emulate the racist and discriminatory character of this decision.[3]

After 1959, starting point of a revolutionary process that eliminated racism and institutionalized racial discrimination, it became contradictory to maintain the same policy in Baptist work. Then the seminary opened its doors to black students; however, currently there is only one black Baptist pastor in the Convention. A similar situation can be confirmed in other Protestant denominations.

MY ENCOUNTER WITH BLACK THEOLOGY

Our personal and familial interest in black liberation theology dates back to the beginning of the 1970s. My wife, Clara María Rodés González, and I graduated from the Seminario Bautista de la Habana, and we went through a deep spiritual crisis. This crisis had several causes. First, we were challenged by the humanist ethics of the Revolution, which emphasized the new man and the new woman – a new human being motivated by a supportive love toward others, especially toward the poor of the Third World. This involved a sense radically different from the conventional bourgeois ethics of human dignity. The demand for social justice and real equality, along with the construction of an alternative society, greatly attracted us. Second, the ecclesiological and theological schema of the Southern Baptist Convention became a barrier to the evangelical option for integration and participation in a new situation, in which God as the Lord of history allowed us to live.

In our experience as a pastoral couple, this mental dilemma dragged us into an agonizing crisis. Theological colonialism made us identify bourgeois ideology with Christian faith. Practically, if we were not part of that ideological package, it implied something like losing our faith. However, we realized that we were in reality recovering the evangelical sense of faith in Jesus of Nazareth by the grace of God and the fellowship of the Holy Spirit.

Third, José Martí's patriotic thought, which lays the foundations for revolutionary work, opened us to the experience of a prophetic ministry in the church. Far from hurting our faith and spirituality, the revolutionary criticism of religion enriched our Christian identity and pastoral vocation. This was so different from Marxist-Leninist criticism – Soviet-style – of religion, which was accompanied by prejudice and discrimination.

Recently, I read an article by James Cone, "Una mirada hacia atrás y una mirada hacia delante. La Teología Negra como teología publica," which describes his experiences during his time as a student of theology.[4] He was passionate about theological debate when he was studying for his PhD in Systematic Theology at Garret and Northwestern University. During his doctoral work in the spring of 1965, he wrote a dissertation based upon Karl Barth's anthropology. And he tells us:

> I thought I had enough knowledge of the Christian faith to communicate it to persons anywhere in the world. Who would not feel adequately endowed after reading twelve volumes of Barth's *Church Dogmatics*? But the Civil Rights and Black Power movements of the 1960s awakened me from my theological slumber. As I became actively involved in the black freedom movement that was exploding in the streets all over America, I soon discovered how limited my seminary education had been. The curriculum at Garret and Northwestern had not dealt with questions that black people were asking as they searched for the theological meaning of their fight for justice in a white racist society.[5]

Along with Dr. James Cone, many of us had to abandon our peaceful sleep as a result of historical circumstances, which had powerfully impacted us in Cuba. On January 1, 1959, we woke up with the news that the Revolution – led by a new generation of youth – had taken power. During the tensest moments of this process, we were filled with uncertainties and questions; however, looking ahead in different contexts a new revolution of the theological task appeared. This was what Dr. Sergio Arce had appropriately called La Teología Cubana en

Revolución (Cuban Theology in Revolution). For us it was of extra-ordinary value to have contact with Dr. Martin Luther King, Jr. and black liberation theology.

This crucial relationship between the animated and directed work of King and the rise of black theology as a prophetic voice in the churches and their theologies constituted an element of great importance for those of us who had to live – thanks to the force of history – our faith to the rhythm of a revolution.

In his letter from his prison in Birmingham, Alabama, King iden-tified the contradiction between a faith based on the Judeo-Christian heritage and social negligence, which stigmatized the Gospel of mod-erate leaders of white churches. Originally written in the margins of the Birmingham newspaper, this letter is one of the greatest prophetic manifestos in the history of humanity. We read over the letter many times within the new revolutionary context in which we lived; we made a decision to break with the reactionary and sectarian tradition of the Southern Baptist Convention. Being placed in a distinct historical situation and living the essentials of a pastoral experience, we asked ourselves similar questions.

That was our first approach to black theology as it relates to the beginnings of liberating theology. Linked to the development of the theological task in Cuba, this experience led us to the option of a dou-ble ministry. Today we can summarize it as follows: Cuban churches can see that it is possible to be revolutionary without ceasing to be Christian. At the same time, Marxist comrades can see that it is pos-sible to be Christian without ceasing to be revolutionary. With the real-ization of prophetic ministry, Dr. King taught us from the beginning that the life and mission of the prophets was being defined in the prac-tice of revolutionary commitment. In the process of becoming aware, a new sense of identity, a sense of self-awareness in the struggle, a com-mitment to compromise and coherence, and all that implies, would be discovered.

I even recall with great emotion our cautious steps in the practice of the new theological and pastoral biblical awareness that we decided to live. We still remained in the Baptist Convention of Western Cuba. Our purpose was to carry out our ministry from within a biblical and theological criticism of what we understood as perversion of the Gospel of Jesus Christ. From April 2 to 4, 1971, we began our first public action with regard to Dr. Martin Luther King, Jr.'s legacy. Every day we met in a different church in the city of Havana. All the congregations supported the idea. We did this until 1973. After that, the practice was extended to different regions of the country. We looked for any texts from Dr. King and discussed them in small groups. As of 1975, the Coordinación Estudiantil Obrera Bautista de Cuba (COEBAC – Working-Class Baptist Scholastic Coordination of Cuba) adopted the idea and began the national journey in honor of Dr. Martin Luther King, Jr. From the beginning, the meetings had two characteristics: the contextualization of King's thought and his contribution to the Cuban revolutionary reality, and for these journeys to culminate in a great meeting in the city of Havana. In 1982, Dr. Jane Cary Peck, who was an associate professor of religion and society at Andover Newton Theological School, Massachusetts, put us in touch with Professor Gayraud S. Wilmore of New York Theological Seminary. In the same year, this extraordinary man of God visited Cuba for the very first time. At that time, I was the Executive Secretary of the Consejo Ecuménico de Cuba (CEC – Ecumenical Council of Cuba) and International Relations Secretary of COEBAC. Both organizations sponsored Dr. Wilmore's visit. Wilmore was in Santiago de Cuba, the birthplace of the Cuban Revolution, and preached at the Second Baptist Church. This church is associated with the name of the revolutionary martyr Frank País, a young Baptist murdered by the Batista dictatorship on July 30, 1957.

Dr. Wilmore was the first African-North American preacher to pro-claim the Word of God from the pulpit of our Baptist church, "Ebenezer," Marianao. The biblical text used at that time was recorded in the historical memory of our church: "even though we are grieving, our sorrow will turn into joy." In this sermon he showed me what later Wyatt Tee Walker would teach me: preaching linked with prayer and hymns constitute the trilogy of the soul of black religion. Later, he offered us a magisterial lecture on the highlights of King's life.

I still remember the shocked reaction to my cautious steps in raising consciousness for a new understanding and practice of faith, which slowly encouraged my theological pilgrimage by listening to Dr. Wilmore's deep analysis of King's life drawn from his criticism of the Vietnam War. This analysis referred us to *La Conciencia y la Guerra de Vietnam*.[6] This text, also read within our revolutionary context and in a moment of awareness, showed me what it was like in the eighth century of the history of Israel to be God's prophet.

Until the end of my life, I will carry within me a profound gratitude toward God for allowing me to cross paths with Dr. Gayraud S. Wilmore. As of that moment, my Christian identity and my pastoral vocation have never been the same. I would say that a new type of missiological relationship began. Until that moment, with rare exceptions, the international relationships of Cuban Protestantism were limited to the mission boards of the historical churches of the United States. For the very first time, we initiated interchanges with leaders of the churches and African-North American movements, and at the same time, a space of biblical-theological dialogue was created.

These exchanges and biblical-theological dialogues were organized and coordinated by the CEC and the COEBAC in Cuba and by the Proyecto de Teologia Negra (BTP-Black Theology Project) from New York. Dr. Wilmore and Dr. Joalynne E. Dodson played an important role in these new relationships. The first major encounter happened from June 22 to 28 of 1984, which was called the Primera Jornada Teológica Dr. Martín Luther King, Jr. in Memoriam (First Theological Journey of Dr. Martin Luther King, Jr., in Memoriam).

THE VISIT OF THE REVD. JESSE JACKSON

It is fair to acknowledge that ecclesiastical hierarchies do not always remember and value positively all that has been done. However, for those of us who have lived these forty-two years of Revolution, the time cannot go unnoticed. In June 1984, the Primera Jornada Teológica coincided with the visit of the Revd. Jesse Jackson to Cuba. His advisors had previously communicated to us his interest in coming and preaching in some of our churches. We then organized an ecumenical public act to pay tribute to Dr. Martin Luther King, Jr. at the Methodist church on K Street and 25 in Vedado. The proclamation of the Word was delivered by the Revd. Jackson and the liturgy was an expression of a deep theological transformation that our churches underwent during this long revolution. An hour before starting, and near the Methodist temple, the Revd. Jackson offered an inspiring speech to approximately 4,000 Havana University students. When this meeting was over, President Fidel Castro accompanied Jackson to the entrance of the church. I waited for the preacher and while I greeted Fidel, I overheard one of his advisors say to him, "Commander, remove your hat, you are about to enter a church." And then they entered the church. Fidel listened carefully to our hymns, our prayers, the Bible readings, and the evangelical message of the ardent black preacher. A young black member of the US delegation approached Fidel and asked him to speak. Surprisingly, he agreed. Those were the times when the so-called scientific atheism of Soviet nuance were made official. And there was a tremendous and significant contradiction with Fidel in front of the pulpit of the Methodist church, the Bible open before him, and an illuminated Cross at his back.

This was the beginning of an increasing openness that exists even today toward the Christian faith and the new spaces for churches in Cuba. The next day, Fidel hosted a reception for the participants and greeted them one by one. These events took place exactly one and a half years before the book *Fidel y la Religión*, written by the Brazilian Dominican priest Frey Betto, a work that gave a major boost to the unity of religious believers and nonreligious believers in Cuba. This is another reason for gratitude shown by Christians in Cuba to the black theology of African Americans.

We always perceived black theology's insights in an instinctive way; we made the road by walking it. Theology that emerges from a concrete reality and breaks with the metaphysical schema of the church is theology that has to live fully in the contemporary reality in which God places us here and now. At the same time, this theology is essentially prophetic. In the Judeo-Christian tradition, the prophetic ministry is not only the voice that announces to the poor God's action in history, but also the denunciation to the oppressor for the unfair structures of society.

In conclusion, in a Cuba isolated by an absurd political blockade, many of these theological elements of the different liberation theologies were instinctive discoveries by the action of the Lord of history in his uncompromising option of accompanying his people every day until the end of days.

LATER STAGES

A second movement can be located in the context of contra-celebrations of the Fifth Centenary. In this space, the campaign "Quinientos años de resistencia indígena, negra y popular" ("Five hundred years of indigenous, black, and popular resistance") was born. In a third continental encounter (Managua, 1992), this campaign was transformed into an indigenous, black, and popular continental movement. From these experiences – today called macro-ecumenical – came the Asamblea Pueblo de Dios (Assembly of God's People), in which we have actively participated ever since its beginning. This rich and significant Indo-Afro-Latin American interchange brought us to the definition of our center as a macro-ecumenical organization of Christian inspiration, and to the development of a new agenda for our social-theological work of communication and popular education.

This macro-ecumenical movement challenged us to begin in our country what was already happening in the Latin American sphere. As a consequence of our participation, a self-critical attitude has become essential.

The path followed since Dr. Wilmore's visit and the richness of the dialogue and biblical-historical-theological thought through the Black Theological Project have been significant accomplishments. These precedents, the experience with the Asamblea Pueblo de Dios, and our friendship with the liberation philosopher and Italian priest of the Salesian order Giulio Girardi, led us to start a dialogic process with our brothers in Afro-Cuban religions.

On July 6, 1996, at the instigation of the Centro Memorial Dr. Martín Luther King, Jr. (Dr. Martin Luther King, Jr. Memorial Center) and the Centro de Estudios del Consejo de Iglesias de Cuba (Center of Studies of the Council of Churches in Cuba), we met at the Catedral Santísima Trinidad de la Iglesia Episcopal de Cuba (Holy Trinity Cathedral of the Episcopal Church in Cuba). From different evangelical and Catholic churches (with followers of the Regla Ocha and the Regla de Palo Monte and the Sociedad Abakuá Ochoa Rule, Palo de Monte Rule, and Abakúa Society), about fifty people had gathered. This encounter, nurtured in an environment of dialogue and mutual confidence, left a positive impact: a better understanding of the Afro-Cuban religions and new perspectives for inter-religious dialogue in Cuba. Even beyond these achievements, it led us to a deep gratitude toward God, which once again led us toward the evangelical *metanoia* of the rectification of our historical sin against the children of Africa.

Since then, we have continued our path of macro-ecumenism. The Centro Memorial Dr. Martín Luther King, Jr. has dedicated an edition of *Caminos*, the Cuban magazine of social-theological thought, to religions of African origin.[7] By doing so, we rightly recognize the importance of a better and greater knowledge of Cuban religious plurality, and make a modest contribution by offering this to our readers – especially to the congregations of the evangelical churches. This is important because without an appreciation of black culture it is difficult to understand Cuba.

The capitalist society of the past with its deep political, economic, and social differences, committed to a permanent acculturation and dependence on the United States, lamentably created not only in Catholicism but also in Protestantism an attitude of exclusion and rejection of everything that smelled like "things of blacks" – as people used to say at that time. This conditioning aspect was a like a network in which many factors converged in order to create a mental schema that would serve the ideological interests of the dominant classes. I can never forget the psychological resources used in many Cuban families in their efforts to intimidate the children not to leave their homes at night. They would simply scare them with the "Coco"; the "Coco" was the black person.

The small town where I was born had a train station in the middle. The freight trains stopped for hours and their workers came down to buy food and drink. They were usually black. The middle-class residents warned the children on the streets – I was one of them – pointing to the railway workers: "Be careful, they are communist witches." The rejection of and disdain for beliefs in African tradition not only claimed biblical and theological foundations, they constituted an essential part of a racist and discriminatory ideology in Cuban society that preceded January 1, 1959.[8]

Notes

1   Pedro Duarte, Joaquin de Palma, Agustín de Santa Rosa, Parmenio Amaya, Juan Bautista Báez, Alberto de Jesús Díaz Navarro, Aurelio Silvera, Enrique Someillán, Evaristo Collazo, Manuel F. Moreno, and Manuel Deulofeu, among others.

2   The process has been widely analyzed by different scholars, both Cuban and American. Among other works, see Rafael Cepeda, "Las iglesias protestantes y el expansionismo norteamericano," *Caminos* 7 (July–September 1997); Harold Greer, "Bautistas en Cuba occidental: de las guerras de independencia a la República," *Caminos* 7 (July–September 1997); Margaret E. Crahan, "La penetración religiosa y el nacionalismo en Cuba: actividades del metodismo norteamericano," *Caminos* 7 (July–September 1997); Louis A. Pérez, "Los misioneros norteamericanos en Cuba y la cultura de la hegemonía," *Caminos* 10–11 (April–September 1998); Louis A. Pérez, "La misión evangélica," *Caminos* 17–18 (January–June 2000).

3   Antonio Hernández Loyola, "Autobiografía" (unpublished manuscript). This work was typed by the author of this chapter. At present, the "Autobiografía" is in the possession of Hernández's son, the Revd. Roberto Hernández Aguiar, who is a Baptist pastor of the "Aposento Alto" Church in Havana. In 1976, when vice-rector of the Seminario Bautista de la Habana, I proposed that a bachelor's degree in theology, *honoris causa*, be awarded to this ordained pastor. The entire faculty accepted the proposal and the degree was granted to him with full honors.

4   James H. Cone, "Looking Back, Going Forward: Black Theology as Public Theology," in Dwight N. Hopkins (ed.), *Black Faith and Public Talk* (Maryknoll, NY: Orbis Books, 1999), p. 250. This is the English version of the article, from which the quotation is taken.

5   Ibid.

6   Speech delivered by Dr. Martin Luther King, Jr., on April 4, 1967, at a meeting of concerned clergy and laity at Riverside Church in New York City. (Translator's note: in English, "Beyond Vietnam: A Time to Break Silence.")

7   *Caminos* 13–14 (January–June 1999). It contains contributions from Lázara Menéndez, Natalia Bolívar, Carmen González, Ivor Miller, Clara Luz Ajo, Yisel Arce Padrón, and Ania Rodríguez Alonso. In addition, there is an excellent piece on the African and Spanish contributions to the national character by Guillermo Rodríguez Rivera.

8   Lázara Menéndez, "Ayé (ki ibo). Tres sin un título," *Caminos* 13–14 (January–June 1999), p. 4.

20 Black theology in Jamaica

NOEL LEO ERSKINE

The roots and praxis of black theology in Jamaica find their antecedents and currency in the teachings of Marcus Mosiah Garvey and the Jah movement of Rastafari. I take the counsel of Lewin Williams seriously that the Christian church in Jamaica missed an opportunity to relate the Gospel of Jesus Christ to the plight of Afro-Jamaicans in their quest for justice in socioeconomic terms because the church unwittingly embraced Euro-American missionary theology. Even when the church was sympathetic to the plight of Afro-Jamaicans, who were severely affected by "persistent poverty," it failed to enter into solidarity with the poor.

There was, in many cases, little difference between the commitments of the church toward the poor and those of the colonizer. The church often aped the ways of the colonizer.[1]

Black theology, as the praxis of black people agitating and protesting for equal rights and the right to choose their own social and political destinies, occurred outside the church. We look therefore to the architects of black theology in Jamaica, Marcus Garvey and the Jah movement of Rastafari. I find it interesting that one of the oldest Christian churches in Jamaica, the Anglican Church, adopted for inclusion in its hymnal two songs of well-known Rastafarians, Bob Marley's "One Love" and Peter Tosh's version of Psalm 27. The rector of St. Mary the Virgin, the Revd. Canon Ernie Gordon, made the announcement and noted that "One Love" was used in an ordination service at St. Andrew Parish Church two years ago. "I don't live in England," he stated, "I live here, [in Jamaica] so my theology and how I think must reflect my cultural morals. You have to interpret the Bible according to where you are. The church in Jamaica is out of date."[2] Rector Gordon is correct in stating that the church in Jamaica is out of date, as the church has to do more than include two songs from reggae artists in its hymnal in carving out a black theology for Jamaica. To go a little further than Rector Gordon, yet taking my cue from him, I suggest that as we craft a black theology

for Jamaica we begin with the father of the Jah movement of Rastafari,
Marcus Mosiah Garvey.

MARCUS MOSIAH GARVEY

Marcus Garvey, founder of the Back-to-Africa movement, was the
foremost prophet of black liberation in the twentieth century. He envisioned the return of black Jamaicans to their homeland, Africa. Black
Jamaicans, like the children of Israel, were captives in the white man's
land, and it was God's will that they experience exodus. "As children
of captivity," Garvey proclaims, "we look forward to a new, yet ever
old, land of our fathers, the land of God's crowning glory." And, he continues, "as the children of Israel, by the command of God, [we will] face
the Promised Land, so in time we shall also stretch forth our hands and
bless our country."[3] Here Garvey makes what was to become the mission statement of his movement. He felt that it was clear as to where
the land was to which white and yellow peoples belonged and that black
people should also be clear as to where their land was – Africa. "Africa
for Africans" was the essence of his cry for the self-awareness and liberation of black people. But Garvey was not unaware of the problems
associated with repatriation. He counseled that Africans in the diaspora
would have to organize, and that even then, freedom would come like a
thief in the night, when least expected.

Born in Jamaica on August 17, 1887, Garvey belonged to both the
nineteenth and twentieth centuries. Like many children growing up in
Jamaica, he could not avoid confrontation with race prejudice. Garvey
tells of not paying attention to questions about race until he was about
fourteen years old. The situation had to do with him becoming a friend
of the missionary's daughter, who confided in him on her departure to
England that she was instructed not to communicate with him while
away because he was a "nigger." As Barrett notes, "Garvey never forgot
this incident," and began to observe "the privilege shown to boys of
white or near white parentage." In contrast to "being sent either to the
few prestigious schools in Jamaica or England to study," Garvey recognized that "the blacker boys were given menial trades as laborers on the
large plantations, or in a few cases, where they were especially bright,
they became teachers in government or private schools."[4]

In response to this dreadful cultural norm, Garvey articulated a
theological base with which to counter the racial discrimination he
experienced in Jamaica. He reminded his audiences that because human
beings were created by God, no one had the right to treat another human

being as a slave or less than human, challenging, as Bennett notes, "all persons of African descent to set themselves the task of building a racial as well as a national consciousness, to liberate themselves from colonialism, to build self-esteem and race pride. These were and remain the imperatives of decolonization."[5] Perhaps Garvey's central contribution to Jamaica and the rest of the African diaspora was not only to keep Africa alive in our consciousness, but to press us to clarify where we stand in relation to Africa.

If the central question of black theology in Jamaica is where we stand in relation to Africa, there is no doubt that Garvey provided the inspiration for the Rastas.[6] Garvey expressed with exquisite beauty a commitment to African redemption: "No one knows when the hour of African's redemption cometh. It is in the wind. It is coming. One day like a storm it will be here." Or Garvey could appeal to his God: "Oh God help the Black man [woman] and rescue him [her] from outrage!" And again: "We have gradually won our way back into the confidence of the God of Africa, and he shall speak with the voice of thunder, that shall shake the pillars of a corrupt and unjust world and once more restore Ethiopia to her ancient glory."[7] Building on the work of Marcus Garvey, and yet departing from Garvey's vision in important areas, the Rastas asked profound questions about the kind of people Jamaicans had decided to become and what that implied. The Rastas, as they looked at Jamaican society from the perspective of the underclass, concluded that criticism of Jamaican society needed to begin with the criticism of the Christian church. They judged the church to be part of the Babylonian establishment that was organized against the poor. It did not help when, during the Ethiopian–Italian war of 1935, the pope gave his blessing to the Italian armed forces. This confirmed their fears that the church, whether Protestant or Catholic, took sides against the poor.

For Rastafari, this meant that the God who these Christians represented did not have the best interests of the poor at heart, and that if the Jamaican underclass – those outside the mainstream who could not measure up to the standards of respectability demanded by the churches – were to have a modicum of respect and dignity, then they had to abolish the God of the Christians. The Rastas saw very early that one of the main criteria of a God who would help deliver them from Babylonian captivity was that this God had to become one of them.

In a profound sense, the Rastas foresaw the need for an incarnational theology. God could no longer be a foreigner representing the interests of Europe and North America; God had to be black and committed to African redemption. Their gaze focused on Haile Selassie in part because Jamaica had a strong Ethiopic tradition, perhaps going back as far as 1784, when George Liele called his church the Ethiopian Baptist Church, and continuing until Marcus Garvey adopted the Ethiopian national anthem as the theme song of the UNIA (Universal Negro Improvement Association). It was not inconceivable that the Rastas would look to Africa in general and to Ethiopia in particular for their emancipator and God. Was Africa not the home of black people and all people of African descent?

In Jamaica, we looked to England for 300 years for our laws, our educational system, our religious liturgies, and in many respects our God. Rastas seized the power to choose their God and, in light of Psalm 68:31, began to look to Africa for help. Further, it was reported that once Garvey, when leaving Jamaica, enjoined his followers to look to Africa, from where a black king would arise who would lead his people out of bondage. There was a confluence of reasons why they would look to Africa and not to the established churches of Europe or North America. To look to Africa for deliverance from the intractable problems of Jamaica was an act of resistance for Jamaicans who lived in a land where the British government ruled supreme and where most public buildings, including educational institutions, were replete with pictures of the British monarch.

RASTA HERMENEUTICS

During the formative years of Rastafari, the cardinal beliefs were laid by Leonard Howell, Archibald Dunkley, Robert Hinds, and teacher Joseph Nathaniel Hibbert – all of whom subscribed to the divinity of their new God, the black man from Ethiopia. Indeed, God had become one of them. Their new God raised the ontological question for all Jamaica: Where do you stand in relation to Africa? The majority of Jamaicans were clear about their response. They rejected Africa – only a handful of Jamaicans sided with the Rastas. Even Marcus Garvey, who in many ways broached this question before the Rastas, had some openness to middle-class values and provided room for a multiclass response to this question. One of Garvey's responses was to run for political office in Jamaica, thereby seeking through political institutions to correct the intractable problems of Jamaica. Garvey felt that liberation was a possibility in Jamaica through political institutions and, of course, the church was one such institution, even if in the end he opted for a nondenominational church. It is quite clear that, for Garvey, the church could serve as an instrument of liberation.

The Rastas, however, looked outside the church and outside political institutions. They argued that the system was corrupt and that repatriation as liberation was the answer. I would like to press the claim, hinted at by the Rastas, that any responsible view of repatriation must include liberation. Included in liberation is the valuing of the self in light of one's vision of God. This means that liberation has to do with the image of God as articulated by the Rastas. To speak of God as black in a society in which the symbols of power are European or North American is an expression of black pride and black dignity. So, for Rastas, the blackness of God not only ensures the dignity and sanctity of the black underclass, but it also serves as a symbol of black empowerment as Rastas connect their emphasis on the "I-and-I consciousness" to the blackness of their God. The notion of "I-and-I consciousness" is a movement from the human subject to the divine and vice versa. It is a model of intersubjectivity in which Rastas are able to share in the divine life and claim sonship and daughtership with God.[8]

To posit the divinity of Haile Selassie and to claim that he is God returned to deliver black people is to begin at the divine pole. It is methodologically to begin with the divine. The Rastas, especially in the early years of the movement, observed that Jamaica – understood as Babylon – was so corrupt and hopeless that liberation could come only through divine intervention, as God would repatriate them to Ethiopia.

This theology, then, had a distinctly millenarian focus: God would intervene and bring forth the new era of justice and peace. Human agency had to take the back seat. But as the theology evolved to include "I-and-I consciousness," in which human life becomes infused with the life of the divine, Rastas began to identify themselves and to see their mission in a new way. They are no longer merely waiting for the in-breaking of the divine in the fullness of time to deliver them. They are now beginning to claim Jamaica as home even as they look toward the promised land of Ethiopia. Their view of eschatology is no longer futuristic as they wait for Jah (Rastas' term for God) to take them out of Babylon, but as they sing about the vision of the end time, this vision impels them to work for change in the here and now. The vision of seeing self within the divine life reminds Rastas that not only is God on their side, but they now have divine agency. In truth, they are Gods.

For the Rastas, new possibilities loom on the horizon as they differentiate between the now and the not-yet and the ways in which the end of history breaks into the midst of history in new and transformative ways. This new vision of their inclusion in the divine life through "I-and-I consciousness" does not soften their assessment of the evils of Jamaica, which they regard as Babylon, but it means that change is possible because of divine agency. This is another way of saying that Rastas do not have to wait for repatriation to Ethiopia to experience the meaning of liberation, but as they work for the changing and building of institutions of justice and peace-making in Babylon, they begin to change the face of Babylon.

This, I believe, is one of the effects of music as a tool for social change. Through music, Rastas begin to move beyond the "I-and-I consciousness," which at its best is still steeped in individualism. This undoubtedly is one of the characteristics of Babylon that is so insidious and subtle that the Rastas do not recognize its potential for setting brother against brother and sister against sister. The weakness of their emphasis on intersubjectivity is their attempt to experience God and each other individually. There is not yet in Rastafari the richness of the African concept of community.

THE BODY IN BLACK THEOLOGY

Aside from this weakness, however, the signal contribution Rastas have made to Jamaican cosmology is in their emphasis on the body; this cannot be emphasized enough. The Rastas have forced us to openly consider issues of shame and guilt, which we are prone to disguise and, through conscience, deem unimportant. One of the issues that Rastas force us to talk about concerns the reality that the body, for several hundred years, was literally owned by the master. The master had the right to flog, sell, and brutalize at will the body of Afro-Jamaicans because they were considered chattel that the slave owner could dispose of as he saw fit. In much of our literature, we do not address this aspect of the body – the sense that the black man and the black woman have never really owned their bodies. We get a sense today of what this must have been like when we examine the present penal system, in which prisoners are not free in relation to their own bodies. In many prison systems, inmates surrender their bodies to the system. They are told when to eat, when to retire, when to work, when to play, and they are punished as the jailor sees fit.

The situation was even worse for women as many were considered the plaything of the master, who would rape and abuse them according to his whim. In the United States it was even more gruesome, as lynchings were very common in the South. What is ironic is that many missionaries who condoned slavery, or felt impotent to affect the system of slavery for good, taught a separation of body and soul. They preached that the soul belonged to God while the body belonged to the master. The missionary sought to save the soul while the master owned the body. What a profound difference it would make if the church recognized that both body and soul belong to God.

An interesting observation is that enslaved Jamaicans practiced an embodied religion as they realized that the body belonged to God. That was one reason why they became impatient with bondage and continually rebelled for freedom. The Maroons of Jamaica are examples of enslaved people who fled to the hills and fought the British in guerrilla warfare until the British signed a treaty acknowledging their right to freedom. I do not need to recount the stories of Sam Sharp or Paul Bogle, leaders of rebellions in Jamaica who demanded freedom not only for their souls, but also for their bodies.

Among some of the reasons why many Jamaicans refuse to focus on body ethics or to see the body and its needs as central in attempts to talk about spirituality is, I believe, the fact that they feel the history of the enslavement of the black body places them in a position to relive the shame. There is a shaming that takes place when we recall and recount the history of oppression, which in many ways was a history of shame for both oppressed and oppressors. One source of the shaming is that we have to face the uncomfortable fact that Africans sold Africans into slavery. I recall visiting Ghana in July 2000 and hearing a stirring lecture by an eminent female professor of history who pointed out that greed was the cause of slavery. Africans sold Africans, and Europeans traded in human cargo for profit. I recall asking her how the children and great-grandchildren of these Africans feel knowing that our parents sold us into slavery. Talk about black bodies and slavery raises the uncomfortable issue of shame.

But Rastas, as they provide important grist for black theology in Jamaica, do not deal with the sexual degradation of the female body in contemporary Jamaican culture. Although Rastas are faithful to their spouses and frown on extramarital relationships, their theology of male superiority does not empower women to regard their bodies as temples of Jah. What is needed is a black theology for the Jamaican context that empowers women to claim the sanctity of their bodies and that treats the female body with respect. Similarly, talk about the human body also forces us to deal with homophobia, which Rastas are not eager to discuss. Black theology in Jamaica must deal with black bodies, reclaiming our bodies for ourselves and not for others. And we must address the ease with which we kill and maim these bodies in our society.

BLACK STORY/BLACK THEOLOGY

Caribbean theologian Kortright Davis speaks of a black story that is common to African American and Caribbean peoples. According to Davis, this story becomes a way of chronicling achievements of ancestry. It is the means whereby succeeding generations can be sure to emulate their parents and at the same time cultivate the will to succeed. Davis reminds us that "Racism was conceived in Europe, incubated in the Caribbean, baptized in America, ordained in North Atlantic trade, and canonized in Southern Africa. So the Caribbean and Americas are a major spiritual center of the Black Story."[9]

If Davis is correct in his assessment, then it becomes logical that the liberation and emancipation of that story also needs to be rooted in Africa. This, undoubtedly, is the strength of the Rasta position in claiming their God as an African. They resolve the ontological problem of God's whiteness and begin to answer the question of where Caribbean people stand in relation to Africa.

The Rastas' claim posits a reversal of values in the Jamaican context in which everything good and beautiful is related to Europe and whiteness, and everything problematic and undesirable is related to blackness and Africa. In the Caribbean we are accustomed to associate problems of ignorance, poverty, and diseases, such as HIV/AIDS, with Africa. Our estimate of blackness is not much different – hence Caribbean people often speak of themselves as "colored" for fear of being associated with blackness, which is a synonym for backwardness. So in finding God in what is despised and rejected (Africa and blackness), Rastas begin to turn the world upside down. For so long the missionaries taught us to rid ourselves of blackness and pray for the heathen in backward Africa. Then we learned from the Rastas that God is black and African.

Have the Rastas broken the rules of the game? Have they invented new rules? How may we address their practice? The Rastas seem to help us understand that we cannot free ourselves with practices that are anchored in the narrative of others. As we begin to take our own story seriously, we begin to value self and discover that we are made in the divine image of blackness.

Ultimately, if we listen to the Rastas or Davis, and to black theology more broadly, the story of black people is the struggle to refuse to allow white structures to be determinative of black existence. The meaning of black life does not depend on the structures of Babylon, for Black Power becomes protest against their attempt to thwart the lives of black people.[10] In his *Exodus* album, Bob Marley reminds us that "we are to open our eyes and look within" and not become satisfied with life in Babylon. Jamaicans are enjoined to leave Babylon as they participate in exodus from practices and traditions that demean human life.[11]

HISTORY AND THE LIBERATION PROJECT

Rex Nettleford, in his important book *Mirror, Mirror*, raises the crucial question as to whether the embrace of African history, which both Garvey and the Rastas advocate, is adequate for the liberation project in Jamaica. African history, it must be granted, explores the ground and goals of family and religion in African tradition, highlights how kinship networks were formed and maintained, and how the community raised children and fashioned their culture. Granted, our roots are in Africa, but are we not Jamaicans? Why should Caribbean people not combine the study of African history with Caribbean history? How well do Jamaican people know Jamaican history, and in what sense could this history serve as a resource for the liberation of Jamaica? Nettleford focuses in on the issue by reminding us that Mboya saw no *"contradiction between black nationalism and, in this case, Jamaican nationalism."* And that it is "reasonable for New World blacks to be concerned with the reconstruction of an African past that can serve their interests of identity wherever they may find themselves."[12]

Black theology in Jamaica, then, must build on the important emphases of Rastafari, and must draw upon African history as source and resource, but it is of first importance that Caribbean (and in particular Jamaican) history is highlighted.

Marcus Garvey and the Rastas have taught us the importance of relating our liberation project to African history. However, Nettleford raises the question of whether this goes far enough. The critical question raised by Garvey and Rastafari – "Where do you stand in relationship to Africa?" – is not yet enough. Africa must also include home; as painful as it is, Africa must include Babylon. We begin to see a move in this direction when we listen to Rasta poetics expressed in reggae music. For example, Bob Marley admonishes Jamaicans in his "No Woman, No Cry" to include friends, family, and local customs as they chronicle their past.[13]

To forget the history of our social locations is to forget friends and families. This is one reason that women have not received their rightful place in our story. In focusing on our roots in Africa we run the risk of forgetting families and friends in Trench Town. The challenge is to see how these histories relate and what questions they raise.

Another problem with focusing on African history at the expense of Jamaican history concerns God, and Rastas' depiction of God, as Ethiopian. I am grateful to the Rastas for bringing God a little closer. In Jamaica I grew up with a European God, so it was timely and helpful to meet a God who knows something about my distant past and knows something about my ancestors. Just as Nettleford explores coupling African history with Jamaican history, I wonder if God would come all the way and be Jamaican. The problem with a God who is totally African is that God runs the risk of being a foreigner and therefore a stranger to the Jamaican situation. According to Rasta theology, Jah is not really invested in liberating Babylon, as Jah will take Rastas and poor people out of Babylon. I have not discovered in Rasta theology any commitment of Jah to work for the liberation of Jamaica. While Rastas are stuck in exile awaiting Jah's arrival, they work for a measure of transformation in Babylon.

The advantage, however, of Rastas linking God to Africa and Ethiopia is that it protects the transcendence of Jah. After all, in some African myths, the African deity receded from the earth because God was tired of the sound of fufu mortars, or of people begging all the time. The sky that was once close to the earth receded from the earth. In this way, Rastas are correct; it is important for God to be in Africa (heaven) as it protects God's otherness. Yet, "since we will be forever loving Jah," it is only a God who is near who can save us. Perhaps, then, God is Afro-Jamaican. If we are made in God's image, as Marcus Garvey contends, then this is logical. To speak of God as Afro-Jamaican would preserve God's transcendence, and yet make Jah "God with us." The affirmation of God's immanence would begin to shift the way Rastas view Babylon. Babylon (Jamaica) would no longer be intractable and perceived as beyond salvation. The nearness of God would place Babylon within the purview of salvation. Hence liberation would be conceived and understood within repatriation. Jah would become one of us and no longer a foreigner. Together with Jah, we would work for the liberation of Jamaica.

Notes

1   Lewin Williams, *Caribbean Theology* (New York: Peter Lang Publishing, 1994), p. 34.
2   *Daily Observer* 13(201) (August 2, 2007): 1.
3   Amy Jacques-Garvey (ed.), *Philosophy and Opinions of Marcus Garvey*, vol. 1 (New York: Atheneum, 1974), p. 121.

4 Leonard E. Barrett, *Soul-Force* (Garden City, NY: Anchor Press/ Doubleday, 1974), p. 130.

5 Hazel Bennett and Phillip Sherlock, *The Story of the Jamaican People* (Kingston, Jamaica: Ian Randall Publishers, 1998), p. 295.

6 Rastas are members of the Rastafari movement, a religious and protest movement that emerged in Jamaica in the 1930s based, among other things, on the belief that Haile Selassie I, former Emperor of Ethiopia (1930–74) was God and Ethiopia was their promised land, the new Zion.

7 Ernest Cashmore, *Rastaman: The Rastafarian Movement in England* (London: George Allen and Unwin, 1979), pp. 23–24.

8 For an in-depth look at the concept of "I-and-I consciousness," see Noel Leo Erskine, *From Garvey to Marley: Rastafari Theology* (Gainesville, FL: University Press of Florida, 2005).

9 Kortright Davis, *Emancipation Still Comin'* (Maryknoll, NY: Orbis Books, 1990), p. 118.

10 Carolyn Cooper, *Noises in the Blood* (London: Macmillan Education, 1993), p. 122.

11 Ibid.

12 Rex Nettleford, *Mirror, Mirror: Identity, Race and Protest in Jamaica* (Kingston, Jamaica: LMH Publishing, 2001), pp. 154, 156.

13 Cooper, *Noises in the Blood*, p. 130.

21 Methodology in an Aboriginal theology

ANNE PATTEL-GRAY

BLACK THEOLOGY AND ABORIGINAL THEOLOGY

The seeds of contemporary black theology of liberation were nurtured in the USA on July 31, 1966, when the ad hoc National Committee of Negro Churchmen (NCNC) published its "Black Power" statement in the *New York Times*. Forty-eight black pastors and church administrators in the NCNC from fifteen different denominations and church offices claimed compatibility between Jesus Christ's words and practice and black American culture. Likewise, they asserted a correlation between Jesus' preferential option for the poor and the need for poor and working-class blacks to have power. Restated, Jesus incarnated in black folk culture and revealed himself in black political power.

Similarly, the contemporary foundation for Aboriginal theology (AT) in Australia emerged in the 1960s. Akin to the motivation of black pastors who crafted black theology of liberation, Aboriginal pastors were tired of white (British-descended) churchmen and missionaries telling the indigenous people they were subhuman. Aboriginal people were fed up with white people (mis)speaking with authority on the indigenous people while labeling their culture as primitive and uncivilized.

More positively, in the 1960s a small group of Aboriginal pastors elevated their culture as an authentic site of the ancestors' and Jesus' revelation. And that sacred culture required Aboriginal people to pursue the right of self-determination or political empowerment. Unknown to many outside of Aboriginal communities, these pastors (and many indigenous people today) referred to themselves as black people working with Jesus against structures of white supremacy in the white (British-descended) church in Australia.

Still, differences existed between US black people and Aboriginal black people. American blacks were brought by violent force as slaves on a Dutch man-of-war. They were not voluntary passengers or military officers on this warship. Their slave owners brought them to Jamestown,

Virginia in August 1619. Then, like hogs, they were bartered to John Rolfe of that British (Church of England) colony. Aboriginals, in contrast, lived freely and occupied the land prior to the British Christian, military, and entrepreneurial context. The April 1770 arrival of British explorer James Cook became a major marker for British incursion onto Aboriginal land.

Therefore, in contrast to the enslaved, British-owned ancestors of current African Americans, the black indigenous of Australia were not forced immigrants. Rather, white people gave them the Bible and stole their land. What is at stake, however, for both black theology of liberation (of African offspring in the USA) and Aboriginal theology (created by the original indigenous "blacks" of the land) is building healthy community and full humanity out of the positive strands of pre-Christianity spiritualities and the revelation of the Jesus movement with the oppressed.

1960S ABORIGINAL THEOLOGY

From its beginnings, Aboriginal theology sought to establish its own methodology, its own way of doing theology. To begin this dynamic of defining our Aboriginal methodology, this process of development has been constructed over many years, by many Aboriginal leaders and theologians. However, because of the limited theological education provided by white Australian churches,[1] these Aboriginal leaders and theologians struggled in their attempts to provide a clear statement of methodological process. And yet, their contribution has been significant in providing the basis from which this methodology has arisen. Thus, we have shared in their courage and passion for the delivery of an authentic Aboriginal theology. Greatly influenced by the various theologies of liberation, specifically black theology of liberation, Aboriginal Christians began to articulate with greater clarity the urgent need for a method of doing Aboriginal theology. This theology would not only affirm them as Aboriginal people, but also would assure them of God's liberating presence in the midst of their suffering and oppression.

Aboriginal theology was, therefore, a radical movement in theology beginning in the late 1960s and becoming more prominent in the early 1970s – one that broke through the barriers and moved forward toward the creation of an indigenous theology that leaned heavily on biblical justice. It was autonomous (post-Western, post-denominational) and emphasized prophetic obedience, action, and liberation. It attempted to hold up Aboriginality as the guiding principle and to maintain traditional

Aboriginal religion as the divine grounding for contemporary faith and identity. It regarded traditional practices (e.g., ceremonies) as potent reminders of important cosmic and temporal truths. And it embraced Aboriginal Dreaming as a timeless guide for active engagement. What these Aboriginal leaders made clear for the Aboriginal Christian was that they themselves, through their lived experience with God from time immemorial, had direct access to God, and that their relationship to Jesus Christ was established a long time before the white invasion of their land.

Of the many Aboriginal Christian leaders involved in the development of an appropriate methodology for an Aboriginal theology, three outstanding Aboriginal Christian leaders most remembered by Aboriginal Christians today are Pastor Don Brady, the Revd. Charles Harris, and Pastor David Kirk. These are considered the pioneers of Aboriginal theology and church. These Aboriginal leaders condemned the dominant white society's subjugation and exploitation of Aboriginal people and also raised important issues of justice and equality. Further, their criticism led them to condemn white missionaries as destructive influences upon the Aboriginal peoples and cultures. In this way they mixed deep faith with political commitment. For our purposes, we will highlight the first of the major Aboriginal Christian leaders of the 1960s.

The Revd. Don Brady was a pivotal figure in Aboriginal religious, social, and political movements.[2] Indeed, Aboriginal people recognized that his life and ministry were essential to the development of Aboriginal theology.[3] Calling for the abolition of the notorious Queensland Aborigines Act, which subjected Aboriginal people to inhumane social, economic, and health conditions, he was the first Aboriginal church leader to lead political marches. This new ministry, indicating a novel turn in how one does theology, was to influence many future generations in their refining of Aboriginal theological methodology.

Pastor Brady was from Palm Island, the former prison compound in Far North Queensland, which was used to contain and control Aboriginal people. He became a Christian there, and eventually was among the first of the male Aboriginal students to receive training through the Aborigines' Inland Mission (AIM). He married fellow student Darlene Willis, of Cherbourg, another Aboriginal mission in southern Queensland. They ministered together within the AIM for a number of years.[4]

The Revd. Brady was a gifted man who was able to see through the lack of effectiveness of mission practice, program, and policy. In the early 1960s, he began a further two years of theological training in the Methodist College at Kangaroo Point. He began his ministry with the Methodist Church in the heart of Brisbane, at Spring Hill. It was enormously popular, particularly among his own Aboriginal people, because his was a (w)holistic ministry. Don was concerned not only about the spiritual, but also the physical and emotional sides of people. He had a way of connecting with people – of seeing brokenness and being able to heal it. The appeal of his ministry extended far beyond the bounds of his own Aboriginal community, as many non-Aboriginal people were also drawn by his charisma.

Brady's prophetic stance grew out of his experiences overseas. He had won a Churchill Fellowship, had traveled to several communities in the United States, and had begun to sense a new direction. In his own words, "In Chicago I heard a call, 'Don arise, you are going to do a new thing'."[5] There he started to see the links between Gospel and culture, and to see what the missions had done to him in Australia. They had robbed him of any semblance of cultural expression in terms of worship and theology. He began to reject the influence of Western mission upon him. This meant, of course, that he had to struggle to find a new identity all by himself: there were no Aboriginal theologians; there was not the emphasis that there is today on culture and Gospel; there were no schools of missiology in the 1960s in Australia; and Brady had no colleagues.

He believed that without culture, Aboriginal people could not identify with Christianity. He believed that it was God who gave the Aboriginal people culture, and God in Aboriginal culture made our Aboriginality that much more authentic. He was trying to put across the idea that to be Christian did not necessarily mean to be white, an idea that was not at all apparent at the time.

The driving force behind Brady's convictions – that which made him get up and challenge and lead his people – was the incarnation of Christ into Aboriginal culture. Whereas when the missionaries came, they could not separate Christianizing from Westernizing, it was Brady who tried to point out the revelation of Christ in Aboriginal culture. This is the source of his radical voice, in challenging white people and churches in their ineffectiveness and inability to incarnate Christ into Aboriginal culture.

Brady was the first of all the Aboriginal pastors and leaders to combine the application of the Gospel with Aboriginal cultural practice. There were two things for which he stood out: he was right at the cutting edge of "Gospel and culture," and he emphasized social justice issues.

His ministry demonstrated the priority of Christ for the poor – Christ's identification with the poor. It was Brady's particular ministry in relation to these two factors that worked so well. Consequently, he tried to bring culture into the church, and this was something that profoundly affirmed Aboriginal people. One of today's Aboriginal church leaders, the Revd. Graham Paulson, remembers Brady's influence: "Brady was right at the cutting edge of Methodist ministry with urban Aboriginal people."[6]

Pastor Brady saw the poverty of his people; he heard their cries. He made the connection with God being on the side of the oppressed and leading his people out of bondage. He raised the question of how he could minister to the spiritual needs of Aboriginal people when they were enslaved by Australian legislation that oppressed them and literally denied them their human dignity and rights. He recognized that, "God is present in the sufferings of [hu]man[ity]. Christ was born in a stable, in humility, in suffering."[7] Brady was firmly committed to the "down and outs." In fact, he earned himself the title "the Punching Parson" by simply going around and picking up those of his homeless people in the parks and other places who were vulnerable to arrest and further abuse by the system. These he would pick up and take back to a refuge – sometimes he would first have to "knock them out," but they always thanked him the next morning. That sort of work, so far as the church was concerned, had never been done before in the history of mission among our people.[8]

Don Brady was a catalyst, in the sense that he created a black church, challenged the institutions, and began a black movement – one that was to be felt right across Australia. He lit the fire in people: he ignited the spark, the will to fight, the need to struggle for justice. He instilled in people the hope, the will to live. He helped to reveal to Aboriginal Christians that the God of justice, who freed the Israelites from the bondage of Egyptian rule, was also with the Aboriginal people as they struggled for freedom from Western oppression, racist laws, and imperialism. Together with other secular Aboriginal movements throughout the country, Brady brought the force of his black church with him, led by the conviction of equality and freedom for all. Black people started to share in the hope that God was on their side, and that God would send the Holy Spirit, the Comforter, to be their strength, hope, and courage in the face of the racist, oppressive evil inflicted upon them by the white Australian society. He raised the consciousness of his people to the realization that Christ came and died for them, and they, too, were free and inheritors of the Kingdom.[9]

Pastor Brady affirmed pride in Aboriginal heritage. This belief was so strong that he supported his children being initiated into traditional Aboriginal culture. It is important to stop here for a moment and to put this action into context. During the mid 1960s, most Aboriginal ministers themselves had absorbed and adopted a white, Western Christianity – one that judged Aboriginal culture, religion, and identity as evil and pagan. Where other church leaders were denying their Aboriginal identity and culture, Brady affirmed that these were God-given. For Brady to support initiation of his own children into Aboriginal culture was a bold and radical move. This, coupled with his theological challenges to and confrontations with the white churches, led to white Christian leaders distancing themselves from Brady's more progressive stance, and urging other conservative Aboriginal Christian leaders to separate themselves from him. Moreover, these white Christian leaders encouraged Aboriginal pastors to feel that "Aboriginal culture is evil."

The pressures on Pastor Brady were absolutely enormous, because he was a lone voice in the Methodist Church at that time: there was simply no one else with him. Brady was saying things that Aboriginal people had never heard before. "No one else had a voice like his."[10] In his own words, "Go forth in the struggle of God, in the power of God. Fight for freedom, for the cause of humanity, for God loves all."[11]

Brady's commitment to social justice led him to question the political system, as exemplified for instance by the Department of Native Affairs in Brisbane and other anti-Aboriginal policies. This meant that the Methodist Church, especially the conservative leaders, began to distance themselves from him. He found himself being more and more isolated by the system that had affirmed him right from the very beginning – that is, until he began to raise questions of justice in terms of social issues. Then the white church started to move away from him and, increasingly, Brady found himself a lonely and deserted leader. Not only that, from his conservative beginnings in the AIM, there were those of his former colleagues who were sniping at him as well. Because they could not understand the clear political dimensions of Jesus' words and practices on behalf of the poor and oppressed, they were trying to spiritualize away all the political, social, and economic issues.[12]

Brady's belief in doing and bringing the Gospel through Christ's action led to severe repercussions. He was spiritually and emotionally shattered, and lost all his drive. The Methodist Church pulled back and "defrocked" him, thereby undermining his status and the basis for his drive in the community. In a sense, the source for justice and morality and integrity was removed from him. The church retreated and thus took from him the very platform on which he was able to stand in order to be the prophet. Consequently, he was a man in the desert by himself, a voice crying in the wilderness. He had no institutional foundation, no status, and no standing from which to launch any action on those particular issues.

In the late 1960s, Brady had worked with the Methodist Church in Queensland. Overcoming tremendous hardships in his own life, he dedicated many years to helping the Aboriginal people of south Brisbane. He was a gifted and passionate preacher, and a tireless campaigner for Aboriginal rights. He was always to be found leading Aboriginal land rights marches. His strong theological stance, combined with his persistent efforts at direct action for justice, eventually led the church to "remove him" from the ministry. This act "broke" him.

The Revd. Graham Paulson states of Brady: "He reminds me of John the Baptist, particularly after he was defrocked – trying to maintain that energy, trying to maintain the drive, without a basis and without support. He lost his economic, emotional, spiritual, personal support. When you pull all of those in one fell swoop, as the church did, then you have a man who is just a shell."[13] But still Brady attempted to minister among his own, continuing to carry the Cross of sacrifice in the hope of securing liberation for his people.

Brady was the Gandhi, the Martin Luther King, Jr., the Malcolm X of the Aboriginal church; but unlike these leaders, who died the quick death of the bullet, Brady was made to suffer the slow death of exclusion and humiliation. Those for whom Brady had given his life and for whom he had struggled, in the hope of breaking the shackles of bondage and oppression, themselves came under the influence of the white church. They also turned their back on him. This was all he could bear, and it became the final nail in his own Cross. Don Brady died a broken man. The church, along with his own people, had successfully crushed his fighting spirit and will to live.

Brady gave his life for what he believed and in obedience to what God called him to do. And even though the church turned against him and tried to silence and discredit him, the legacy of his ministry was to be continued and made visible in the lives and ministries of those that were to follow. Brady's efforts were not wasted; on the contrary, his influence lives on in those who have the courage and the conviction to carry the Cross of sacrifice today. David Thompson, a lifelong friend of Pastor Brady's, describes him as "a man ahead of his time," and "a man of strength, character, and vision, who laid the foundations for the future."[14]

While Aboriginal theology's founders have been passionate about justice and the need for liberation of their people, they have nevertheless failed to address the particular concerns of oppression suffered by Aboriginal women, youth, and the disabled.[15] Indeed, all of the emerging theologians starting in the 1960s were weighed down by Western patriarchal structures and sexist attitudes and actions. Thus historic strides toward advancing a new theological methodology were lacking as a result of an internal gender critique.

AN ABORIGINAL METHODOLOGY

Drawing on the lives of black or Aboriginal pastors from the 1960s and 1970s, this chapter endeavors to provide a clear, systematic statement of methodology that will be instrumental in furthering the course of the development of an Aboriginal theology. The process continues the discourse on constructing an appropriate hermeneutical method that will enable Aboriginal Christians to incorporate their traditions and spirituality into the formulation of an Aboriginal theology. Furthermore, such a discussion on hermeneutical freedom to acculturate and contextualize the biblical narratives through our own cultural epistemology and ontological understanding becomes the praxis of my theological construction. Hopefully, the methodology for blacks doing Aboriginal theology will be a gift to and engagement with black theology of liberation globally.

My methodological process consists of seven consecutive applications, and these include the following: (1) indigenous research; (2) the New Reformation; (3) a rereading of the biblical narratives; (4) a postcolonial reflection on Christian mission and colonialism; (5) a postcolonial reading of Christian ethics; (6) the process of inculturation; and (7) Western dichotomy/Aboriginal wholeness. Each process of application is covered further within this chapter in what follows.

Indigenous research: practice and protocol

For over two centuries, Australian indigenous people have been the subject and object of study by many disciplines within the academic world. Aboriginal research has been dominated by Euro-Australians, many earning PhDs, becoming renowned as "white experts" on indigenous knowledge, publishing literally thousands of studies on their interpretations and so-called "expertise" in indigenous lifeways, and gathering knighthoods, Royal Society memberships, and other Western accolades along the way.

Reflected in a great deal of this literature, however, are imperialistic attitudes, bigotry, and social Darwinist views that support and perpetuate the dehumanization of Aboriginals and their relegation to the lowest rung of humanity. Such so-called scholars assume the right to interpret indigenous ancestral narratives, songs, and dances. They draw heavily on secondary sources, without appropriately citing the primary sources, the indigenous people themselves.

Their research requires no field exposure, instead, the "armchair scholars" remain in their ivory towers and undertake their so-called "research" by reading and engaging "the literature." Other "scholars," the "hit-and-run field researchers," see the flaws of the "armchair approach" and instead take the two or three months they feel necessary to give academic credibility to inquire into indigenous knowledge.[16] Such "scholars" assume that they can interview any Aboriginal person they "need" on any street or in any community, and that this will represent the "Aboriginal viewpoint" on a given subject.

One of the more obvious problems with this approach is that, while Euro-Australian researchers are usually pursuing and intruding upon secret/sacred areas with their many assumptions and hypotheses, not all indigenous people have total knowledge of all aspects of their culture, especially the secret/sacred areas, because they may not yet have completed all stages of initiation – a process that can take a lifetime. Another not-so-obvious problem is that when Euro-Australian researchers do actually cite the primary sources, the indigenous people, they remain faceless and nameless subjects of their so-called scholarship. Inevitably, this creates great difficulties for current indigenous scholars to check the source, accuracy, and validity of the information.

With regard to oral testimonies, Western scholars continually gather information from the primary sources, but fail to cite the precise sources; that is, the *names* of the "informants," the authority of the informants, or the extent of the informants' knowledge and their "ownership" of it. Instead, they take such knowledge and label it as "their" findings. Subsequently, Aboriginal people then find themselves unable to access the knowledge that has been recorded by these people, as they no longer "own" it because they "told" it to someone who has copyrighted it as "theirs." If Aboriginal people are not cited, then who owns the information? Here we begin to move into the area of cultural property and intellectual copyright. Who owns traditional and contemporary Aboriginal material? Do "outsiders" have the right to claim ownership over others' knowledge? Indeed, do they have any rights at all over indigenous intellectual property?

In order to undertake reliable academic research, one needs to identify a series of stages. With particular regard to secret and sacred areas, one needs to identify the keeper, or keepers, of the ceremonies with specific authority over certain sections of the rituals and ceremonies, and which persons are recognized as owners. This is primarily elders, fully initiated men and women.

Scholars should have an adequate understanding and knowledge of the language, as our people often have a limited or a simplified understanding of the English language. Even beyond this, some Aboriginal people speak what Oodgeroo Noonuccal has described as "Aboriginal English" in the national education curriculum, which makes the communication process nearly impossible. Even though they are speaking "English," European scholars still do not understand them.

To limit one's research only to the spoken word, in particular in English, is not only to impose imperialism, but also to miss out on the depth and breadth of the indigenous languages, which range beyond the verbal. Specifically, the nonverbal is highly developed within Aboriginal societies and is often overlooked by many Western scholars. To undertake a research project within indigenous communities can take several years; it cannot be assumed that you can do "hit-and-run" fieldwork, because what inevitably happens in this situation is either the acquisition of false information or confinement to superficial interpretations. If indigenous people do not know you, or respect you, they will not give you important or extensive information about anything at all. If scholars limit their research to secondary sources, they are also prone to fall into the trap of undermining the credibility and authority of their research, as there is every possibility that they will regurgitate misconceptions, errors, untruths, and biases.

A better method is offered by Paulo Freire, the Brazilian theoretician and practitioner of pedagogical methodology. In his classic *Pedagogy of the Oppressed*, he discusses various kinds of participatory techniques for self-empowerment and consequent revolutionary action of oppressed and marginalized peoples.[17] Freire considers that his methodology is not just a process of imparting knowledge. It enhances transformation and empowerment of the oppressed by way of conscientization. He states,

That's what conscientization is: a seizing of reality; and for that very reason, for the very utopian strain that permeates it, we can call it a reshaping of reality. Conscientization demythologizes. Obvious and impressive as the fact may be, an oppressor can never be conscientized for liberation. (How would I possibly demythologize if I am an oppressor?) A humanizing endeavour can only be an endeavour to demythify. Conscientization, then, is the most critical approach conceivable to reality, stripping it down so as to get to know it and know the myths that deceive and perpetuate the dominating structure ... A conscientizing – and therefore liberating – education is not that transfer of neatly wrapped knowledge in which there certainly is no knowledge; it is a true act of knowing. Through it, both teacher and pupils simultaneously become knowing subjects, brought together by the object they are knowing. There is no longer one who thinks, who knows, standing in front of others who admit they don't know, that they have to be taught. Rather, all of them are inquisitive learners, avid to learn.[18]

This methodology that Freire has developed is critical to the process I have undertaken based on participatory and action research, which can be defined as research where the researcher and the researched constructively cooperate to seek ways in which to transform the subjects/ actors into aware transformers and cocreators of their lives. By using this method, greater opportunities are given to various Aboriginal elders while doing oral history research. In my oral history sessions, which were undertaken in various Aboriginal communities (both traditional and urban), each elder took turns to speak. Everyone had a chance to tell their life story without being interrupted, judged, prompted, helped, or ridiculed by the other members of the group. As each Aboriginal elder completed his/her turn, the oral testimony (or rather subject matter) was open to comments and questions (but not criticism) by the other elders of the group; these questions and comments would often serve as starting points for the next narration.

The New Reformation

What Christians are witnessing today throughout the world and in particular within the global church is the revolution by those who were and some who would still be considered by the West the subjects or objects of Western Christian missionary evangelism. This revolutionary movement is a world-wide phenomenon for such people who have found themselves dispossessed, disenfranchised, oppressed, exploited, and made criminals, just by the color of their skins. And they are committed to the process of a "New Reformation." This reformation requires the dismantling of both church and state racism, classism, sexism, and homophobia ingrained in their many institutions. Such

Western imperialism has led to the establishment of unjust social systems and structures, and inequitable social culture based on their many isms, which has led to the oppression of many people throughout the world. The point of critique among indigenous peoples is the failure of the West to see its classical theology as contextual and influenced by the social and political environment and the experiences of any given time throughout history. The failure of the West to consider its theology as "contextual" rather than universal is surely because it is blinded by its so-called "superiority."

Justo L. González, in his book *Mañana*, takes context seriously. González provides five points that introduce a critical analysis for the Third-World context, an analysis pointing toward a methodology in the New Reformation.

The first critique offered by González concerns the "three self." These goals, suggested by Roland Allen, call for self-support, self-government, and self-propagation. What the West did not include or intend, however, was for the non-Western churches to forge a methodology calling for the right to self-interpretation and self-theologizing. The expectation from the West, therefore, was for non-Western Christians to continue to proclaim the Gospel from the perspective given by the West.[19]

The second critical analysis provided by González rises out of a post-Constantinian perspective. Rather than fearing the post-Constantinian era, González states that it "is leading us to a deeper understanding of the biblical message. Scripture is better understood from the perspective of the early church than from that of the Constantinian church."[20] As González effectively points out, those who have experienced slavery, alienation, bondage, oppression, and poverty bring a radical challenge to Western classical theology. From the underside of history, indigenous and minority people are finding liberation through the rereading of the Bible within their context.[21]

The third aspect raised by González concerns the question of truth. For Aboriginal people this question of truth is considered to be of a critical nature in any given context. For example, from whose perspective is the "truth" being defined: Is it the West that has total authority to set in concrete the terms and definition of truth to which all the universe must submit, or is truth open for all to interpret for themselves? Truth can have so many meanings and can be understood in different ways. The question is not who is right and who is wrong, but rather from whose point of view and from whose context is this perspective on truth being defined?[22]

For Aboriginal theology and black theology of liberation, truth is found in the liberating works of God and through the lived example provided by Jesus of Nazareth, who was born in human form and who proclaimed the "Good News" of God's reign of justice, liberty, healing, hope, and eternal life. This Jesus said that the Kingdom was obtainable to all who believed here and now and also in the future.[23] The fourth dimension concerns ecumenism. Today, in the presenet reformation, the issues of the sixteenth century do not hold very much importance for us in the current movements of liberation throughout the world of oppressed peoples or in the radical ecumenical movements. In the sixteenth century, the debate engaged salvation as either a faith stance or a works practice. Our understanding of salvation in our current situation is vastly different from that of the sixteenth century. Now salvation concerns the entire earth, especially accenting the poor. Today's ecumenical process includes anyone on earth who lifts up justice.

The fifth and final characteristic of the New Reformation proposed by González challenges the Western theological methodology of so-called "universals" or "universality"; that is to say, Western theology is not for the whole world. Rather, like all theologies, its method is contextual and local to its European context. What spreads it globally is not the power of its ideas or the force of its argument. On the contrary, the force of imperialist economic, military, and cultural systems gives it the false and dangerous appearance of disinterested, objective logic. González, therefore, articulates quite accurately the views shared by those from the underside of life and community.

In characteristic fashion, this question of the nature of universals is not being asked in purely logical or philosophical terms but rather in terms of justice, power, and human relations. The new theology being done by those who are aware of their traditional voicelessness is acutely aware of the manner in which the dominant is confused with the universal. North Atlantic male theology is taken to be basic, normative, universal theology, to which women, other minorities, and people from the younger churches may then add their footnotes. White theologians do general theology; black theologians do black theology ... Such a notion of "universality" based on the present unjust distribution of power is unacceptable to the new theology.[24]

A rereading of the biblical narratives

As a scholar and also a black Aboriginal woman, I have spent many years wrestling with the question that undergirds all theological concepts regarding the contextualization of one's Christian faith. Since the

1960s, oppressed peoples of color have been deconstructing Western cultural domination and interpretation of the biblical scriptures and Christian faith. The Western assumption concerning its authority over the expression of the Christian faith has been for some time questioned by those who have been subjugated by colonial and Christian expansion throughout the world.[25] As African American theologian Professor Robert E. Hood points out in his book *Must God Remain Greek?*, the ideas and conceptual character at play in the Western framework have been largely influenced by Graeco-Roman metaphysical and philosophical thought, which is intimately linked to cultural and social ideas of Greek and Roman antiquity.[26] At the same time, this Graeco-Roman tradition and culture is also the foundation of what can be called Eurocentric cultures and intellectual history, meaning Western civilization and its colonial offspring throughout the world.[27]

From a different cultural and biblical context, we have seen the rise of black theology of liberation in the USA, where African Americans try to understand God's liberating presence in the exodus narrative and the incarnation of Christ in black culture. This biblical hermeneutical method allows them to see Jesus as one of them.[28]

To put it succinctly, we need to reread the Bible from a black Aboriginal perspective, recognizing the need for criticism and self-criticism.

A postcolonial reflection on Christian mission and colonialism

Critical to the development of an indigenous methodology is the application of postcolonial criticism and theory. Part of this entails the deconstruction of colonial and mission history from the viewpoints of those who were made subjects and objects of Western colonialism and Western missions during the nineteenth and early twentieth centuries.

African American womanist theologian Jacquelyn Grant provides a perfect example for us in a story she presented in *The Kairos Covenant*.

There was a little boy in an African village who customarily came home from the mission school with excitement about his learning of the day. On one particular day, he came home with a look of puzzlement on his face. And when he came into his house his father inquired about his puzzlement. The little boy said, "Father, I don't understand this. I go to school every day and the teacher often tells us the story about this lion who they say is the king of the jungle. But this ferocious and strong beast always seems to get killed by the hunter in the story. I don't understand it. If the lion is so strong, why does the hunter always kill the lion?" The father responded, "Well, son, until lions learn how to write books, that's the way the story will always end."[29]

This is a good analogy for Aboriginal people to ponder over. We indigenous people must write books presenting our unrepresented critique of Western colonialism and mission, which will "lend itself to a 'reading' and a 'counter-reading'; that is, reading traditionalist Western interpretation and a rereading from a colonized viewpoint."[30]

A postcolonial reading of Christian ethics

A further aspect for us to note in the construction of indigenous methodology is the question of ethics, that which determines human identity, action, morals, and obedience.[31] But this is not to say that identity is static, because if this was the case, transformation would never occur, thereby limiting the power of the Creator to bring about a new creation, both personally and socially. "Just as identity is socially acquired, so also identity is *socially transformed*. As the above discussion has implied, identity, including moral identity, is not fixed once and for all but is to varying degrees flexible, subject to change. And such changes occur through a social process."[32]

So the basis for the development of any kind of Aboriginal methodology must make identity the primary focus with which to begin reconstruction through the process of inculturation and theological application. Identity helps to reaffirm the human dignity of Aboriginal people today, a pressing need resulting from the existential suffering of our people as a result of the oppressive force of white colonialism and missionization. An indigenous, black reconfiguring of identity has deep implications for Christian ethics.

The process of inculturation

To aid in this process of developing a methodology in Aboriginal theology, the process of inculturation is critical. The importance I give to this dynamic is not just limited to superficial cultural dressing, but rather a deeper process that has been described as incarnational. This was first described by Father Pedro Arrupe in 1981. He states:

> Inculturation is the incarnation of Christian life and of the
> Christian message in a particular cultural context, in such a way
> that this experience not only finds expression through elements

proper to the culture in question, but becomes a principle that animates, directs and unifies the culture, transforming and remaking it so as to bring about *"a new creation."*[33]

The original Word was made flesh in the life of Jesus, in a particular time, place, and context, among a particular people, life situation, and culture, and has been recorded within biblical scripture for us to read. The task of indigenous Christians and theologians today is to incarnate the *living* Word not only into our cultural life and context, but also to enable the *living* Word to take shape in the blood, sweat, and tears of Aboriginal people. This kind of reinterpretation is a necessary process of inculturation, through which the Word of God is made relevant to indigenous peoples and contexts.[34]

Faith as understood by Aboriginal people is their response to God's self-revelation. Faith is a commitment shown in life through action, and, therefore, faith for Aboriginal people is a lived experience. Faith, for an Aboriginal person, is to be proclaimed and celebrated, and the proclamation happens primarily in the context of a celebration. Through the enactment of rituals, Aboriginal people become consciously aware of and affirm their faith in narrative and ritual. The community is empowered in word and symbolic action and especially through the rites of passage. Aboriginal people see their faith as questioning their lived experience and their experience questioning their faith; this enables critical reflection. Such reflection is always context-specific and is conditioned by space and time, because both the experience and the tools of reflection provided by culture are local. Three dimensions of faith keep interacting mutually: life challenges our convictions and the truth of our celebration; celebration challenges life prophetically in the context of tradition and provokes reflection; and reflection gives rise to new options for praxis and new and more effective symbols for celebration.

Aboriginal spirituality and identity are given by the Creator God and are the foundation of our Aboriginal faith. So, if we believe in Jesus Christ as incarnated of God, then our Christology is a natural process in the development of our Aboriginal theology. Orthodox Christian theology holds that God is incarnated in Christ Jesus, making the Word flesh and a living example for us to follow. Is it not possible, then, also to say that Christ is our ancestor, since, as argued above, the Creator God interacted in creation through our spirit ancestors in a living form? Christ is the divine link between the old lifeways of the Aboriginal people and the Creator God, and the nexus to the new lifeways. Just as we say that Christ is the New Covenant of the Bible – and the Old

Covenant of Moses has been transcended through Christ – we can also say that, through our ancestor Christ, we, the Aboriginal people, are embarking upon our New Covenant, as Christ enables us to transcend our own cultural limitations, through the ability to critique our own culture and position in society.

Aboriginal methodology, therefore, begins with the nature of God in our creation, spirituality, land, and identity. It is in this respect that we can truly grapple with being made in the image of God, and the implication that has for our humanity, laws, faith, and identity in our relationship with the Creator God. It is only when Aboriginal people begin to draw upon the old ancestral lifeways and the interaction of the Creator God in the old ways that we can sustain and maintain our spirituality and the reflected divinity of God, encompassed in our identity. This is where Aboriginal people find their strength and the affirmation of their identity and self-worth, through the acts of the Creator God. From here we can struggle against the negative aspects of colonization and missionization, and counteract the destructive impact and legacies of this history.

Western dichotomy/Aboriginal wholeness

The final aspect of Aboriginal theological methodology concerns the notion of hierarchical polarity. Western theologians have for centuries wrestled with their own perception of the dichotomy of the body and spirit, yet within the indigenous *Weltanschauung* there is no dichotomy. Instead, the oneness is reinforced within our religious and spiritual life, because from my indigenous exegetical and hermeneutical application of the biblical text, I am able to interpret the text and draw upon my own Aboriginal epistemology in rereading the scriptures. That process enables the creation of (w)holism to emerge.

In Genesis we find the narrative relating to the Creator God's actions in creation, creating humanity from the earth and breathing life into male and female, made in the image of God. Here we find the integrity of humanity, possessing the breath of the divine spirit of God, and reflecting the image of God in human flesh. For the West, the body is made to be subordinate to the spirit, but I have a different interpretation. The flesh or body is as important as the spirit, because it is through the flesh that we can experience the Spirit of God. Indeed, if we look at the meaning of the *logos* (i.e., Jesus the Christ), and the Word becoming flesh, it is in Jesus the Anointed One where we begin to see the (w)holism found in the union of the body and spirit.

It was through Mary that the Word became flesh; through the human form of Mary did the spirit of God create new life. Chosen by God, Mary conceived the Word; during her time of pregnancy, Mary brought about the miracle of incarnation in the birth of Jesus. God did not choose to create Jesus from the soil of the earth, but instead chose a humble maiden named Mary to process and give life to the Word. The incarnation was not possible without Mary; through the spirit of God did Mary conceive the divine spirit and through her flesh was the incarnation of the *logos* able to take form. Through the womb of Mary was the incarnation made possible, the Word, cradled in her womb, nurtured and nourished, made of her flesh, took life in human form in the birth of Jesus. So it is with this in mind that I regard Mary as the Mother of Incarnation.[35] As fully incarnated, she embodied holistically mind, spirit, and body.

Like this biblical story of a comprehensive way of doing faith, a black Aboriginal theology from Australia seeks to contribute to global discussions on new methodology – itself a doing of or path toward faith. In particular we understand commonalities with black theology of liberation as it, too, has journeyed along a similar path of its own indigenous research, rereading of the Bible, postcolonial analysis of contextualization, inculturation of Jesus' movement within black US culture, and appreciating the need for a (w)holistic, all-embracing method of doing theology for the twenty-first century. In this sense, Aboriginal theology is also a form of black theology.

Notes

1 See, e.g., Andrew Dutney, "Teaching the Teacher ...," in Anne Pattel-Gray (ed.), *Martung Upah: Black and White Australians Seeking Partnership* (New York: HarperCollins, 1996), pp. 248–62.

2 This section is based upon personal knowledge as well as on interviews with several persons who knew and/or worked with Pastor Brady: Marceil Lawrence, David Thompson, the Revd. Charles Harris, and the Revd. Graham A. Paulson; interviews by the author, Sydney, NSW, 1987–97.

3 From the author's interview with Charles Harris, Sydney, NSW, 1988.

4 From the author's interview with Cecil Grant, Sydney, NSW, November, 1995.

5 Don Brady, "Sermon Quotes," in *Racism in Australia: Tasks for General and Christian Education: Report of Southport Conference, November 19–24, 1971* (Melbourne: Australian Council of Churches, Division of Christian Education, 1971), p. 39.

6   From the author's interview with Graham Paulson, Sydney, NSW, November, 1995.

7   Brady, "Sermon Quotes," p. 39.

8   "Pastor Burns and Spits on Aboriginal Act," *Courier-Mail* (January 10, 1970): 1.

9   From the author's interview with Charles Harris, Lismore, NSW, 1991.

10 Ibid.

11 Brady, "Sermon Quotes," p. 39.

12 From the author's interview with Charles Harris, Lismore, NSW, 1991.

13 From the author's interview with Graham Paulson, Sydney, NSW, November, 1995.

14 From the author's interview with David Thompson, Sydney, NSW, 1995.

15 In terms of organizations in this group, the Aboriginal and Islander Commission (AIC) of the National Council of Churches in Australia is currently taking unprecedented and dramatic strides toward discerning and embodying an indigenous, autonomous theology. In 1991, it organized the participation of Aboriginal and Islander People in the World Council of Churches 7th Assembly in Canberra, in which the Indigenous People of Australia opened the Assembly with a traditional smoking ceremony and made significant contributions to the worship, business, and informal times of the gathering. See Anne Pattel-Gray, *Cry for Justice* (Sydney: Aboriginal and Islander Commission, 1991). More recently, the AIC has moved to the forefront of organizing a national Aboriginal church women's movement. See, e.g., Anne Pattel-Gray (ed.), *Tiddas Talkin' Business* (Garbutt, Australia: Centre for Indigenous and Religious Research, 1999), p. ???.

16 Vine Deloria, Jr., *Custer Died for Your Sins* (New York: Macmillan, 1969; repr. Norman: University of Oklahoma Press, 1988).

17 Paulo Freire, *Pedagogy of the Oppressed* (New York: Continuum, 1993; first edn. 1970).

18 Paulo Freire, "Conscientizing as a Way of Liberating," in Alfred T. Hennelly (ed.), *Liberation Theology: A Documentary History* (Maryknoll, NY: Orbis Books, 1990), pp. 5–13, at p. 9.

19 Justo L. González, *Mañana: Christian Theology from a Hispanic Perspective* (Nashville, TN: Abingdon Press, 1991), p. 49.

20 Ibid.

21 Ibid., pp. 49–50.

22 Ibid., p. 50.

23 Ibid., pp. 50–51.

24 Ibid., pp. 51–52.

25 See Garry W. Trompf (ed.), *The Gospel Is Not Western: Black Theologies of the Southwest Pacific* (Maryknoll, NY: Orbis Books, 1987).

26 Robert E. Hood, *Must God Remain Greek? Afro-Cultures and God-Talk* (Minneapolis, MN: Fortress Press, 1990), pp. 245–46.

27 Ibid., p. 245.

28 Wesley Ariarajah, *Gospel and Culture: An Ongoing Discussion within the Ecumenical Movement*, Gospel and Cultures Pamphlets 1 (Geneva: WCC Publications, 1994), pp. 36–37.

29 Wills H. Logan (ed.), *The Kairos Covenant* (New York: Friendship Press, 1988), p. 131.
30 Jacob S. Dharmaraj, *Colonialism and Christian Mission: Postcolonial Reflections* (Delhi: ISPCK, 1993), p. xv.
31 Hunter P. Mabry (ed.), *Christian Ethics: An Introductory Reader* (Serampore: Indian Theological Library, 1987), pp. 29–30.
32 Ibid., p. 30.
33 Pedro Arrupe, "Letter on Inculturation," in J. Aixala, SJ (ed.), *Jesuit Apostolates Today* (Anand: Gujarat Sahitya Prakash, 1981), p. 173.
34 Ibid.
35 The Rt. Revd. V. Devasahayam also used this concept during his sermon at the United Theological College, Bangalore, India, July 28, 1999.

22 Black theology and postcolonial discourse
EDWARD P. ANTONIO

I want to suggest that there are at least five discursive areas where the "postcolonial" opens up spaces of possible articulation with black theology. First, I argue that slave protests, resistance, and contestation of colonial slavery by slaves are situated in and sustained by images of a future society characterized by freedom. Though not named "postcolonial," this society will answer to that description in its capacity to represent social and political arrangements that have transcended colonial slavery itself. Second, black theology and postcolonial discourse encounter each other in the emergence and development of black critical social theory represented by a long line of black thinkers such as Alexander Crummell, Edward Blyden, Sojourner Truth, W. E. B. DuBois, and many others whose thought sustained the postcolonial imaginary through the production of theory in literature, philosophy, history, religion, and so forth. Third, I shall make reference to certain black movements of thought such as Pan-Africanism, Negritude, and the civil rights movements, which inspired a global vision of a world without colonial domination, as another area of articulation between black theology and postcolonial discourse. Fourth, I propose that we take seriously the global presence of black theology as already securing the relationship between black theology and postcoloniality. Fifth and finally, I conclude the chapter by discussing an important example of black theology's direct participation in postcolonial discourses of the twentieth century through the work of James Cone.

The relationship between black theology and postcolonial discourse is best approached by situating it in the larger context of Western modernity. There are, of course, interminable debates about the meaning of modernity or about what modernity stands for. For my purposes, it is not necessary to attribute to modernity any singularity in meaning in order to endorse the argument that has been made by different scholars that whatever other elements belong to its makeup, race and racism must be counted among the structural formations of modernity.

Race and racism represent two contiguous formations in modernity's understanding of human selves and the social structures they create and inhabit. Despite its declared intentions to instantiate and propagate universal justice, it plays the role of a totalizing and a reductive philosophical anthropology that privileges white humanity and reduces everything else to figures of being that are at best represented as marginal to what it means to be human.

This is the context in which slavery, colonialism, postcolonialism, and global imperialism must be situated if we are to understand not only how black thought, including black theology, emerged but also how black theology is connected to postcolonial discourse. For all four moments are distinguished by their historical function in the movement of Western modernity to the ends of the earth, a movement in which race and racism are intrinsic, that is, are defining operations at every level of social being. It is now a common story that race and racism are at the heart of slavery; that they undergird justifications of the colonial expropriation of lands and territories or the denigration of non-Western cultures and thus the imposition of Western "civilization"; and that they define human selves and determine their existential possibilities. It is simply remarkable how race and racism are repeatedly and routinely produced and reproduced throughout modernity's vast historical and geographical network of colonial territories and practices simultaneously associated with the slave trade, with different European empires, and later with American capitalistic imperialism. They express and articulate a desire for a world dominated by whiteness.

POSTCOLONIALITY AS UTOPIAN PRACTICES OF RESISTANCE

The form of the historical trajectory of race and racism that I am proposing here is important. I begin with modernity, but it is really within the historical specificities of slavery, colonialism, postcolonialism, and globalization as expressions of Western modernity that we must account for both scientific and philosophical doubts about black beings and the ubiquitous representation of *other* human beings as racially *other* and thus, often, as inferior. It is against this background of cross-cultural, cross-geographical, and transhistorical colonialism as a system of domination (direct and discursive) that we must try to address the connections between black theology and postcolonial discourse.[1] Why is this so? There are three reasons. First, this is because the postcolonial can only speak in and through its parasitic relationship on the "colonial."

Second, this is so fundamentally because the movement from slavery through to global imperialism was actively mediated through colonialism itself. For example, slavery was practiced in the New World colonies possessed and controlled by the British, Portuguese, the French, the Spanish, the Dutch, and the Danes;[2] in other words, it had as its context the territories expropriated from the indigenous populations of Africa, the Americas, and the Caribbean, the accompanying disruption of local cultures and ecologies, as well as a strong militaristic and mercantile capitalism that massively depended on exploiting the labor of millions of slaves imported from thousands of miles away in Africa.

Third, the necessity of colonialism for understanding black theology's relationship to postcolonialism stems from the fact that insofar as black theology is somehow aligned or wishes to align with the postcolonial it must take seriously the colonial as a key moment in its self-understanding. Now, as it happens, black theology is historically already mapped onto the colonial in two different ways: (1) through the role colonial slavery played in creating and constituting black subjects as beings whose humanity was open to systemic doubt, disdain, and repudiation; and (2) black theology is also mapped onto the colonial through the role slave religion played in protesting, challenging, resisting, and subverting slavery and its colonial underpinnings long before its formalization into the academic discourse of theology. The point I wish to argue here is that the manner in which black theology is defined by these two elements of coloniality provides its incipient connections with postcolonial discourse. I want to argue that the "dialectic" between colonial slavery and black resistance is the historical framework out of which slave religion and later black theology emerge doubly marked as both colonial and postcolonial. The figure of the colonial exists here as a historical fact and there is nothing controversial in the claim that slave religion and by extension black theology are concrete discursive effects, produced by and in the context of colonial violence. However, it is not uncontroversial to suggest, as I have also just done, that these effects, concurrent with their location in colonial slavery, also attest to the existence of postcoloniality. In what possible way might slave religion have been postcolonial? In what respects can black theology today be said to have inherited and continued the postcolonial legacy of slave religion? After all, postcolonial discourse is a twentieth-century phenomenon associated in the minds of many with struggles to end colonialism and to locate and position colonial subjects in a time register of the "after" of colonial domination. This being so, is there not a danger of historical anachronism in my suggestion? The problem is further complicated by the difficulty of theorizing both the colonial and the postcolonial in the singular when we know that there are, in fact, many different forms of colonialism and postcolonialism.[3]

I believe these problems can be got around by rethinking postcolonialism not as a cluster of historical moments individually or collectively representing the immediate or gradual overcoming or demise of institutionalized colonialism, and thus marking the end of the colonial event. Rather, if I had the space to do so here in detail, I would rethink the postcolonial as a discursive structure of moral, political, and religious/theological protest situated not beyond the colonial but within it. That slaves challenged, critiqued, and rejected slavery and white domination has been well documented, and will not detain us here.[4] It is not the historical fact of such protest that interests me at this point but rather what it represents or its teleology or purpose, namely freedom and emancipation. There are at least four features of slave protests worth noting. First, rebellions and protests were generally framed in Christian religious terms. Slaves were critical of the religion of the slave master, which they saw and experienced as oppressive because it justified their enslavement and contradicted its own proclamation of universal equality and freedom. But they also critically appropriated Christianity precisely in order to redeem its promise of equality for all before God, and in the process transformed it into "slave religion" for all human beings. This religious or theological moment of slave protest will become a fundamental source for black theology in the twentieth century. Second, slave protests were characterized by a utopian desire for freedom and liberation. What I want to argue here is that this desire for freedom and emancipation is imaginatively organized and articulated around the transformative possibilities for the creation of a world of justice beyond the constraints of colonial slavery.[5] I call this the utopian dimension of slave religion and protest. It is this utopian aspect that gives postcoloniality the moral status of a sociopolitical reality beyond the subjugating horizon of colonialism. Slaves were not merely critical of existing social institutions, their many acts of insurrection and protest were not merely ad hoc or tactical "practices of freedom" dependent on indeterminate "auspicious" circumstances. My argument is that intrinsic to their acts of rebellion was an imaginative yearning for a different social order, which can be rendered as genuinely "postcolonial" not completely in the sense overdetermined by current usages of the term but in the rhetorical and moral sense in which the achievement of structural or systemic justice for slaves and the oppressed laboring under the dystopian conditions of

racial domination involves vanquishing the ordering structures of colonial governmentality. Something perhaps along the lines of what Paul
Gilroy calls the "politics of fulfillment."[6] The general implication of
my argument is that postcoloniality has a primary utopian dimension
that serves as motivation for struggling against the injustices of slavery,
and provides a different vision of the social world. Third, this way of
thinking about postcoloniality as a utopian moment inherent in social
critique supplies an ethical or moral framework for positing interpretive continuity between earlier and later forms of postcoloniality. If we
look ahead to postcolonial movements of the twentieth century we see
the struggle for freedom and justice linked to some vision of a future
society or vision of a universal humanistic ethic among virtually all of
them. Negritude, for example, was quite explicit in its articulation of
a black humanism beyond the shackles of an oppressive white civilization. This brings me to the third feature of slave protests to which
I want to draw attention, namely, the way in which these protests and
the oppositional praxis they inscribe initiate and continue a genealogy
of a black critical social theory.

POSTCOLONIALITY AS BLACK UTOPIAN CRITICAL SOCIAL THEORY

Second, then, the impulse toward freedom and the acts of resistance
it inaugurated gave rise to a distinctive black critical social theory in the
speeches, writings, poems, and sermons of a long line of thinkers such
as Sojourner Truth, Frederick Douglass, Ida B. Wells Barnett, Martin
Delany, Nat Turner, Anna Julia Cooper, David Walker, Henry Highland
Garnet, Alexander Crummell, Harriet Tubman, Edward Wilmot Blyden,
William Edward Burghardt DuBois, Marcus Mosiah Garvey, Léopold
Sédar Senghor, George Padmore, Julius Nyerere, Franz Fanon, Aimé
Césaire, and Cheikh Anta Diop.

This critical social theory not only theorized the struggles of blacks
in modernity, it was also premised upon the need for a revolutionary
dissolution of existing social and political arrangements inasmuch as
it demanded equality, justice, and the recognition of black humanity – social practices conspicuously absent under slavery and colonialism. The absence of racial justice and equality in colonial slavery and
throughout modernity bespoke a moral and political hiatus between
modernity's promise of freedom and justice, on the one hand, and its
failure to fulfill that promise, on the other. Black critical social theory took this hiatus as the impetus to mount a critique of modernity

characterized by three features: (1) a hermeneutic of suspicion about the effectiveness of relying on modernity's inner norms to overcome its racism; (2) the emergence of a critique of modernity that drew from African humanistic sources and was combined with modernity's own promise of freedom to propose a different way of thinking about politics and human relationships (an alternative modernity, no less); and (3) a postcolonial imaginary that came into being not just as an effect of slave protest and resistance but also as the enunciation of utopian and eschatological desires for emancipation, freedom, and equality. In short, because practices of racial justice and freedom were absent in racist and colonial modernity, their achievement, therefore, presupposed a postcolonial order as a social ideal. My argument does not depend on deciding whether such an ideal was imagined in historical terms as an actually attainable state of affairs or whether it was posited only morally or regulatively. The idea of utopia is important for the kind of critical social theory I am describing here, because, as Maeve Cooke has pointed out, without it, without "the idea of an alternative, better social order," we cannot make sense of critical theory's criticism of a given social context.[7]

In saying this I do not mean to suggest that history is unimportant to utopian images of a future postcolonial society, for this would lead to bad utopianism "defined as lack of connection with the actual historical process, and 'finalism' defined as closure of the historical process." To portray black critical social theory and the acts of protest it represents as utopian is not to say that postcoloniality is unattainable, and as just remarked it is not to disconnect black resistance from history. Rather, the ideal of a world that has overcome colonialism is provoked and informed by the experience of wrestling with existing historical conditions. I am proposing that in this regard we think of postcoloniality as an imagined moral vision of a social formation characterized by racial justice and peace. In other words, slave protests were often driven by an imaginative utopian impulse that gestured toward postcoloniality and in so doing inscribed its moral and rhetorical possibility.

POSTCOLONIALITY AS PAN-AFRICAN HUMANISM

The historical connections between this vision and postcolonial critical social thought on the one hand, and history, on the other, can be seen at work in the black social movements in which postcolonialism in the sense in which I have characterized it is connected with the formal emergence of historical postcolonialism through a whole range of critical discursive practices carried out as part of the anticolonial and decolonizing struggles of the twentieth century throughout Africa and other parts of the black world.

This brings us to our third area of possible articulation between black theology and postcolonial discourse. I have in mind how black critical social theory gave rise to anticolonial international communities and movements of struggle and solidarity such as Pan-Africanism, Garveyism, the civil rights movement, the Rastafarian movement, Black Power and Black Consciousness movements, Negritude, and many others that agitated for the dissolution of colonialism and thus for the establishment of a social order outside colonial regulation not just at the level of the imagination but as a real historical possibility.

Although these movements reflect serious differences in historical context, in culture, politics, and the experience of racism, that is, although they are not governed by a single unifying teleology, they more or less belong to a strong structure of family resemblances whose phenomenological possibility derives first from the constitutive role of colonial modernity in producing race and racism as paramount modes of determining and understanding human identities, second from resistance to racism, and third from imagining orders of being that transcend coloniality.

Indeed, they represent genuine, creative historical experiments in rethinking freedom in terms of what Gordon Lewis has called "Africana humanistic traditions." These movements provided a space in which Africans in Africa and Africans in the diaspora could think together about a world and a future without racism, a future modeled on African hospitality. This was a space in which historically Franz Fanon, Léopold Sédar Senghor, Aimé Césaire, Nnamdi Azikiwe, Kwameh Nkrumah, C. L. R. James, and many others, claimed their place in history along with Edward Wilmot Blyden, W. E. B. DuBois, Nat Turner, Sojourner Truth, and Alexander Crummell – a long line of thinkers (invoked earlier) who worked to undo the negative effects of colonial modernity and modern coloniality by rethinking blackness as a source of struggle and freedom. What I want to suggest here is that in different ways these thinkers represent a genealogical meeting place for black theology and postcolonial theory both in the sense in which I have characterized postcolonial discourse as moral protest and as an imagined future, as well as in the sense anticipating the actual, historical postcolonial movements of the nineteenth and twentieth centuries.

POSTCOLONIALITY AS BLACK GLOBAL SOLIDARITY

The Pan-Africanist movements I have just been discussing pre-supposed the existence of a common and shared, and thus global, burden of slavery, colonial oppression, and racism. Thus, fourth, another space where black theology and postcoloniality encounter each other is this global experience of racism and colonialism that has produced black Christian religious thought in Africa, Australia, the Americas, the Caribbean, Europe, and Asia. The globality of black theology is as much a function of anticolonial as it is of postcolonial hopes. The global character of black theology is important for understanding the play of solidarity at work in the relationship between postcoloniality and black theology itself. The social and political demands of black theology are echoed on every continent and in most countries with the experience of racist colonial domination. This global presence calls for an analysis of its discursive formation as constituted by colonialism and black resistance to colonialism. To be sure such an analysis must engage the full plurality of historical and theological difference as well as expression of black resistance in the modern world if it is going to properly describe the globality of black theology and its conditions of possibility. Of course, I do not have the space to offer such an analysis here but I want briefly to touch very directly on an example of one of the ways in which black theology has actively participated in postcolonial discourses of the twentieth century through the work of James Cone, the progenitor of black theology in the USA. I choose Cone because as a progenitor and leading protagonist of black theology he models this participation in a manner historically consistent with the understanding of postcolonialism I have been describing in this essay. Cone has participated in many of the leading conversations of the Ecumenical Association of Third World Theologians (EATWOT). While this organization is not historically part of the Pan-Africanist movement, it has been an important gathering place for theologians from many countries with the direct experience of colonialism and racism, including many whose histories intersect with the histories and concerns of the Pan-Africanist and civil rights movements. Cone's participation in EATWOT meetings explicitly enunciates the points of articulation between black theology and postcoloniality that I have been arguing for. He begins from the claim that "The history of American blacks cannot be completely separated from the history of Africa" and makes several points to support his claim. First, he appeals to history. He says historically there was a time when the distinctions between Africans and Africans in diaspora did not exist. Second, now that these distinctions exist, they require that we recognize "the interrelation of our histories" and how the structure of this interrelation is a critical frame of reference for addressing both "our present realities and the shaping of our future hopes and dreams" because it secures African and black nationalism as an instrument of liberation from international political and economic domination. Cone envisages a nationalism rooted in the unity of the black world: "there is some sense in which the Black World is one, and this oneness lays the foundation and establishes the need for serious dialogue." Here Cone invokes Pan-Africanism and the thinking associated with Marcus Garvey, W. E. B. Dubois, George Padmore, and Kwame Nkrumah to support his claim.[8]

For Cone black unity functions as a political metaphor for the global unity of all oppressed peoples. Thus he speaks of how US minorities have much in common with the Third World peoples of Africa, Asia, and Latin America. Again, "We are your brothers and sisters and feel hurt when you reject us. We are culturally, politically and economically Third World peoples living in the first World."[9] Cone's argument traces two different trajectories: the historical connection of African Americans to Africa, and the sociopolitical connection of African Americans to other oppressed peoples around the world. These two trajectories are built on his belief that:

> All Third World theologies began as a reaction to the dominant theologies of Europe and North America. Whether one speaks of Latin American, African, Asian or Caribbean theologies – all of these recent theological developments in the churches and seminaries of the Third World signal the rejection of the missionary theologies of their former colonizers.[10]

Thus by making African American religious protest against racism fit into a broader movement of global protest against racist colonialism, Cone locates black theology firmly in the context of postcolonial discourse both in the moral, rhetorical, and utopian sense I have argued for, as well as in the specifically historical sense of being part of the solidarity of efforts to precipitate or shore up the actualization of empirical postcolonial regimes through the anticolonial movements for self-determination and political independence that profoundly marked the history of the twentieth century.

In addition to all of this it is important to note in passing some of the other ways in which black theology has connected with postcolonial discourse. Two related points can be made. First, the globalization of black theology referred to earlier has been built on various histories of critical engagement with long legacies of imperial and colonial domination. This is the case with black theology in places such as South Africa, Britain, and the Caribbean, for example. In other words, black theology's critical engagement with the varied legacies of colonialism anticipates a postcolonial ethico-political imperative as the context from which to read the end of colonialism itself.

Second, black theology, in many of its forms, makes claims and continues to claim privileged historical and hermeneutical connections with Africa. Africa, with its complex colonial history and its history of participation in the slave trade, is an important hermeneutical trope for black theology. This hermeneutical trope has allowed black theology to participate in the articulation of shared themes, concerns, goals, and objectives around a possible postcolonial Africa. It is for this reason that many black theologies seek models of community, of being human, and of friendship, as well as of notions of the divine and of salvation and freedom that in some form or another reconnect with Africa.

Notes

1 Stephen Slemon, "The Scramble for Post-colonialism," in Chris Tiffin and Alan Lawson (eds.), *De-Scribing Empire: Post-colonialism and Textuality* (London: Routledge, 1994), pp. 15–32.

2 Robin Blackburn, *The Overthrow of Colonial Slavery* (London: Verso, 1989), p. 5.

3 Vijay Mishra and Bob Hodge, "What Is Post(-)colonialism?" in Patrick Williams and Laura Chrisman (eds.), *Postcolonial Discourse and Postcolonial Theory: A Reader* (New York: Columbia University Press, 1994), pp. 276–90.

4 Albert Raboteau, *Slave Religion: The "Invisible" Institution in the Antebellum South* (Oxford University Press, 2004), pp. 289ff. See also his *Canaan Land: A Religious History of African Americans* (Oxford University Press, 2001); Dwight Hopkins, *Down, Up, and Over: Slave Religion and Black Theology* (Minneapolis, MN: Fortress Press, 1999).

5 Whether this meant an entirely other world, a transcendent reality somehow disconnected from history (which of course is always one of the major issues utopian discourse frequently runs into) or the creation of a future society out of the structures of modernity and its promise of universal freedom, is a question my argument must at some stage engage. Although I do not have the space to do so here, it is nevertheless important to emphasize the extent to which postcolonialism as I have described it here exists and is thoroughly situated within modernity and, as such, within the colonial itself, even as it looks beyond both. This means that the utopian moment in the postcolonial is not completely cut off from history. Indeed, it draws some of its resources

from the language of modernity. This means that postcoloniality and postcolonial critique are situated in three crucial moments that must be taken together if we are to properly represent the differentiated and complex structure of the relationship between black theology and postcolonial discourse. These three moments are: (1) the history of colonial slaves (and I presuppose here, as I have done throughout this essay the centrality of colonial modernity as a racist project). This pertains to the aspect of memory as an important hermeneutical resource for imagining the postcolonial; (2) the present as the moral and political framework within which the desire for postcoloniality is posited and reenacted as an ongoing sign of struggle for racial justice; and (3) the future as the achievement (proleptic, deferred, or actualized) of the goals and aspirations of the historical struggles to overcome colonialism.

To be sure, each of these moments requires much deeper historical and theological engagement than I have given them here. That is work for another occasion.

6 Paul Gilroy, *The Black Atlantic: Modernity and Double Consciousness* (London: Verso, 1993), p. 37.

7 Maeve Cooke, "Redeeming Redemption: The Utopian Dimension of Critical Social Theory," *Philosophy and Social Criticism* 30(4) (2004): 413–29, at p. 413.

8 James H. Cone, "A Black American Perspective on the Future of African Theology," in Kofi Appiah-Kubi and Sergio Torres (eds.), *African Theology en Route* (Maryknoll, NY: Orbis Books, 1979), pp. 176–86.

9 James H. Cone, "A Statement from US Minorities," in K. C. Abraham (ed.), *Third World Theologies: Commonalities and Divergences* (Maryknoll, NY: Orbis Books, 1990), pp. 129–31.

10 James H. Cone, "Reflections from the Perspective of US Blacks: Black Theology and Third World Theology," in Virginia Fabella, MM, and Sergio Torres (eds.), *Irruption of the Third World: Challenge to Theology* (Maryknoll, NY: Orbis Books, 1983), pp. 235–45.

23 The future of black theology

JAMES H. EVANS, JR.

INTRODUCTION

In the late 1960s, black theology was the answer to some of the critical questions of the age. Chief among these were: Can I be authentically black and Christian at the same time? Does the Gospel have anything to say to those who are struggling against racial oppression? How is Christianity as practiced historically by the oppressors any different from that practiced by their victims? These and similar questions focused the conversations among early black theologians. As we look back on those years, the works produced strike us in two distinctly different ways. First, those texts can appear to be somewhat rough and unpolished when seen through the lens of more than forty years of the refining fire of debate, conversation, and research. At the same time, these works continue to convey the urgency, passion, and commitment of their authors. There is nothing dispassionate about these texts. They are written as if the very future of the Gospel and the race were at stake. In a sense, they were. At the time, the United States and its allies were engaged in a never-to-be-won war in Southeast Asia; the nation was still reeling from a decade of public assassinations and secret wars on various political resistance movements. The main-line churches were just beginning their slow decline and right-wing Christian groups were about to awaken from a cultural slumber. Black theology addressed questions of power, race, and justice because these were exactly the issues and problems with which black people were dealing.

As the essays in this volume reveal, the times have changed and the questions have changed in form if not in content. What made black theology so powerful was that it addressed the real, concrete questions that African Americans were asking at the time. In fact, as Reinhold Niebuhr has observed, "Nothing is so incredible as an answer to an unasked question." This is the key to the challenges and the opportunities that confront black theologians at this moment in history. One can no longer assume that the presenting question will always and everywhere be framed as an unambiguous query about race and racism. Black theologians will have to listen again and listen carefully to the cries of the dispossessed and not be too quick to respond with familiar and stock answers. Black theologians will have to listen with new ears to the mingled cries of the poor and the dispossessed, and provide responses that can speak to the complexity of life for the oppressed in the twenty-first century without being overwhelmed by that complexity.

The purpose of what follows is to reflect on and respond to those mixed and mingled cries. Certainly, within the scope of this chapter it will not be possible to address this topic in a comprehensive manner. That task must await another occasion. However, it is the aim of this essay to contribute to the richly textured task of exploring the challenges and opportunities that lie ahead. This essay will address three distinct sets of questions and concerns. The first set emerges from the relationship or lack thereof between black theology and other forms of intellectual discourse. Has black theology stagnated and reverted to insularity without engagement with recent theoretical developments in the academy? How might black theology take on, in a creative and constructive fashion, other forms of modern theologies? What role will theory and metaphysics play in the future development of black theology? The second set emerges from the relationship or lack thereof between black theology and recent ecclesial developments. How does black theology address contemporary cults of materialism? How does black theology respond to the new global phenomenon of neocharismatic pro-capitalist missionaries flooding developing nations and communities of color? How does black theology respond to these developments within its own communities? The third set emerges from the relationship or lack thereof between black theology and its social, political, economic, and cultural environment. How do present-day developments in politics, culture, psychology, economics, and globalization impact black theological discourse? What is the significance of inter-religious dialogues for black theology? What vibrancy does black theology have given the rise of one cultural and economic superpower? To be sure, there are a host of other questions that could be added to this list. However, these questions will provide a more than adequate point of entry for our inquiry.

A NEW FOUNDATIONAL THEOLOGY

Contemporary black theological discourse is confronted with a fundamentally altered intellectual context at the beginning of the twenty-first century. This changed scholarly and academic environment brings with it new questions and concerns. What is the relationship or lack thereof between black theology and other forms of intellectual discourse? Has black theology stagnated and reverted to insularity without engagement with recent theoretical developments in the academy? How might black theology take on, in a creative and constructive fashion, other forms of modern theologies? Although black theologians have in recent years become more visible conversation partners with other disciplines in the academy, including history, economics, political science, and cultural studies, there are critical conversations that need to take place at this moment concerning the production, evaluation, and application of knowledge. Conversations taking place in major research centers continue to have a profound impact on the lives of people of African descent. It is incumbent on black theologians to engage these conversations on at least three levels: those of scientific discourse, technological discourse, and philosophical discourse. For the purposes of this essay, we will address the first of these three, leaving the other two for another occasion.

Black theologians need to participate in conversations regarding research in the physical and biological sciences. A chief concern ought to be current developments in the field of genetics. In the mid 1980s, the Human Genome Project was launched with great excitement about its potential to dramatically improve life and to reduce or eliminate some of the most difficult diseases and maladies. "The objective of the Human Genome Project is simple to state, but audacious in scope: to map and analyse every single gene within the double helix of humanity's DNA. The project will reveal a new human anatomy – not the bones, muscles and sinews, but the complete genetic blueprint for a human being."[1] But as promising as this research is, it is accompanied by a sinister sibling, eugenics. "The term eugenics, meaning 'wellborn,' was coined in 1883 by Francis Galton, the scion of an upper-class British family and a cousin of Charles Darwin."[2] Eugenics refers to the science of genetic manipulation in the population by selective breeding. From the very outset, the development of eugenics as a field of inquiry was beset with potential racist and classist applications. Galton, drawing on the achievements of Darwin's *Origin of Species*, saw this science as a means of weeding out undesirables within the population. It has been well documented that the idea of natural selection was the foundation of nineteenth-century scientific theories of the racial inferiority of people of African descent. While a utopian vision of a society free from genetically based diseases and maladies may drive the science of genetics, the specter of a eugenically based ethnic cleansing continues to be the nightmare of people of color. Is the agenda of eugenics in play within the African American community today? How is it related to the crisis in urban school districts and educational policies within the African American community? One writer suggests that the rigid imposition of standardized testing is driven by the eugenics agenda. "High-stakes testing has its origins in the eugenics movements and racist assumptions about IQ. We forget, at our own peril, that this legacy hangs over current demands for increased testing."[3] Is the eugenics agenda served by the prison industry? One writer argues that while Hitler's use of eugenics to effect the racial purification of Germany occurred in the past,

> government-sanctioned eugenics did not end with the fall of the Third Reich, however; it only became less obvious. Today, it is more subtle. Cleverly packaged with the popular "tough on crime" crusade, eugenics is now practiced by imprisoning those individuals whom society deems to be less desirable … By using the criminal justice system to legitimize the selection and removal of undesirables from the nation's breeding stock, we have progressed from eugenics-in-theory to eugenics-in-practice.[4]

Moreover, black theologians must consider the fact that eugenics, while potentially a powerful weapon in the hands of racists, has been a part of the solution to "the Negro Problem" for some African American intellectual leaders. Consider the tentative embrace of eugenics by W. E. B. DuBois. He argued that within the black race as within the white race there are those who are fit for intellectual endeavor and those who are fit for manual labor. He argued that intentional and careful selection of mates, including intermarriage among blacks and whites, would lead to an increase in the number of the "Talented Tenth."[5]

Black theologians should be a part of these so-called "objective" analyses because they deal with the foundational theological question of what it means to be human. There are two fundamental theological/ philosophical questions that black theologians should bring to this conversation. First, the question of Psalm 8:4, "What is man, that thou art mindful of him?" compels the theologian to frame the discussion of human nature with a different and broader context. Is the essence of humanity determined by the genetic code? Second, a question that lies at the heart of much traditional African philosophical thought is: At what point does the individual become a person? In traditional African philosophical thought one's personhood is determined not by one's chronological age but by a constellation of social, cultural, and environmental factors. By bringing these and similar questions to the table, black theologians can help ensure that the voices of the voiceless are heard through the din of the production of knowledge.

A NEW ECCLESIAL THEOLOGY

Black theological discourse is confronted with a radically changed ecclesial situation at the beginning of the twenty-first century. Among the new questions to be addressed is: How does black theology address contemporary cults of materialism? How does black theology respond to the new global phenomenon of neocharismatic pro-capitalist missionaries flooding developing nations and communities of color? How does black theology respond to these developments within its own communities? Ecclesial life around the globe is being influenced by the appearance of new religious movements, or NRMs, but perhaps nowhere is that influence more critical than in communities of the African diaspora.

The single canopy under which many of these emerging ecclesial communities find their identity is that of the so-called "prosperity gospel." The prosperity Gospel refers to the belief that the acme of the Christian life is material wealth and affluence. While traditional African American denominations reject prosperity preaching as crass materialism, its allure continues to grow and to fascinate a materialistic and celebrity-obsessed culture.[6] The central purveyors of this prosperity preaching unashamedly display their wealth with opulent lifestyles that include multimillion-dollar residences, jewelry, automobiles, expensive clothing, and private jets for their personal use. They routinely claim tens of thousands of devotees and worship in large arena-like settings. These preachers defend their material gain as quite biblical. Almost to a person, these preachers proclaim that God's people were not meant to be poor, but to prosper. Moreover, what is required, they maintain, to realize these blessings is simply to verbally claim them. While the attractiveness of prosperity preaching is powerful, it is not necessarily new. In fact, one need only recall the critique that W. E. B. DuBois leveled against Booker T. Washington at the beginning of the twentieth century when he referred to Washington's philosophy as a "gospel of wealth."

This is not just about styles of worship or the extravagance of celebrity preachers. These emerging ecclesial communities are giving rise to theological affirmations and claims that are different from and, in many instances, diametrically opposed to the historical affirmations and claims that have been identified with the black churches. Just as any ministry is supported by implicit or explicit theological claims, these prosperity ministries are undergirded by certain theological claims that run counter not only to the historical witness of the black church in America, but also to the historical claims of the broader Christian community. The historical witness of the black church in America has traditionally emphasized the collective well-being of the community. That is, unless all enjoyed the fruits of freedom and wholeness, none truly possessed them. Prosperity preaching has abandoned the emphasis on collective liberation in favor of personal aggrandizement. This materialistic preaching asserts that one can have personal prosperity without social justice. One of the theological questions raised here is whether biblical definitions of prosperity support this view, or whether secular notions of prosperity have simply been given a Christian veneer. One of the most problematic aspects of prosperity preaching is its revisionist Christology. How can one claim a Christ whom the church has historically described as a poor and oppressed member of a poor and oppressed community and still hold on to the notion of material prosperity as an ultimate value? At least two resolutions to this dilemma have been appropriated by prosperity preachers. First, many of them have simply excised Jesus from their preaching altogether. They have resorted to delivering motivational, self-help sermons, which rarely, if ever, mention Jesus, especially in his social, political, and economic setting. In this case, what emerges is a new form of docetism in which Christ becomes an ephemeral figure posing no threat to the sociopolitical oppression of poor people and people of color.

Concomitantly, preaching in this case becomes an exercise in a new form of gnosticism, where the key to wealth is access to some secret knowledge, and the prosperity preacher is the avenue to that knowledge. Second, some prosperity preachers, recognizing that for many African American Christians Jesus is an essential part of any authentic worship experience, have reinterpreted Jesus to suit the Gospel that they preach. In this instance, preachers have claimed that Jesus was not actually poor, and that he was, in reality, the son of a middle-class business owner. Given the fact that portrayals of Jesus have historically been subject to cultural distortions, critical attention must be given to the ways in which Jesus has been and is being portrayed in these new ecclesial communities.

Prosperity preaching has not only affected the African American community, but has significantly affected white American Christian communities, as well. In fact, many of the first televised preachers of the prosperity Gospel were white ministers who took the language of Pentecostalism and evangelicalism and combined it with an entrepreneurial drive. From this fertile combination ecclesial empires have been built. The property holdings of these empires are extraordinary and extravagant. White prosperity preachers, for the most part, have shied away from overly conspicuous displays of opulence. However, unlike their white counterparts, many black prosperity preachers make no attempt to hide their wealth, but proudly display it as an unmistakable sign of God's favor. Black theology must address the influence of prosperity preaching by both black and white preachers, because in both cases these ministries are supported in varying degrees by poor African Americans seeking a way to access the blessings they see on television.

Prosperity preaching is also a global phenomenon, and nowhere is its influence more powerfully felt than the continent of Africa. In the midst of poverty and a myriad of social and environmental challenges, prosperity preaching has found a firm foothold.[7] In sub-Saharan Africa:

> [P]rosperity-tinged Pentecostalism is growing faster not just than other strands of Christianity, but than all religious groups, including Islam. Of Africa's 890 million people, 127 are now "revivalists" (a term that includes both Pentecostals and charismatics) ... They make up more than a fourth of Nigeria's population, more than a third of South Africa's, and ... 56 percent of Kenya's.[8]

This Pentecostal and charismatic base has been almost totally infiltrated by Western-style prosperity preaching. The Gospel of health and wealth is preached by leaders who emulate American jet-setters and entrepreneurs. This Gospel is spread through well-funded television broadcasting facilities. A message of opulence and conspicuous consumption bombards a continent mired in an economic and public health crisis. Widespread poverty and malnutrition mark the existence of tens of millions of Africans, and certainly it is plausible that this Gospel would be attractive in this context.

However, there is another element that bears upon the attractiveness of prosperity preaching in Africa. Traditional African religious values strongly link material and spiritual blessings. The lack of a rigid separation between the spiritual and the material dimensions of life ensures receptivity to the Gospel of wealth and health. Another African value is a strong, visible, and charismatic leader. "The African 'Big Man' ideal honors rich, powerful leaders such as prosperity preachers."[9] This means that these churches are not democratically governed and are heavily dependent on the charisma of their leaders. These leaders often present themselves as larger-than-life figures, symbols of both what can be achieved by a select few and what is clearly out of reach for the masses. There is a third African value that undergirds the popularity of the prosperity Gospel in Africa. One scholar suggests that "an ancient urge, trumping even promises of material provision, animates the continent's prosperity movement: a desire for communication with the supernatural."[10] Many of these prosperity preachers place a great deal of emphasis on the power and meaning of dreams. In African traditional thought dreams are often believed to be the means through which communication with the divine takes place. Through the valuing and interpretation of these dreams the promise of prosperity gains strength. These dreams are sometimes seen as oracles of future riches or warnings against potential calamity. But it is the fact that dreams are valued that permits prosperity preachers to ignore the reality of the social, economic, and political vulnerability of their congregants and proclaim a future reality of heavenly bliss. It is a version of the American Dream built on the flimsy rhetoric of ready riches. And the social, political, and economic "dream" of a beloved community articulated by Dr. Martin Luther King, Jr. is nowhere to be found.

Black theology must reevaluate and rearticulate its essential affirmations in light of this changed and changing ecclesial reality. What black theologians say about God, Christ, church, humanity, and hope must respond to these and other social forces. Is God to be understood as the provider of material wealth and what does this say about the purpose of God's creation? Is Christ to be understood as provider of motivation for personal enrichment and what does this say about his life, death, and resurrection? Is the church the gathering of wealth-seeking individuals and what does this say about its mission to be the community that had all things in common? Are human beings to be understood solely in material terms and what does that say about the ubiquity of sin? Is hope totally exhausted by the expectation of a financial windfall and what does that say about hope being the evidence of things unseen? Black theology will need to continue to refract and refine these and similar questions in order to speak a relevant word in our time.

A NEW PRACTICAL THEOLOGY

Contemporary black theological discourse must contend with a host of contextual issues and questions. While the political, cultural, psychological, economic, and global environment exerts a powerful influence on any attempt to speak of God, Christ, and humanity, this is especially true of black theology. There is one theme, one thread that ties these questions and concerns together: the reality of life under the hegemony of an empire. Empire is and has been a more or less permanent feature of human existence in our time. Historically, some empires (and emperors) have been more benign, and perhaps more benevolent, than others. Yet an empire is still an empire. Unlike regimes, empires are characterized by a rapacious appetite for power and conquest. Until the latter part of the twentieth century, it was not common to refer to "an American empire," but the reality of the unrivaled economic, military, and cultural influence of the United States has brought into sharp relief not only its imperial present but also its imperial past. It is this past, this present, and the immediate future that should be the practical focus of black theology.

What makes this a theological task proper and not solely a political, social, or economic concern is that Christianity bears within its own history and development the marks of imperial hegemony. That is, Christianity, itself, was shaped in the midst of and in response to the influence of an empire. Contemporary scholarship has demonstrated that the influence of the Roman Empire affected every aspect of the life of the early church and especially its claim that Jesus is King and Lord. As Jaroslav Pelikan observes, it is not only impossible to understand the history of Jesus apart from the development of the West, it is also impossible to understand the history of the West apart from the history of Jesus. "To trace the historical variations and permutations of the kingship of Jesus in its interaction with other political themes and symbols is to understand a large part of what is noble and a large part of what is demonic in the political history of the West."[11] Christianity has never been apolitical, acultural, or immune from the social and economic forces of the day. This was not just a matter of the application of Christian principles in the public realm but reflects the fact that Christianity itself was shaped on the anvil of imperial politics. As Pelikan again notes, even the central affirmation of the early Christian community that Jesus is Lord must be understood in this context:

Thanks to the careful work of recent social and political historians of late antiquity, we are beginning to understand better the complex of political, social, economic, psychological, and ideological factors that, along with the religious factors, underlay the Roman persecution of Christians. Nevertheless, as those scholars have also shown, it does remain necessary to conclude that the image of Jesus as King and Lord repeatedly came into conflict with the sovereignty of Caesar as king and lord.[12]

It is not just the affirmations of the early church that must be understood in light of imperial realities, but even the life of Jesus must be understood in this context. Richard A. Horsley observes that:

> The Romans determined the conditions of life in Galilee where Jesus lived and carried out his mission … Roman governors such as Pontius Pilate appointed and deposed the high priests who ruled Judea from their base in Jerusalem Temple. When the Pharisees and the Herodians wanted to trap Jesus into incriminating himself, they asked him whether it was lawful to pay tribute to the Roman emperor. Jesus was executed by order of the Roman governor, and he was killed by crucifixion, a form of execution that the Romans used to intimidate subject peoples, by publically torturing to death their rebel leaders. Even to begin to understand Jesus in historical context, we must have a clearer sense of how Roman imperial practices affected the people of Galilee.[13]

Whether overt or covert, empires are sustained by violence. Only when absolutely necessary is that violence made visible. Subtle, silent, and invisible violence are more suited to sustained imperial supremacy. It is particularly within the context of this violence that the life and death of Jesus is best understood. As John Dominic Crossan notes:

> In Jesus, the radicality of God became incarnate, and the normalcy of civilization's brutal violence (our sins, or better, Our Sin) executed him. Jesus' execution asks us to face the truth that, across human evolution, injustice has been created and maintained by violence while justice has been opposed and avoided by violence.[14]

This imperial context is important to black theology because it was in the context of empire that Africans were introduced to the New World. One great empire in North America and several smaller, but no less brutal, empires in Europe were funded by the Atlantic slave trade. In spite of claims to the contrary, the conquest of Africa bore all of the marks of an imperial invasion. Its people were subjugated. Its wealth was stolen. Its cultures were corrupted.

The Atlantic slave trade and the continued enslavement of African peoples were sustained by imperial mechanisms. Among these imperial mechanisms were the establishment of centralized structures of government designed to sustain imperial aims, the expansion of imperial influence into every part of the empire, the romanticization of the subjected peoples, the glorification of conquest, the use of terror and humiliation to solidify its hegemonic position, and the unspoken, but very real, final solution of the extermination of the "other."[15] The American Southern Confederacy represented a centralized structure of government specifically designed to institutionalize the culture of slavery. The Fugitive Slave Law of 1850 effectively extended the reach of slavery into even the so-called free states by protecting the interests of slaveholders anywhere and everywhere. Even while they were bought and sold, Africans were often viewed as quaint and romantic oddities in polite social circles. The kidnapping of Africans was often celebrated with festivals of departure and festivals of return, where the captains of the slave ships were honored as if they were noble mariners. Slavery could not be sustained without the intentional and focused employment of terror and humiliation. The chief instruments of terror and humiliation were lynching and rape. The fact that such a fate could await every African man, woman, boy, or girl served to ensure submission and deference to imperial power. The ultimate insanity of slavery was that the very asset that enriched the slaveholder, he paradoxically sought to eliminate. The neurosis created by the quest for empire led to the psychological need to eliminate the conquered.

Black theology has before it the task of speaking truth to imperial power. Racial oppression can no longer be adequately understood as ignorance as to the humanity of black people or as the failure to apply the rules of civil justice to the black community. Racial oppression has to be seen as the foundation of and the result of imperial conquest. In a historical moment when the growing insecurity and xenophobia of the West have provided the fertile soil for tyrannical forms of governance, black theology must affirm that empire is not order and that freedom is not chaos. Black theology needs to recover the resistance traditions of the early church and the black church in slavery in order to assist present-day African American Christians to realize that in Christ "we are more than conquerors through him who loved us."

CONCLUSION

Black theologians stand in a position to participate in the critique and reshaping of our understanding of the world and one another. The bravery, courage, and commitment that fueled the passion of the first generation of black theologians need to be applied to the contemporary challenges that confront us. One question that needs to be honestly faced is whether black theological discourse has found too comfortable a place in seminaries and universities. Has this accommodation led to stagnation and a lack of creativity among black theologians? These are difficult questions. We must face the fact that a certain degree of stagnation has set in. It is easy to substitute whimsical and folksy conversation for hard theological work. To the extent that this has occurred, we need to face it and change our focus.

On the other hand, when we engage theological conversations being carried out in the seminaries and divinity schools, we must resist the burden of apologetics. That is, there is no need to apologize for doing theology out of concern for a specific community and within a specific tradition. Moving beyond stagnation and defensiveness, black theologians can speak with confidence, whether critiquing the excesses of radical orthodoxy, for example, or expanding the vision of eco-theologies. The freedom that lies before black theologians today will permit the joyous telling, retelling, and foretelling of stories of faith, hope, and love in the African American community. Moreover, black theologians are then permitted to explore heretofore neglected regions of our own historical experiences. We can recover our indigenous ascetic and contemplative resources. We can turn our attention to the devotional dimensions of our theological work. We can celebrate the "apophatic" and positive character of our faithwork. Black theologians ought to stand before the great challenges and opportunities of our time, fully convinced of the authority of our vocation and that, in the words of scripture, "the earth is the Lord's and the fullness thereof" (Ps. 24:1).

Notes

1   Tom Wilkie, *Perilous Knowledge: The Human Genome Project and Its Implications* (Berkeley, CA: University of California Press, 1993), p. 1.
2   Ruth Hubbard, "Eugenics, Reproductive Technologies and 'Choice'," http://genetics.live.radicaldesigns.org (accessed November 26, 2007).
3   Alan Stoskepf, "The Forgotten History of Eugenics," www.rethinking-schools.org/archive/13_03/eugenic.shtml, p. 1 (accessed November 26, 2007).

4 C. C. Simmons, "Eugenics by Imprisonment," *The Touchstone* 15(1) (January 2005): 1.

5 W. E. B. DuBois, "The Marrying of Black Folk," *The Independent* 69 (October 13, 1910): 812–13.

6 See "Black Believers Debate Prosperity Gospel," www.christianpost. com/pages/print.htm?aid=29037 (accessed October 23, 2007).

7 See "Gospel Riches: Africa's Rapid Embrace of Prosperity Pentecostalism Provokes Concern – and Hope," www.christianitytoday.com/ct/article_ print.html?=46571 (accessed October 23, 2007).

8 Ibid., p. 1.

9 Ibid., p. 3.

10 Ibid., p. 5.

11 Jaroslav Pelikan, *Jesus through the Centuries: His Place in the History of Culture* (New York: Harper and Row, 1985), p. 47.

12 Ibid., p. 49.

13 Richard A. Horsley, *Jesus and Empire: The Kingdom of God and the New World Disorder* (Minneapolis, MN: Fortress Press, 2003), p. 15.

14 John Dominic Crossan, *God and Empire: Jesus against Rome, Then and Now* (New York: HarperCollins, 2007), p. 140.

15 Horsley, *Jesus and Empire*, pp. 16–34. Horsley identifies these features as constitutive of the Roman Empire. These features highlight the fact that the slavocracy of the eighteenth and nineteenth centuries was a form of empire.

Further reading

Ad Hoc National Committee of Negro Churchmen. "1966 Black Power: Statement by the National Committee of Negro Churchmen." In James H. Cone and Gayraud S. Wilmore (eds.), *Black Theology: A Documentary History*, vol. I, *1966–1979*, 2nd edn. Maryknoll, NY: Orbis Books, 1993.

Akbar, Na'im. *Breaking the Chains of Psychological Slavery*, rev. edn. Tallahassee, FL: Mind Productions and Associates, 1996.

Andrews, Dale. *Practical Theology for Black Churches: Bridging Black Theology and African American Folk Religion*. Louisville, KY: Westminster John Knox Press, 2002.

Antonio, Edward P. "Culture and Politics in Black and African Theologies." In Dwight N. Hopkins and Sheila Greeve Davaney (eds.), *Changing Conversations: Cultural Analysis and Religious Reflection*. New York: Routledge, 1996.

Ashby, Homer U., Jr. *Our Home Is Over Jordan: A Black Pastoral Theology*. St. Louis, MO: Chalice Press, 2003.

Baer, Hans. *The Black Spiritual Movement: A Religious Response to Racism*, 2nd edn. Knoxville, TN: University of Tennessee Press, 2001.

Baker-Fletcher, Garth. *Bible Witness in Black Churches*. New York: Palgrave, 2009.

Baldwin, James. *Nobody Knows My Name*. New York: Dell, 1967.

Beckford, Robert. *Dread and Pentecostal: A Political Theology for the Black Church in Britain*. Eugene, OR: Wipf and Stock, 2011.

Jesus Is Dread: Black Theology and Black Culture in Britain. London: Darton, Longman and Todd, 1998.

Boesak, Allan Aubrey. *Farewell to Innocence: A Socio-Ethical Study on Black Theology and Black Power*. Maryknoll, NY: Orbis Books, 1976.

The Tenderness of Conscience: African Renaissance and the Spirituality of Politics. Glasgow: Wild Goose Publications, 2008.

Boff, Leonardo and Clodovis Boff. *Introducing Liberation Theology*. Maryknoll, NY: Orbis Books, 2007.

Bonhoeffer, Dietrich. *The Cost of Discipleship*, 2nd edn. New York: Macmillan, 1959.

Brittan, Arthur and Mary Maynard *Sexism, Racism, and Oppression*. Oxford and New York: Blackwell Publishing, 1984.

Brown, Michael Joseph. *Blackening of the Bible: The Aims of African American Biblical Scholarship*. Harrisburg, PA: Trinity Press International, 2004.

Burkett, Randall K. and Richard Newman (eds.), *Black Apostles: Afro-American Clergy Confront the Twentieth Century.* Boston, MA: G. K. Hall & Company, 1978.

Butler, Judith. "Merely Cultural," *New Left Review* 1(227) (January/February 1998): 33–44.

Chikane, Frank. *Black Theology Revisited: Conference Report, 1983.* Cape Town, South Africa: Institute for Contextual Theology, 1983.

"EATWOT and Third World Theologies: An Evaluation of the Past and Present." In K. C. Abraham (ed.), *Third World Theologies: Commonalities and Divergences.* Maryknoll, NY: Orbis Books, 1990.

No Life of My Own: An Autobiography. Eugene, OR: Wipf and Stock, 2010.

Cone, Cecil Wayne. *The Identity Crisis in Black Theology.* Nashville, TN: AMEC, 1975.

Cone, James H. *Black Theology and Black Power.* New York: Seabury Press, 1969.

A Black Theology of Liberation. Philadelphia, PA: J. B. Lippincott, 1970.

For My People: Black Theology and the Black Church. Maryknoll, NY: Orbis Books, 1984.

God of the Oppressed. New York: Seabury Press, 1975.

Martin and Malcolm and America: A Dream or a Nightmare. Maryknoll, NY: Orbis Books, 1991.

My Soul Looks Back. Nashville, TN: Abingdon, 1982.

Risks of Faith: The Emergence of a Black Theology of Liberation, 1968–1998. Boston, MA: Beacon Press, 1999.

Speaking the Truth: Ecumenism, Liberation, and Black Theology. Grand Rapids, MI: William B. Eerdmans Publishing Co., 1986.

Cone, James H. and Gayraud S. Wilmore (eds.), *Black Theology: A Documentary History*, vol. I, *1966–1979*, 2nd edn. Maryknoll, NY: Orbis Books, 1993.

Black Theology: A Documentary History, vol. II, *1980–1992*, 2nd edn. Maryknoll, NY: Orbis Books, 1993.

Davis, Cyprian. *The History of Black Catholics in the United States.* Chestnut Ridge, NY: Crossroad, 1995.

Davis, Cyprian and Diana L. Hayes (eds.), *Taking Down Our Harps: Black Catholics in the United States.* Maryknoll, NY: Orbis Books, 1998.

Davis, Cyprian and Jamie Phelps (eds.), *"Stamped with the Image of God": African Americans as God's Image in Black.* Maryknoll, NY: Orbis Books, 2003.

Douglas, Kelly Delaine Brown. *The Black Christ.* Maryknoll, NY: Orbis Books, 1994.

"Womanist Theology: What Is Its Relationship to Black Theology?" In James H. Cone and Gayraud S. Wilmore (eds.), *Black Theology: A Documentary History*, vol. II, *1980–1992*, 2nd edn. Maryknoll, NY: Orbis Books, 1993.

Earl, Riggins, Jr. *Dark Salutations: Ritual, God, and Greetings in the African-American Community.* Harrisburg, PA: Trinity Press International, 2001.

Dark Symbols, Obscure Signs: God, Self and Community in the Slave Mind. Knoxville, TN: University of Tennessee Press, 2003.

Edwards, Herbert O. "Black Theology and Liberation Theology." In Sergio Torres and John Eagleson (eds.), *Theology in the Americas.* Maryknoll, NY: Orbis Books, 1976, pp. 177–91.

Ela, Jean-Marc. *African Cry.* Maryknoll, NY: Orbis Books, 1986.

Erskine, Noel. *Decolonizing Theology: A Caribbean Perspective.* Trenton, NJ: African World Press, 1998.

Evans, James H. *We Have Been Believers: An African American Systematic Theology.* Minneapolis, MN: Fortress Press, 1993.

We Shall All Be Changed: Social Problems and Theological Renewal. Minneapolis, MN: Fortress Press, 1997.

Franklin, John Hope and Evelyn Brooks Higginbotham. *From Slavery to Freedom,* 9th edn. New York: McGraw-Hill, 2010.

Fraser, Nancy. "From Redistribution to Recognition? Dilemmas of Justice in a 'Post Socialist' Age," *New Left Review* 1(212) (July/August 1995): 68–93.

Gonzalez, Michelle A. *Afro-Cuban Theology: Religion, Race, Culture, and Identity.* Gainesville, FL: University Press of Florida, 2006.

Grant, Jacquelyn. *White Women's Christ and Black Women's Jesus: Feminist Christology and Womanist Response.* Atlanta, GA: Scholars Press, 1989.

Harnett, Ann Marie, S.N.J.M. *et al.* "A Theological Quest. Synthesis of the First Stage of Theology in the Americas." In Sergio Torres and John Eagleson (eds.), *Theology in the Americas.* Maryknoll, NY: Orbis Books, 1976, pp.242–52.

Hopkins, Dwight N. *Being Human: Race, Culture, and Religion.* Minneapolis, MN: Fortress Press, 2005.

Black Theology USA and South Africa: Politics, Culture, and Liberation. Maryknoll, NY: Orbis Books, 1989.

Down, Up, and Over: Slave Religion and Black Theology. Minneapolis, MN: Fortress Press, 1999.

Heart and Head: Black Theology–Past, Present, and Future. New York: Palgrave Macmillan, 2002.

Introducing Black Theology of Liberation. Maryknoll, NY: Orbis Books, 1999.

Shoes That Fit Our Feet: Sources for a Constructive Black Theology. Maryknoll, NY: Orbis Books, 1993.

Hopkins, Dwight N. (ed.). *Black Faith and Public Talk: Critical Essays on James H. Cone's "Black Theology and Black Power."* Maryknoll, NY: Orbis Books, 1999.

Kalu, Ogbu. *African Pentecostalism: An Introduction.* Oxford University Press, 2008.

Kee, Alistair. *Domination and Liberation: The Place of Religion in Social Conflict.* London: SCM Press, 1986.

King, Martin Luther, Jr. *Where Do We Go from Here? Chaos or Community.* New York: Harper & Row, 1967.

Kunnie, Julian. *Models of Black Theology: Issues in Class, Culture, and Gender.* Harrisburg, PA: Trinity Press International, 1994.

Lincoln, C. Eric. *The Black Church since Frazier.* New York: Schocken Books, 1974.

Magubane, B. "Race and Class Revisited: The Case of North America and South Africa," *Africa Development* 12(1) (1987): 5–42.

Maimela, Simon S. *Proclaim Freedom to My People.* Johannesburg, South Africa: Skotaville Publishers, 1987.

Maimela, Simon S. (ed.). *Culture, Religion, and Liberation.* Pretoria, South Africa: Penrose Book Printers, 1994.

Mbiti, John S. *African Religions and Philosophy.* Portsmouth, NH: Heinemann, 1992.

Introduction to African Religion. Portsmouth, NH: Heinemann, 1991.

Mofokeng, Tokatso. *The Crucified among the Cross-Bearers: Towards a Black Christology.* Kampen: Kok, 1983.

Moore, Basil. "Theological Perspectives on Racism." Paper delivered at the AAC Consultation at Lincoln College, North Adelaide, South Australia, May 30, 1978.

Mosala, Itumeleng. *Biblical Hermeneutics and Black Theology in South Africa.* Grand Rapids, MI: William B. Eerdmans Publishing Company, 1989.

Motlhabi, Mokgethi. *African Theology/Black Theology in South Africa: Looking Back, Moving On.* Pretoria, South Africa: University of South Africa Press, 2009.

"The Historical Origins of Black Theology." In I. J. Mosala and B. Tlhagale (eds.), *The Unquestionable Right to Be Free.* Johannesburg, South Africa: Skotaville Publishers, 1986; Maryknoll, NY: Orbis Books, 1986.

Niebuhr, Reinhold. *The Nature and Destiny of Man: A Christian Interpretation,* vol. 1. New York: Charles Scribner's Sons, 1941.

Pattel-Gray, Anne. *The Great White Flood: Racism in Australia.* Atlanta, GA: American Academy of Religion, 1998.

Through Aboriginal Eyes: The Cry from the Wilderness. Geneva, Switzerland: World Council of Churches Publications, 1991.

Phan, Peter. "Method in Liberation Theologies," *Theological Studies* 61 (2000): 40–63.

Phelps, Jamies T. (ed.). *Black and Catholic: The Challenge and Gift of Black Folk.* Milwaukee, WI: Marquette University Press, 1997.

Reddie, Anthony G. *Black Theology in Transatlantic Dialogue.* New York: Palgrave Macmillan, 2006.

Working against the Grain: Black Theology in the 21st Century. Sheffield, UK: Equinox Publishing, 2008.

Reddie, Anthony G. and Michael N. Jagessar (eds.), *Black Theology in Britain: A Reader.* Sheffield, UK: Equinox Publishing, 2007.

Postcolonial Black British Theologies: New Textures and Themes. London: Epworth Press, 2007.

Rex, John. *Race Relations in Sociological Theory.* London and New York: Routledge and Kegan Paul, 1983.

Roberts, J. Deotis. *A Black Political Theology.* Philadelphia, PA: Westminster John Knox Press, 1974.

Black Theology in Dialogue. Philadelphia, PA: Westminster John Knox Press, 1987.

Black Theology Today: Liberation and Contextualization. New York: Edwin Mellen Press, 1983.

Liberation and Reconciliation: A Black Theology. Philadelphia, PA: Westminster John Knox Press, 1971.

Roots of a Black Future: Family and Church. Philadelphia, PA: Westminster Press, 1980.

Rolison, G. L. "An Exploration of the Term Underclass as It Relates to African-Americans," *Journal of Black Studies* 21(3) (March 1991): 287–301.

Sebidi, Lebamang. "The Dynamics of the Black Struggle and Its Implications for Black Theology." In I. J. Mosala and B. Tlhagale (eds.), *The Unquestionable Right to Be Free.* Johannesburg, South Africa: Skotaville Publishers, 1986; Maryknoll, NY: Orbis Books, 1986.

Silva, Silvia Regina de Lima. "Black Latin American Theology: A New Way to Sense, to Feel, and to Speak of God." In Dwight N. Hopkins (ed.), *Black Faith and Public Talk: Critical Essays on James H. Cone's "Black Theology and Black Power."* Maryknoll, NY: Orbis Books, 1999.

Suárez, Joel. "Baptists and Popular Education in Cuba: Interview with Joel Suárez," December 2006, www.yesmagazine.org/issues/latin-america-rising/baptists-and-popular-education-in-cuba-an-interview-with-joel-suarez.

Trompf, G. W. (ed.). *The Gospel Is Not Western: Black Theologies from the Southwest Pacific.* Maryknoll, NY: Orbis Books, 1987.

Van der Berghe, Pierre. *Race and Racism: A Comparative Perspective.* New York: John Wiley and Sons, 1967.

West, Cornel. "Black Theology and Marxist Thought." In James H. Cone and Gayraud S. Wilmore (eds.), *Black Theology: A Documentary History*, vol. I, *1966–1979.* Maryknoll, NY: Orbis Books, 1979.
"The North American Blacks." In Sergio Torres and John Eagleson (eds.), John Drury (trans.), *The Challenge of Basic Christian Communities. Papers from the International Ecumenical Congress of Theology, February 20–March 2, 1980, São Paulo, Brazil.* Maryknoll, NY: Orbis Books, 1981.

Wiley, Dennis W. "Black Theology, the Black Church, and the African American Community." In James H. Cone and Gayraud S. Wilmore (eds.), *Black Theology: A Documentary History*, vol. II, *1980–1992.* Maryknoll, NY: Orbis Books, 1993.

Williams, Delores S. *Sisters in the Wilderness: The Challenge of Womanist God-Talk.* Maryknoll, NY: Orbis Books, 1993.

Wilmore, Gayraud S. *Black Religion and Black Radicalism: An Interpretation of the Religious History of African Americans*, 3rd edn. Maryknoll, NY: Orbis Books, 1998.

Wilson, W. J. *Power, Racism, and Privilege: Race Relations in Theoretical and Sociological Perspective.* New York: The Free Press, 1973.

Wright, Jeremiah A., Jr. "An Underground Theology." In Dwight N. Hopkins (ed.), *Black Faith and Public Talk: Critical Essays on James H. Cone's "Black Theology and Black Power."* Maryknoll, NY: Orbis Books, 1999.

Index

THE CAMBRIDGE COMPANION TO PURITANISM
edited by John Coffey and Paul Lim (2008)
9780521860888 hardback   9780521678001 paperback

THE CAMBRIDGE COMPANION TO ORTHODOX CHRISTIAN
THEOLOGY
edited by Mary Cunningham and Elizabeth Theokritoff (2008)
9780521864848 hardback   9780521683388 paperback

THE CAMBRIDGE COMPANION TO PAUL TILLICH
edited by Russell Re Manning (2009)
9780521859899 hardback   9780521677356 paperback

THE CAMBRIDGE COMPANION TO JOHN HENRY NEWMAN
edited by Ian Ker and Terrence Merrigan (2009)
9780521871860 hardback   9780521692724 paperback

THE CAMBRIDGE COMPANION TO JOHN WESLEY
edited by Randy L. Maddox and Jason E. Vickers (2010)
9780521886536 hardback   9780521714037 paperback

THE CAMBRIDGE COMPANION TO CHRISTIAN PHILOSOPHICAL
THEOLOGY
edited by Charles Taliaferro and Chad Meister (2010)
9780521514330 hardback   9780521730372 paperback

THE CAMBRIDGE COMPANION TO MUHAMMAD
edited by Jonathan E. Brockopp (2010)
9780521886079 hardback   9780521713726 paperback

THE CAMBRIDGE COMPANION TO SCIENCE AND RELIGION
edited by Peter Harrison (2010)
9780521885386 hardback   9780521712514 paperback

THE CAMBRIDGE COMPANION TO GANDHI
edited by Judith Brown and Anthony Parel (2011)
9780521116701 hardback   9780521133456 paperback

THE CAMBRIDGE COMPANION TO THOMAS MORE
edited by George Logan (2011)
9780521888622 hardback   9780521716871 paperback

THE CAMBRIDGE COMPANION TO MIRACLES
edited by Graham H. Twelftree (2011)
9780521899864 hardback   9780521728515 paperback

THE CAMBRIDGE COMPANION TO FRANCIS OF ASSISI
edited by Michael J. P. Robson (2011)
9780521760430 hardback   9780521757829 paperback

THE CAMBRIDGE COMPANION TO CHRISTIAN ETHICS,
SECOND EDITION
edited by Robin Gill (2011)
9781107000070 hardback   9780521164832 paperback

THE CAMBRIDGE COMPANION TO BLACK THEOLOGY
edited by Dwight N. Hopkins and Edward P. Antonio (2012)
9780521879866 hardback   9780521705691 paperback

Forthcoming

THE CAMBRIDGE COMPANION TO NEW RELIGIOUS MOVEMENTS
edited by Olav Hammer and Mikael Rothstein

THE CAMBRIDGE COMPANION TO THE CISTERCIAN ORDER
edited by Mette Birkedal Bruun

Made in the USA
San Bernardino, CA
18 January 2018